HARBRACE
ESSENTIALS

WITH RESOURCES FOR WRITING IN THE DISCIPLINES

SECOND EDITION

CHERYL GLENN

The Pennsylvania State University

LORETTA GRAY

Central Washington University

CENGAGE
Learning·

Australia • Brazil • Mexico • Singapore • United Kingdom • United States

CENGAGE
Learning·

Harbrace Essentials
with Resources for Writing in
the Disciplines, **Second Edition**
Cheryl Glenn, Loretta Gray

Product Director: Monica Eckman

Product Manager: Christopher Bennem

Managing Developer: Leslie Taggart

Content Developer: Kristin Bowen

Associate Content Developer: Danielle Warchol

Product Assistant: Kerry Devito

Media Developer: Cara Douglass-Graff

Market Development Manager: Erin Parkins

Content Project Manager: Rosemary Winfield

Art Director: Marissa Falco

Manufacturing Planner: Betsy Donaghey

Intellectual Property Analyst: Ann Hoffman

Production Service: Thistle Hill Publishing Services

Text Designer: Cenveo® Publisher Services

Cover Designer: Sarah Bishins

Compositor: Cenveo® Publisher Services

Library of Congress Control Number: 2013954420
ISBN-13: 978-1-285-45181-7
ISBN-10: 1-285-45181-3

Cengage Learning
200 First Stamford Place, 4th floor
Stamford, CT 06902
USA

Cengage Learning is a leading provider of custom-ized learning solutions with office locations around the globe, including Singapore, the United Kingdom, Australia, Mexico, Brazil, and Japan. Locate your local office at **international.cengage.com/region**.

Cengage Learning products are represented in Canada by Nelson Education, Ltd.

For your course and learning solutions, visit **www.cengage.com**.

Purchase any of our products at your local college store or at our preferred online store **www.cengagebrain.com**.

Instructors: Please visit **login.cengage.com** and log in to access instructor-specific resources.

Printed in the United States of America
3 4 5 6 7 17 16 15 14

Preface

Whether you are writing for school or on the job, *Harbrace Essentials with Resources for Writing in the Disciplines* provides the practical advice, helpful strategies, and examples of effective writing that will help you make your writer's voice heard.

Finding What You Need

Harbrace Essentials with Resources for Writing in the Disciplines puts all the information you need at your fingertips.

- **Brief Contents.** Use the brief table of contents on the inside front cover to find the chapter you need. For quick reference, the brief table of contents also provides a guide to the color-coded parts of the book—you'll find the color for each part on related page tabs.
- **Contents.** When you need to quickly locate more specific information, consult the detailed table of contents on the inside back cover. Then you can flip to the section you need, such as 4a or 15c, using the section locators at the top of each page.
- **User-Friendly Index.** You can find the specific pages on which any topic is mentioned by consulting the index (p. 543). The index includes entries that reflect the terminology of the book (for example, *conjunction*) as well as entries in everyday language for when you're not certain what topic to check (such as *and*). It provides not only page numbers but also chapter and section references for each topic.
- **Advice on MLA, APA, CMS, and CSE.** For quick access to documentation styles, open to the tab that says MLA and then scan the next page for the style you are using. At the end of the book (p. 569), a directory of Citation Maps guides you

to the Citation Maps in each documentation chapter, which walk you through the process of citing common sources in each style. The chapter on MLA documentation is preceded by a tabbed divider for quick access.

- **Help for Writing in the Disciplines.** For advice on responding to an assignment or working with sources for courses in literature, the social sciences, humanities, natural sciences, or business, refer to one of these style- and discipline-specific chapters.
- **Glossaries.** If you need help with words that are commonly confused or misused (such as *accept* and *except*), consult the Glossary of Usage on page 515. The Glossary of Terms (p. 531) defines grammatical and rhetorical terms, including those that appear in boldface throughout the book.
- **Revision Symbols.** If your instructor gives you feedback that includes revision symbols, use this list to lead you to sections of the book that offer strategies and detailed help for revision. The list appears on p. 570, one page in from the inside back cover.
- **Resources for Multilingual Writers.** Refer to the checklists and tips throughout the book for key advice on special topics. For quick access to grammar help designed especially for multilingual writers, the directory at the end of the book (p. 569) points you to help with specific topics throughout the book.
- **Answers to Exercises.** *Harbrace Essentials with Resources for Writing in the Disciplines* offers answers to even-numbered exercise items so that you can work through material and test your own understanding.

Although we believe *Harbrace Essentials* will help you answer any question you may have about writing, if you have suggestions for improving the next edition or if we can assist you in any way, don't hesitate to write to us c/o Cengage Learning, English Editorial, 20 Channel Center Street, Boston, MA 02210.

Cheryl Glenn
Loretta Gray

Teaching and Learning Resources

Answer Key and Instructor Manual

Available for easy download on the book's password-protected companion website, the Answer Key and Instructor Manual provides instructors with answers to all exercises in the handbook as well as a variety of pedagogical and teaching materials.

Online College Workbook

A great companion to the handbook, the Online College Workbook covers grammar, punctuation, usage, style, and writing. It provides supplemental exercises and includes clear examples and explanations. The workbook is available as a downloadable PDF on the password-protected companion website for instructors. The Answer Key for the workbook is also available on the website.

Multimedia eBook

ISBN: 9781285451541

Students can do all of their reading online or use the multimedia eBook available for *Harbrace Essentials*. The eBook includes the full text of the print version while also providing user-friendly navigation, search, and highlighting tools, and links to videos that enhance the handbook content.

Enhanced InSite for *Harbrace Essentials*

Printed Access Card (1 semester):
9781285451701
Instant Access Code (1 semester):
9781285451688
Printed Access Card (2 semester): 9781285451572
Instant Access Code (2 semester): 9781285451565

From a single, easy-to-navigate site, you and your students can manage the flow of papers online, check for originality, and conduct peer reviews. Students can access a multimedia eBook with text-specific workbook, private tutoring options, and resources for writers that include anti-plagiarism tutorials and downloadable grammar podcasts. **Enhanced InSite**™ provides the tools and resources you and your students need plus the training and support you want. Learn more at **www.cengage.com/insite**. (*Access card/code required.*)

Write Experience

writ⊕xperience

Printed Access Card:
9781285836232
Instant Access Code:
9781285836225

Cengage Learning's Write Experience is a technology product that allows you to assess written communication skills without adding to your workload. This new product utilizes artificial intelligence not only to score student writing instantly and accurately but also to provide students with detailed revision goals and feedback on their writing. Write Experience is the first product designed and created specifically for the higher education market through an exclusive agreement with McCann Associates and powered by e-Write IntelliMetric Within™. IntelliMetric is the gold standard for automated scoring of writing and is used to score the Graduate Management Admissions Test® (GMAT®) analytical writing assessment. Better Writing. Better Outcomes. Write Experience. Visit **www.cengage.com/writeexperience** to learn more.

Questia

quest⊕a

Printed Access Card (6-month subscription):
9781428277441
Instant Access Code (6-month subscription):
9781428277434
Printed Access Card (12-month subscription):
9781285079172
Instant Access Code (12-month subscription):
9781285079202

Questia is the online library that provides 24/7 access to the web's premier collection of full-text books and academic journal and periodical articles in the humanities and social sciences. And, it is more than a vast collection of online sources. Questia can help your students in the entire research process, from topic selection and research to organization of their notes and proper citations. Questia will help your students by providing a wider array of scholarly sources and enabling them to organize what they've learned into a better-thought-out paper.

Additional Resources

Resources for Writers
Printed Access Card: 9781133044390
Instant Access Code: 9781133044383

Resources for Writers offers a variety of activities for students to practice and refine their understanding of key concepts via interactive grammar and proofreading exercises, anti-plagiarism tutorials, writing and research modules, multimedia activities, and downloadable grammar podcasts.

Merriam-Webster's Collegiate Dictionary (eBook)
ISBN: 9781285054360

America's best-selling dictionary delivers accurate, up-to-date information to students as they work on writing assignments. This edition of *Merriam-Webster's Collegiate Dictionary* contains thousands of new words and meanings from all areas of human endeavor, including electronic technology, the sciences, and pop culture. This indispensable tool will give your students fast and easy access to the words they need to know today.

Turnitin
Printed Access Card (1 semester): 9781413030181
Printed Access Card (2 semester): 9781413030198

This proven, online plagiarism-prevention software promotes fairness in the classroom by helping students learn to correctly cite sources and allowing instructors to check for originality before reading and grading papers. (*Access code/card required.*)

InfoTrac® College Edition
ISBN: 9780534558536

This online research and learning center offers over 20 million full-text articles from nearly 6,000 scholarly and popular periodicals. The articles cover a broad spectrum of disciplines and topics—ideal for every type of researcher. Learn more at **www.cengage.com/infotrac.** (*Access code/card required.*)

Acknowledgments

We would like to thank our colleagues who reviewed this handbook during the course of its development. Their astute comments and thoughtful suggestions helped shape this second edition.

Nancy Applegate, *Georgia Highlands College*; Craig Barrette, *Brescia University*; Kirsten Benson, *University of Tennessee*; Jesse Bishop, *Georgia Highlands College*; Laura Bowles, *University of Central Arkansas*; Janice Brantley, *University of Arkansas at Pine Bluff*; Kimberly Del Bright; *Penn State University*; Ron Brooks, *Oklahoma State University*; Jeffrey Cain, *Sacred Heart University*; Michael Callaway, *Mesa Community College*; Beth Capo, *Illinois College*; Allan Carter, *College of Dupage*; Liz Dennis, *Barton College*; Jason DePolo, *North Carolina A&T State University*; Anthony Edgington, *University of Toledo*; Christopher Ervin, *Western Kentucky University*; Lynee Gaillet, *Georgia State University*; Rebecca Gidjunis, *Eastern University*; Margaret Gillio, *Finger Lakes Community College*; Rebecca Godwin, *Barton College*; Charlotte Gordon, *Endicott College*; Jean Grace, *University of Pittsburgh*; Loren Gruber, *Missouri Valley College*; Barbara Heifferon, *Louisiana State University*;

John Hyman, *American University*; Elizabeth Imafuji, *Anderson University*; Maria Jerenic, *University of Nevada-Las Vegas*; Leslie Johnston, *Georgia Highlands College*; Amelia Keel, *Lone Star College-Kingwood*; Kristie Kemper, *Georgia Highlands College*; Bridget Kozlow, *North Carolina State University*; Jessica Lindberg, *Georgia Highlands College*; Elaine Marshall, *Barton College*; Brett McInelly, *Brigham Young University*; Kevin McKelvey, *University of Indianapolis*; Betty Mealy, *Southern Wesleyan University*; Joe Moxley, *University of South Florida*; Roxanne Munch, *Joliet Junior College*; Jill Parrott, *Eastern Kentucky University*; Jonathan Purkiss, *Pulaski Technical College*; Alex Reid, *University at Buffalo*; Jennifer Richardson, *SUNY Potsdam*; John-Michael Rivera, *University of Colorado*; Leigh Ryan, *University of Maryland*; Jasna Shannon, *Coker College*; Dixie Shaw-Tillmon, *The University of Texas at San Antonio*; Patricia Taylor, *University of Connecticut*; Paul Walker, *Murray State University*; Rachel Wall, *Georgia Highlands College*; Shevaun Watson, *UW-Eau Claire*; Linda Weeks, *Dyersburg State Community College*; Kristen Weinzapfel, *North Central Texas College*; Kim Welborn, *Southern Wesleyan University*; Mary Wright, *Christopher Newport University*

W

WRITING

1 Writing and Reading Rhetorically

Whether you are reading textbooks or e-mails, writing assignments for class, text messaging your friends, or composing with words or visuals, you are actively using your knowledge of **rhetoric**, the purposeful use of language. In fact, you are purposefully using language to address your **rhetorical situation**, the set of circumstances within which a person writes or reads a text.

1a Understanding the rhetorical situation

You already intuitively know the basic elements of the rhetorical situation: **opportunity**, **writer**, **audience**, **message**, **stance**, and **context**. To communicate effectively, writers must analyze their particular situation and respond appropriately to their intended audience. Therefore, in academic and other formal rhetorical situations, you will want to allow time to consider the basic elements of the situation:

- **Opportunity.** What problem or issue is the writer taking the opportunity to resolve or address?
- **Writer.** What do you know about the writer (or author), whether yourself or the person whose work you are reading?
- **Audience.** Who is the writer's audience? How might this audience help the writer resolve or address the problem? Will the audience understand, be influenced (to change behavior or opinion), be entertained?
- **Purpose.** How does the writer's purpose connect with the audience? Does the writer want to entertain, inform,

explain, describe, or argue a point? How does the purpose connect with the opportunity?

- **Message.** What specific assertions, examples, and support does the writer use? How is the message delivered? Via a visual text, a verbal text, or a combination? Is it print or electronic? In what ways are both the content and the delivery of the message appropriate for the audience?
- **Stance.** What is the writer's stance? What opinions, hopes, or experiences does the writer connect with the purpose and the message itself?
- **Context.** In what context is the communication between writer and audience taking place? Context includes the time and place, the writer and audience, the medium of delivery—as well as the social, political, historical, geographical, and cultural factors that influence the context, whether helping or hindering successful communication.

1b Applying rhetorical knowledge

When you write rhetorically, you consider the best ways of reaching your audience—the best way to deliver an appropriate, purposeful, and convincing message. When you read rhetorically, you allow yourself to consider the writer's message. Rhetorical readers often begin with a **preview**, skimming over the message to locate its major points (title and headings, for example), and then they read through it carefully (including author biography, preface, index, and bibliography) to determine the credibility and reputation of the author as well as the amount of research that went into the message itself. During the preview and close reading, rhetorical readers watch for **transitional** words that indicate important points of purpose, result, summary, causation, repetition, exemplification, or intensification (**3d**).

1c   Academic writing

Academic writing, the writing expected of you as a student, will vary according to the assignments you receive within various academic disciplines. Much academic writing, though, shares several features: a thesis statement, purposefully organized supporting details and examples (often drawn from outside sources), and conventional grammar, spelling, punctuation, and mechanics. In other words, academic writing is carefully planned out and seriously delivered—unlike casual, social writing.

(1) Expectations for academic writing

Although assignments across courses and disciplines may differ, the expectations for academic writing remain fairly constant. Academic writing demonstrates an essential set of skills, including your ability to:

- respond appropriately to the assignment
- think critically
- apply outside sources (your research, practice, observations, readings) as you join the scholarly conversation
- organize and develop your material effectively and logically
- communicate with clarity, purpose, and a sense of audience
- edit and proofread with an eye to conventions of formatting, documentation, grammar, punctuation, mechanics, and tone (or level of formality)
- deliver your knowledge and researched information in a number of ways (orally, visually, electronically, verbally)

(2) Analyzing assignments

To meet the expectations for academic writing, you need to understand every assignment. Ideally, assignments will be communicated in writing and explained and discussed in class. For each assignment, make sure you understand the following requirements.

- **Task.** What task does the assignment ask you to complete? What verb does the assignment use? The imperative verb (*argue, describe, explain*) should direct you toward the expected purpose. Are you to solve a problem, research an issue, answer a question, remember and retell a significant event, support a thesis, explain a process, define a concept?
- **Role and audience.** What stance are you expected to or allowed to take with regard to your audience? Are you being asked to assume the role of expert, explainer, questioner, arguer? Are you writing from a position of knowledge and power, from that of a learner, or from an opposing point of view?
- **Format.** What are the instructor's expectations with regard to length, manuscript form (electronic or print? verbal or visual?), documentation style, and so on? What manuscript format should you follow (that of a report, an essay, an oral delivery)?
- **Process to be followed.** Are you expected to conduct library or laboratory research? What is the schedule for completion of research, drafts, peer reviews, workshops, revisions, and so forth? Are you expected to submit your rough drafts with the final draft?
- **Criteria for evaluation.** How will the final product be graded? What are the criteria for success?

1d Genres and formats of academic writing

You may already be familiar with many of the genres of academic writing, such as the personal essay, the case study, and the lab report. Each of these has a distinctive purpose, format, and tone.

Once you decide on the appropriate genre and format for your academic writing, you can choose to deliver it in print, online, verbally, or visually (or some combination). Just as your choice of medium shapes how you produce your message, that choice also offers you opportunities for experimenting with its delivery and reach. Writing specifically for online media can extend the range of your project by reaching a wider audience outside your classroom and campus.

(1) Web pages

Writing material for a web page is different from writing a traditional academic essay or report. Web material requires a rethinking of organization, design, and style. The writer must determine a hierarchy of content emphasis (with related links to additional information), develop a clear, pleasing organization, and include useful links and other tools for navigation.

(2) Blogs

Writing a blog requires you to aim toward a specific, often limited, audience who will be receptive to your topic(s), your stance (your attitude toward your subject and your audience), and your ability to engage intelligently and frequently.

(3) Wikis

Wikis—collaborative online texts—allow you to share huge amounts of information with colleagues. All wiki writers expect to receive both positive and negative feedback from one another.

(4) Audio and video

The possibilities of audio and video delivery allow you to compose podcasts, YouTube videos, documentaries, and short films—all sorts of multimedia genres, including mash-ups that integrate music, visuals, information, and data. You can use these media to enhance your print texts or as stand-alone compositions.

2 Planning and Drafting Essays

Writing is a process, a series of manageable steps. Effective writers know they cannot possibly do everything at once, so they generate, organize, develop, and clarify their ideas as well as polish their prose in separate—but often overlapping—stages.

2a Stages of the writing process

Prewriting is the initial stage of the writing process. Consider your intended audience, purpose, and context. Then jump-start your thinking about your topic by talking with others working on the same assignment, keeping a journal, freewriting, or questioning.

Drafting involves writing down as much as you can with regard to your topic. Academic writing calls for evidence to support your assertions and your opinions. At this stage, then, you will need to determine the kinds of evidence your writing calls for (facts, testimony, personal experience, library, archival, laboratory or field research) and set about collecting that evidence. The more information you get down, the more options you will have as you begin to clarify your thesis (or guiding question) and purpose for writing. Progress is your goal at this stage, not perfection.

Revising offers you the opportunity to focus your purpose for writing, establish a clear thesis statement or governing idea, and organize your ideas accordingly. During revision, you work to stabilize the overall structure of your essay and individual paragraphs. You also shape your introduction and conclusion. Revising often means producing another draft for yet further revision and editing.

Editing and **proofreading** focus on surface features: punctuation, spelling, word choice, sentence structure, and all the rest of the details of academic English.

CHECKLIST FOR ASSESSING A TOPIC

- Why are you interested in the topic?
- What audience might be interested in the topic? How is the topic appropriate for your audience?
- What is your purpose in writing about this topic to your intended audience?
- How can you do justice to the topic in the time and space available to you? Should you narrow it or expand it?
- Do you have the information you need to address this topic? If not, what additional information might you need?

2b   Developing a thesis statement

Once you decide on a topic, ask yourself what you would like to say about it. By combining your topic (for example, studying another language) with your point about that topic (it's important because it prepares students to participate in a global economy), you will create a thesis statement, an explicit declaration of the overarching idea of your paper. A thesis statement keeps your writing on target, unifies your writing, and guides your readers through the content that follows at the same time that it showcases your originality.

To bring your topic into focus, consider your individual interests, your purpose, the needs of your audience, and the time and space available. Look over your prewriting and drafting to determine where, exactly, your interests took hold. Often, your interest provides the most fruitful site for sharpening your focus, developing a tentative thesis, and then drafting an essay.

TIPS FOR DEVELOPING A THESIS STATEMENT

- Decide which feature of the topic interests you most.
- Write down your point of view or assertion about it.
- Draft a thesis statement that includes the topic and your assertion about it.
- Mark the passages in your rough draft that support your position to see how well this thesis fits with ideas you've been developing.
- Ask yourself whether your thesis is too broad or too narrow to be sufficiently developed given the constraints of your project.
- After completing a draft, ask yourself whether the scope of your thesis should be adjusted to reflect the direction your essay has taken. Qualify your thesis if necessary, acknowledging any conditions where your assertion may not hold up.
- If you are still unhappy with your thesis, start again with the first tip and be even more specific.

2c Creating an outline

Many writers need a working plan to direct their ideas and keep their writing on course. Others rely on outlines to organize their writing, as in this example:

TENTATIVE THESIS STATEMENT: Students who study another language become better communicators, both in their own language and with people from other cultures.

I. Many Americans don't think they need to learn another language.

    A. English is the language of global communication.

    B. English speakers always have an advantage in intercultural communication.

(Continued on page 10)

(Continued)

II. English-only speakers miss out on benefits of learning another language.

   A. Learning another language is not just about being able to talk to people in different countries.

   B. Studying another language increases a student's knowledge of another culture and so promotes tolerance and understanding.

   C. Knowing the language enriches a student's stay in a foreign country.

III. Students who take another language do better on standardized tests.

   A. Students can compare grammars to better remember the rules of their own language.

   B. Studying another language opens up a student's mind to different ways of speaking and expressing ideas.

   C. Studying another language helps students acquire better reading skills.

3 Developing Paragraphs

You compose a draft by developing the information that will constitute the individual paragraphs of your essay. Every paragraph serves a purpose: whether it is the introduction, the support for a main point, or the conclusion, each paragraph guides your reader through your piece of writing.

3a Stating the main idea

Effective paragraphs are unified around one main idea, often stated in a topic sentence. A **topic sentence** states the main idea of the paragraph clearly, and all the other sentences in the paragraph relate to that idea. Topic sentences often appear at the start of a paragraph to focus readers on what the paragraph is about. Whether a paragraph is long or short, it should focus on one main idea or point.

In the following paragraph about business at Hollywood movie studios in the late 1960s, the topic sentence appears at the beginning of the paragraph. The support sentences mention the consequences of the event described in the topic sentence.

> *Between August 1964 and March 1965, four new movies sold so many tickets and made so much money that, collectively, they pointed toward a dramatic shift in the tastes of American moviegoers and suggested an entirely new way for the studios to do business.* Hollywood did not react well. Historically, the only event more disruptive to the industry's ecosystem than an unexpected flop is an unexpected smash, and, caught off guard by the sudden arrival of more revenue than they thought their movies could ever bring in, the major studios resorted to three old habits: imitation, frenzied speculation, and panic.   —MARK HARRIS, *Pictures at a Revolution*

3b Developing the main point

(1) Using details

The following well-developed paragraph uses details to bring an idea to life:

> My hair was one of those odd, amazing, unbelievable, stop-you-in-your-tracks creations—not unlike a zebra's stripes, an armadillo's ears, or the feet of the electric-bluefooted boobie—that the Universe makes for no reason other than to express its own limitless imagination. . . . It never thought of lying down. It sought more and more space, more light, more of itself. It loved to be washed; but that was it.   —ALICE WALKER, "Oppressed Hair Puts a Ceiling on the Brain"

(2) Providing examples

Like details, examples contribute to paragraph development by making specific what otherwise might seem general and hard to grasp. The author of the following paragraph uses both details and examples:

> It began with coveting our neighbor's chickens. Lily would volunteer to collect the eggs, and then she offered to move in with them. Not the neighbors, the chickens. She said if she could have some of her own, she would be the happiest girl on earth. What parent could resist this bait? Our lifestyle could accommodate a laying flock; my husband and I had kept poultry before, so we knew it was a project we could manage, and a responsibility Lily could handle largely by herself. I understood how much that meant to her when I heard her tell her grandmother, "They're going to be just my chickens, grandma. Not even one of them will be my sister's." To be five years old and have some other life form entirely under your control—not counting goldfish or parents—is a majestic state of affairs.
>
> —BARBARA KINGSOLVER, *"Lily's Chickens"*

3c   Choosing methods for developing paragraphs

When drafting an essay, you can develop paragraphs using various **rhetorical methods**. The method you choose will depend on how you want to achieve the purpose of your paragraph. Your paragraph might make sense of a person, place, or event (narration and description); think critically about a process (process analysis or cause-and-consequence analysis); investigate similarities or differences (comparison or contrast); organize concepts (classification and division); establish boundaries (definition); or convince someone (argument). These rhetorical methods are already second nature to you. You use them every day to understand the world around you.

By using these rhetorical methods of development, you will make your writing more understandable to your audience. Take care to use the one(s) best suited to supporting your thesis, fulfilling your purpose, and reaching your audience. As you draft and revise, check to see that each paragraph is anchored in your thesis statement.

(1) Narration

A **narrative** discusses a sequence of events, normally in **chronological** order (the order in which they occur), to develop a particular point or set a mood. Narrative often includes a setting, characters, dialogue, and description and makes use of transition words or phrases such as *first*, *then*, *later*, *that evening*, and so forth to guide readers from one incident to the next. Whatever its length, a narrative must remain focused on the main idea. The narrative in this paragraph traces the history of the *Beaver*, a replica of the original Boston Tea Party ship:

> In 1972, three Boston businessmen got the idea of sailing a ship across the Atlantic for the tea party's bicentennial. They bought a Baltic schooner, built in Denmark in 1908, and had her rerigged as an English brig, powered by an anachronistic engine that was, unfortunately, put in backwards and caught fire on the way over. Still, she made it to Boston in time for the hoopla. After that, the bicentennial *Beaver* was anchored at the Congress Street Bridge, next to what became the Boston Children's Museum. For years, it was a popular attraction. In 2001, though, the site was struck by lightning and closed for repairs. A renovation was planned. But that was stalled by the Big Dig, the excavation of three and a half miles of tunnel designed to rescue the city from the blight on interstate 93, an elevated expressway that, since the 1950s, had made it almost impossible to see the ocean, and this in a city whose earliest maps were inked with names like Flounder Lane, Sea Street, and Dock Square. . . . In 2007, welders working on the Congress Street Bridge accidentally started another fire, although by then, the *Beaver* had already been towed, by tugboat, twenty-eight miles to Gloucester, where she'd been ever since, bereft, abandoned, and all but forgotten.   —JILL LEPORE, "Prologue: Party Like It's 1773"

(2) Description

Descriptions make your writing come alive. Predominantly visual, descriptions can also include the details of what you hear, smell, taste, and touch; that is to say, descriptions appeal to your senses. In the following paragraph, Ishmael Beah employs vivid descriptive details to convey what he saw and heard as he walked through a small town in Sierra Leone that had been devastated by rebels.

> I am pushing a rusty wheelbarrow in a town where the air smells of blood and burnt flesh. The breeze brings the faint cries of those whose last breaths are leaving their mangled bodies. I walk past them. Their arms and legs are missing; their intestines spill out through the bullet holes in their stomachs; brain matter comes out of their noses and ears. The flies are so excited and intoxicated that they fall on the pools of blood and die. The eyes of the nearly dead are redder than the blood that comes out of them, and it seems that their bones will tear through the skin of their taut faces at any minute. I turn my face to the ground to look at my feet. My tattered *crapes* [sneakers] are soaked with blood, which seems to be running down my army shorts. I feel no physical pain, so I am not sure whether I've been wounded. I can feel the warmth of my AK-47's barrel on my back; I don't remember when I last fired it. It feels as if needles have been hammered into my brain, and it is hard to be sure whether it is day or night. The wheelbarrow in front of me contains a dead body wrapped in white bedsheets. I do not know why I am taking this particular body to the cemetery.   —**ISHMAEL BEAH**, *A Long Way Gone: Memoirs of a Boy Soldier*

(3) Process analysis

In explaining how something is done or made, process paragraphs often use both description and narration. You might describe the items used in a process and then narrate the steps of the process chronologically. See how Sam Swope explains the process by which an elementary school assistant principal tried (unsuccessfully) to intimidate students into snitching on a fellow student.

> Later that day, a frowning assistant principal appeared in the doorway, and the room went hush. Everyone knew why he was there. I'd known Mr. Ziegler only as a friendly, mild-mannered fellow with a comb-over, so I was shocked to see him play the heavy. His performance began calmly, reasonably, solemnly. He told the class that the administration was deeply disappointed, that this theft betrayed the trust of family, teachers, school

and country. Then he told the children it was their duty to report anything they'd seen or heard. When no one responded, he added a touch of anger to his voice, told the kids no stone would go unturned, the truth would out; he vowed he'd find the culprit—it was only a question of time! When this brought no one forward, he pumped up the volume. His face turned red, the veins on his neck bulged, and he wagged a finger in the air and shouted, "I'm not through with this investigation, not by a long shot! And if any of you know anything, you better come tell me, privately, in private, because they're going to be in a lot of trouble, *a lot of trouble!*"   —SAM SWOPE, "The Case of the Missing Report Cards"

(4) Cause-and-consequence analysis

Writers who analyze cause and consequence raise the question *Why?* and must answer it to the satisfaction of their audience. In this type of analysis, writers often differentiate the **primary cause** (the most important one) from **contributory causes** (which add to but do not directly cause an event or situation) and the **primary consequence** (the most important result) from **secondary consequences** (which are less important). Writers who analyze cause and consequence also usually link a sequence of events along a timeline, always keeping in mind that just because one event happens before—or after—another event does not necessarily make it a cause or consequence of that event. The following paragraph catalogues the consequences of a recent ruling in favor of air-passenger rights.

The turning point [in air-passenger rights] came last April when a new Department of Transportation rule went into effect prohibiting lengthy tarmac delays on domestic flights at large and midsize hub airports. It requires that airlines provide food, water, and working toilets within two hours of delaying a plane on the ground and, after three hours, that passengers be allowed to safely leave the plane.   —MARK ORWOLL, "Revolution in the Skies"

(5) Comparison and contrast

A **comparison** points out similarities, helping readers see a relationship they might otherwise miss, while a **contrast** points out differences, establishing useful distinctions to better understand an issue or make a decision. Comparison and contrast can be arranged in at least two ways: The paragraph can discuss all the details about one subject and then cover the other. Or the paragraph might shift back and forth to discuss both subjects, point by point. In the following paragraph, the writer employs the second method, using descriptive details to compare humankind with the monster known as Frankenstein:

> "Hateful day when I received life!" I exclaimed in agony. "Accursed creator! Why did you form a monster so hideous that even you turned from me in disgust? God, in pity, made man beautiful and alluring, after his own image; but my form is a filthy type of yours, more horrid even from the very resemblance. Satan had his companions, fellow-devils, to admire and encourage him; but I am solitary and abhorred."   —**MARY SHELLEY**, *Frankenstein*

Another kind of comparison is the **analogy**, which compares two subjects that may seem dissimilar or compares an unfamiliar subject or item with a familiar one, as in the following paragraph:

> And she was happy right now, it was true. Jane Houlton, shifting slightly inside her nice black coat, was thinking that, after all, life was a gift—that one of those things about getting older was knowing that so many moments weren't just moments, they were gifts.   —**ELIZABETH STROUT**, *Olive Kitteridge*

(6) Classification and division

Classification is a way to understand or explain something by establishing how it fits within a category or group. Book classifications, for instance, include such categories as reference, fiction, and nonfiction. And those same classifications can be further broken down, with fiction subclassified into historical, suspense, mystery, Western, literary, and so on. **Division**, in contrast, separates something into component parts and examines the relationships among them. *Murder as a Fine Art*, David Morrell's latest novel, can be discussed in terms of its components: plot, setting, characters, theme. Thus, classification and division offer two different perspectives: classify things into groups or divide things into subclasses. In the following paragraph, both classification and division are used to differentiate the two versions of the cowboy icon. Like many paragraphs, this one mixes rhetorical methods; the writer uses description, comparison, contrast, and classification to make her point.

> First, and perhaps most fundamentally, the cowboy icon has two basic incarnations: the cowboy hero and the cowboy villain. Cowboy heroes often appear in roles such as sheriff, leader of a cattle drive, or what I'll call a "wandering hero," such as the Lone Ranger, who appears much like a frontier Superman wherever and whenever help is needed. Writers and producers most commonly place cowboy heroes in conflict either with "Indians" or with the cowboy villain. In contrast to the other classic bad guys of the Western genre, cowboy villains pose a special challenge because they are essentially the alter ego of the cowboy hero; the cowboy villain shares the hero's skill with a gun, his horse-riding maneuvers, and his knowledge of the land. What distinguishes the two, of course, is character: the cowboy hero is essentially good, while the cowboy villain is essentially evil.   —JODY M. ROY, "The Case of the Cowboy"

(7) Definition

By defining a concept or term, you efficiently clarify your meaning and so develop an idea. You also immediately connect with your readers when they know what you are and are not talking about. Definitions are usually constructed in a two-step process: the first step locates the term by placing it in a class or general category; the second step differentiates this particular term from other terms in the same class. This paragraph defines volcanoes by placing them into a class ("landforms") and then distinguishes them ("built of molten material") from other members of that class. The definition is clarified by examples.

> Volcanoes are landforms built of molten material that has spewed out onto the earth's surface. Such molten rock is called lava. Volcanoes may be no larger than small hills, or thousands of feet high. All have a characteristic cone shape. Some well-known

mountains are actually volcanoes. Examples are Mt. Fuji (Japan), Mt. Lassen (California), Mt. Hood (Oregon), Mt. Etna and Mt. Vesuvius (Italy), and Paricutín (Mexico). The Hawaiian Islands are all immense volcanoes whose summits rise above the ocean, and these volcanoes are still quite active.   —JOEL AREM, *Rocks and Minerals*

3d | Making paragraphs unified and coherent

When a paragraph flows, sentences and details are arranged in a way that is easy for readers to follow. When every sentence relates to the main idea, the paragraph is **unified**.

TIPS FOR STRONG, UNIFIED PARAGRAPHS

Identify	Identify the topic sentence, if there is one, making sure that it both highlights the main idea of the paragraph and connects the paragraph to the thesis statement. If the main idea is not stated in a topic sentence, what is the implied main idea of the paragraph?
Relate	Read each sentence in a paragraph and determine how it relates to and develops the main idea.
Eliminate	Eliminate any sentence that does not relate to the main idea or violates the unity of the paragraph. Or consider adding clarifying details or a transitional word or phrase to make the relationship clear.
Connect	Check to see how your sentences fit together. What specific words or phrases help your reader move from one idea to the next?
Clarify	Clarify the relationship between each sentence and the main idea by using details, examples, and other evidence that bring the main idea of the paragraph to life. Without details and examples, broader statements in the paragraph can seem abstract or hollow.
Rewrite	If more than one idea is conveyed in a single paragraph, either split the paragraph in two or rewrite the paragraph so that it establishes a relationship between both ideas.

(1) Using patterns of organization

When sentences are arranged in such a way that the relationship among ideas is clear as is the progression of those ideas, then the paragraph is **coherent**. The following patterns of organization are useful for creating unity and coherence.

- **Chronological order** (particularly useful in narration) arranges ideas according to the order in which things happened.
- **Spatial order** (effective in description) orients the reader's focus from right to left, near to far, top to bottom, and so on.
- **Emphatic order** (useful in expository and persuasive writing) arranges information in order of importance, usually from least to most important, which helps readers understand logical relationships.
- **Logical order** presents information from specific to general or from general to specific, as in the following paragraph.

> It was not the only disappointment my mother felt in me. In the years that followed, I failed her so many times, each time asserting my own will, my right to fall short of expectations. I didn't get straight As. I didn't become class president. I didn't get into Stanford. I dropped out of college.   —AMY TAN, "Two Kinds"

(2) Using pronouns

Instead of repeating names or key words, use pronouns such as *both*, *their*, and *they* to keep references within a paragraph clear.

> Jim Springer and Jim Lewis were adopted as infants into working-class Ohio families. **Both** liked math and did not like spelling in school. **Both** had law enforcement training and worked part-time as deputy sheriffs. **Both** vacationed in Florida, **both** drove Chevrolets. Much has been made of the fact that **their** lives are marked by a trail of similar names. **Both** married and divorced women named Linda and had second marriages

with women named Betty. **They** named **their** sons James Allan and James Alan.

(3) Using repetition

Repeating words, phrases, structures, or ideas can help you link a sentence to those that precede it. Here the repetition of the pronoun *they* and references to *No Child Left Behind* link sentences.

> I recently encountered a mother who told me that her school "had some of those **Nickleby** kids" . . . in reference to **No Child Left Behind** kids. **NCLB**. It was said in a derogatory way, like the school was being dragged down because of these children. So who are these "**Nickleby**" kids? The voiceless ones who slipped through the system because **they** were someone else's problem. **They** were in someone else's school. But you know what? **They** weren't. And aren't. **They** are in almost every school. Your child's school. My daughters' schools. And **they** are gifted young people with much to offer our communities, our country, and our world.
>
> —MARGARET SPELLINGS, "Spellings Addresses PTA Convention"

(4) Using transitions

Even if your sentences are arranged in a seemingly clear sequence, they may be hard for readers to follow without transitions and other necessary connections.

Conjunctions and other transitional words or phrases indicate the logical relationship between ideas.

➤ The toddler cried, **and** he listened helplessly.

➤ The toddler cried **while** he introduced her to the babysitter.

➤ The toddler cried **because** he was putting on his coat.

➤ The toddler cried, **so** he gave her a cookie.

COMMONLY USED TRANSITIONS

Addition	and, and then, further, furthermore, also, too, again, in addition, besides
Alternative	or, nor, either, neither, on the other hand, conversely, otherwise
Comparison	similarly, likewise, in like manner
Concession	although this may be true, even so, still, nevertheless, at the same time, notwithstanding, nonetheless, in any event, that said
Contrast	but, yet, or, yet, however, on the contrary, in contrast
Exemplification	for example, for instance, in the case of
Intensification	in fact, indeed, moreover, even more important, to be sure
Place	here, beyond, nearby, opposite to, adjacent to, on the opposite side
Purpose	to this end, for this purpose, with this objective, in order to, so that
Repetition	as I have said, in other words, that is, as has been noted, as previously stated
Result or cause	so, for, therefore, accordingly, consequently, thus, thereby, as a result, then, because, hence
Sequence	next, first, second, third, in the first place, in the second place, finally, last, then, afterward, later
Summary	to sum up, in brief, on the whole, in sum, in short
Time	meanwhile, soon, after a few days, in the meantime, now, in the past, while, during, since

4 Revising and Editing Essays

Revising entails reviewing your writing in light of your overall purpose: your success at addressing your audience, the clarity of your thesis, the effectiveness of your arrangement, the development and detailed support of your assertions. When you are **editing**, you are polishing your writing: choosing precise words, shaping distinct prose, and structuring effective sentences. When you are **proofreading**, you focus even more: you eliminate surface errors in grammar, punctuation, and mechanics, and you check the formatting and documentation of your sources. If you set aside your writing for twenty-four hours, you will more likely return to it with a critical eye.

CONCERNS FOR REVISION

Look at your draft with a critical eye, considering the following areas closely.

- **Opportunity for writing.** Why are you writing on this topic in the first place?
- **Audience and purpose.** How does your purpose align with your audience?
- **Introduction.** How does it grab the reader?
- **Thesis statement.** How do you declare your purpose?
- **Organization.** According to what specific purpose is your information arranged?
- **Reasons and evidence.** What reasons, evidence, examples, and details do you use to support or extend your thesis?
- **Transitions.** How do you move your reader from one point to the next?

> **CONCERNS FOR REVISION**
>
> - **Conclusion.** How do you describe the consequences of your argument in a final attempt to encourage your audience to consider (if not commit to) a particular course of action?

4a Revising for unity and coherence

When revising the body of an essay, writers are likely to discover ways to make the essay itself more **unified** by relating the assertions and support of each individual paragraph to the thesis statement. After deleting, expanding, or compressing the information in each paragraph accordingly, writers concentrate on **coherence**, ordering their paragraphs purposefully (chronologically, spatially, emphatically, logically) so that a reader can easily follow the connections from one idea, sentence, and paragraph to the next **(3d)**.

4b Revising and editing paragraphs

Just as every paragraph should align itself with the thesis statement, each paragraph should have its own main idea, which often appears as a topic sentence **(3a)**. Every sentence in a paragraph should then align with the main idea or topic sentence. Sometimes, the main idea is implied by the cumulative effect of all the sentences in the paragraph. More often, writers open their paragraphs with an explicit topic sentence. Still, strong paragraphs can end with a topic sentence as well, as in the following paragraph:

> The first time I visited Texas, I wore a beige polyester-blend lab coat with reinforced slits for pocket access and mechanical-pencil storage. I was attending a local booksellers' convention, having just co-written a pseudo-scientific book . . . , and my publicist suggested that the doctor getup would attract attention. It did.

Everyone thought I was the janitor. *Lesson No. 1: When in Texas, do not dress down.*   —PATRICIA MARX, "Dressin' Texan"

CHECKLIST FOR REVISING PARAGRAPHS

For more advice about developing and editing strong paragraphs, see chapter **3**.

- Does each paragraph include a topic sentence that states (or clearly implies) the main idea of the paragraph?
- Does every sentence in the paragraph align with the paragraph's main idea? Eliminate those that do not relate, or consider using them elsewhere.
- Check the detailed support in each paragraph. Are the reasons, evidence, examples, and details effective? What kinds of detailed support might be missing?
- What method or methods have been used to develop the paragraph? What other methods might also be effective, maybe more effective?
- What effective transitions are used to connect sentences?

4c   Getting response

Before you submit your work to an instructor, take advantage of other opportunities for getting response to it. Consult with readers—at the writing center, in your classes, or in online writing groups—asking them for responses to your writing. The following questions will help your readers focus their responses as they read your draft closely.

- How does the draft fulfill all the requirements of the assignment?
- What rhetorical opportunity does the draft address?

- Who is the specific audience? How is that audience appropriate for the assignment?
- How is the tone appropriate? How does it align with the draft's audience and purpose? Is the stance on the topic made clear?
- What is the thesis statement? How is it focused? What assertions support the thesis statement? What evidence, examples, and details are used?
- What makes the arrangement of paragraphs effective? How might the organization be improved?
- What specifically makes the introduction effective? How is it engaging?
- How is the conclusion appropriate? How does it draw the draft together?

4d Editing and proofreading

If you are satisfied with the revised structure of your essay and the content of your paragraphs, you can edit individual sentences for clarity, effectiveness, and variety. Once you have revised and edited, then you must proofread the entire draft, making sure the final product is free from error.

CHECKLIST FOR EDITING SENTENCES

Sentences

- What is the unifying idea of each sentence (23)?
- How have you varied the lengths of your sentences? If your sentences tend to be the same length (whether long or short), revise them for variation (27a).
- How many of your sentences use subordination? Coordination? If you overuse any one sentence structure, revise for variation (24).

(Continued on page 26)

CHECKLIST FOR EDITING SENTENCES   *(Continued)*

- Which sentences might be strengthened with parallel structure? Check that lists and series are in parallel form (**25**).
- Check that each verb agrees with its subject (**20f**). Check that every pronoun agrees with its antecedent (**21c**). Reread your sentences with these agreement issues in mind, revising accordingly.

Diction

- Check that you have not unintentionally repeated any words (**30**).
- Which general words can you make more specific (**29**)?
- How exactly is the vocabulary you have chosen appropriate for your audience, purpose, and context?
- Which technical or unfamiliar words have you defined for your audience?

CHECKLIST FOR PROOFREADING

Spelling

- Have you double-checked the words you frequently misspell and any the spell checker may have missed (**36**)? For example, check for misspellings that still form words (such as *form* for *from*).
- If you used a spell checker, did it overlook homophones (such as *there/their*, *who's/whose*, and *it's/its*)?
- Have you double-checked the spelling of all foreign words and all proper names?

Punctuation and Capitalization

- Check that each sentence has appropriate closing punctuation. Check that you use only one space after each end punctuation mark (**35**).
- Check that all punctuation within sentences—commas, semicolons, apostrophes, hyphens, and dashes—is used appropriately and placed correctly (**31, 32, 33**).

5 Critical Reading and Textual Analysis

In your academic work, you will be called on to read a variety of complex visuals and texts that make arguments to support a position. You will need to identify the argument, the claims it makes, and the evidence it uses. To engage these texts fully, you must learn to read them actively and critically.

5a Critical reading

Because you cannot always take a message at face value, when you read critically, you concentrate, ask good questions, and comment thoughtfully on or about the text itself. Whether the text is print, electronic, spoken, visual, or some combination, you need to interpret it critically.

You already use this skill in your personal life when you are considering a friend's text message, a child's excuse, or a popular movie. For example, when you go to *Skyfall*, you watch the complex plot quickly unfold, asking yourself how the London

bombing, the Shanghai paradise, the Macau casino all connect with M, with Silva, with James Bond himself. All during
the movie, you use similar critical skills, posing questions and
making comments to yourself as you figure out the connections. In your academic life, you use the same questioning and
commenting skills, whether you are reading finance problem
sets, your political science textbook, or a speech class podcast.

Reading critically helps you establish what you already know
about a topic or author, what you are likely to learn from the
text, and what information is lacking. Reading critically also
helps you gauge the expertise and credibility of the writer. In addition, the process helps you distinguish between actual content
and your expectations for that content, a process that prepares
you to handle a heavy academic reading and writing load.

CHECKLIST FOR CRITICAL READING

- **Consider your purpose.** What is your purpose for reading?

- **Preview the text.** What information does the title convey? What
  do you already know about the topic? What opinions do you hold
  about the topic?

- **Consider the author.** What do you know about the credibility of
  the author or creator? What is the author's purpose?

- **Read the text.** Identify the key parts of the text itself. How do
  they relate to one another? What parts do you find informative?
  Confusing?

- **Annotate.** Identify the key terms or characters in the text. How
  do they contribute (or not) to your understanding of the text?

- **Analyze the text.** With what parts of the text do you agree?
  Disagree? Does the author achieve his or her purpose? Why or
  why not?

- **Consider the effects of the text.** What parts of the text rein-
  forced what you already knew? What you already value? What
  parts of the text surprised you? Why? What else would you like
  to know?

When you analyze, you take care to evaluate the claims and positions of written and visual texts, whether they are advertisements, accounts of current events, or excuses for breaking a date (**6c**). Textual analysis is an intellectual skill closely aligned with argumentation, in that it serves as a mechanism for recognizing and examining the arguments of others as well as for formulating and then examining your own. Most communication is to some extent an argument, intended to influence the attitudes or actions of an audience. Writing is recognized as argumentative when it clearly supports a position. A résumé is an argument for a job interview, just as a warm welcome is an argument for you to enjoy an evening with friends.

Effective arguments are well developed, broken into strong assertions that are supported by intelligent and appropriate **evidence**. Effective arguments also take into consideration the **reasons** others might disagree. For readers to take the ideas in an argument seriously, the writer must communicate the reasons that have led to a position as well as the values and **assumptions** (assumed shared beliefs, often unstated) that underlie the writer's thinking.

Although many arguments are based on the use of assertions and support, some, like those of Stephen Toulmin, are rooted in a logical progression. The Toulmin method for understanding an argument provides yet another way for you to consider the elements of an argument for analysis.

FEATURES OF A TOULMIN ARGUMENT

The philosopher Stephen Toulmin defined **argument** as a logical progression, from the **data** (accepted evidence or reasons that support a claim), to the **claim** (a debatable or controversial statement), based on the **warrant** (the underlying assumption, like the major premise). If the warrant is controversial, it requires **backing** (independent support or justification).

(Continued on page 30)

FEATURES OF A TOULMIN ARGUMENT *(Continued)*

Starting with a general statement and then reasoning toward a conclusion, Toulmin's method establishes a reasonable relationship between the data and the claim, as in the following argument:

➤ Universities should not sell naming rights to buildings because education, not pleasing corporate sponsors, should be the universities' primary goal.

Data (support)	Selling naming rights to buildings makes pleasing the sponsors a top priority.
Claim	Universities should not sell naming rights to buildings.
Warrant	Education is the first priority of universities.

TIPS FOR ANALYZING AN ARGUMENT

- Read through the argument carefully. Determine the author's main point or thesis.

- Map out the supporting evidence that the author uses to support that thesis.

- Identify the kinds of sources the author uses. How reliable, current, and effective are they?

- Determine the author's qualifications, assumptions, and values. Identify evidence that supports the credibility (or lack thereof) of the author.

- Weigh your opinions against the author's, identifying places you agree and disagree with the author, assumptions you share and do not share.

- Evaluate the quality of the supporting examples or evidence the author uses to reinforce the position. Whether visual, verbal, or a combination, the reasons should be good ones, reasonable, practical, and ethical. What objections might be made to this series of good reasons?

- Identify the assumptions the author makes about the intended audience. How does the author reach out to that audience?

> **TIPS FOR ANALYZING AN ARGUMENT**
>
> - Consider your overall impression of the argument. What does the author want readers to do in response to the argument? If you were successfully, partially, or unsuccessfully persuaded by this argument, identify the passages that were effective or weak. How might the author strengthen those passages?

5c Basic appeals in an argument

Effective arguments always incorporate a combination of persuasive strategies, which include three general types of **appeal**.

(1) Ethical appeals

The most important appeal is the **ethical appeal** because it establishes the writer's credibility and trustworthiness. An ethical appeal demonstrates goodwill toward the audience, good sense or knowledge of the subject at hand, and good character. To identify the ethical appeal, look for the way the writer strives to establish common ground with readers in the introduction. Then, look for ways that the writer demonstrates a thorough knowledge of the topic to establish credibility. Also check biographical information that may accompany the text for personal and professional information about the author (qualifications, credentials, and experiences), all of which help establish good sense and moral character.

(2) Logical appeals

By providing good reasons (practical, moral, even aesthetic reasons) in the body of a text, an author establishes the **logical appeal**. Evidence, examples, statistics, comparisons, facts, expert opinions, and personal experiences or observations all constitute good logical appeals—if they are trustworthy, effective, and judicious. Evaluate these pieces of evidence and check facts; you cannot assume that all logical appeals are built on valid facts and sources.

(3) Emotional appeals

An **emotional appeal** connects the writer's beliefs and feelings with those of the audience. To identify an emotional appeal, look for language (examples, possible consequences, and so on) designed to stir emotions, build connections, and invoke shared values. Like the ethical and logical appeals, emotional appeals should also be trustworthy, never manipulative.

6 Writing Arguments

If everyone agreed on everything, there would be no need for **argument**, for taking a position, whether gently or forcefully. Therefore, a good deal of the writing you will do in school, at home, or at work will require you to take an arguable position on a topic. Arguments serve three basic purposes: (1) to analyze a complicated issue or question an established belief, (2) to express or defend a point of view, (3) and to invite or convince an audience to change a position or adopt a course of action.

6a   Considering differing viewpoints

Behind any effective argument is a question that can generate more than one reasonable answer. Answers differ because people approach questions with various backgrounds, experiences, and assumptions, and they are often tempted to use reasoning that supports what they already believe. As a writer, employing such reasoning is a good place to start. However, as you expand your argument, you will want to demonstrate not only that you are knowledgeable about your topic but also that you have given fair consideration to other views about it.

When you choose a topic for argumentation, you will want to take a stance that provides you with a reason for writing, a problem to address or resolve (chapter **1**). At the same time, you must establish **common ground** with your audience, stating a goal toward which you both want to work or identifying a belief, assumption, or value that you both share. First, focus on a topic, on the part of some general subject that you will address in your essay, and then pose a question about it. Consider what you know about the topic and the following:

- your own values and beliefs with respect to the question
- how your assumptions might differ from those of your intended audience
- how you might establish common ground with members of your audience while respecting any differences between your opinion and theirs

The question you raise will evolve into your **thesis**, an arguable statement. To determine whether a topic might be suitable, make a statement about the topic.

"I believe strongly that . . . "

"My view is that . . . "

Then check to see if that statement can be argued.

6b   Distinguishing between fact and opinion

When you develop your thesis statement into an argument, you use both facts and opinions. **Facts** are reliable pieces of information that can be verified through independent sources or procedures. **Opinions**, on the other hand, are assertions or inferences that may or may not be based on facts. Opinions that are widely accepted may seem to be factual when they are not; rather, they are assumptions. Facts are significant only when they are used responsibly to support a claim; otherwise, a thoughtful and well-informed opinion might have more impact and forge a stronger connection with your audience.

6c | Taking a position or making a claim

When making an argument, a writer takes a position (called the **claim**) on a particular topic, which clearly states what the writer wants the audience to do with the information being provided. The central claim is the thesis for your argument and is articulated in your thesis statement.

Claims can be absolute or moderate, large or limited. Absolute claims assert that something is always true or false ("The sun will rise tomorrow"), completely good or bad ("All professional athletes dope"); moderate claims make less sweeping assertions ("It looks like rain" or "Unfortunately, some professional athletes have admitted to doping").

ABSOLUTE CLAIM   College athletes are never good students.

MODERATE CLAIM   Most colleges have low graduation rates for their athletes.

The stronger the claim, the stronger the evidence needed to support it. Be sure to consider the quality and the significance of the evidence you use—not just its quantity.

Claims may assert that something exists or is evident. Without making a value judgment, such a claim makes a point that can be supported by evidence.

➤ The job market for those who just received an MBA appears to be unlimited.

➤ The post office is raising rates again.

Claims may assert evaluations—that something has a specific quality, is good or bad, effective or ineffective, attractive or unattractive, successful or unsuccessful.

➤ The graduation rate for athletes at Penn State is very high compared with that at the other Big Ten universities.

➤ The public transportation system in Washington, DC, is reliable and safe.

Claims may also call for a specific action.

➤ We must find the funds to keep our successful and well-qualified high school teachers.

➤ We need to build a light-rail system linking downtown with the airport and the western suburbs.

6d Providing evidence for an effective argument

(1) Establishing reasons for the claim

If you want readers to take your ideas seriously, you must communicate the reasons that have led to your position as well as the values and **assumptions** (the underlying beliefs) of your thinking. When you are exploring your topic, make a list of the reasons that have led to your belief. If it is likely that your readers will not share an assumption, consider giving your reasons and offer supporting evidence. For example, when Anna Seitz was working on her argumentative essay (**6g**), she listed the following reasons for her belief that universities should not allow individuals or corporations to buy naming rights to campus buildings:

1. By purchasing naming rights, donors gain influence over educational policy decisions, even though they are not qualified to make such decisions.

2. Significant donations can adversely affect overall university finances by replacing existing funding sources.

3. Donors who purchase naming rights are associated with the university, in spite of the fact that they or their corporations may subscribe to a different set of values.

Although it is possible to base an argument on one good reason (such as "The selling of naming rights distracts from the educational purposes of universities"), doing so can be risky. When you show that you have more than one reason for believing as you do, you increase the likelihood that your audience will find some measure of merit in your argument. Sometimes, however, one reason is more appropriate than several others you could advance. To develop an argument for which you have only one good reason, explore the bases underlying your reason: the assumptions that led you to take your stand.

Whether you have one reason or several, be sure to provide sufficient evidence from credible sources to support your claim: facts, statistics, examples, and testimony from personal experience or professional expertise. This evidence must be accurate, representative, and sufficient. Accurate information should be verifiable by others. Recognize, however, that even if the information a writer provides is accurate, it may not be representative or sufficient if it was drawn from an exceptional case, a biased sample, or a one-time occurrence. Whatever form of evidence you use, you need to make clear to your audience exactly *why* and *how* the evidence supports your claim.

(2) Responding to diverse views

Effective arguments consider and respond to other points of view, fairly and respectfully. The most common strategy for addressing opposing points of view is **refutation**: you introduce diverse views and then respectfully demonstrate why you disagree with or accept each of them. When you find yourself agreeing with a point that supports another side of the issue, you can benefit from offering a **concession**, which can demonstrate your fair-mindedness. If you admit that others are partially right, they are more likely to admit that you could be partially right as well.

(3) Using visuals

Visuals, such as tables, charts, graphs, photographs, and maps can strengthen your argument by offering evidence as well as organizing and describing facts and data.

TIPS FOR THINKING CRITICALLY ABOUT VISUALS

Before you incorporate a visual into your project, analyze the argument it makes and its purpose.

- Study the visual until you understand its claim.

- Determine the trustworthiness and accuracy of the visual. How does the creator of the visual establish credibility? What sources are used? Are they current and reliable?

- Determine if—and how—the visual incorporates rhetorical appeals: ethical, logical, or emotional (**5c**).

- Determine the purpose of the visual: to organize facts, present data, illustrate a piece of background, demonstrate authority.

- Identify the intended audience. What assumptions does the visual make about viewers? What background knowledge or attitudes would the audience likely have?

- If the visual includes words and images, consider how they work together. How do the words and visual elements relate to one another?

- Look closely at composition and the design of the visual. What colors, lines, shapes, positions of objects, or expressions of people do you notice? How do these elements relate to one another to make a point or serve the purpose of the visual?

Make clear how the visual supports the claim you are making in your text. Check the disciplinary conventions and models in your field for the kinds of visuals that are considered appropriate.

6e   Using appeals to ground your argument

Effective arguments always incorporate a combination of three persuasive strategies: the **appeals** of ethos, logos, and pathos (**5c**). **Ethos** (an ethical appeal) establishes the speaker's or writer's credibility and trustworthiness. An ethical appeal demonstrates goodwill toward the audience, good sense or knowledge of the subject at hand, and good character. Establishing common ground with the audience is another feature of ethos. **Logos**, a logical appeal consisting of good reasons, demonstrates an effective use of reason and judicious use of evidence, whether that evidence consists of facts, statistics, comparisons, anecdotes, expert opinions, personal experiences, or observations. Good reasons should be practical, moral, and aesthetic (meaning they should have a pleasing outcome). You employ your good reasons in the process of supporting claims, drawing reasonable conclusions, and avoiding rhetorical fallacies. **Pathos** (an emotional appeal) involves using language that will engage (not manipulate) the feelings of the audience by establishing empathy and authentic understanding. The most effective arguments combine these three persuasive appeals responsibly and knowledgeably.

6f   Organizing an effective argument

No single organization is right for every written argument. The decisions you make about arrangement should be based on several factors: your topic, your audience, and your purpose. You can develop a good plan by listing the major points you want to make, deciding what order to put them in, and determining where to include refutation or concession. You must also decide where to place your thesis statement or claim.

Your conclusion should move beyond what has already been stated to reinforce your rhetorical purpose: the course of action you want your audience to take, an invitation to further understanding, or the implications of your claim.

FEATURES OF THE CLASSICAL ARRANGEMENT

One way to organize your argument is to use classical arrangement, which assumes that an audience is prepared to follow a well-reasoned argument.

Introduction	Introduce your issue and capture the attention of your audience. Begin establishing your credibility (using ethos) and common ground with your audience.
Background information	Provide your audience with a history of the situation and state how things currently stand. Define any key terms. Draw the attention of your audience to those points that are especially important and explain why they are meaningful.
Proposition	Introduce the position you are taking: present the argument itself and provide the basic reasons for your belief. Frame your position as a thesis statement or a claim.
Proof or confirmation	Discuss the reasons that have led you to take your position. Each reason must be clear, relevant, and representative. Provide facts, expert testimony, and any other evidence that supports your claim.
Refutation	Recognize and disprove the arguments of people who hold a different position and with whom you continue to disagree.
Concession	Concede any point with which you agree or that has merit; show why this concession might affect yet does not damage your own case.
Conclusion	Summarize your most important points and appeal to your audience's feelings, making a personal connection. Describe the consequences of your argument in a final attempt to encourage your audience to consider (if not commit to) a particular course of action or belief.

6g   Sample argument

As you read the following essay by Anna Seitz, note her use of ethical, logical, and emotional appeals; reasoning; and arrangement. Also, identify the kinds of evidence she uses (facts, examples, testimony, or authority).

Seitz 1

Anna Seitz

Professor Byerly

English 102

30 November 2012

Naming Opportunities: Opportunities for Whom?

All over the nation, football stadiums, business schools, law schools, dining halls, and even coaching positions have become naming opportunities (also known as "naming rights" and "legacy opportunities"). Since the first college deal in 1979—when Syracuse University signed a deal with the Carrier Corporation for

Introduction   lifetime naming rights to its sports stadium, the Carrier Dome— naming has become a common practice with an alleged two-fold payoff: universities raise money, and donors get their names writ large. Universities use the money from naming opportunities to hire more faculty, raise salaries, support faculty research, provide travel opportunities for students, and build stadium suites and boxes for game watching. Reser Stadium (Oregon State), The Donald Bren School of Law (University of California–Irvine), or the KFC Yum! Center (University of Louisville)—all these naming opportunities

Seitz 2

seem like a good solution for raising money, especially at a time when state legislatures have cut back on university funding and when wealthy alumni are being besieged for donations from every college they have ever attended. Naming opportunities seem like a good solution for donors, too, because their donations will be broadly recognized. While naming opportunities may seem like a perfect solution for improving colleges and universities and for simplifying funding, in reality they are not. Therefore, I argue against naming opportunities on college and university campuses because they create more problems than they solve.

The naming of sports stadiums is a familiar occurrence. After all, universities commonly highlight the sponsors of their athletic programs. But naming opportunities in other spheres of academic life are unfamiliar to most people, even though such naming is an established practice. A quick search of the web pages of university libraries reveals that many of them, especially those in the midst of major development campaigns, have created a price list just for naming opportunities. Entire buildings are available, of course. For example, a $3 million donation earns the right to name the music library at the University of Colorado Boulder (Williams). But even parts of buildings are also available these days. North Carolina State University is willing to name an exhibit case according to the donor's wishes for only $10,000 or put a specific name on a table in their reading room for $3,500 (Mulvey).

Background information

Seitz 3

Naming opportunities can clearly bring in a good deal of money. It has become commonplace for schools to offer naming opportunities on planned construction in exchange for 51 percent of the cost of the building! That is a big head start to a building project, and naming opportunities may be what allow some schools to provide their students with better facilities than their unnamed counterparts. In fact, donors are often recruited for the opportunity to pay for named faculty chairs, reading rooms, or major library or art collections—all of which enhance student life.

Background information

Clearly the more opportunities and resources any university can offer current and potential students and even alumni, the more that university enhances its own growth and that of its faculty. Library donors and recipients say that if it is possible for a library to pay for a new computer lab just by adding a sign with someone's name over the door, the advantages often seem to outweigh the disadvantages. Proponents of naming opportunities point out that small donors are often hailed as library supporters, even when big donors are maligned as corporate flag-wavers.

Few would argue that these donations necessarily detract from the educational mission of the institution. However, selling off parts of a university library, for example, does not always please people, especially those whose responsibility includes managing

Seitz 4

that donation. The curator of rare books and manuscripts at a
prominent state university told me that one of the most frustrating
parts of her job is dealing with "strings-attached" gifts, which
is what too many library donations turn out to be (and why she
wishes to remain anonymous). Some major donors like to make
surprise visits, during which they monitor the prominence of their
"legacy opportunity." Others like to create rules which limit the use
of their funds to the purchase of certain collections or subjects;
still others just need constant personal maintenance, including
lunches, coffees, and regular invitations to events. But meddling
in their donation after the fact is just a minor inconvenience
compared to some donors' actions.

    Donors who fund an ongoing educational program and give
money on a regular basis often expect to have regular input.
Because major donors want major prestige, they try to align
themselves with successful programs. Doing that can result in
damage to university budgets. First, high-profile programs can
become increasingly well funded, while less prominent, less
glamorous ones are ignored. Second, regularly available corporate
or private funds can erode existing funding sources. Simply put, if
a budgeted program becomes funded by donation, the next time
the program needs funding, the department or unit will likely

Background information

Proposition

be told that finding a donor is their only option. Essentially, once donor-funded, always donor-funded.

Proposition

Additionally, many academics feel that selling off naming rights can create an image problem for a university. While buildings, schools, endowed chairs, even football stadiums were once named for past professors, university presidents, or others with strong ties to the university, those same facilities are now named for virtually anyone who can afford to donate, including corporations. A close relationship with or input from a corporation creates the appearance of a conflict of interest in a university, which is exactly the reason such arrangements are so often vehemently opposed by the university community. The University of Missouri arranged to name a new sports arena after Paige Laurie, whose parents are heirs to part of the Walmart fortune and donated $25 million (Dunn). In 2004, reports of a scandal surfaced that Laurie was guilty of extensive academic misconduct as an undergraduate at USC that forced her to return her diploma. The negative press related to the ethics scandal and the Laurie donation pressured the university to rename the Paige Arena, which quickly became the Mizzou Arena.

Proof

Given these drawbacks, many universities are establishing guidelines for the selection of appropriate donors for named gifts. To that end, fundraising professional Robert Hoak suggests that naming opportunities should be mutually beneficial for the donor (whether a corporation or an individual) and the organization (university, for instance) and that these opportunities should be

Seitz 6

viewed as the start of a long-term relationship between the two,
not the final gift. Additionally, he cautions that even if the donor
seems the right fit for the organization, it is in the best interest
of both parties to add an escape clause to the contract in order to
protect either side from potential embarrassment or scandal. He
provides the example of Seton Hall University, which regrettably
had both an academic building and the library rotunda named for
Tyco CEO Dennis Kozlowski. When Kozlowski was convicted of grand
larceny, the university pulled the names (Hoak).

Proof

Although many people prefer that naming be a recognition
of an accomplished faculty member or administrator, most realize
that recruiting named gift donors is good business. Whether it is
"good education" is another question. Naming university property
for major donors should not be merely a sales transaction. New
College in Cambridge, Massachusetts, was just that—until local
clergyman John Harvard died and left half his estate and his entire
library to what would soon become Harvard College. Modern naming
opportunities, however, do not necessarily recognize and remember
individuals who had significant influence on university life; rather,
they create obligations for the university to operate in such a way
as to please living donors or their descendants. Pleasing wealthy
donors should not replace educating students as a university's
primary goal.

Refutation

Seitz 7

Works Cited

Dunn, Paul. "When a Donor Becomes Tainted." *Nonprofit Quarterly*

17.1 (2010): n. pag. Web. 26 Nov. 2012.

Hoak, Robert. "Making the Most of Naming Opportunities." *on*

Philanthropy. Changing Our World, 28 Mar. 2003. Web. 25

Nov. 2012.

Mulvey, Jim. "Donors Can Find Many Naming Opportunities for the

D. H. Hill Library," *Focus Online* 25.2 (2005): 7. Web. 25 Nov.

2012.

Williams, James F. "Naming Opportunities." *CU University Libraries/*

Dean's Office. U of Colorado Boulder, 2012. Web. 25 Nov.

2012.

Works Cited page follows MLA style

7 Designing Documents

Consistent, thoughtful use of design and effective visual elements in your writing—whether reports, essays, articles, or news stories—can enhance your message, engage your readers, and thus create an appropriate overall impression. The elements of design include typeface, layout, lists, headings, and color. The visual elements of writing can include tables, pie charts, line graphs, bar graphs, diagrams, photographs, maps, and even cartoons. For academic writing, be sure to check the formatting guidelines for your discipline. This handbook provides advice for formatting essays and other projects using style guides sponsored by the Modern Language Association (MLA), the American Psychological Association (APA), the *Chicago Manual of Style* (CMS), and the Council of Science Editors (CSE). If you are unsure of which style to follow, check with your instructor.

7a Elements of design

No matter what you compose, your first design decisions center on layout and typeface. Other choices, from those of headings to use of color, come later.

(1) Layout

Layout, also referred to as formatting, is the arrangement of the text on a page or screen, the **spacing**, and the **margins**. Final drafts of your academic projects will often be double-spaced, with indented paragraphs (usually one-half inch or five spaces, following the style of your discipline). Other documents, including lab reports and business documents (such as memos, résumés, and letters) will be single-spaced and use an extra line space to indicate a new paragraph instead of indentation. Texts you create to be read online should also be single-spaced.

Appropriate use of margins and white space in your document guides readers and creates a sense of control and readability. Most of the writing (essays and reports) you do in school will be formatted for 8½-by-11-inch paper, usually with one-inch margins throughout. Use additional space around block quotations (often indented one inch), headings, and visuals, such as graphs and tables. MLA, APA, and other documentation styles offer specific guidelines for margins and the amount of space around block quotations, headings, and other visuals.

(2) Fonts or typefaces

The fonts and sizes of type used in a document can greatly affect readability. For most of your academic essays, professional reports, and other print documents, use serif fonts, such as Times New Roman, Garamond, or Century. Regarded as most readable for printed works (including this book), these fonts include serifs, those little tails that elongate the tips of most of the letters. Fonts without serifs (sans serif fonts), such as Arial, Lucida Sans, and Calibri, are said to be easier to read on the screen, so they are the popular typeface choice for web texts. For print documents using multiple fonts, sans serif fonts are effective when used in headings, subheadings, or captions.

For most academic work, you will use 10-, 11-, or 12-point type. A wide variety of fonts are available. Use the decorative or amusing ones (such as ALGERIAN, *Blackadder*, and Curlz MT) sparingly because they are difficult to read in large passages.

Use **bold**, *italicized*, or underlined text options for emphasis. For example, bold can be useful to distinguish headings, and italic type is used to set off titles and words being defined.

Your use of type style often depends on your academic discipline, so be sure you follow the appropriate formatting rules— MLA, APA, CMS, or CSE—for your field.

(3) Headings

Headings provide visual signposts for your audience that offer help navigating your text and understanding its organization. Consider the wording of your headings carefully, making sure they are concise and consistent throughout your document. Word your headings informatively so they relay the essence of the text they accompany. Use grammatically parallel structures, either a noun (*Vaccination*), phrases with gerunds (*Mandating Vaccination*), or questions (*Should States Mandate Additional Vaccinations?*). In many cases, the wording of headings will be dictated by the documentation style you use (for example, *Abstract* or *References* in APA style).

Your discipline may also have guidelines for the placement and format of your headings, for example, requiring that they be centered. (APA style offers specific instruction for the style and placement of headings.) In most academic writing, you might

Center and Use Boldface for Your First-Level Heading

Align Left Your Second-Level Heading or Subheading

<u>Underline and Merge Your Third-Level Heading</u> with the paragraph information that follows. However you use headings, position them consistently and follow the guidelines of your discipline.

(4) Lists and examples

Purposeful lists and examples also enhance your design. Many writers use bullets, numbers, or letters to highlight lists and examples. Choose bulleted lists when the items are related but may appear in any order. Use numbered or lettered lists when the sequential order of items is important (as in "first, do this; second, do that"). Lists are always indented, at least one-half inch, and single-spaced. Leave white space around your list, on both sides as well as above and below.

(5) Color

To use color appropriately in your documents, first consider the conventions in your discipline and assignment, along with your purpose and audience. Use of color helps you draw attention to headings or to other elements on a page, including graphs, charts, or other visuals. Position colors thoughtfully, keeping the number of colors to a minimum, and use them consistently throughout. Choose legible colors that offer contrast, and check that colors you choose will work well in the final product. Color combinations that are strong and legible on your screen may look different to your readers when printed or projected.

7b   Using visuals

Many academic and professional documents that are primarily composed of text also make substantial use of visuals, or **graphics**, to clarify written material. Because they are fully integrated into the overall argument of the text, such visuals are much more than decoration. Used purposefully, they organize and clarify evidence or establish credibility. All visuals should be cited carefully and used ethically.

TIPS FOR USING VISUALS EFFECTIVELY

- Choose images that have a clear purpose and that relate clearly to a point you are making in your text.

- Insert visuals following or near the text that refers to them. Give each visual a number (*Figure 1* or *Fig. 1*), and number tables separately. Include a title for each.

TIPS FOR USING VISUALS EFFECTIVELY

- Identify the visual in your text, clarifying the connection or purpose for including it (*Fig. 2 presents the number of children with high lead levels over time*).

- Following the rules of your discipline, include documentation for each visual in your bibliography. For visuals you create using data or information in a source, you must cite the source of that information.

- Obtain permission to include visuals from other sources if you plan to publish your work online or outside your course.

- Resize, crop, and edit images if necessary, taking care not to alter meaning or distort the original point of a visual you find in another source. Check to be sure for any maps, charts, diagrams, or graphs that all elements of the graphic and its labels are clear, so that readers will understand the information.

(1) Tables

Tables use a row-and-column arrangement to organize data (numbers or words) spatially. They are especially useful for presenting great amounts of numerical information in a small space, enabling the reader to draw direct comparisons among pieces of data or even to locate specific items. When you design a table, be sure to label all of the columns and rows accurately and to provide both a title and a number for the table. The table number and title traditionally appear above the table body, as table 7.1 demonstrates, and any notes or source information should be placed below it.

(2) Charts and graphs

Charts and graphs display relationships among statistical data in visual form by using lines, bars, or other visual elements rather than just letters and numbers. **Pie charts** are especially useful for showing the relationship of parts to a whole (see fig. 7.1), but they can only be used to display sets of data that add up to 100 percent (a whole).

Table 7.1

Identified Prevalence of Autism Spectrum Disorders Autism and Developmental Disabilities Monitoring Network 2000–2008 Combining Data from All Sites				
Surveillance Year	Birth Year	Number of ADDM Sites Reporting	Prevalence per 1,000 Children (Range)	This is about 1 in X children . . .
2000	1992	6	6.7 (4.5–9.9)	1 in 150
2002	1994	14	6.6 (3.3–10.6)	1 in 150
2004	1996	8	8.0 (4.6–9.8)	1 in 125
2006	1998	11	9.0 (4.2–12.1)	1 in 110
2008	2000	14	11.3 (4.8–21.2)	1 in 88

Source: "Data and Statistics," *Autism and Spectrum Disorders,* CDC (http://www.cdc.gov/ncbddd/autism/data.html).

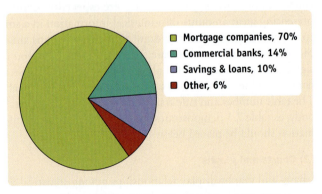

Mortgage companies, 70%
Commercial banks, 14%
Savings & loans, 10%
Other, 6%

Figure 7.1. Pie chart showing issuers of mortgage-based securities.
Copyright © Cengage Learning®

Bar charts show correlations between two variables that do not change smoothly over time. For instance, a bar chart might

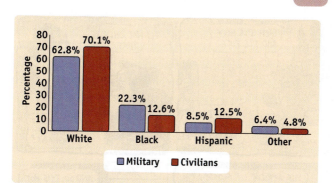

Figure 7.2. Bar chart illustrating the composition of the U.S. military.
Copyright © Cengage Learning®

illustrate the relative speeds of various computer processors or statistics about the composition of the U.S. military (see fig. 7.2).

(3) Maps

Historical, economic, and geographic accounts often call for the use of maps (see fig. 7.3).

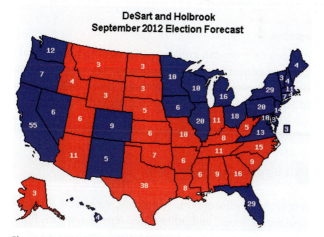

Figure 7.3. 2012 Presidential election forecast map.
Source: DeSart, Jay, and Thomas Holbrook

Figure 7.4. Cartoon (*Our Moral*, by Tim Eagan) **illustrating a political idea.**
Source: Tim Eagan/Cagle Cartoons

(4) Cartoons

Sometimes a cartoon can enhance your writing, as political, medical, and educational humor often brings home a point even better than words do. In the cartoon shown in figure 7.4, the reader is asked to separate the alleged policies from the message itself.

7c   **Using pictures effectively**

Pictures include photographs, sketches, technical illustrations, paintings, icons, and other visual representations. Photographs are often used to reinforce textual descriptions or to show a reader exactly what something looks like. But photographs are not always the most informative type of picture. Compare the two images in figure 7.5. Although the photograph is a more realistic image of a small wind turbine, the

A

B

Figure 7.5. A photo and a drawing of a small wind turbine.
Sources: photo (A)—© Bergey Windpower Co., National Renewable Energy Laboratory, http://images.nrel.gov; illustration (B)—National Renewable Energy Laboratory, http://plainswindeis.anl.gov/guide/basics/index.cfm

illustration more clearly shows the wind turbine's important features: rotor, gearbox, generator, and so forth. Line drawings enable the designer of a document to highlight specific elements of an object while de-emphasizing or eliminating unnecessary information.

R

RESEARCH

8 Planning Research

Research is much more than the act of searching for information. It consists of posing intriguing, challenging questions. Seeking information is a response to these questions. In fact, thinking of research as **inquiry**, as asking questions and finding answers, will help you to craft a research question, or a set of related questions, as well as to create a plan that focuses your attention and makes your work efficient.

8a Considering your assignment

When you are given an assignment that calls for research, begin by asking yourself why you are doing this research and who will benefit from your research findings. Common purposes for doing research include the following:

- **To inform an audience.** The researcher reports current thinking on a specific topic, including opposing views, factual information, and credible evidence.
- **To analyze and synthesize information and then offer possible solutions.** The researcher analyzes a topic and synthesizes the available information about it, looking for points of agreement and disagreement and for gaps in coverage. Sometimes the researcher offers possible ways to address any problems found.
- **To convince or issue an invitation to an audience.** The researcher states a position and backs it up with data, statistics, testimony, corroborating texts or events, or supporting arguments. The researcher's purpose is to persuade readers to take the same position.

Next, consider your audience. Who are your readers, and what do they most need to know? What kinds of sources and evidence will they find reliable? Also important is consideration of your stance (or attitude). Will you be able to keep an open mind as you do your research? Will you be able to take into account multiple points of view?

Before you start to write, be sure you understand your instructor's expectations for length, format, due date, and other practical matters. Creating a research plan will help you meet these expectations and complete your work on time (**8d**).

8b Formulating research questions

Research questions often arise when you try to relate what you are studying to your own experience. For instance, you may start wondering about voting regulations while reading about past elections for a history class and, at the same time, noticing news stories about the role technology plays in current elections or the unfair practices reported in some states. Each of these observations may give rise to a different question. Focusing on the influence of technology may prompt you to inquire, "What are the possible consequences of having only electronic ballots?" However, if you focus on unfair voting practices, you may ask, "How do voting procedures differ from state to state?" Because you can ask a variety of research questions about any topic, choose the one that interests you the most and allows you to fulfill your assignment.

To generate useful research questions, you may find it helpful to ask yourself about causes, consequences, processes, definitions, or values.

What caused the power outage during the 2013 Super Bowl in New Orleans?

What are the consequences of taking selective serotonin reuptake inhibitors (SSRIs) for a long period of time?

How do musicians decide whether to charge for access to their music online?

Do psychiatrists agree on a definition for Internet addiction?

Should the federal minimum wage be raised?

Although choosing just one question will make your research efficient, you may find it beneficial to answer more than one question when you write your paper. For example, if you explain the debate over the minimum wage, you may also decide to define *federal minimum wage*. Regardless of how many questions you ask, the best research questions are challenging, focused, and connected to current facts or events. A question such as *Do psychiatrists agree on a definition for Internet addiction?* is much more focused than *What is Internet addiction?*

TIPS FOR FINDING A CHALLENGING RESEARCH QUESTION

First find a topic.

- What problem or issue from one of your classes would you like to address?
- What have you read or observed recently that piqued your curiosity?
- What local or school problem would you like to explore or help solve?
- Is there anything (lifestyles, political views, global events) that you find unusual or intriguing enough to investigate?

Once you have a topic, jot down all the questions you have about that topic. (Think about causes, consequences, processes, definitions, and values.) Choose the most specific question that will interest both you and your audience and that will help you address your assignment. Be sure the question cannot be easily answered with a *yes* or *no*.

8c   Testing research questions

You can test your research question to see whether it is effective by first making sure you and others are sincerely interested in answering this question. At the same time, double-check your assignment for length restrictions and decide whether your research question is specific enough to be addressed in the space available. Finally, because any assignment comes with deadlines, determine whether you have the time and resources available to answer the question by the due date.

TIPS FOR TESTING YOUR RESEARCH QUESTION

To test your research question, start a conversation about it by having a friend or classmate interview you about its potential. If no one is available, sharpen your ideas by *writing* your answers.

- Why is it important for you to answer this research question?
- Are there more than two ways of answering this question?
- Why is it important for your audience to know the answer to the question?
- Why does the answer to your question require research?
- What type of research might help you answer your question?
- Will you be able to carry out the necessary research in the amount of time and space allowed?

After you have a strong research question, you are ready to start gathering information and exploring sources. Your preliminary reading of appropriate sources will help you go from your research question to a tentative or working thesis statement (**8d**).

8d   Creating a research plan

As you craft your research question, you may find it helpful to draft a plan for your research project as well.

1. Create a research question.   *Due:* _____

It is easy to rush to answer your question, even before you have done any research. Try to keep an open mind until you have consulted some of your sources (**8a, 8b**).

2. Note the assignment's requirements.   *Due:* _____

Clarify your instructor's expectations. *What is the due date? What is the approximate length of the research project? What style manual should you use (MLA, APA, CMS, CSE)? What point of view is appropriate (first person, third person, a combination)? What is the medium of delivery? Are you expected to print out a document? Post a document online? Prepare an oral presentation? Incorporate visuals?* If you have not already received sufficient information about your assignment, ask your instructor these questions as soon as possible.

3. Establish your audience and purpose.   *Due:* _____

Knowing who your readers are and what your purpose is will help you not only to decide what types of sources to use but also to establish an appropriate tone. Your instructor will be one of your readers. *Does your assignment expect you to consider other readers as well?*

4. Decide which types of sources to use.   *Due:* _____

Assignments differ. *Will your research require the use of a wide range of sources—books, articles, and websites? Or does your assignment call for the use of historical archives?* If you are having trouble determining which sources to use, ask your instructor or a reference librarian for help.

5. Find, review, and evaluate sources.   *Due:* _____

Chapters **9** and **10** provide guidance in finding and evaluating sources. Be sure to give yourself plenty of time to locate your sources, read them, and take notes.

6. Develop a tentative thesis statement and an outline or description of the overall structure of your paper.
                                        Due: _____

Once you have done sufficient research, you are ready to answer your question in the form of a thesis statement (**2b**). This statement will form the governing idea of your essay. Remember that thesis statements are related to your purpose. *Are you providing your audience with general information? Are you reporting on your analysis of information? Are you proposing a solution to a problem? Are you persuading your audience to change their opinion or take action?* The thesis statement generally appears in the first paragraph or two of a research project. The subsequent paragraphs serve as support for the thesis statement.

7. Write a first draft.   *Due:* _____

As you write, keep your thesis statement in mind, revising it if you need to. Be willing to do additional research if necessary.

8. Get the response of readers.   *Due:* _____

Allow time before you turn in your final draft to get feedback from other readers—students in your class or tutors at a writing center.

9. Revise.   *Due:* _____

Use reader feedback to revise your work (**4c**).

10. Edit, proofread, and polish (**4d**).   *Due:* _____

9 Finding Appropriate Sources

Whenever you do research, you can choose from a wide variety of sources—books, articles, online material, even your own fieldwork. Choosing appropriate sources depends on your assignment and research question. If you are unsure of what types of sources to use, ask a reference librarian or clarify the assignment with your instructor.

9a   Considering kinds of sources

As you consider which sources might be the most useful for your project, remember that there are significant differences among kinds of sources.

(1) Primary and secondary sources

Primary sources provide firsthand information. In the humanities, primary sources may include documents such as archived letters, historical records, and papers, as well as literary, autobiographical, and philosophical texts. Primary sources do not have to be in written form. Artwork, photographs, and audio and video recordings are also considered primary sources. In the social sciences, primary sources can be field observations, case histories, survey data, and interviews. In the natural sciences, primary sources are generally empirical and include field observations and experimental results. **Secondary sources** are commentaries on or descriptions of primary sources. They may offer summary or interpretation and appear as reviews, reports, scholarly biographies, and surveys of the work done on a specific topic.

(2) Scholarly and popular sources

Scholarly books and journals contain reports of original research written by experts for an academic audience. Professional or trade books and magazines feature articles written by staff writers or industry specialists. Popular books, magazines, and newspapers are generally written by staff writers, though scholars are frequently invited to contribute articles written for a lay audience.

(3) Current and older material

When writing about current issues, you will need to use up-to-date sources. However, to place an issue in a historical context, search for older sources and documents from the appropriate historical period.

(4) Biased or impartial sources

You will find the best support for your assertions by using sources that are impartial, that is, sources that treat all points of view fairly (chapter **10**). Nonetheless, including a clearly biased source can be useful to bring in other viewpoints or to demonstrate that certain ways of discussing an issue are faulty in some way (**6c**).

9b Searching electronically

Whenever you are searching for sources—either electronic or print material—you will need to know how to use online search tools. Your library's website will likely have a search tool for its catalog of print sources and various search tools connected to the library's **databases**. The better you are at using these tools, the more efficient your research will be. If you are working in the library, a reference librarian will be able to help you learn to use these tools.

Whether you are using a popular **search engine** (such as Bing, Google, or Yahoo!), a **subject directory** designed for academic research (such as Internet Public Library or The WWW Virtual

Library), or a search tool on your library's website, you will be able to narrow your findings by conducting an **advanced search**.

Searches generally start with **keywords**, so choosing just the right word or phrase is important. If you start with a keyword search and find that you are not locating useful sources, you could first try a related term or a synonym, for example, using *wind energy* for *wind power*. You could also try using terms that are more specific or more general. If you were interested in sources of wind energy, a search for *wind farms* would be more specific than *wind energy* and more general than *wind turbines*. Most online search tools allow you to filter your results by searching for sources that match (1) the exact phrase, (2) some words but not others, (3) words related in form, or (4) alternative spellings of a word. When you know the name of an author or the title of a work, you will be able to search for the author or title directly.

TIPS FOR REFINING KEYWORD SEARCHES

The options for refining your search will vary depending on the database or search engine you choose, but most will include the following methods.

- Use **quotation marks** around terms to search for exact phrases. If you find that many search results are irrelevant when you do a general search, enclose a phrase in quotation marks to narrow results.

- Combine words or phrases using the connectors AND, OR, or NOT (sometimes called **Boolean operators**) to limit or widen a search. For example, you could try *Marion AND Ohio* for results that include both keywords, *Buckeye OR Ohio* for results that contain information about either keyword, or *Marion NOT Ohio* for results that exclude mention of Ohio.

- Use **truncation** to broaden a search so that results will include various forms of a word (for example, *manage, management, manager*). Use the root of the words you are searching for and place an asterisk after it (*manag**).

TIPS FOR REFINING KEYWORD SEARCHES

- Use **wildcards** (such as a question mark: *industriali?ation*) to broaden a search so that the results will include various spellings (for example, *industrialization* and *industrialisation*).

- Use **parentheses** around terms to further customize and group one term with keywords: *obesity AND (childhood OR preschoolers)*.

Most search tools have features that allow you to perform advanced searches and thus limit the results in a number of ways. The ProQuest database shown in figure 9.1, for example, shows a few ways one user has limited a search by source type and date, among other options.

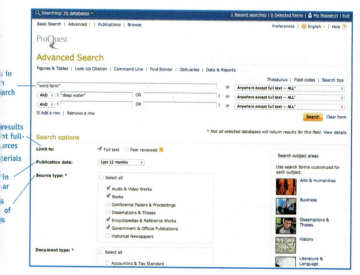

Figure 9.1. Advanced search using keywords in a database.
Source: ProQuest

9c   Locating reference works

To begin a research project, you may find it useful to consult general or specialized reference works, including the encyclopedias, dictionaries, bibliographies, atlases, almanacs, and other resources available at your library. These works—many available online—will help you find background information about people, events, and concepts related to your topic. Especially helpful are specialized reference works—such as the *Encyclopedia of Psychology* or the *Dictionary of American History*—which not only provide in-depth information on a topic but also offer extensive lists of other sources to consult. *Wikipedia* is a popular source for information, but it is sometimes considered unreliable because contributors are not always experts in a field and because facts are not always verified before they are published.

9d   Locating articles

Articles in **periodicals** (publications that appear at regular intervals) offer information that is often more recent than that found in books. Periodicals include journals, magazines, and newspapers and can be published in print, online, or both.

To find articles, you may search the web, but such a general search will most likely yield unreliable sources as well as others that charge a fee for you to access an article. A better way to locate articles is to access your library's **databases**, which are collections of articles indexed according to author, title, date, keywords, and other features (**9b**). The databases you may access include general databases covering a wide range of subject areas and specialized databases and indexes that offer material specific to one subject or discipline. For older articles that are not online, you should consult a print index at your library.

GENERAL DATABASES

Academic Search Complete: Multidisciplinary database of journals and magazines, many full-text versions, via EBSCOhost

Expanded Academic ASAP: Database of journals and periodicals covering a wide variety of disciplines

Google Scholar: Search tool for articles, books, and other documents from academic sources and other sites, though it may be necessary to access the full text via your library

InfoTrac: Database of articles on a wide variety of subjects from journals and magazines

JSTOR: Database for digital library books, primary sources, and articles from journals in the arts, humanities, sciences, and social sciences

LexisNexis Academic: Database strong in coverage of legal as well as local, national, and world news sources

ProQuest: Large database of news and academic sources, in areas ranging from arts, literature, and social sciences to business, technology, medicine, and natural sciences

SUBJECT-SPECIFIC DATABASES

ERIC: Database for information on education

MLA International Bibliography: Database of research in literature, language, and film

PsycINFO: Database for psychology research

ScienceDirect: Database for research in the physical, life, health, and social sciences

To search a database, you will usually begin with a keyword search for terms related to your research question. If your list of results is too large, use the tips for refining keyword searches (**9b**).

9e Locating books

Books published by reputable companies provide comprehensive and authoritative coverage of a topic. You can find books related to your research question by using your library's online catalog and conducting searches using a keyword, author, or title. Experiment with keywords, choosing a word or phrase you think might be found in the title of a book or in notes in the catalog's records. You can also try a subject search by entering words related to your topic; if the search does not yield any results, ask a reference librarian for a subject-heading guide. (A source's detailed record in your library catalog will feature subject headings that you may also use to expand your search.) Once you find the online catalog record for a book you would like to use, write down its **call number**, which indicates where the book is shelved. Some library catalogs will also allow you to send yourself a text message that includes the call number.

Take time when you reach the shelves to scan for related books nearby that may offer additional information.

9f Locating online sources

Material on the web varies greatly in its reliability. Although the facts provided on some websites have been carefully checked, facts on other websites have not undergone close examination.

Colleges, universities, and individual scholars may have reliable websites, blogs, or other information related to your topics. But quality can vary, so take time to evaluate any online source you are thinking of using (**10c**).

By sifting through your search results, you will be able to find a great deal of useful information, for example, current news events, maps, historical documents, and government reports, statistics, and legislative materials. Here is a list of types of websites to consider as you do your research:

- **Government sites.** Federal, state, and local governments provide an abundance of information. USA.gov directs you to sources on topics ranging from art to zoos.
- **News sites.** Newspapers, magazines, radio, and television stations sponsor websites that provide frequently updated news reports. Archived news stories are also sometimes available (though your library may offer easier access via a database).
- **Discussion lists and forums.** You may be able to find experts on topics by joining newsgroups, discussion groups, forums, or online mailing lists. To find such groups or access archived discussions, use a search engine or specialized service such as Google Groups.
- **Digital archives.** Archives are of particular interest if you need artifacts from the past—maps, speeches, drawings, documents, and recordings. The National Archives and the Library of Congress are good places to start.
- **Blogs and wikis.** As starting points, blogs and wikis can provide overviews of topics or issues as well as links to primary sources. However, because they are not generally reviewed by experts, they are often not considered reliable academic sources. Avoid using information from these sources without your instructor's approval.

9g Keeping track of your sources

As you start gathering sources, be sure to keep them organized. For online and other non-print sources, it is a good idea to keep a separate record of the **access date** (the date on which you visited the source) and the **publication date** (the date on which the source was published or last modified). The publication date generally appears on the bottom of the website's home page.

- **Bookmarks.** Bookmark any sources you find on the web, using the most stable URL you can find, which in the case of online journals, magazines, and newspapers is a home page.
- **Database and library accounts.** Your library site may allow you to use your personal account to collect and organize sources using bookmarking tools. Some databases also offer this service, which will allow you to save and retrieve your search history.
- **Downloads.** If you decide to download PDFs or other materials, be sure to label them and place them in folders clearly labeled for your project.
- **Photocopies and printouts.** Keep printouts together by stapling them and placing them in clearly labeled file folders.
- **Reference management systems.** To organize your bibliographic entries, consider using a reference management system such as EndNote, RefWorks, or Zotero. Check to see which system your library supports.

9h   Doing field research

Interviews, observations, and surveys are the most common methods of **field research**.

(1) Interviews

Interviews can take place in person, via e-mail, or over the phone.

1. **Arrange the interview.** E-mail or phone to request an interview. Be sure to introduce yourself, briefly describe your project, and explain your reasons for requesting the interview. Try to accommodate the person you hope to

interview by asking him or her to suggest an interview date. If you intend to record your interview, ask for permission.

2. **Prepare for the interview.** Consult sources on your topic, especially any written by the person you will be interviewing. Start preparing your list of questions before the day of the interview, using a blend of open (or broad) questions and focused (or narrow) questions that begin with *why, when, what, who, where*, or *how.*

3. **Conduct the interview.** Before the interview begins, remind the person that you are interviewing that you will be recording the conversation or taking notes. Although you will have prepared questions, do not feel that you must ask all your questions in the order you wrote them. Listen closely to responses and follow up with related questions, perhaps even ones you had not thought of beforehand. If responses are elaborate, you may find that you do not have to ask each of your questions.

4. **Reflect on the interview.** Review and expand your notes or transcribe the relevant parts of the recording. Write extensively about the interview, asking yourself what you found most important, most surprising, and most puzzling. Send your thanks via a written note or an e-mail message.

(2) Observations

Observations yield detailed information about human activity.

1. **Establish the goals of your observation.** With a clear purpose in mind, you will be able to focus your attention.

2. **Set up an appointment, if necessary.** In some settings, such as in a school or hospital, you will need to obtain permission for your observation.

3. **Take detailed notes.** A helpful method for note-taking during observations is to divide each page of your paper in half vertically. Keep your notes on the left side of the page and leave space on the right side of the page for later commentary.

4. **Analyze your observation.** Review your notes looking for both patterns and behaviors or events that veer from the ordinary. On the right side of your notebook page, write down your comments; whenever possible, explain the patterns and deviations you have found.

(3) Surveys

Whereas an interview elicits information from one person whose name you know, a survey provides information from a number of anonymous people.

1. **Compile a list of questions.** To be effective, a survey questionnaire should be short and focused. If the list of questions is too long, people may not be willing to take the time to answer them all. If the questions are not focused on your research topic, you will find it difficult to integrate the results into your project.

2. **Decide who you would like to participate and how you will contact them.** Some surveys are done in person or by phone. Others are sent to participants via regular mail or e-mail. Surveys conducted through e-mail often include a link to a web service such as SurveyMonkey.

3. **Design the survey to introduce your purpose and review your distribution method.** Begin your survey questionnaire with an introduction stating the purpose of the questionnaire, how the results will be used, and how many questions it contains or approximately how

long it should take to complete. In the introduction, assure participants that their answers will remain confidential. Before you distribute your questionnaire, check with your instructor or the institutional review board (IRB) on your campus to make certain that you have followed appropriate guidelines. It is often helpful to ask a few friends to "test-drive" your questionnaire to see whether all the questions are clear.

4. **Analyze your results.** Once the questionnaires have been completed and returned, tally the results for all but the open questions. Read through the open questions and look for patterns in the responses. Try to create categories for the responses that will help you tally the answers.

10 Evaluating Print and Online Sources

After you find sources that seem to address your research question, you will need to judge their credibility.

10a Credibility of authors

Credible (or trustworthy) authors present facts accurately, support their opinions with compelling evidence, connect their ideas reasonably, and demonstrate respect for any opposing views. To evaluate the credibility of authors whose work you might like to use, consider their credentials, examine their values and beliefs, and note the response they receive from other readers. Credentials include academic or professional training, publications, and experience. The author's credentials may be found on the jacket or in the preface of a book, in a note in an article, or on a page in the journal or on the website devoted to providing background on contributors. Some search tools will allow you to see the influence of the author's work by including a link to other sources that cite articles or books written by the author.

CHECKLIST FOR ASSESSING AN AUTHOR'S CREDENTIALS

- Does the author's education or profession relate to the subject of the work?
- With what institutions, organizations, or companies has the author been affiliated?
- What awards has the author won?
- What other works has the author produced?
- Do other experts speak of the author as an authority or link to the author's work? Check Google Scholar, for example, for works by the author and then review the listed "cited by" information.

An author's values and beliefs underpin his or her research and publications. To determine what these values and beliefs are, consider the author's purpose and intended audience. For example, on the subject of malpractice suits, a lawyer may write an article to convince patients to sue health providers, a doctor may write an essay for other doctors to highlight the frivolous nature of malpractice claims, while a linguist might prepare a conference paper that reveals miscommunication to be at the core of malpractice suits. By identifying the underlying values and beliefs, you can responsibly discuss information in your sources.

CHECKLIST FOR DETERMINING AN AUTHOR'S BELIEFS AND VALUES

- What is the author's educational and professional background?
- With what types of organizations do the author and publisher affiliate themselves?
- What is the author's stance? What is the stance of the organization publishing the author's work? How conservative, moderate, or liberal does the publisher appear to be?
- What, if any, signs of bias on the part of the author or the publisher can you detect in the language used? In the title? In the advertising? Is the information presented factual? Objective?
- To what types of websites do any links lead?
- How can you use the source? As fact? Opinion? Example? Authoritative testimony? Material to be refuted?

Published reviews often include information for determining whether an author is credible. Though a work by any credible author may get some negative responses, use carefully the work of a writer whom more than one reviewer characterizes as biased, ill-informed, or careless with facts.

10b Credibility of publishers

When doing research, consider not only the credibility of authors but also the credibility of the media through which their work is made available to you. The facts in some types of publications are checked more carefully than those in others.

When evaluating books and articles, you can usually assume that publishers associated with universities demand a high standard of scholarship, including review of the work by other scholars in the field. Work published in popular magazines and newspapers is generally reliable and may provide useful overviews of a topic, but such publications do not require scholarly review and may not include bibliographies or citation of sources for other researchers to consult. Because magazines and newspapers often report research results that were initially published elsewhere, try to find the original source to ensure the accuracy of their reports.

10c Online sources

If you are evaluating an online source that also appears in print, you can follow the guidelines for print-based sources. But if you are evaluating a web or other online source, you need to consider additional features of the medium. For help locating important information, see figures 10.1 and 10.2, which show the top and bottom of the same web source.

Figure 10.1. Top of a web page from Global Journalist.
Source: Global Journalist

findings, it was "a terrible year" for personal online privacy against governments' cyberintelligence.

EFF researchers found that states around the world "are obtaining detailed logs of our entire lives online, and they are doing so under weaker legal standards than ever before. Several laws and proposals now afford many states warrantless snooping powers and nearly limitless data collection capabilities." The report contains examples to support the contention that digital privacy is under attack.

None of that bodes well for journalists.

BBC World Affairs producer Stuart Hughes believes certain protective techniques should be a standard practice for the media. "You wouldn't leave your notebook on a park bench or a train, so why would you leave your data wide open for all to see," Hughes wrote in a blog. He advises: "Be Paranoid."

 Sherry Ricchiardi

Sherry Ricchiardi, Ph.D., is a writer for American Journalism Review, specializing in international issues. She is also a media development specialist, working with journalists in the Middle East and South Asia.

Home Stories Free Press Watch Opinions Radio Blogs About Us

Global Journalist is produced by the **Missouri School of Journalism**

Copyright © 2013

Figure 10.2. Bottom of a web page from Global Journalist.
Source: Global Journalist

1. Check the URL for information about the sponsoring organization. Colleges and universities are indicated by the suffix *.edu*, government departments and agencies by *.gov*, professional and nonprofit organizations by *.org*, and businesses by *.com*. As you access the various types of sites to evaluate their content, keep in mind that every site is shaped to achieve a specific purpose and to address a specific audience.

2. Locate the name of the sponsor. This information is generally found at the bottom of the page.

3. Determine the organization's or company's stance on your research question. You will be able to find out more information on an "About Us" or "Our Vision" page. Links may be found at the top of the page, at the bottom of the page, or both.

4. Examine the author's credentials. If the author's name is not given near the title, look at the bottom of the page. Information about the author's credentials can often also be found at the bottom of the page. Because this information is provided by the author, sponsor, or publisher, it is always a good idea to search elsewhere for additional information about the author (**10a**).

5. Identify the date of publication. Some articles place the publication date (or date of most recent update) near the title, but often it is at the bottom of the page. Determine whether the date is sufficiently current.

6. Check links and cited sources. By examining the sources the author uses, you will be able to gauge the reliability of the information provided. Consider unreliable any web source that does not provide a link or enough bibliographic details for you to track down the original source for information presented as factual.

CHECKLIST FOR EVALUATING ONLINE SOURCES

- Who is the author? Is this author credible? (**10a**)

- Who is the sponsor? A government agency? An institution of higher education? A business? An individual? Is the sponsor credible? (**10b**)

- To what extent has the source's information been reviewed by others?

- Is there a list of original sources available so that you can consult them to check facts?

(Continued on page 80)

CHECKLIST FOR EVALUATING ONLINE SOURCES *(Continued)*

- When was the source last updated? Is the information up to date? How current are the source's links? If it includes dead links, the source may not be recent enough to be useful.

10d Reading closely and critically

Once you have determined that the sources you have collected might be useful, allow yourself time to read them closely. Not only will you educate yourself about your topic, but you will also be able to discuss the strengths and weaknesses of what you have read, and you will find it easier to write about it later on. Approach each source with an open mind, but at the same time be prepared to question your sources. By reading critically, you will pay attention to both the claims an author makes and the support for those claims.

CHECKLIST FOR READING CLOSELY AND CRITICALLY

How do you know that you have read each article closely and with an open mind?

- What is the author's argument? (chapter **6**)
- What is the purpose of the argument? Who is its audience?
- What specific claims does the author make? What evidence does the author use to support these claims?
- What are the author's assumptions? Do you share these assumptions?
- Does the author represent diverse points of view? Does the author respond to divergent points of view?
- After reading the article, do you find yourself agreeing with the author? Disagreeing with the author? Agreeing with some points and disagreeing with others?
- What questions would you like to ask the author?

11 Using Sources Critically and Responsibly

For your research project, you will have to discuss what others have discovered, creating a conversation in which you play an essential role: you will decide how the different ideas in your sources connect to each other and to your own views. To make a smooth transition between the words you read and the words you write, you will need to develop a system for managing all the information you have found.

11a Taking and organizing notes

Managing information is critical for a research project in which you will have to attribute specific words and ideas to others while adding your own ideas. Most research projects start with note-taking. Choose the method that best meets the requirements of your project and your own working style:

- take notes in a notebook
- write notes on index cards
- type notes into computer files
- write notes directly on pages you have photocopied or printed out from an online source

Remember that your notes will be most useful to you when it comes time to begin your draft if they are comprehensive and accurate.

TIPS FOR TAKING AND ORGANIZING NOTES

- **Subject heading.** Use a short descriptive phrase to summarize the content of the note. This phrase will help you retrieve information later.

- **Type of note.** Indicate whether the note is a quotation (**11d**), a paraphrase (**11e**), a summary (**11f**), or your own thoughts. Place quotations between quotation marks (**34**). Indicate any changes to quotations with square brackets (**35f**) or ellipsis points (**35g**). If you are using a computer to take notes, you can change font color to indicate your own thoughts.

- **Bibliographic information.** Provide complete bibliographic information in a working bibliography (**11b**). Jot down the author's name and/or the title of the source. If the source has page numbers, indicate which pages your notes refer to.

- **Computer folders.** Create a master folder (or directory) for the project. Within that folder, create separate folders for your notes, drafts, and bibliography. In your notes folder, create a separate file for each source.

11b   Creating a working bibliography

Effective research depends in part on meticulous record keeping. By creating a **working bibliography**, you will have a record of the sources you might use in your final project. A working bibliography contains all the information you might need in your final bibliography. For each work it should include title, authors' names, and publication date, along with other information needed to locate the source. Note that not all documentation styles require you to include the URLs for online sources in your final bibliography, but you will do well to record them for quick access later.

Creating a working bibliography can also help you evaluate the quality of your research. If you find that your most recent source is ten years old, for example, or that you have relied exclusively on information from magazines or websites, you may need to find some other sources.

Right from the start entries should follow the bibliographic format you have been instructed to use. This book covers the most common formats: MLA (chapter **13**), APA (chapter **14**), CMS (chapter **15**), and CSE (chapter **16**).

If you are asked to prepare an **annotated bibliography** (also called an **annotated list of works cited**), provide a bibliographic entry for and a summary of each of your sources. You may also wish to include comments or personal responses on how information in the source is related to your research question or to that in other sources. These comments will be helpful when you are drafting. Check with your instructor to find out whether your annotated bibliography should include both summaries and commentaries.

A working bibliography is equivalent to a rough draft. In final form, you will have to make sure that you have placed in conventional order each element of the bibliographic entry (author, title, date, and so on).

TIPS FOR CREATING AN ANNOTATED BIBLIOGRAPHY

- Find out which documentation style you should use: MLA, APA, CMS, or CSE.

- Provide a complete bibliographic entry for each of your sources in the required documentation style.

- Summarize the content of each source in two or three sentences. Refer to the main point of the source (*What is it about?*). If relevant, describe the intended audience or the scope of the source (*What is the range of subtopics included? What historical period does the source cover?*).

- In writing your summaries, use your own words instead of inserting quotations. That way, when you consult your annotations, you will not inadvertently use quotations as your own words (**11f**).

- Comment on the sources by connecting the information you find to your research question and to the information you find in other sources.

The following sample annotated bibliography entry was written for a research project (following MLA style) on the question of whether the minimum wage should be raised for restaurant servers.

Alderman, Liz. "Minimum Wage in Europe Offers Ammunition in U.S. Debate." *New York Times.* New York Times, 13 Feb. 2013. Web. 15 Feb. 2013.

Prov com bibl entr

In this newspaper article, written in response to the debate over President Obama's proposal to increase the federal minimum wage, Liz Alderman reports that European countries are having a similar debate. Alderman focuses on countries with advanced economies such as France, which has a minimum wage, and Germany, which does not. Although Alderman does not state her opinion, she does quote Simon Tilford, an economist at the Centre for European Reform, who believes that a balance has to be found. A minimum wage that is too low increases poverty levels; a minimum wage that is too high increases production costs so companies find it difficult to be competitive.

Sun the

Additional comments focus on information related to the research question

With regard to restaurant servers, Alderman mentions that in Germany some people working in food service commonly earn €6 an hour, approximately $8.00, an amount considered low in Europe but high in the United States. According to the United States Department of Labor, the national minimum cash wage for workers who receive tips, which applies to most restaurant servers, is $2.13. It is important to remember, though, that tipping customs differ from country to country.

Con inf in sou inf fou els

For some assignments, this entry would have to be condensed for the final draft of the annotated bibliography:

In response to the debate over President Obama's proposal to increase the federal minimum wage, Liz Alderman describes similar debates taking place in a few European countries. Part of the debate focuses on providing an adequate wage without adversely affecting businesses.

11c   Acknowledging your sources

You can integrate sources into your own writing in a number of ways: quoting exact words, paraphrasing sentences, and summarizing longer pieces of text or even entire texts. Whenever you use ideas from a source, you must give credit to that source. The way in which you introduce your source will depend on which documentation style you follow. Most style manuals offer two options: In MLA style, you may (1) put the author's name in parentheses at the end of the sentence or (2) introduce the author's name within a sentence. In either case, place a page number, if one is available, in parentheses (**13a**). The author's name refers the reader to the full bibliographic citation at the end of your essay.

Use the first method (author's name in parentheses) when you are using statistics or statements to support a major idea in your paragraph.

> Displaying body art, especially tattoos, is gaining in popularity (Grief, Hewitt, and Armstrong 371). However, little is known about the reasons college-age students obtain tattoos. Some students use body art to identify themselves with a specific group (Craig 37). Others see body art as self-expression (Armstrong 230), perhaps suggesting their adventurous nature (Duke 243). Still others use body art, especially tattoos, to remember a significant event (Reams 72). The purpose of this study is to explore whether these are typical reasons for students at this university to have tattoos and whether other reasons exist as well.

Cite the author's name in the text if you are going to discuss the source's statistics or ideas in more detail. It is common to first introduce the author's full name and include any important information about the author. For example, in an essay on the origins of literacy, the following statement becomes more credible if readers are given the added information about Oliver Sacks's background.

➤ *professor of neurology and psychiatry at Columbia University,*
  According to Oliver Sacks, ⌃ "The origin of writing and reading
  cannot be understood as a direct evolutionary adaptation" (27).

In subsequent references to the author, use just the last name.
Other style guides such as APA require use of just the last
names of authors for first and subsequent references.

➤ According to Sacks (2010), "The origin of writing and reading
  cannot be understood as a direct evolutionary adaptation" (p. 27).

Phrases such as *According to Oliver Sacks* and *from the author's
perspective* are called **signal phrases** because they indicate the
source (both author and publication) from which the information
was taken. In academic writing, most signal phrases consist of the name of an author (or a related noun or pronoun)
and a verb such as *states*, *reports*, or *argues*.

SIGNAL PHRASES FOR QUOTING, PARAPHRASING, AND SUMMARIZING

Signal phrases indicate which source you are using and alert readers
that the words or ideas that follow are from a source and are not your
own.

- In "Cybersecurity Today" Chris Allen states that _____.
- According to Allen, _____.
- In Allen's view, _____.
- The writer points out that _____. She also stresses that _____.

The following is a list of verbs commonly found in signal phrases.

admit	conclude	find	reject
advise	deny	imply	reply
argue	disagree	indicate	state
believe	discuss	insist	suggest
claim	emphasize	note	think
concede	explain	observe	

Most often signal phrases begin a sentence, but they can also appear in the middle or at the end of a sentence.

➤ **According to Jim Cullen**, "The American Dream would have no drama or mystique if it were a self-evident falsehood or a scientifically demonstrable principle" (7).

➤ "The American Dream," **claims Jim Cullen**, "would have no drama or mystique if it were a self-evident falsehood or a scientifically demonstrable principle" (7).

➤ "The American Dream would have no drama or mystique if it were a self-evident falsehood or a scientifically demonstrable principle," **asserts Jim Cullen in his book *The American Dream: A Short History of an Idea That Shaped a Nation*** (7).

The placement of the signal phrase will depend on what part of the sentence you would like to emphasize and on how the sentence connects to surrounding sentences.

Signal phrases can include neutral, objective verbs (*Cullen stated*) or verbs that are more descriptive and subjective (*Cullen insists*). If your assignment allows the insertion of your opinion, you can use descriptive verbs or add an adverb to the verb in the signal phrase: *persuasively* argues, *inaccurately* represents. The appropriate verb tense for the signal phrase—simple present tense (*the author states*), the simple past tense (*the author stated*), or the present perfect (*the author has stated*)—will depend on the context of the sentence (**20b–c**) and on the guidelines for your discipline (chapters **13–16**).

If you include visuals or graphics as sources, you must introduce and label them as figures and assign them Arabic numbers (**7b**). You can then refer to them within the text in a parenthetical comment, as in this example (following APA style): "The Maori of New Zealand are also well-known for their hand-carved facial tattoos, known as *Moko* (see Figure 1)." Include a title or caption with the figure number.

11d Using direct quotations

Direct quotations draw attention to key passages. Include a direct quotation only if

- you want to retain the beauty or clarity of someone's words
- you need to reveal how the reasoning in a specific passage is flawed or insightful
- you plan to discuss the implications of the quoted material

Keep quotations as short as possible and make them an integral part of your text.

Place any quotation of another person's words in quotation marks. However, if you set off the material as an indented **block quotation**, leave the quotation marks out. The length of a passage determines whether it should be set off as a block quotation. According to MLA style, a quotation longer than four lines should be set off (chapter **13**). If you are following APA style, quotations are set off when they include forty or more words (chapter **14**). The general rule for CMS is to use block quotations for passages of one hundred words or more (chapter **15**). CSE does not specify a word or line limit.

If you need to clarify a quotation by changing it in any way, place square brackets around the added or changed words (**35f**).

➤ The critic notes that in this role, "he [Robin Williams] successfully conveys a diverse range of emotion" (23).

If you want to omit part of a quotation, replace the deleted words with ellipsis points (**35g**).

➤ When asked about the future of the industry, Owens responded, "Overseas markets . . . are critical to the financial success of Hollywood films" (54).

When modifying a quotation, be sure not to alter its essential meaning.

Each quotation you use should also have a signal phrase to help readers understand why the quotation is important. A sentence that consists of only a quotation is called a **dropped quotation**. Notice how the signal phrase improves the dropped quotation below:

➤ ~~Compromises~~ *Joel Achenbach recognizes that compromises* must be made to promote safer sources of energy~~.~~ : "To accommodate green energy, the grid needs not only more storage but more high-voltage power lines" (~~Achenbach~~ 137).

Readers want to know how a quotation is related to your point, so whenever possible provide a sentence or two before or after the quotation explaining its relevance.

➤ Joel Achenbach recognizes that compromises must be made to promote safer sources of energy: "To accommodate green energy, the grid needs not only more storage but more high-voltage power lines" (137). If we are going to use green energy to avoid depending on types of energy that cause air pollution, we may have to tolerate visual pollution in the form of power lines strung between huge towers.

CHECKLIST FOR USING DIRECT QUOTATIONS

- Have you copied all the words and punctuation accurately?
- Have you attributed the quotation to a specific source?
- Have you used square brackets around anything you added or changed in a direct quotation? (**35f**)
- Have you used ellipsis points to indicate anything you omitted? (**35g**)
- Have you included a signal phrase with the quotation?
- Have you included a sentence or two before or after a quotation to indicate its relevance? Have you made it an integral part of the text?
- Have you used quotations sparingly? Rather than using too many quotations, consider paraphrasing or summarizing the information instead.

11e   Paraphrasing

A **paraphrase** is a restatement of someone else's ideas in approximately the same number of words. Paraphrasing allows you to demonstrate that you have understood what you have read; it also enables you to help your audience understand it. Paraphrase when you want to

- clarify difficult material by using simpler language
- use another writer's idea but not his or her exact words
- create a consistent tone for your work
- interact with a point that your source has made

Your paraphrase should be entirely in your own words and should accurately convey the content of the original passage. As you compare the source below with the paraphrases that follow, note the similarities and differences in both sentence structure and word choice.

Source

Zimmer, Carl. *Soul Made Flesh: The Discovery of the Brain—and How It Changed the World.* New York: Free, 2004. (page 7)

> The maps that neuroscientists make today are like the early charts of the New World with grotesque coastlines and blank interiors. And what little we do know about how the brain works raises disturbing questions about the nature of our selves.

Inadequate paraphrase

> The maps used by neuroscientists today resemble the rough maps of the New World. Because we know so little about how the brain works, we must ask questions about the nature of our selves (Zimmer 7).

If you simply change a few words in a passage, you have not adequately restated it. You may be committing plagiarism (**12a–b**) if the wording of your version follows the original too closely, even if you provide a page reference for the source.

Adequate paraphrase

> Carl Zimmer compares today's maps of the brain to the rough maps made of the New World. He believes that the lack of knowledge about the workings of the brain makes us ask serious questions about our nature (7).

In the second paraphrase, both vocabulary and sentence structure differ from those in the original. This paraphrase also includes a signal phrase (*Carl Zimmer compares*).

Any paraphrase must accurately maintain the sense of the original. If you unintentionally misrepresent the original because you did not understand it, you are being *inaccurate.* If you deliberately change the gist of what a source says, you are being *unethical.* Compare the original statement below with the paraphrases.

Source

Hanlon, Michael. "Climate Apocalypse When?" *New Scientist* 17 Nov. 2007: 20.

> Disastrous images of climate change are everywhere. An alarming graphic recently appeared in the UK media showing the British Isles reduced to a scattered archipelago by a 60-metre rise in sea level. Evocative scenes of melting glaciers, all-at-sea polar bears and forest fires are routinely attributed to global warming. And of course Al Gore has just won a Nobel prize for his doomsday flick *An Inconvenient Truth,* starring hurricane Katrina. . . .
>
> There is a big problem here, though it isn't with the science. The evidence that human activities are dramatically modifying the planet's climate is now overwhelming—even to a former paid-up sceptic like me. The consensus is established, the fear real and justified. The problem is that the effects of climate change mostly haven't happened yet, and for journalists and their editors that presents a dilemma. Talking about what the weather may be like in the 2100s, never mind the 3100s, doesn't sell.

Inaccurate or unethical paraphrase

> Evocative scenes of melting glaciers, landless polar bears, and forest fires are attributed to global warming in Al Gore's *An*

Inconvenient Truth. The trouble is that Gore cannot predict what will happen (Hanlon 20).

Accurate paraphrase

According to Michael Hanlon, the disastrous images of climate change that permeate the media are distorting our understanding of what is actually happening globally and what might happen in the future (20).

Although both paraphrases include a reference to an author and a page number, the first focuses misleadingly on Al Gore, whereas the second paraphrase notes the much broader problem, which can be blamed on the media's focus on selling a story.

11f   Summarizing

When you summarize, you condense the main point(s) of your source. Although a summary omits much of the detail used by the writer of the original source, it accurately reflects the essence of that work. In most cases, then, a **summary** reports a writer's main idea and the most important support given for it.

Whereas the length of a paraphrase (**11e**) is usually close to that of the original material, a summary is shorter than the material it reports. When you paraphrase, you restate an author's ideas to present or examine them in detail. When you summarize, you present the gist of the author's ideas, without including background information and details. Summaries can include short quotations of key words or phrases, but you must always enclose another writer's exact words in quotation marks when you blend them with your own.

Source

Marshall, Joseph M., III. "Tasunke Witko (His Crazy Horse)." *Native Peoples* Jan./Feb. 2007: 76-79.

The world knows him as Crazy Horse, which is not a precise translation of his name from Lakota to English. *Tasunke Witko* means "his crazy horse," or "his horse is crazy." This slight mistranslation of his name seems to reflect the fact that Crazy Horse the man is obscured by Crazy Horse the legendary warrior. He was both, but the fascination with the legendary warrior hides the reality of the man. And it was as the man, shaped by his family, community and culture—as well as the events in his life—that he became legend.

Summary

The Lakota warrior English speakers refer to as "Crazy Horse" was actually called "his crazy horse." That mistranslation may distort impressions of what Crazy Horse was like as a man.

This example reduces five sentences to two, retaining the key idea but eliminating the source author's analysis and speculation. A writer who believes that the audience needs to understand the analysis might decide to paraphrase rather than summarize the passage.

EXERCISE 11.1

Find a well-developed paragraph in one of your recent reading assignments. Rewrite it in your own words, varying the sentence structure of the original. Make your paraphrase approximately the same length as the original. Next, write a one-sentence summary of the same paragraph.

11g Analyzing and responding to sources

Though quotations, paraphrases, and summaries are key to academic writing, thinking critically involves more than referring to someone else's work. Quotations, paraphrases, and summaries call for responses. Your readers will want to know what you think about an article, a book, or another source. They will expect you to indicate its strengths and weaknesses and to mention the impact it has had on your own ideas.

Your response to a source will be based on your analysis of it. You can analyze a source according to its rhetorical situation (**1a**), its use of rhetorical appeals (**5c**), or its reasoning (**6d1**). You can also evaluate a source by using some common criteria: timeliness, coverage, and reliability.

(1) Considering the currency of sources

Depending on the nature of your research, the currency of sources may be an important consideration. Using up-to-date sources is crucial when researching most topics. Historical research may also call for sources from a specific period in the past. When you consider the currency of a source, start by looking for the date of its publication. Then, examine any data reported. Even a source published in the same year that you are doing research may include data that are several years old and thus possibly irrelevant. In the following example, the writer questions the usefulness of an out-of-date statistic mentioned in a source:

> According to Jenkins, only 50 percent of all public schools have web pages (23); however, this statistic is taken from a report published in 1997. A more recent count would likely yield a much higher percentage.

(2) Noting the thoroughness of research

Coverage refers to the comprehensiveness of research. The more comprehensive a study is, the more convincing are its findings. Similarly, the more examples an author provides, the more compelling are his or her conclusions. Claims or opinions that are based on only one instance are often criticized for being merely anecdotal or otherwise unsubstantiated. The writer of the following response suggests that the author of the source in question may have based his conclusion on too little information:

> Johnson concludes that middle-school students are expected to complete an inordinate amount of homework given their age,

but he bases his conclusion on research conducted in only three schools (90). To be more convincing, Johnson needs to conduct research in more schools, preferably located in different parts of the country.

(3) Checking the reliability of findings

Reliability is a requirement for reported data. Researchers are expected to report their findings accurately and honestly, not distort them to support their own beliefs or claim others' ideas as their own. To ensure the reliability of their work, researchers must also report all relevant information and refrain from excluding any that weakens their conclusions. When studies of the same phenomenon give rise to disputes, researchers should discuss conflicting results or interpretations. The writer of the following response focuses on the problematic nature of her source's methodology:

> Jamieson concludes from her experiment that a low-carbohydrate diet can be dangerous for athletes (73), but her methodology suffers from lack of detail. No one would be able to confirm her experimental findings without knowing exactly what and how much the athletes consumed.

Researchers use common phrases when responding to sources. The following list includes a few examples.

COMMON PHRASES FOR RESPONDING TO SOURCES

Responding, in agreement

- Recent research confirms that <u>Baron</u> is correct in asserting that _____.
- <u>Moore</u> aptly notes that _____.
- I agree with <u>Gyasi</u> that _____.

(Continued on page 96)

> **COMMON PHRASES FOR RESPONDING** *(Continued)*
> **TO SOURCES**
>
> Responding, in disagreement
>
> - Several of <u>Bender's</u> statements are contradictory. He asserts that _____, but he also states that _____.
> - In stating that _____, <u>Porter</u> fails to account for _____.
> - I disagree with <u>Lurie</u> on this point. I believe that _____.
>
> Responding, in agreement and in disagreement
>
> - Although I agree with <u>Blake</u> that _____ and that _____, I disagree with his conclusion that _____.
> - In a way, the author is correct: _____. However, from a different perspective, _____.
> - Though <u>Day</u> may be right that _____, I must point out that _____.

11h Synthesizing sources

While *thesis* is typically defined as a claim, an informed opinion, or a point of view, *synthesis* refers to combinations of claims, opinions, or points of view. When you synthesize sources, you combine them, looking for similarities, differences, strengths, weaknesses, and so on.

In the following excerpt, the writer reports two similar views on the topic of ecotourism.

> The claim that ecotourism can benefit local economies is supported by the observations of Ellen Bradley, tour leader in Cancun, Mexico, and Rachel Collins, county commissioner in Shasta County, California. Bradley insists that ecotourism is responsible for creating jobs and improved standards of living in Mexico (10). Likewise, Collins believes that ecotourism has provided work for people in her county who had formerly been employed by the timber industry (83).

Notice that the writer uses the transition *likewise* (**3d2**) to indicate a comparison. In the next excerpt, on the topic of voting fraud, the writer contrasts two different views, using the transition *although*.

> Although Ted Kruger believes voting fraud is not systematic (45), that does not mean there is no fraud at all. Kendra Berg points out that voter rolls are not updated often enough (18), which leaves the door open for cheaters.

In both examples, the writers not only summarize and respond to sources but synthesize them as well. Below, you will find common phrases for synthesizing sources.

COMMON PHRASES FOR SYNTHESIZING SOURCES

- The claim that _____ is supported by the observations of <u>Blair</u> and <u>Jones</u>. <u>Blair</u> insists that _____. Likewise, <u>Jones</u> believes that _____.

- <u>Perez</u> asserts that _____. <u>Mehan</u> supports this position by _____.

- Although <u>Miller</u> believes that _____, this interpretation is not held universally. For example, <u>Klein</u> notes that _____.

- <u>Kim</u> asserts that _____; however, she fails to explain _____. <u>Lee</u> points out that _____.

11i | **Critical thinking**

At some point in your studies, you will undoubtedly come across the term *critical thinking*. Although there are a variety of models used to describe what it means to think critically, the one that is relevant to writing research projects was initially developed in 1956 by Benjamin Bloom and his colleagues. Known as the *Bloom Taxonomy*, this model has evolved over the years, but six main skills remain at its core: remembering, understanding, applying, analyzing, evaluating, and creating.

When you summarize sources, you demonstrate your ability to remember and understand. When you respond to sources, you apply your understanding of a topic and/or evaluate the work of others. When you analyze and synthesize sources, you evaluate the ideas of others and then tie them together, along with your own thoughts. In so doing, you create something new.

12 Crediting Others and Avoiding Plagiarism

When you do research, your work depends on the research that was done before you, and the research you are working on has the potential to influence future research. An essential part of this scholarly tradition is the acknowledgment of previous work—not just prior scientific research but artistic, political, philosophical, religious, and other work as well. In fact, acknowledging the contributions of others is so highly valued that copyright and patent laws exist to protect intellectual property. Before you start drafting your project, be sure you understand what to acknowledge, how to acknowledge it, and how to avoid **plagiarism**—the presentation of someone else's ideas as your own.

12a Determining what to acknowledge

Although you will need to acknowledge the great majority of your sources, it is not necessary to credit information that is **common knowledge**—well-known facts, noncontroversial information, or information that is available in a variety of sources. For example, writing *The* Titanic *hit an iceberg and sank on its maiden voyage* is not problematic: this event has been the subject of many books and movies, so the general outline of the event is considered common knowledge. However, if you are preparing a research project about the *Titanic* and wish to include new information about its sinking, such as the role of the tides, you will be providing information or ideas that must be documented. By carefully recording your own thoughts as you take notes, you should have little difficulty distinguishing between what you knew to begin with and what you have learned through research.

Here are two questions you can ask yourself to decide whether information is considered common knowledge:

- Can the information be found in a number of sources? Check several to find out. These sources should not refer to other sources.
- Is the information commonly known among other students taking the course?

If you have any doubts about whether information is common knowledge, err on the side of caution and acknowledge your source. Taking even part of someone else's work and presenting it as your own can result in charges of plagiarism.

Plagiarism is illegal, and penalties range from receiving a failing grade on an essay or in a course to being expelled from school. Never compromise your integrity or risk your future by submitting someone else's work as your own.

CAUTION

Although it is fairly easy to copy material from a source or even to purchase a paper online, it is just as easy for a teacher or employer to locate that same material and determine that it has been plagiarized. Your instructors routinely use search engines such as Google or special services such as Turnitin when they see abrupt changes in writing or shifts within an essay that lead them to suspect that a student has submitted work that was plagiarized, downloaded, or written by others. Take extra care to avoid such deceptive, deliberate plagiarism.

Rules for **fair use**—the section of U.S. copyright law that permits material to be used without permission—covers most of the writing you will do in your courses. You are required to cite and document your source material, but you do not have to seek written permission from authors. If, however, you decide to post your research online, you will have to seek permission for images or extensive portions of text. In such situations, ask your instructor for guidance.

MATERIALS THAT SHOULD BE ACKNOWLEDGED

- Written works, both published and unpublished
- Opinions and judgments that are not your own
- Statistics and other facts that are not widely known
- Images and graphics, such as works of art, drawings, charts, graphs, tables, photographs, maps, and advertisements
- Personal communications, such as interviews, letters, and e-mail messages
- Electronic communications, including television and radio broadcasts, motion pictures and videos, sound recordings, websites, blogs, wikis, and online discussion groups

12b Citing quoted or paraphrased material

To draw responsibly on the words and ideas of others, consider the following examples (in MLA style).

Source

> We propose that while social network use does make people feel better about themselves, these increased feelings of self-worth can have a detrimental effect on behavior.

Wilcox, Keith, and Andrew T. Stephen. "Are Close Friends the Enemy? Online Social Networks, Self-Esteem, and Self Control," page 90.

Quotation with documentation

> Keith Wilcox and Andrew T. Stephen, both professors of business, claim that "while social network use does make people feel better about themselves, these increased feelings of self-worth can have a detrimental effect on behavior" (90).

Quotation marks show where the copied words begin and end; the number in parentheses indicates the exact page on which those words appear (**11d**). The authors' names are identified in the sentence, although their names could have been omitted at the beginning of the sentence and noted within the parenthetical reference instead:

> Although users of social networks may experience an increase in self-esteem, "these increased feelings of self-worth can have a detrimental effect on behavior" (Wilcox and Stephen 90).

Paraphrase with documentation

> Keith Wilcox and Andrew T. Stephen, both professors of business, claim that using social networks may increase self-esteem but that such increased positive feelings can adversely affect behavior (90).

This example, in MLA style, includes both authors' names and a parenthetical citation, which marks the end of the paraphrase and provides the page number where the information can be found. Remember that your paraphrases must be both accurate and ethical (**11e**).

Patchwriting. Be sure to review any paraphrase closely to make sure that both the words and the ordering of words differ significantly from those of the source material. Just as you cannot falsely represent someone else's ideas as your own, you cannot pass off someone else's writing style as your own. **Patchwriting** refers to paraphrases that are too close to the wording of the source. If you have trouble thinking of new ways to express the original information, move away from your desk for an hour or more. When you return, write down what you remember without looking at the source. You may find it easier to use your own words and style without the original material in front of you. If you are still having trouble, spend some time rereading your source so that you thoroughly understand it.

12c   Understanding citation and documentation

Citation and documentation go hand in hand. When you mention someone else's work by quoting, paraphrasing, or summarizing it, you are *citing* that work. Documentation refers to the information you include in parentheses, footnotes, or bibliographies that allows readers to find the material you used.

Systems for documentation vary according to discipline. Each system provides two main sets of guidelines. First are guidelines for citing each instance of quotation, paraphrase, or summary of a source *in* the text. These are generally referred to as in-text citation or in-text documentation guidelines. They are usually shortened forms, including just the author's name and page number, for example.

Second is a system of documentation that requires complete bibliographic information about sources. In most cases, the bibliographic information is included in a list at the end of a work. This book covers four documentation systems: MLA (chapter **13**), APA (chapter **14**), CMS (chapter **15**), and CSE (chapter **16**).

D

DOCUMENTATION

13) **MLA Documentation**

The Modern Language Association (MLA) provides guidelines for documenting research in literature, languages, linguistics, and composition studies. The *MLA Handbook for Writers of Research Papers*, 7th ed., is published specifically for undergraduates.

13a MLA-style in-text citations

(1) Citing material from other sources

The citations you use within the text of a research project refer your readers to the list of works cited at the end of the paper, tell them where to find the borrowed material in the original source, and indicate the boundaries between your ideas and those you have borrowed. In the following example, the parenthetical citation guides the reader to page 88 of the book by Pollan in the works-cited list.

In-text citation

Since the 1980s virtually all the sodas and most of the fruit drinks sold

in the supermarkets have been sweetened with high-fructose corn syrup

(HFCS)—after water, corn sweetener is their principal ingredient (Pollan 88).

Works-cited entry

Pollan, Michael. *The Omnivore's Dilemma: A Natural History of Four Meals*. New

York: Penguin, 2006. Print.

MLA guidelines suggest reserving numbered notes for supplementary comments—for example, when you wish to explain a point further but the subject matter is tangential to your topic. When numbered notes are used, superscript numbers are inserted in the appropriate places in the text, and the notes are gathered at the end of the paper on a separate page titled "Notes." Each note begins with an indent.

In-text note number

Most food found in American supermarkets is ultimately derived from corn.[1]

Notes entry

1. Nearly all farm animals—from cows and chickens to various kinds of farmed fish—are fed a diet of corn.

An in-text citation usually provides two pieces of information about borrowed material: (1) information that directs the reader to the relevant source on the works-cited list and (2) information that directs the reader to a specific page or section within that source. The author's last name and a page number suffice. To create an in-text citation, place both the author's last name and the page number in parentheses or introduce the material being cited by giving the author's name in the sentence and supply only the page number in parentheses.

A "remarkably narrow biological foundation" supports the variety of America's supermarkets (Pollan **18**).

Pollan explains the way corn products "feed" the familiar meats, beverages, and dairy products that we find on our supermarket shelves (**18**).

When referring to information from a range of pages, separate the first and last pages with a hyphen: (34-42). If the page numbers have the same hundreds or thousands digit, do not repeat it when listing the final page in the range: (234-42) or (1350-55) but (290-301) or (1395-1402). If you refer to an entire work or a work with only one page, no page numbers are necessary.

The following examples are representative of the types of in-text citations you might be expected to use.

1. Work by one author named in a signal phrase
Signal the material being cited by mentioning the author's name in your sentence.

Susan J. Rosowski argues that Westerns often reveal a "pattern of linguistic regression" (170).

2. Work by one author named in parentheses
If your sentence does not name the author, include the author's name before the page reference in parentheses.

Set on the frontier and focused on taciturn characters, Westerns often reveal a "pattern of linguistic regression" (Rosowski 170).

3. More than one work by the same author

Provide a shortened title in a signal phrase or in parentheses that identifies the relevant work. Use a comma to separate the author's name (or names) from the shortened title (usually the first word or phrase) when both are in parentheses.

According to one neurological hypothesis, "feelings are the expression of human flourishing or human distress" (Damasio, *Looking* 6).

OR

Antonio Damasio believes that "feelings are the expression of human flourishing or human distress" (*Looking* 6).

4. Work by two or three authors

Some environmentalists seek to protect wilderness areas from further development so that they can both preserve the past and learn from it (Katcher and Wilkins 174).

Use commas to separate the names of three authors: (Bellamy, O'Brien, and Nichols 59).

5. Work by more than three authors

Use either all the authors' last names or the first author's last name followed by the abbreviation *et al.* (Latin meaning "and others"). Use the same format for the names in the corresponding works-cited entry (see item 3, pp. 120–21).

In one important study, women graduates complained more frequently about "excessive control than about lack of structure" (Belenky et al. 205).

OR

In one important study, women graduates complained more frequently about "excessive control than about lack of structure" (Belenky, Clinchy, Goldberger, and Tarule 205).

6. Works by different authors with the same last name

When your works-cited list includes works by different authors with the same last name, provide a first initial and last name in parenthetical citations, or use the author's first and last name in the text.

Pre-Aristotelian rhetoric still has an impact today (T. Enos 331-43).

If two authors have the same last name and first initial, spell out each author's first name in a parenthetical citation.

7. Work by a corporate author

A work has a corporate author when individual members of the group that created it are not identified. If the corporate author's name is long, you may use common abbreviations for parts of it—for example, *Assn.* for "Association" and *Natl.* for "National."

Strawbale constructions are now popular across the nation (Natl. Ecobuilders Group 2).

8. Two or more works in the same citation

When two sources provide similar information or when you combine information from two sources in the same sentence, cite both sources, separating them with a semicolon.

Agricultural scientists believe that crop productivity will be adversely affected by solar dimming (Beck and Watts 90; Harris-Green 153-54).

9. Multivolume work

When you cite material from more than one volume of a multivolume work, include the volume number (followed by a colon and a space) before the page number.

Katherine Raine claims that "true poetry begins where human personality ends" (2: 247).

You do not need to include the volume number in a parenthetical citation if your list of works cited includes only one volume of a multivolume work.

10. Anonymous work

The Tehuelche people left their handprints on the walls of a cave, now called Cave of the Hands ("Hands of Time" 124).

Use the title of an anonymous work in place of an author's name. If the title is long, provide a shortened version. For example, the shortened title for "Chasing Down the Phrasal Verb in the Discourse of Adolescents" is "Chasing Down."

11. Indirect source

If you need to include material that one of your sources quoted from another work because you cannot obtain the original source, use the following format (*qtd.* is the abbreviation for "quoted").

The critic Susan Hardy Aikens has argued on behalf of what she calls "canonical multiplicity" (qtd. in Mayers 677).

A reader turning to the list of works cited should find an entry for Mayers, the source consulted, but not for Aikens.

12. Poetry, drama, and sacred texts

When you refer to poetry, drama, or sacred texts, you should give the numbers of lines, acts, and scenes or of chapters and verses, rather than page numbers. This practice enables readers to consult an edition other than the one you have used. Act, scene, and line numbers (all Arabic numerals) are separated by periods with no space before or after them.

The following example illustrates a citation referring to lines of poetry.

Emily Dickinson alludes to her dislike of public appearance in "I'm Nobody! Who Are You?" (5-8).

The following citation shows that the famous "To be, or not to be" soliloquy appears in act 3, scene 1, lines 56-89, of *Hamlet.*

In *Hamlet,* Shakespeare presents the most famous soliloquy in the history of the English theater: "To be, or not to be . . ." (3.1.56-89).

MLA guidelines recommend treating biblical chapters and verses similarly; the progression is from larger to smaller units. Citations of biblical material identify the book of the Bible, the chapter, and the pertinent verses. In the following example, the writer refers to the creation story in Genesis, which begins in chapter 1 with verse 1 and ends in chapter 2 with verse 22.

The Old Testament creation story, told with remarkable economy, culminates in the arrival of Eve (*New American Standard Bible*, Gen. 1.1-2.22).

Mention in your first citation which version of the Bible you are using. List only book, chapter, and verse in subsequent citations. Note that the names of biblical books are neither italicized nor enclosed in quotation marks.

13. Constitution

When referring to the U.S. Constitution, use the document title, and do not italicize or enclose it in quotation marks. The following are common abbreviations for in-text citations:

UNITED STATES CONSTITUTION	US Const.
ARTICLE	art.
SECTION	sec.

The testimony of two witnesses is needed to convict someone of treason (US Const., art. 3, sec. 3).

14. Works with numbered paragraphs or sections

If paragraphs in an electronic source (or online publication) are numbered, cite the number(s) of the paragraph(s) after the abbreviation *par.* (for one paragraph) or *pars.* (for more than one). If a section number is provided, cite that number after the abbreviation *sec.* (or *secs.* for more than one). Do not cite page numbers unless the source is a PDF, which has stable numbering.

Alston describes three types of rubrics for evaluating customer service (pars. 2-15).

Hilton and Merrill provide examples of effective hyperlinks (sec. 1).

If a source includes no numbers distinguishing one part from another, you should cite the entire source. In this case, to establish that you have not accidentally omitted a number, avoid using a parenthetical citation by providing what information you have within the sentence that introduces the material.

Raymond Lucero's *Shopping Online* offers useful advice for consumers who are concerned about transmitting credit card information over the Internet.

(2) Guidelines for in-text citations and quotations

PLACEMENT OF IN-TEXT CITATIONS

When you acknowledge your use of a source by placing the author's name and a relevant page number in parentheses, insert this parenthetical citation directly after the information you used, generally at the end of a sentence but *before* the final punctuation mark.

Oceans store almost half the carbon dioxide released by humans into the atmosphere (Wall 28).

However, you may need to place a parenthetical citation earlier in a sentence to indicate that only the first part of the sentence contains borrowed material. Place the citation after the clause containing the material but before a punctuation mark (a comma, semicolon, or colon).

Oceans store almost half the carbon dioxide released by humans into the atmosphere (Wall 28), a fact that provides hope for scientists studying global warming but alarms scientists studying organisms living in the oceans.

If you cite the same source more than once in a paragraph, with no intervening citations of another source, you can place one parenthetical citation at the end of the last sentence in which the source is used: (Wall 28, 32).

LENGTHY QUOTATIONS

When a quotation is more than four lines long, set it off from the surrounding text by indenting it one inch from the left margin, keeping it double-spaced. The right-hand margin is not indented, nor does the passage appear in quotation marks.

In *Reimagining Equality: Stories of Gender, Race, and Finding Home*, Anita Hill describes the somewhat disappointing results of her genealogical research:

> When I began to explore my family history, I was in search of the perfect past. What I found were surprises and a messy, complicated reality that forced me to abandon the myths that filled my head about family, progress, and success. I was stunned to find that my grandmother had a child before marrying my grandfather and becoming mother to a total of fifteen children. I accepted that neither of my grandparents could read or write when they married in 1890, but I was disappointed that my grandmother never gained those skills, even though her husband managed to do so, perhaps by teaching himself or picking them up from his children. (34)

Hill's discoveries about her forebears elucidated the racist and sexist nature of early-twentieth-century schooling in the United States.

Note that the period precedes the parenthetical citation at the end of an indented (block) quotation. Note, too, how the writer introduces and then comments on the block quotation from Hill, explaining the significance of the block quotation to the writer's larger essay.

Rarely will you need to quote more than a paragraph, but if you do, indent the first line of each additional paragraph an extra quarter inch.

PUNCTUATION WITHIN CITATIONS AND QUOTATIONS

Punctuation marks clarify meaning in quotations and citations. The following list summarizes their common uses.

- A colon separates volume numbers from page numbers in a parenthetical citation.

   (Raine 2: 247)

- A comma separates the author's name from the title when it is necessary to list both in a parenthetical citation.

(Pipher, *Writing to Change the World*)

A comma also indicates that page or line numbers are not sequential.

(44, 47)

- Ellipsis points indicate an omission within a quotation.

"They lived in an age of increasing complexity and great hope; we in an age of . . . growing despair" (Krutch 2).

- A hyphen indicates a continuous sequence of pages or lines.

(44-47)

- A period separates acts, scenes, and lines of dramatic works.

(3.1.56)

- A question mark placed inside the final quotation marks indicates that the quotation is a question. Notice that the period after the parenthetical citation marks the end of the sentence.

Peter Elbow asks, "What could be more wonderful than the pleasure of creating or appreciating forms that are different, amazing, outlandish, useless—the opposite of ordinary, everyday, pragmatic?" (542).

When placed outside the final quotation marks, a question mark indicates that the quotation has been incorporated into a question posed by the writer of the research project.

What does Kabat-Zinn mean when he advises people to practice mindfulness "as if their lives depended on it" (305)?

- Square brackets enclose words that have been added to the quotation as clarification and are not part of the original material.

"The publication of this novel [*Beloved*] establishes Morrison as one of the most important writers of our time" (Boyle 17).

13b | **MLA list of works cited**

All of the works you cite should be listed at the end of your paper, beginning on a separate page with the heading *Works Cited*. For sample lists of works cited, see pages 46, 157-58.

TIPS FOR PREPARING A LIST OF WORKS CITED

- Center the heading *Works Cited* one inch from the top of the page.
- Arrange the list of works alphabetically by the author's last name.
- If a source has more than one author, alphabetize the entry according to the last name of the first author.
- If you use more than one work by the same author, alphabetize the works by the first major word in each title. For the first entry, provide the author's complete name (last name given first), but substitute three hyphens (---) for the author's name in subsequent entries. However, if that author is also the first author in a collaboration, write out the author's name in full.
- For a work without an author or editor, alphabetize the entry according to the first important word in the title.
- Type the first line of each entry flush with the left margin and indent subsequent lines one-half inch (a hanging indent).
- If your list includes entries with URLs, enclose them in angle brackets and turn off any automatic hyperlink formatting inserted by your word processor. If the URLs are long enough to run onto a second line, make sure to break them only after a slash.
- For entries including a publisher's name, include a shortened form of the name omitting articles, abbreviations (Co., Inc.), and words such as Books, Press, or Publishers. To cite something from a university press, however, include abbreviations as in U of Missouri P.
- Double-space equally throughout—between lines of an entry and between entries.

MLA

When writing down source information for your bibliography, be sure to copy the information directly from the source.

AUTHORS

1. One author

Rose, Mike. *Why School? Reclaiming Education for All of Us.* New York: New, 2009. Print

Note that the publisher, the New Press, has been shortened to the first word *New*.

2. Two or three authors

Type the first author's name in inverted order (last name first), followed by a comma, and the name of the other author(s) in normal order.

Eagly, Alice H., and Linda L. Carli. *Through the Labyrinth: The Truth about How Women Become Leaders.* Cambridge: Harvard Business School P, 2007. Print.

Spinosa, Charles, Ferdinand Flores, and Hubert L. Dreyfus. *Disclosing New Worlds: Entrepreneurship, Democratic Action, and the Cultivation of Solidarity.* Cambridge: MIT P, 1997. Print.

3. Four or more authors

Bullock, Jane A., George D. Haddow, Damon Cappola, Erdem Ergin, Lissa Westerman, and Sarp Yeletaysi. *Introduction to Homeland Security.* Boston: Elsevier, 2005. Print.

OR

Bullock, Jane A., et al. *Introduction to Homeland Security*. Boston: Elsevier, 2005. Print.

4. No author listed

Primary Colors: A Novel of Politics. New York: Warner, 1996. Print.

Begin the entry with the title. Do not use *Anonymous* or *Anon.*

5. Corporate author

Institute of Medicine. *Blood Banking and Regulation: Procedures, Problems, and Alternatives*. Washington: Natl. Acad., 1996. Print.

6. Two or more works by the same author

Joy, Camden. *Boy Island: A Novel*. New York: Quill-Morrow, 2000. Print.

---. *Lost Joy*. Seattle: TNI, 2002. Print.

List entries alphabetically by title, giving the author name in the first entry. For subsequent entries, type three hyphens in place of the author's name followed by a period.

ARTICLES (PRINT)

A **journal** is a publication written for a specific discipline or profession. **Magazines** and **newspapers** are written for the general public. You can find most of the information required for a works-cited entry for a journal article on the first page of the journal (citation map 13.1) or at the bottom of the first page of the article you are citing.

Title of article and name of periodical
Put the article title in quotation marks with a period inside the closing quotation marks. Italicize the name of the periodical; do not add any punctuation following the name. Capitalize all major words (nouns, pronouns, verbs, adjectives, adverbs, and subordinating conjunctions). Omit the word *A*, *An*, or *The* from the beginning of the name of a periodical.

"Into the Void." *New Scientist*

Volume and issue numbers

In an entry for an article from a journal, provide the volume number. If the issue number is available, put a period after the volume number and add the issue number.

Contemporary Review 194   *Studies in the Literary Imagination* 26.3

Date

For journals, place the year of publication in parentheses after the volume and issue number. For magazines and newspapers, provide the date of issue after the name of the periodical. Note the day first (if provided), followed by the month (abbreviated except for May, June, and July) and year.

JOURNAL	*American Literary History* 20.1-2 (2008)
MAGAZINE	*Economist* 20 Apr. 2013
NEWSPAPER	*Chicago Tribune* 24 July 2002

Page numbers

Use a colon to separate the date from the page number(s). Note all the pages on which the article appears, separating the first and last page with a hyphen: 21-39. If the page numbers have the same hundreds or thousands digit, do not repeat it when listing the final page in the range: 131-42 or 1680-99. Magazine and newspaper articles are often interrupted by advertisements or other articles. If the first part of an article appears on pages 45 through 47 and the rest on pages 92 through 94, give only the first page number followed by a plus sign: 45+.

Medium of publication

Be sure to include the medium (*Print*) at the end of the entry.

7. Article in a journal

Caillouet, Ruth R. "Everything I Need to Know about Teaching I Learned from
    Beowulf." English Journal 98.1 (2008): 42-46. Print.

8. Article in a monthly magazine

Keizer, Garret. "How the Devil Falls in Love." *Harper's* Aug. 2002: 43-51. Print.

CITATION MAP 13.1: ARTICLE IN A JOURNAL, MLA STYLE

To cite an article from a journal, include the following elements.

FIRST PAGE OF JOURNAL

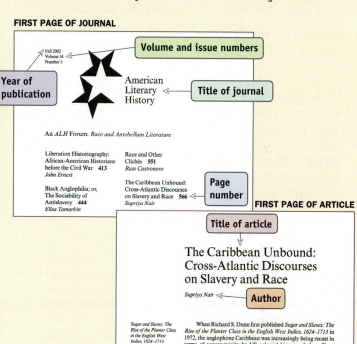

Volume and issue numbers

Fall 2002
Volume 14
Number 3

Year of publication

American Literary History

Title of journal

An *ALH* Forum: *Race and Antebellum Literature*

Liberation Historiography: African-American Historians before the Civil War 413
John Ernest

Black Anglophilia; or, The Sociability of Antislavery 444
Elisa Tamarkin

Race and Other Clichés 551
Russ Castronovo

The Caribbean Unbound: Cross-Atlantic Discourses on Slavery and Race 566
Supriya Nair

Page number

FIRST PAGE OF ARTICLE

Title of article

The Caribbean Unbound: Cross-Atlantic Discourses on Slavery and Race

Supriya Nair

Author

*Sugar and Slaves: The Rise of the Planter Class in the English West Indies, 1624–1713
By Richard S. Dunn
University of North Carolina Press, 1972, 2000*

When Richard S. Dunn first published *Sugar and Slaves: The Rise of the Planter Class in the English West Indies, 1624–1713* in 1972, the anglophone Caribbean was increasingly being recast in terms of consanguinity by US colonial history scholars. Since then other major publications and new scholarly trends and terminologies—postcolonial, black Atlantic, circum-Atlantic, New World—have continued to map the islands as a crucial, even orig-

M L A

WORKS-CITED ENTRY FOR AN ARTICLE IN A JOURNAL

Author

Title and subtitle of article

Nair, Supriya. "The Caribbean Unbound: Cross-Atlantic Discourses on Slavery and Race." *American Literary History* 14.3 (2002): 566-79. Print.

Title of journal

Volume number

Year of publication

Medium of publication

Issue number

Page numbers

9. Article in a weekly magazine or newspaper

Chown, Marcus. "Into the Void." *New Scientist* 24 Nov. 2007: 34-37. Print.

10. Article in a daily newspaper

Moberg, David. "The Accidental Environmentalist." *Chicago Tribune* 24 Sept.

2002, final ed., sec. 2: 1+. Print.

When the name of the city is not part of a locally published newspaper's name, it should be given in brackets after the title: *Star Telegram* [Fort Worth]. If a specific edition is not identified on the masthead (natl. ed., final ed.), put a colon after the date and then provide the page reference. Specify the section by inserting the letter and/or number as it appears in the newspaper (A7 or 7A, for example).

11. Unsigned article or wire service article

"View from the Top." *National Geographic* July 2001: 140. Print.

12. Editorial in a newspaper or magazine

Beefs, Anne. "Ending Bias in the Human Rights System." Editorial. *New York Times* 22 May 2002, natl. ed.: A27. Print.

13. Book or film review in a magazine

Denby, David. "Horse Power." Rev. of *Seabiscuit*, dir. Gary Ross. *New Yorker* 4 Aug. 2003: 84-85. Print.

Include the name of the reviewer, the title of the review (if any), the phrase *Rev. of* (for "Review of"), the title of the work being reviewed, and the name of the author, editor, or director.

14. Book or film review in a journal

Graham, Catherine. Rev. of *Questionable Activities: The Best*, ed. Judith Rudakoff. *Canadian Theatre Review* 113 (2003): 74-76. Print.

BOOKS (PRINT)

15. Basic format for a book

Min, Anchee. *The Cooked Seed: A Memoir.* New York: Bloomsbury, 2013. Print.

CITATION MAP 13.2: BOOK, MLA STYLE

Include the following elements when citing a book.

TITLE PAGE

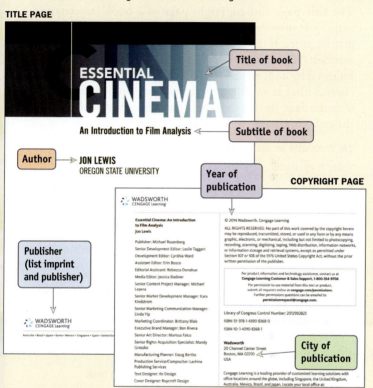

Title of book

ESSENTIAL
CINEMA

An Introduction to Film Analysis ← Subtitle of book

Author → JON LEWIS
OREGON STATE UNIVERSITY

Year of publication

COPYRIGHT PAGE

WADSWORTH
CENGAGE Learning

Essential Cinema: An Introduction
to Film Analysis
Jon Lewis

Publisher: Michael Rosenberg
Senior Development Editor: Leslie Taggart
Development Editor: Cynthia Ward
Assistant Editor: Erin Bosco
Editorial Assistant: Rebecca Donahue
Media Editor: Jessica Badiner
Senior Content Project Manager: Michael Lepera
Senior Market Development Manager: Kara Kindstrom
Senior Marketing Communication Manager: Linda Yip
Marketing Coordinator: Brittany Blais
Executive Brand Manager: Ben Rivera
Senior Art Director: Marissa Falco
Senior Rights Acquisition Specialist: Mandy Groszko
Manufacturing Planner: Doug Bertke
Production Service/Compositor: Lachina Publishing Services
Text Designer: Ke Design
Cover Designer: Roycroft Design

© 2014 Wadsworth, Cengage Learning

ALL RIGHTS RESERVED. No part of this work covered by the copyright herein may be reproduced, transmitted, stored, or used in any form or by any means graphic, electronic, or mechanical, including but not limited to photocopying, recording, scanning, digitizing, taping, Web distribution, information networks, or information storage and retrieval systems, except as permitted under Section 107 or 108 of the 1976 United States Copyright Act, without the prior written permission of the publisher.

For product information and technology assistance, contact us at
Cengage Learning Customer & Sales Support, 1-800-354-9706

For permission to use material from this text or product, submit all requests online at **cengage.com/permissions.**
Further permissions questions can be emailed to **permissionrequest@cengage.com.**

Library of Congress Control Number: 2012950823
ISBN-13: 978-1-4390-8368-0
ISBN-10: 1-4390-8368-1

Wadsworth
20 Channel Center Street
Boston, MA 02210
USA

City of publication

Cengage Learning is a leading provider of customized learning solutions with office locations around the globe, including Singapore, the United Kingdom, Australia, Mexico, Brazil, and Japan. Locate your local office at:

Publisher
(list imprint
and publisher)

WADSWORTH
CENGAGE Learning

Australia • Brazil • Japan • Korea • Mexico • Singapore • Spain • United Kingdom

M L A

WORKS-CITED ENTRY FOR A BOOK

Author   Title   City of publication

Lewis, Jon. *Essential Cinema: An Introduction to Film Analysis.* Boston:
Wadsworth-Cengage, 2014. Print.

Publisher   Year of   Medium of
             publication   publication

The title page and copyright page of a book (see citation map 13.2) provide the information needed to create a bibliographic entry. If more than one city is listed on the title page, mention only the first. Place a colon after the name of the city, followed by a shortened form of the publisher's name with a comma after it and then the copyright date. Place a period after the date. Be sure to include the medium of publication at the end of the entry, followed by a period.

16. Book with an author and an editor

Stoker, Bram. *Dracula*. Ed. Glennis Byron. Peterborough: Broadview, 1998. Print.

Include both the name of the author and the name of the editor (preceded by *Ed.* for "Edited by").

17. Book with an editor instead of an author

Kachuba, John B., ed. *How to Write Funny*. Cincinnati: Writer's Digest, 2000.

Print.

For a book with one editor include the abbreviation *ed.* and use *eds.* for "editors."

18. Edition after the first

Zinsser, William. *On Writing Well*. 5th ed. New York: HarperCollins, 1995. Print.

19. Introduction, preface, foreword, or afterword to a book

Olmos, Edward James. Foreword. *Vietnam Veteranos: Chicanos Recall the War*.

By Lea Ybarra. Austin: U of Texas P, 2004. ix-x. Print.

Begin the entry with the author of the section of the book. Then give the title of the section. Place the page numbers of the section after the year of publication.

20. Translated book

Garrigues, Eduardo. *West of Babylon*. Trans. Nasario Garcia. Albuquerque: U of

New Mexico P, 2002. Print.

Place the abbreviation *Trans.* for "Translated by" before the translator's name.

21. Graphic novel or illustrated book

Helfer, Andrew, writer. *Malcolm X: A Graphic Biography*. Illus. Randy DuBurke.

New York: Hill and Wang, 2006. Print.

Bechdel, Alison. *Fun Home: A Family Tragicomedy*. New York: Houghton, 2006. Print.

For a book that relies on visuals, cartoons, or illustrations, start with the person and role you want to emphasize: the writer, artist, or illustrator. If the writer and illustrator are the same, cite just as you would a book.

22. Publisher's imprint

Fey, Tina. *Bossypants*. New York: Reagan Arthur-Little Brown, 2011. Print.

23. Republished book

Alcott, Louisa May. *Work: A Story of Experience*. 1873. Harmondsworth:

Penguin, 1995. Print.

After the title of the book, provide the original publication date, followed by a period.

24. Book with a title within a title

Coontz, Stephanie. *A Strange Stirring:* The Feminine Mystique *and American*

Women at the Dawn of the 1960s. New York: Basic, 2011. Print.

25. Anthology

Buranen, Lisa, and Alice M. Roy, eds. *Perspectives on Plagiarism and Intellectual*

Property in a Postmodern World. New York: State U of New York P, 1999. Print.

Cite an anthology (a collection of works by different authors) as you would a book, beginning with the name(s) of the editor or editors, followed by *ed.* or *eds.*

26. Work originally published in an anthology or chapter in a book with an editor

Rowe, David. "No Gain, No Game? Media and Sport." *Mass Media and Society*.

Ed. James Curran and Michael Gurevitch. 3rd ed. New York: Oxford UP,

2000. 346-61. Print.

Cite the author(s) of the selection; place the title of the article, essay, story, poem, or play in quotation marks; and italicize the title of the anthology in which the selection was published for the first time. Use *Ed.* for "edited by" to identify the editor(s) of the anthology, and note the edition if it is not the first. List the publication data for the anthology, the range of pages on which the individual selection appears, and the medium of publication.

27. Two or more selections from the same anthology

Clark, Irene L. "Writing Centers and Plagiarism." Buranen and Roy 155-67.

Howard, Rebecca Moore. "The New Abolitionism Comes to Plagiarism."

   Buranen and Roy 87-95.

The entry for the entire anthology will include all publication data; therefore individual citations include only the name(s) of the author(s) of the selection, the title of the work, the name(s) of the editor(s), and the inclusive page numbers.

28. Work from a journal reprinted in a textbook or an anthology

Webb-Sunderhaus, Sara. "A Family Affair: Competing Sponsors of Literacy in

   Appalachian Students' Lives." *Community Literacy Journal* 2.1 (2007):

   5-24. Rpt. in *The Norton Book of Composition Studies.* Ed. Susan Miller.

   New York: Norton, 2009. 1600-43. Print.

Use the abbreviation *Rpt.* for "Reprinted."

29. Work from an edited collection reprinted in a textbook or an anthology

Brownmiller, Susan. "Let's Put Pornography Back in the Closet." *Take Back

   the Night: Women on Pornography.* Ed. Laura Lederer. New York: Morrow,

   1980. 252-55. Rpt. in *Conversations: Readings for Writing.* By Jack

   Selzer. 4th ed. New York: Allyn, 2000. 578-81. Print.

See item 27 for information on citing more than one work from the same anthology.

30. Multivolume work

Young, Ralph F., ed. *Dissent in America.* 2 vols. New York: Longman-Pearson,

   2005. Print.

Cite the total number of volumes in a work when you have used material from more than one volume. Include the year the volumes were published. If the volumes were published over a span of time, provide inclusive dates: 1997-99 or 1998-2004.

If you have used only one volume, include that volume's number (preceded by the abbreviation *Vol.*) in place of the total number of volumes.

Young, Ralph F., ed. *Dissent in America*. Vol. 1. New York: Longman-Pearson,

2005. Print.

The publisher's name is hyphenated: the first name is the imprint; the second is the publisher.

31. Article in a multivolume work

Provide the author's name and the title of the article in quotation marks. Note the page numbers for the article after the date of publication.

Baxby, Derrick. "Jenner, Edward." *Oxford Dictionary of National Biography*. Ed. H. C. G.

Matthew and Brian Harrison. Vol. 30. Oxford: Oxford UP, 2004. 4-8. Print.

If required by your instructor, include the number of volumes and the inclusive publication dates after the medium of publication: Print. 60 vols. 2004-2008.

32. Book in a series

Sumner, Colin, ed. *Blackwell Companion to Criminology*. Malden: Blackwell,

2004. Print. Blackwell Companions to Sociology 8.

When citing a book that is part of a series, add the name of the series and, if one is listed, the number. Abbreviate words in the series name according to the MLA guidelines; for example, the word *Series* is abbreviated *Ser.*

33. Dictionary entry

When citing a specific dictionary definition for a word, use the abbreviation *Def.* (for "Definition") and indicate which one you used if the entry has two or more.

"Reactive." Def. 2a. *Merriam-Webster's Collegiate Dictionary*. 10th ed. 2001. Print.

34. Sacred text

Begin with the title of the work, rather than information about editors or translators.

New American Standard Bible. Anaheim: Foundation, 1997. Print.

The Qur'an. Trans. Muhammad A. S. Abdel Haleem. Oxford: Oxford UP, 2004.

Print.

ONLINE SOURCES

Many of the guidelines for documenting online sources are similar to those for print sources. For sources found online, provide electronic publication information and access information.

Electronic publication information

Indicate the author's name, the title of the work, the title of the website, the site's sponsoring organization (usually found at the bottom of the site's home page; see citation map 13.4), the date of publication, and the medium of publication (*Web*). All of this information precedes the access information.

Access information

When you document an online source, you must include the date of access: the day, month, and year on which you consulted the source. Either keep track of the date of access or print out the source so that you have a record.

If your readers can easily locate the online source by searching for the author's name and the title of the work, no URL is necessary. Otherwise, you should provide the complete and accurate URL (between angle brackets) following the date of access after a period and a space. When the URL does not fit on a single line, break it only after a slash. The closing angle bracket should be followed by a period.

The following formats apply to articles available only online.

35. Article in an online journal

Bowdon, Melody, and Russell Carpenter. "Introduction: Digital Media and

Community Literacy." *Community Literacy Journal* 6.1 (2011): 1-4. Web.

9 Feb. 2013.

When page numbers are not provided for online journals, write *n. pag.* (for "no pagination"). If they are provided, place them after the colon that follows the date of publication.

36. Article in an online magazine

Dickerson, John. "Karl Rove's Courage: Why It Was Brave—and Smart—for

Him to Challenge the Tea Party." *Slate.com*. Washington Post Company,

8 Feb. 2013. Web. 9 Feb. 2013.

37. Newspaper article

"Damages Sought for Accident at Bank." *Santa Fe New Mexican*. Santa Fe New

Mexican. 8 Feb. 2013. Web. 8 Feb. 2013.

When no author is identified, begin with the title of the article. If the article is an editorial, include *Editorial* (not italicized) after the title: "America's Promises." Editorial. (In the sample entry, the first mention of *Santa Fe New Mexican* is the title of the newspaper's website, and the second, which is not italicized, is the name of the site's sponsor.)

38. Book available only online

Ames, James Barr, Jeremiah Smith, and Roscoe Pound. *A Selection of Cases on

the Law of Torts*. Cambridge: Harvard UP, 1919. U of Toronto Lib. Web.

3 Aug. 2013.

Note that in this example the name of the sponsoring organization, the University of Toronto Libraries, is included.

39. Book available online and in print

Rohrbough, Malcolm J. *Days of Gold: The California Gold Rush and the

American Nation*. Berkeley: U of California P, 1997. *History E-book

Project*. Web. 17 Feb. 2005.

Begin the citation with print citation information: the author's name, the title of the work, city of publication, publisher, and date. Follow this information with the title of the database or website (italicized), the medium of publication (*Web*), and the date of access.

To cite books available via devices such as the Kindle, follow the relevant guidelines for a book (whether an actual or online book) including relevant publication information. Finally, include the format *(Kindle, Kindle file, or Kindle AZW file).*

Mankell, Henning. *Treacherous Paradise.* New York: Knopf, 2013. Kindle.

40. Part of an online book

Strunk, William, Jr. "Elementary Rules of Usage." *The Elements of Style.*

Ithaca: Humphrey, 1918. N. pag. *Bartleby.com.* Web. 6 June 2003.

DATABASES

Many print materials are available online through a database (JSTOR, Project MUSE, ERIC, PsycINFO, Academic Universe, LexisNexis, ProQuest, InfoTrac, SilverPlatter, or EBSCO). To cite material from a database, begin with the author, the title of the article (in quotation marks), the title of the publication (in italics), the volume and issue numbers, the year of publication, and the page numbers (or the abbreviation *n. pag.*). Then add the name of the database (in italics), the medium of publication consulted (*Web*), and the date of access. You can find most of the information you need for a works-cited entry on the abstract page of the article you select.

41. Article through ERIC

Taylor, Steven J. "Caught in the Continuum: A Critical Analysis of the

Principle of the Least Restrictive Environment." *Research and Practice*

for Persons with Severe Disabilities 29.4 (2004): 218-30. *ERIC.* Web. 3

Mar. 2009.

CITATION MAP 13.3: ARTICLE IN A DATABASE, MLA STYLE

Include the following elements when citing an article in a database.

WORKS-CITED ENTRY FOR AN ARTICLE IN A DATABASE

42. Article through EBSCO

Folks, Jeffrey J. "Crowd and Self: William Faulkner's Sources of Agency in *The Sound and the Fury*." *Southern Literary Journal* 34.2 (2002): 30+. *EBSCO.* Web. 6 June 2013.

For sources that list only the page number on which a work begins, include that number followed by a plus sign.

43. Article through LexisNexis

Suggs, Welch. "A Hard Year in College Sports." *Chronicle of Higher Education* 19 Dec. 2003: 37. *LexisNexis.* Web. 17 July 2004.

44. Article through ProQuest

Fabel, Robin F. A. "The Other War of 1812: The Patriot War and the American Invasion of Spanish East Florida." *Alabama Review* 57.4 (2004): 291-92. *ProQuest.* Web. 30 June 2013.

45. Article through InfoTrac

Priest, Ann-Marie. "Between Being and Nothingness: The 'Astonishing Precipice' of Virginia Woolf's *Night and Day*." *Journal of Modern Literature* 26.2 (2002-03): 66-80. *InfoTrac.* Web. 12 Jan. 2004.

46. Article through JSTOR

Blum, Susan D. "Five Approaches to Explaining 'Truth' and 'Deception' in Human Communication." *Journal of Anthropological Research* 61.3 (2005): 289-315. *JSTOR.* Web. 3 Mar. 2009.

47. Article through Project MUSE

Muñoz, Alejandro Anaya. "Transnational and Domestic Processes in the Definition of Human Rights Policies in Mexico." *Human Rights Quarterly* 31.1 (2009): 35-58. *Project MUSE.* Web. 3 Mar. 2013.

48. Abstract from a database

Landers, Susan J. "FDA Panel Findings Intensify Struggles with Prescribing of Antidepressants." *American Medical News* 47.37 (2004): 1-2. *ProQuest Direct.* Web. 7 Feb. 2005.

49. Entire website

McGann, Jerome, ed. *The Complete Writings and Pictures of Dante Gabriel Rossetti*. Inst. for Advanced Technology in the Humanities, U of Virginia, n.d. Web. 16 Mar. 2009.

Include the name of the author, editor, compiler, director, or translator, followed by the title of the site (italicized), the version or edition (if given), the publisher or sponsor (if not available, use *N.p.*), the date of publication (if not available, use *n.d.*), the medium of publication (*Web*), and the date of access.

50. Website with untitled work

Breastcancer.org. N.p., 2 Feb. 2008. Web. 5 Feb. 2008.

If a website does not provide all the information usually included in a works-cited entry, list as much as is available.

51. Section of a website

Altman, Andrew. "Civil Rights." *Stanford Encyclopedia of Philosophy*. Ed. Edward N. Zalta. Center for the Study of Lang. and Information, Stanford U, 3 Feb. 2003. Web. 12 June 2003.

Mozart, Wolfgang Amadeus. "Concerto No. 3 for Horn, K. 447." *Essentials of Music*. Sony Music Entertainment, 2001. Web. 3 Mar. 2009.

52. E-mail

Socarides, Alexandra. "Scholarships for Women." Message to the author. 15 Feb. 2013. E-mail.

53. Posting to a discussion forum

Schipper, William. "Re: Quirk and Wrenn Grammar." *Ansaxnet*. N.p., 5 Jan. 1995. Web. 12 Sept. 1996.

If the posting is untitled, identify the genre (e.g., *Online posting*) instead of providing the title.

54. Entire blog

Sullivan, Andrew. *The Dish*. N.p. 2013. Web. 1 July 2013.

CITATION MAP 13.4: WORK FROM A WEBSITE, MLA STYLE

Include the following elements when citing a document you find on the web.

Sponsor of site

Title of site

Title of short work

Author

Date of publication

Source: Environmental Protection Agency (EPA)

WORKS-CITED ENTRY FOR A SHORT WORK FROM A WEBSITE

Author

Title of short work

Rogers, Kim. "Research in Action: Nanosilver and Consumer Products."
Exposure Research. United States Environmental Protection Agency,
9 Aug. 2013. Web. 3 Sept. 2013.

Title of site

Date of publication

Medium of publication

Date of access

Sponsor of site

Cite as you would a website. If a blog has no sponsor or publisher, include *N.p.* (for "no publisher") after the title.

55. Blog entry

Silver, Nate. "As More Attend College, Majors Become More Career-Focused."

FiveThirtyEight. New York Times, 25 June 2013. Web. 1 July 2013.

56. Entry in an online reference work

"Iran." *Encyclopaedia Britannica Online*. Encyclopaedia Britannica, 2002. Web.

6 Mar. 2004.

57. Wiki entry

"Buddy Love." *WikiScreenplay*. WikiScreenplay, 5 Dec. 2009. Web. 1 July 2013.

58. Online congressional document

United States. Cong. Senate. Special Committee on Aging. *Global Aging:*

Opportunity or Threat for the U.S. Economy? 108th Cong., 1st sess. S.

Hrg. 108-30. GPO, 2003. *GPO Access*. Web. 7 Jan. 2005.

Provide the number and session of Congress and the type and number of publication. (*S* stands for "Senate"; *H* or *HR* stands for "House of Representatives.")

59. Online government document

United States. Dept. of State. Bur. of Democracy, Human Rights, and Labor.

Guatemala Country Report on Human Rights Practices for 1998. Feb.

1999. Web. 1 May 1999.

Begin with the name of the country, state, or city whose government is responsible for the document and the department or agency that issued it. If a subdivision of the larger organization is responsible, name the subdivision. If an author is identified, provide the name, preceded by the word *By*, between the title and the date of issue of the document.

60. Online legal source

Tennessee v. Lane. 541 US 509. Supreme Court of the US. 2004. *Supreme*
Court Collection. Legal Information Inst., Cornell U Law School, n.d.
Web. 28 Jan. 2005.

61. Online public law

Individuals with Disabilities Education Act. Pub. L. 105-17. 104 Stat. 587-698.
Thomas. Lib. of Cong., 4 June 1997. Web. 29 Jan. 2005.

62. Online sacred text

Sama Veda. Trans. Ralph T. H. Griffith. 1895. *Sacred-Texts.com.* Ed. John B.
Hare. N.p., 2008. Web. 6 Mar. 2008.

ONLINE AUDIO AND VISUAL SOURCES

63. Digital file (PDF, JPEG)

Digital files include PDFs, JPEGs, MP3s, and other documents, images, or recordings that can exist independently
from the web.

National Center for Emerging and Zoonotic Infectious Diseases. "CDC and
the Food Safety Modernization Act." CDC Division of Foodborne,
Waterborne, and Environmental Diseases, May 2011. PDF file.

64. Sound recording

Moran, Jason. "Jump Up." *Same Mother.* Blue Note, 2005. *Blue Note.* Blue
Note Records. Web. 7 Mar. 2005.

In this entry, "Blue Note" is the manufacturer of the CD, *Blue*
Note is the title of the website where the song was accessed,
and "Blue Note Records" is the sponsor of that site.

65. Podcast

"Episode 402: David Sedaris." Host Marc Maron. *WTF with Marc Maron.* WTF,
1 July 2013. MP3 file.

"Out Loud: Justice and Ruth Bader Ginsburg." Narr. Margaret Talbot, Jeffrey
Toobin, and Amy Davidson. *New Yorker.* New Yorker. Conde Nast,
4 Mar. 2013. Web. 23 May 2013.

Podcasts found online are cited much like short works from a website (see item 51). Cite a podcast you download as you would a digital file (see item 63), ending with the file type (*MP3*).

66. Online speech

Malcolm X. "The Ballot or the Bullet." Detroit. 12 Apr. 1964. *American*

> *Rhetoric: Top One Hundred Speeches*. Ed. Michael E. Eidenmuller. N.p.,

> 2005. Web. 14 Jan. 2005.

"12 Apr. 1964" is the date the speech was delivered, "2005" is the year of the speech's electronic publication, "Web" is the medium, and "14 Jan. 2005" is the date of access.

67. Online video

Riefenstahl, Leni, dir. *Triumph of the Will*. Reichsparteitag-Film, 1935.

> *Movieflix.com*. MovieFlix, 2005. Web. 17 Feb. 2005.

"1935" is the year in which the movie was originally released, "2005" is the year in which it was made available online, and "17 Feb. 2005" is the date of access.

To cite a YouTube clip following the MLA guidelines for a video, begin with author name (or poster's username), followed by the title of the image or video (in quotation marks), the media type, name of website (in italics), name of website's publisher, date of posting, medium, and date accessed.

SciShow. "Is Sharknado Possible?" Online video. *YouTube*, 31 July 2013. Web.

> 3 Aug. 2013.

68. Online television or radio program

"Religion and the American Election." Narr. Tony Hassan. *The Religion Report*.

> ABC Radio National, 3 Nov. 2004. Web. 18 Feb. 2005.

69. Online interview

McLaughlin, John. Interview by Wolf Blitzer. *CNN.com*. Cable News Network,

> 14 July 2004. Web. 21 Dec. 2004.

70. Online review

Dombal, Ryan. "Kanye West, *Yeezus.*" *Pitchfork*. Pitchfork Media, 18 June
2013. Web. 30 June 2013.

71. Online editorial

"A Bump in the Road for Tesla." Editorial. *Washington Post*. Washington Post,
13 June 2013. Web. 30 June 2013.

72. Online work of art

Vermeer, Johannes. *Young Woman with a Water Pitcher*. c. 1660. Metropolitan
Museum of Art, New York. *The Metropolitan Museum of Art*. Web. 2 Oct.
2002.

73. Online photograph

Marmon, Lee. *Engine Rock*. 1985. *Lee Marmon Gallery*. Web. 9 Feb. 2009.

74. Online map or chart

"Virginia 1624." Map. *Map Collections 1544-1996*. Lib. of Cong. N.d. Web.
26 Apr. 1999.

United States. Dept. of Health and Human Services. Centers for Disease
Control and Prevention. "Daily Cigarette Smoking among High School
Seniors." Chart. *National Center for Health Statistics*. 27 Jan. 2005. Web.
25 Feb. 2005.

75. Online advertisement

Milk Processor Education Program. "Got Milk?" Advertisement. *MilkPEP*.
MilkPEP, n.d. Web. 16 Feb. 2005.

76. Online cartoon or comic strip

Cagle, Daryl. "Social Security Pays 3 to 2." Cartoon. *Slate.com*. Newsweek
Interactive, 4 Feb. 2005. Web. 5 Feb. 2005.

OTHER SOURCES

77. Government publication

United States. Office of Management and Budget. *A Citizen's Guide to the
Federal Budget*. Washington: GPO, 1999. Print.

List the author, if given. Otherwise, begin with the name of the government, followed by the agency. Italicize the title of a book or pamphlet. Indicate the city of publication. Federal publications are usually (but not always) printed by the Government Printing Office (GPO). For an online government publication, follow the guidelines for an entire website or for a section of a website (items 49 and 51).

When the name of an author, editor, or compiler appears on a government publication, you can begin the entry with that name, followed by the abbreviation *ed.* or *comp.* if the person is not the author. Alternatively, insert that name after the publication's title and introduce it with the word *By* or the abbreviation *Ed.* or *Comp.*

78. Historical document

Eisenhower, Dwight D. Farewell Address. 1961. *Our Documents: 100 Milestone*

   Documents from the National Archives. Foreword by Michael Beschloss.

   New York: Oxford UP, 2003. 217-19.

79. Law case

Chavez v. Martinez. 538 US 760. Supreme Court of the US. 2003. *United*

   States Reports. Washington: GPO, 2004. Print.

Include the last name of the first plaintiff, the abbreviation *v.* for "versus," the last name of the first defendant, data on the law report (volume, abbreviated name, and page or reference number), the name of the deciding court, and the year of the decision. Although law cases are italicized in the text of a paper, they are *not* italicized in works-cited entries.

80. Public law

No Child Left Behind Act of 2001. Pub. L. 107-10. 115 Stat. 1425-2094.

   8 Jan. 2002. Print.

Include the name of the act, its public law number, its Statutes at Large cataloging number and page numbers, the date it was enacted, and the medium of publication. Notice the use of abbreviations in the example.

81. Pamphlet, bulletin, or report

Stucco in Residential Construction. St. Paul: Lath & Plaster Bureau, 2000. Print.

If the pamphlet has an author, begin with the author's name, as you would for a book.

82. Published dissertation

Fukuda, Kay Louise. *Differing Perceptions and Constructions of the Meaning of Assessment in Education*. Diss. Ohio State U, 2001. Ann Arbor: UMI, 2002. Print.

After the title of the dissertation, include the abbreviation *Diss.*, the name of the university granting the degree, the date of completion, and the publication information. In the example, *UMI* stands for "University Microfilms International," which publishes many dissertations.

83. Published letter

Jackson, Helen Hunt. "To Thomas Bailey Aldrich." 4 May 1883. *The Indian Reform Letters of Helen Hunt Jackson, 1879-1885*. Ed. Valerie Sherer Mathes. Norman: U of Oklahoma P, 1998. 258-59. Print.

In general, treat a published letter like a work in an anthology, adding the date of the letter and the number (if the editor assigned one).

84. Personal letter

Lethem, Jonathan. Letter to the author. 30 June 2013. TS.

To cite an unpublished letter you received, include the phrase *Letter to the author*, followed by the date, and the medium of deliver (*MS* for "manuscript" or *TS* for "typescript," meaning a typed letter).

85. Cartoon or comic strip

Cheney, Tom. Cartoon. *New Yorker* 9 June 2003: 93. Print.

Trudeau, Garry. "Doonesbury." Comic strip. *Daily Record* [Ellensburg] 21 Apr.

2005: A4. Print.

After the creator's name, place the title of the work (if given) in quotation marks and include the descriptor *Cartoon* or *Comic strip*.

86. Map or chart

Cincinnati and Vicinity. Map. Chicago: Rand, 2008. Print.

87. Advertisement

Nu by Yves Saint Laurent. Advertisement. *Allure* June 2003: 40. Print.

88. Live performance

Proof. By David Auburn. Dir. Daniel Sullivan. Walter Kerr Theater, New York.

8 Oct. 2002. Performance.

Cite the date of the performance you attended.

89. Lecture or presentation

Guinier, Lani. Barbara Jordan Lecture Ser. Schwab Auditorium, Pennsylvania

State U, University Park. 4 Oct. 2004. Address.

Scharnhorst, Gary. English 296.003. Dane Smith Hall, U of New Mexico,

Albuquerque. 30 Apr. 2013. Guest lecture.

Identify the site and the date of the lecture or presentation. Use the title if available; otherwise, provide a descriptive label.

90. Conference paper in published proceedings

Crosetto, Alice. "Food in Children's Literature: An Exploration of Use and

Meaning." *Proceedings of the 54th Annual Midwest Modern Language*

Association, November 8-11, 2012. Chicago: MMLA, 2012. Print.

91. Interview

Furstenheim, Ursula. Personal interview. 16 Jan. 2003.

Sugo, Misuzu. Telephone interview. 20 Feb. 2003.

If the interview was conducted by someone else, add the name of the interviewer, a title or a descriptive label, and the name of the source.

Harryhausen, Ray. Interview by Terry Gross. *Fresh Air*. Natl. Public Radio.

WHYY, Philadelphia. 6 Jan. 2003. Radio.

92. Film

My Big Fat Greek Wedding. Dir. Joel Zwick. IFC, 2002. Film.

When you want to highlight the contribution of a specific person, list the contributor's name first. Other supplementary information may be included after the title.

Gomez, Ian, perf. *My Big Fat Greek Wedding*. Screenplay by Nia Vardalos. Dir.

Joel Zwick. IFC, 2002. Film.

93. Radio or television program

When referring to a specific episode, place quotation marks around its title. Italicize the title of the program.

"'Barbarian' Forces." *Ancient Warriors*. Narr. Colgate Salsbury. Dir. Phil

Grabsky. Learning Channel. 1 Jan. 1996. Television.

To highlight a specific contributor or contributors, begin the entry with the name or names and note the nature of the contribution.

Abumrad, Jad, and Robert Kulwich, narrs. "Choice." *Radiolab*. New York Public

Radio. WNYC, New York. 14 Nov. 2008. Radio.

94. Painting or other artwork

Gauguin, Paul. *Ancestors of Tehamana*. 1893. Oil on canvas. Art Inst. of

Chicago, Chicago.

Identify the artist's name, the title of the work (italicized), the date of composition (if known; otherwise, write *N.d.*), the medium of composition, the organization or individual holding the work, and the city in which the work is located. For a photograph or reproduction of a work of art, provide the preceding information followed by complete publication information for the source, including medium of publication. For works you locate online, omit the medium of composition. Include the name of the website, medium, and date of access.

Gaugin, Paul. *Ancestors of Tehamana*. 1893. Art. Inst. of Chicago. Web.

    3 Aug. 2013.

95. Photograph

Marmon, Lee. *White Man's Moccasins*. 1954. Photograph. Native American

    Cultural Center, Albuquerque.

96. CD-ROM

"About *Richard III*." *Cinemania 96*. Redmond: Microsoft, 1996. CD-ROM.

Jordan, June. "Moving towards Home." *Database of Twentieth-Century African*

    American Poetry on CD-ROM. Alexandria: Chadwyck-Healey, 1999. CD-ROM.

97. DVD or Blu-ray

A River Runs through It. Screenplay by Richard Friedenberg. Dir. Robert

    Redford. 1992. Columbia, 1999. DVD.

Cite relevant information about the title and director as you would for a film. Note the release date for the DVD or Blu-ray and include the original release date of the film when relevant.

98. Clip or section from DVD

"From Script to Screen." Prod. Allison Abbate. *Fantastic Mr. Fox*. Dir. Wes

    Anderson. Twentieth Century Fox, 2009. DVD. Disc 1.

End with information about the DVD including the disc number, if appropriate.

99. Sound recording on CD

Franklin, Aretha. *Amazing Grace: The Complete Recordings*. Atlantic, 1999. CD.

When citing a recording of a specific song, begin with the name of the performer and place the song title in quotation marks. Identify the author(s) after the song title. If the performance is a reissue from an earlier recording, provide the original date of recording (preceded by *Rec.* for "Recorded").

Horne, Lena. "The Man I Love." By George Gershwin and Ira Gershwin. Rec.

15 Dec. 1941. *Stormy Weather*. BMG, 1990. CD.

13c Sample MLA-style paper

(1) Submit a title page if your instructor requires one

The MLA recommends omitting a title page and instead providing identifying information on the first page of the essay, including your name, the instructor's name, the name of the course with its section number, and the date. If your instructor requires a separate title page, follow the specific directions for doing so.

(2) Sample MLA-style paper

Interested in the controversy surrounding prison reform, Marie Heller explores the issue in the MLA-style essay that follows.

TIPS FOR PREPARING AN MLA-STYLE ESSAY

- Double-space throughout.
- Number all pages (including the first one) with an Arabic numeral in the upper right-hand corner, one-half inch from the top. Put your last name before the page number.
- On the left side of the first page, one inch from the top, type a double-spaced heading that includes your name, the name of your instructor, the course number, and the date of submission.
- Double-space between the heading and the title of your essay and the line(s) of your title. Center your title.
- Double-space between your title and the first line of the text.
- Indent the first paragraph and every subsequent paragraph one-half inch.

Marie Heller

Professor Browne

Liberal Arts 101H, Section 014

9 January 2013

Prison Problems: Correctional System Reform

Proposal for Congress

In George Orwell's dark vision of a future fascist state, *Nineteen Eighty-Four*, all of the government institutions are precisely named for what they are not. The Ministry of Love tortures its citizens; the Ministry of Peace orchestrates wars; the Ministry of Truth fabricates propaganda; and the Ministry of Plenty rations all food. Just as Orwell's readers are rightfully suspicious of those names, I am suspicious of "Department of Corrections," the term used to describe prison systems in this country. After all, the *Oxford English Dictionary* tells us that "corrective" means "having the property or function of correcting or setting right what is erroneous or faulty." Given that definition, how could our prisons be considered correctional when they are actually and primarily punitive? Either we should drop the pretense and call the system the "Department of Punishment," or we should reexamine and reform the way we run the US prison system.

Reform is needed urgently. At present, there are nearly 2.5 million Americans locked behind bars (see fig. 1), a rise in the

The writer's last name and the page number

Heading

Center the title

Writer opens with an attention-getting statement

Double-space throughout

Use one-inch margins on both sides of the page

1 inch

1/2 inch

1 inch

M L A

Heller 2

number of convicts not reflected in an increased number of prison

cells. While our prisons are bursting at the seams, we should consider it our duty as a society to see that criminals are reformed at the same time they are punished and treated humanely and with respect.

Fig. 1. Number of incarcerated Americans between 1920 and 2006. Sources: Justice Policy Institute. "The Punishing Decade." *US Bureau of Justice Statistics Bulletin*. NCJ [National Criminal Justice] 219416-Prisoners in 2006. N.d. Web. 3 Jan. 2013.

Before discussing potential reforms, however, I want to outline the current state of America's prison system and assess its effectiveness as a correctional tool. An examination of trends in the past decade alone yields interesting data about incarceration.

Prison inmates constitute only 0.7% of the total population, a seemingly negligible percentage except that those prisoners live in

Heller 3

cramped conditions, within an overextended prison system ("Prisoner

Statistics" 1). In 2009, 743 out of every 100,000 Americans were

incarcerated ("Correctional" 2). That number might seem relatively

insignificant until we consider that it is one of the highest

incarceration rates in the world. The world's highest incarceration rate

in modern times belongs to the Soviet Union and its Gulag system

of prison camps and colonies, where, from 1934 to 1953, over a

million people were imprisoned, at a rate of 800 out of every 100,000

(Rosefielde 117). As recently as 2008, the United States was ranked

first as the world's leading jailer, now followed by Russia (see fig. 2).

Citation of a work by an organization

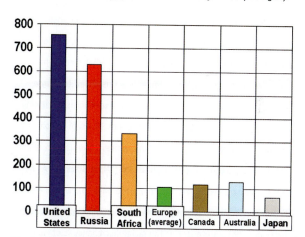

Fig. 2. The United States remains the world's leading jailer.
Source: Roy Walmsley. *World Prison Population List, 2009*. 8th ed.
International Centre of Prison Studies. King's College. 2008. Web.
3 Jan. 2013.

Indent each paragraph one-half inch

These dire statistics frame the discussion for prison reform by defining the shape and magnitude of the current US prison system. In terms of the causes for these incarcerations, the rate of violent crimes has been decreasing for decades with 49% of criminals convicted of nonviolent crimes ("Incarcerated America"). Some scholars argue that this steep drop in violent crimes in relation to the high incarceration rate can be attributed to the "war on drugs" in the United States and the concomitant implementation of three-strike laws, mandatory minimum sentencing, and similar social policy legislation.

The writer supplies details about the US prison population

Refers to two sources in one parenthetical reference

An examination of the characteristics of the US prison population brings to light a deep racial and economic divide. A 2007 report by the Associated Press reveals that blacks and Hispanics are more likely to be found in a prison cell than in a college dorm room ("More Blacks"). While blacks account for only 13.6% of the US population, they constitute 39.4% of prison population. Furthermore, non-Hispanic whites make up 37% of the US prison population, and Hispanics 19% ("More Blacks"). As far as Hispanics are concerned, they represent only 16.3% of the total US population yet 20.6% of jail and prison populations (*American FactFinder*; "Prison Inmates"). The racial discrepancy is obvious.

Just a cursory racial profile of the US prison population indicates a systemic problem of legal and judicial racism. Such legal

racism intersects with three-strike laws, mandatory minimum
sentencing, and the associated incarceration of nonviolent offenders,
thereby causing the huge increase in the US prison population.
With the overcrowding of prisons comes more cause for releasing
prisoners. And with more release of prisoners comes the question of
a prison's correctional efficacy, defined by its recidivism rate.

Perhaps the best measurement of a prison's correctional
efficacy lies in its recidivism rates. Recidivism, defined as
"relapsing into crime, or reoffending, especially habitually," is
difficult to measure. The recidivism rates in the United States
are incredibly fuzzy. Despite the implementation of recidivism-
incentive programs, state correctional departments are not required
to report them. In fact, the most recent available US Department
of Corrections recidivism statistics are from 1994, with very
few states providing those statistics since then. Nevertheless,
recidivism rates are often linked to the effectiveness of a
correctional facility. In terms of such links, however, no researcher
has yet definitively determined the likelihood of an inmate's
relapse. One study finds no evidence to link one incarceration
with repeated incarcerations (Langan). On the other hand, the
researchers for "Incarcerated America" argue that extended prison
stays gradually destroy the positive social networks inmates have
on the outside, the friends, family, and employees who can offer

Direct quotation of a phrase from a cited work

MLA

positive yet informal social pressure, pressure that helps keep
them from committing further crimes, from relapsing. Without
that informal social control, inmates are more likely to relapse
("Incarcerated America"). In the absence of firm findings that
connect prison policies and practices with low rates of recidivism,
the US public has no sense of whether our correctional facilities
actually succeed in transforming criminal behavior.

Oregon, however, has taken the initiative to report its
recidivism rates as well as to improve those rates. Oregon has a
30% recidivism rate, compared with other states, most of which
have 50% or higher rates (Baer). The state has made it a point to
implement social and judicial policies aimed toward incentivizing
good recidivism rates for Oregon prisons. For instance, in 2003,
the Oregon legislature passed a bill that mandated state prisons
use rehabilitation programs that were proven effective. As a result,
"between 2004 and 2007, Oregon's recidivism rate dropped 22.8
percent" (Baer). Oregon made decisions about who should and
should not be spending time behind bars in order to both lower
their recidivism rate and save taxpayer money. Adam Gelb, leader of
the Pew Study on State Recidivism Rates, suggests alternatives:

> In some cases, that means diverting offenders to
> community corrections programs instead of state prisons.
> In others, it means training offenders in decision-making

MLA

The writer
examines
the reasons
for the lack
of firm
findings

Writer
indents
a block
quotation
one-inch
on the left
margin only

and thinking skills, instead of just sending them through
drug treatment programs that may or may not stick.

(qtd. in Baer)

While creating a compromise between the needs of society and
those of the prisoner seems almost impossible, some correctional
facilities succeed at not only sufficiently caring for their inmates
but achieving unbelievable rehabilitation rates like the ones
found in Oregon. Rehabilitation *is* possible and should be actively
pursued.

So how do we fix the US prison system? The problem with
changing the current corrections system is that radical reforms
may be necessary. Therefore, a more practical approach might help
to gradually improve the current corrections system, by gradually
transitioning US prison policies and practices away from those that
make the United States the world leader in incarcerations.

The most obvious and perhaps least controversial reform
would be to reduce the length of sentencing or eliminate it
altogether for the majority of nonviolent crimes. Instead, nonviolent
offenders might be better served by conducting mandated community
service, participating in support groups tailored to their specific
conviction (anger-management courses, drug-education courses),
and enrolling in educational programs that teach critical thinking
and long-term planning skills. Diverted from the prison system,

Abbreviation *qtd. in* indicates quotation of Gelb appears in a source written by someone else

M L A

The writer offers some steps toward prison reform

The writer offers solutions in emphatic order, from least to most controversial and effective

minor offenders will be able to maintain their social support network and any informal control that such a network might provide. In addition, when nonviolent yet convicted criminals become involved in community projects, they have the opportunity to become more integrated into their community and to feel more invested in the welfare of that community.

Another reform, more controversial than the previous one, would include bipartisan congressional reconsideration. Might conservatives want to cut the massive cost of the "war or drugs"? Might liberals want to keep people out of prison and in drug-rehabilitation programs? Both sides of the aisle could agree that the current situation is not productive, let alone effective. Therefore, they might also agree that our nation now deserves a public exchange on the possibilities for the decriminalization of nonviolent offenses. The decriminalization of nonviolent offenses would reduce the strain on our prisons and—more important—the strain on (mostly poor) communities, families, and individuals. When nonviolent charges are decriminalized, nonviolent criminals can be diverted to community-service projects. For instance, among the nonviolent crimes might be "low-quantity possession," which might merit an addiction-education program rather than years of imprisonment.

Perhaps Americans will come to support even more radical reforms of our prison systems, especially if they see that practical approaches can make a difference. This discussion of crimes, prisons, and recidivism is one that the American public and their elected representatives desperately need to have, given that our current prison policies and practices are not working to reduce recidivism on a national scale. The US legal system has locked prisoners away to the point that they are living in overcrowded conditions with little hope of rehabilitation.

Therefore, we must refocus the current prison system from punitive to correctional. I am not arguing that criminal offenders, let alone violent criminals, should be coddled. However, they should be treated with respect and compassion, particularly when they are nonviolent offenders. As we work to reform our current prisons, we should model them after effective international rehabilitation correctional facilities, like those found in Oregon and also in Pennsylvania. The Pennsylvania Department of Corrections has made good progress toward reform, having established a recidivism-risk-reduction-incentive program for state prisons in 2010. According to the RRRI [Recidivism Risk Reduction Incentive], "the Commonwealth has saved approximately $37.1 million (an estimated $10,693 per RRRI inmate) due to reduced prison stays," reads the 2012 RRRI report ("RRRI"). These numbers serve as proof that a correctional system can be beneficial to the inmates as well as to the taxpayers who invest in the prison system.

MLA

Heller 10

Conclusion sums up argument and restates thesis

Congress has a duty to American citizens, both incarcerated and free, to make sure the prison system is the best it can be. By keeping nonviolent criminals out of the general prison population, the US prison system could move from a position of struggling to punish inmates housed at overcapacity to one of focusing on true correctional and rehabilitation practices and programs. After all, a more effective prison system means a more effective society overall, with more citizens contributing to their local and national communities.

1 inch

Works Cited

American FactFinder. 10 Apr. 2012. Web. 7 Jan. 2013.

Baer, April. "Pew Study Finds Low Recidivism Rate in Oregon
　　Prisons." *Oregon Public Broadcasting*. OPB News, 13 Apr.
　　2011. Web. 30 Dec. 2012.

"Correctional Populations in the United States, 2009." *Bureau
　　of Justice Statistics (BJS)—Total Correctional Population*.
　　Bureau of Justice Statistics, n.d. Web. 30 Dec. 2012.

"Corrective." Def. 1a. *OED Online*. Oxford University Press. March
　　2012. Web. 7 Jan. 2013.

"Incarcerated America, April 2003." *Human Rights Watch*. Apr.
　　2003. Web. 7 Jan. 2013.

Langan, Patrick A., and David J. Levin. "Recidivism of Prisoners
　　Released in 1994." Bureau of Justice Statistics, 2 June 2002.
　　PDF file.

"More Blacks, Latinos in Jail Than College Dorms." *MSNBC*. 27 Sept.
　　2007. Web. 5 Jan. 2013.

"Prison Inmates at Midyear 2009—Statistical Tables." *Bureau of
　　Justice Statistics (BJS)*. Bureau of Justice Statistics, 23 June
　　2010. Web. 5 Jan. 2013.

"Prisoner Statistics." *Correctional Population in the United States,
　　2011*. Bureau of Justice Statistics, 2011. Web. 7 Jan. 2013.

Center the
heading

Alphabetize
the entries
according to
the authors'
last names
or the name
of the article
itself

Indent
second and
subsequent
lines of each
entry one-
half inch

M L A

The writer
includes the
medium of
publication
for every
entry

Heller 12

"Recidivism." *OED Online*. Oxford University Press. March 2012.

> Web. 5 Jan. 2013.

Rosefielde, Steven. *The Russian Economy: From Lenin to Putin*.

> Malden, MA: Blackwell, 2007. Print.

"RRRI 2012 Report." *Research & Statistics*. Pennsylvania Department

> of Corrections, 2012. Web. 30 Dec. 2012.

14 APA Documentation

The American Psychological Association (APA) publishes a style guide entitled *Publication Manual of the American Psychological Association* (currently, the sixth edition). Its documentation system (called an *author-date system*) is used in psychology and many other disciplines, including education, economics, and sociology.

14a APA-style in-text citations

APA-style in-text citations usually include just the last name(s) of the author(s) of the work and the year of publication. If you do not know the author's name, use a shortened version of the source's title instead.

Be sure to specify the page number(s) for any quotations you use in your paper. The abbreviation *p.* (for "page") or *pp.* (for "pages") should precede the number(s). If visible paragraph numbers are provided instead of page numbers, use the abbreviation *para.* For documents that have neither page nor paragraph numbers, include the name of the section or an abbreviated heading. Then determine the number of the paragraph and include that number.

The following examples are representative of the types of in-text citations you can expect to use.

1. Work by one author

Yang (2006) admits that speech, when examined closely, is a "remarkably messy means of communication" (p. 13).

OR

When examined closely, speech is "a remarkably messy means of communication" (Yang, 2006, p. 13).

Use commas to separate the author's name from the date and the date from the page number. Include page numbers only when quoting from the source.

2. Work by two authors

According to Goodie and Fortune (2013), "impaired control . . . is a gambler's belief that he or she cannot control his or her own problematic gambling behaviors" (p. 2).

OR

Many compulsive gamblers believe they have no control over their behaviors (Goodie & Fortune, 2013).

When the authors' names are in parentheses, use an ampersand (&) to separate them.

3. Work by more than two authors

Interference between conversation and driving occurs because both are

"complex, multimodal, attention-demanding tasks" (Bergen, Medeiros-Ward,

Wheeler, Drews, & Strayer, 2013, Introduction section, para. 2).

For works with three to five authors, cite all the authors the first time the work is referred to, but in subsequent references give only the last name of the first author followed by *et al.* (meaning "and others").

The research of Bergen et al. (2013) confirms previous studies

"demonstrating that language use, even without a handheld device,

interferes with successful control of a vehicle" (Discussion section, para. 2).

For works with six or more authors, provide only the last name of the first author followed by *et al.* in both the first and subsequent citations.

4. Anonymous work

Use a shortened version of the title to identify an anonymous work.

Chronic insomnia often requires medical intervention ("Sleep," 2009).

This citation refers to an article identified in the bibliography as "Sleep disorders: Standard methods of treatment."

If the word *Anonymous* is used in the source itself to designate the author, it appears in place of an author's name.

The documents could damage the governor's reputation (Anonymous, 2009).

5. Two or more works by different authors in the same parenthetical citation

Smokers frequently underestimate the long-term effects of smoking

(O'Conner, 2005; Polson & Truss, 2007).

Arrange the citations in alphabetical order, using a semicolon to separate them.

6. Two or more works by the same author in the same parenthetical citation

The amygdala is active when a person experiences fear or anger (Carey, 2001, 2002).

Jameson (2007a, 2007b) has proposed an anxiety index for use by counselors.

Order the publication dates of works by the same author from earliest to most recent; however, if the works have the same publication date, distinguish the dates with lowercase letters (a, b, c, and so on) assigned according to the order in which the entries for the works are listed in your bibliography.

7. Personal communication

State educational outcomes are often interpreted differently by teachers in the same school (J. K. Jurgensen, personal communication, May 4, 2009).

Letters, memos, e-mail messages, interviews, and telephone conversations are cited in the text only, not in the reference list.

8. Indirect source

Korovessis (2002) points out Toqueville's description of the "strange melancholy" (p. 63) exhibited by citizens living amid abundance.

Toqueville (as cited in Korovessis, 2002) observed the "strange melancholy" (p. 63) exhibited by citizens living amid abundance.

In the reference list, include a bibliographic entry for the source read, not for the original source. Use an indirect source only when you are unable to obtain the original.

14b   APA-style reference list

All of the works you cite should be listed at the end of your paper, beginning on a separate page with the heading "References." The following tips will help you prepare your list.

TIPS FOR PREPARING A REFERENCE LIST

- Center the heading "References" one inch from the top of the page.

- Include entries for only those sources you explicitly cite in your paper but not for personal communications or original works cited in indirect sources.

- Arrange the list of works alphabetically by the author's last name or by the last name of the first author. For a work without an author, alphabetize the entry according to the first important word in the title.

- If you use more than one work by the same author(s), arrange the entries according to the date of publication, placing the entry with the earliest date first. (See item 6.) If two or more works by the same author(s) have the same publication date, the entries are arranged so that the titles of the works are in alphabetical order, according to the first important word in each title; lower-case letters are then added to the date (2013a, 2013b) to distinguish the works. (See item 7.)

- When an author's name appears both in a single-author entry and as the first name in a multiple-author entry, place the single-author entry first.

- Type the first line of each entry flush with the left margin and indent subsequent lines one-half inch or five spaces (a hanging indent).

- Double-space between lines of each entry and between entries.

Directory to APA Entries for the Reference List

AUTHORS IN REFERENCE ENTRIES

APA

A P A

AUTHORS IN REFERENCE ENTRIES

Citations begin with the authors' last names, followed by initials for first and middle names. Consult this section when deciding how to list different numbers of authors.

1. One author

Read, A. (2013, May). Rural sustainability: Factors and resources for

communities to consider. *Public Management 95*(4), 14–17. Retrieved

from http://icma.org/en/press/pm_magazine/about_pm

2. Two to seven authors

Zenz, G., Tahmasebi, N., & Risse, T. (2013). Towards mobile language
    evolution exploitation. *Multimedia Tools and Applications 66*(1),
    147–159. doi:10.1007/s11042-011-0973-0

Invert the last names and initials of all authors. Use a comma
after each last name and after each set of initials except the last.
Use an ampersand (in addition to the comma) before the last
author's name.

3. Eight or more authors

Kawakami, K., Phills, C. E., Greenwald, A. G., Simard, D., Pontiero, J., Brnjas,
    A., . . . Dovidio, J. F. (2012). In perfect harmony: Synchronizing the
    self to activated social categories. *Journal of Personality and Social
    Psychology, 102*(3), 562–575.

List the first six names followed by a comma and three ellipsis
points and then the last author's name.

4. No author listed

Atlas of the world (19th ed.). (2012). New York, NY: Oxford University Press.

Start the entry with the title.

5. Corporate author

American Psychiatric Association. (1995). *American Psychiatric Association
    capitation handbook*. Washington, DC: Author.

When the author and the publisher are the same, use the word
Author as the publisher at the end of the entry.

6. Two or more works by the same author.

The book published first is listed first.

Eagleman, D. (2009). *Sum: Tales from the afterlives*. Edinburgh, Scotland:
    Canongate Books.

Eagleman, D. (2011). *Incognito: The secret lives of the brain*. New York, NY:
    Pantheon Books.

7. Two or more works by the same author published in the same year

If works appear in the same year, list them alphabetically by title and add letters (*a*, *b*, and so on) to the year.

Wheelen, C. (2013a). *The centrist manifesto.* New York, NY: Norton.

Wheelen, C. (2013b). *Naked statistics: Stripping the dread from the data.*

New York, NY: Norton.

ARTICLES (PRINT)

8. Article in a journal paginated by volume

North, M. S., & Fiske, S. T. (2013). Act your (old) age: Prescriptive,

ageist biases over succession, consumption, and identity.

Personality and Social Psychology Bulletin, 39, 720–734.

doi:10.1177/0146167213480043

Capitalize only the first word of the title and subtitle (if there is one) and any proper nouns. Italicize the name of the journal; capitalize all major words, as well as any other words consisting of four or more letters. Some journals include a DOI (digital object identifier) on the first page of an article, in both print and electronic versions. Include the DOI at the end of the entry.

9. Article in a journal paginated by issue

Hall-Lew, L., & Stephens, N. (2013). Country talk. *Journal of English*

Linguistics, 40(3), 256–280.

Provide the issue number (placed in parentheses) directly after the volume number (italicized).

10. Abstract of a journal article

Huang, H. D., & Hung, S. A. (2013). Comparing the effects of test anxiety

on independent and integrated speaking test performance [Abstract].

TESOL Quarterly, 47(2), 244–269.

CITATION MAP 14.1: ARTICLE IN A JOURNAL, APA STYLE

To cite an article from a journal, include the following elements. If an issue number is provided, include that as well.

FIRST PAGE OF ARTICLE

Tricksters and the Marketing of Breakfast Cereals → **Title of article**

THOMAS GREEN → **Author**

BREAKFAST CEREALS ARE SOLD BY TRICKSTERS. FROM LUCKY THE Leprechaun to the Cookie Crook to the mischievous live-action squirrels who vend General Mills Honey Nut Clusters, an astounding number of Saturday morning television commercials feature 30-second dramatizations of trickster tales that are designed to promote breakfast cereals. True, breakfast cereals are not the only products sold by tricksters, and not all cereals are sold by tricksters—especially in the last decade. But the association is common enough to persist as an unexamined assumption that seems obvious to most Americans once it is pointed out. Naturally, breakfast cereals are often sold by animated tricksterish mascot characters, and naturally such commercials feature motifs and narrative patterns that are common in trickster tales. But the perception of an inherent internal logic in this scheme overlooks a couple of key questions. Why, for example, are tricksters considered a particularly appropriate or effective means of marketing breakfast cereals? And why breakfast cereals in particular (and a few other breakfast products), almost to the exclusion of tricksters in other types of marketing campaigns? The answers to these questions, it turns out, may lie back in the semi-mystical, pseudoreligious origins of prepared breakfast foods and the mating of the mythology of those foods with the imperatives of the competitive, prepared-foods marketplace.

Title of journal | **Volume number** | **Issue number**

The Journal of Popular Culture, Vol. 40, No. 1, 2007 ← **Year of publication**
© 2007, Copyright the Authors
Journal compilation © 2007, Blackwell Publishing, Inc.

REFERENCES LIST ENTRY FOR AN ARTICLE FROM A JOURNAL

Author | **Year of publication** | **Title of article**

Green, T. (2007). Tricksters and the marketing of breakfast cereals. *The Journal of Popular Culture, 40*(1), 49–68.

Title of journal | **Volume number** | **Issue number** | **Page numbers**

11. Article in a monthly, biweekly, or weekly magazine

Finkel, M. (2013, June). First Australians. *National Geographic, 223*(6), 66–83.

For monthly publications, provide both the year and the month. For magazines published weekly or biweekly, add the day of the issue: (2013, May 8).

12. Article in a newspaper

Simon, S. (2007, October 14). Winning hearts, minds, homes. *Los Angeles Times*, p. A1.

Include both the section letter and the page number.

13. Letter to the editor

Budington, N. (2010, July 20). Social class and college admissions [Letter to the editor]. *The New York Times*, p. A26.

14. Editorial

Editorial: Print is dead! Or is it? [Editorial]. (2012). *New Oxford Review, 79*(10), 4–7.

15. Book review

Orford, J. (2007). Drug addiction and families [Review of the book *Drug addiction and families*, by M. Barnhard]. *Addiction, 102,* 1841–1842.

If the review does not have its own title, use the title of the book, but do not italicize it.

BOOKS (PRINT)

When preparing an entry for the reference list, be sure to copy the bibliographic information directly from the title page of the book (see citation map 14.2).

16. Book with author(s) listed

Pollan, M. (2013). *Cooked: A history of transformation*. New York, NY: Penguin.

Edwards, M., & Titman, P. (2010). *Promoting psychological well-being in children with acute and chronic illness*. London, England: Jessica Kingsley.

CITATION MAP 14.2: BOOK, APA STYLE

Include the following elements when citing a book.

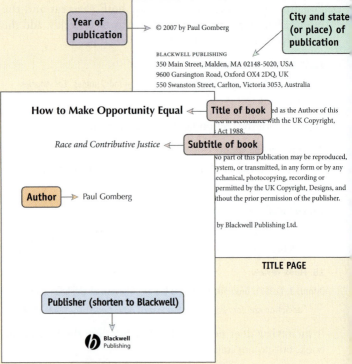

Year of publication → © 2007 by Paul Gomberg

City and state (or place) of publication

BLACKWELL PUBLISHING
350 Main Street, Malden, MA 02148-5020, USA
9600 Garsington Road, Oxford OX4 2DQ, UK
550 Swanston Street, Carlton, Victoria 3053, Australia

How to Make Opportunity Equal ← **Title of book** ed as the Author of this
ted in accordance with the UK Copyright,
Act 1988.

Race and Contributive Justice ← **Subtitle of book**
No part of this publication may be reproduced,
ystem, or transmitted, in any form or by any
echanical, photocopying, recording or
permitted by the UK Copyright, Designs, and
ithout the prior permission of the publisher.

Author → Paul Gomberg

by Blackwell Publishing Ltd.

TITLE PAGE

Publisher (shorten to Blackwell)
↓
ⓑ Blackwell
Publishing

COPYRIGHT PAGE

REFERENCES LIST ENTRY FOR A BOOK

Author | **Year of publication** | **Title and subtitle of book**
↓ | ↓ | ↓

Gomberg, P. (2007). *How to make opportunity equal: Race and contributive justice.* Malden, MA: Blackwell.
↑ ↑
City and state (or place) of publication | **Name of publisher**

Capitalize only the first word and any proper nouns in the title and subtitle. Italicize both title and subtitle. Include the city of publication and the United States Postal Service two-letter state abbreviation. For books published outside the United States, include the country.

17. Book with editor(s)

Wolfe, D. A., & Mash, E. J. (Eds.). (2005). *Behavioral and emotional disorders in adolescents: Nature, assessment, and treatment.* New York, NY: Guilford Press.

Provide only enough of the publisher's name so that it can be identified clearly. Omit *Publishers, Inc.,* and *Co.,* but retain *Books* and *Press.*

18. Edition after the first

Lycan, W., & Prinz, J. (Eds.). (2008). *Mind and cognition* (3rd ed.). Malden, MA: Blackwell.

19. Translation

Rank, O. (2002). *Psychology and the soul: A study of the origin, conceptual evolution, and nature of the soul* (G. C. Richter & E. J. Lieberman, Trans.). Baltimore, MD: Johns Hopkins University Press. (Original work published 1930)

20. Multivolume work

Hawthorne, N. (1962–1997). *The centenary edition of the works of Nathaniel Hawthorne* (Vols. 1–23). Columbus: Ohio University Press.

If the multivolume work was published over a period of more than one year, use the range of years for the publication date. If the publisher is a university press whose name mentions a state, do not include the state abbreviation.

21. Government report

Executive Office of the President. (2003). *Economic report of the President, 2003* (GPO Publication No. 040-000-0760-1). Washington, DC: Government Printing Office.

22. Chapter or article from an edited book

Empson, R. (2007). Enlivened memories: Recalling absence and loss in
Mongolia. In J. Carsten (Ed.), *Ghosts of memory: Essays on remembrance
and relatedness* (pp. 58–82). Malden, MA: Blackwell.

23. Selection from a reference work

Wickens, D. (2001). Classical conditioning. In *The Corsini encyclopedia of
psychology and behavioral science* (Vol. 1, pp. 293–298). New York,
NY: Wiley.

24. Republished book

Petersen, J. (2009). *Our street* (B. Rensen, Trans.). London, England: Faber.
(Original work published 1938)

25. Book with a title within its title

Wheen, F. (2007). *Marx's* Das Kapital: *A biography*. New York, NY: Atlantic
Monthly Press.

A title within a book title is not italicized.

ONLINE SOURCES

The APA guidelines for online sources are similar to those for
print sources. Many scholarly journals use a Digital Object
Identifier (DOI) to simplify searching for an article. The DOI
is listed on the first page of the article, which usually contains
the abstract. Citation map 14.3 shows the location of a DOI
and other pertinent bibliographic information on the first
page of an online journal. If available, insert the DOI (without
a period following it) at the end of the entry.

To cite an article without a DOI, use the URL for the periodical's home page. If the URL has to continue on a new line,
break it before a punctuation mark or other special character.
Do not add a period after the URL.

26. Article from a database

Hill, E. J., Erickson, J. J., Holmes, E. K., & Ferris, M. (2010). Workplace flexibility, work hours, and work-life conflict: Finding an extra day or two. *Journal of Family Psychology, 24*(3), 349–358. doi:10.1037 /a0019282

Acocella, J. (2008, May 26). A few too many. *The New Yorker, 84*(15), 32–37. Retrieved from http://www.newyorker.com

27. Article from an online journal

Buhrmester, M. D., Blanton, H., & Swann, W. B., Jr. (2011). Implicit self-esteem: Nature, measurement, and a new way forward. *Journal of Personality and Social Psychology, 100*(2), 365–385. doi:10.1037 /a0021341

Tuladhar-Douglas, W. (2007). Leaf blowers and antibiotics: A Buddhist stance for science and technology. *Journal of Buddhist Ethics, 14*, 200–238. Retrieved from http://www.buddhistethics.org

28. Article from an online magazine

Saletan, W. (2008, August 27). Unfinished race: Race, genes, and the future of medicine. *Slate.* Retrieved from http://www.slate.com

29. Article from an online newspaper

Shellenbarger, S. (2010, July 21). Kids quit the team for more family time. *The Wall Street Journal.* Retrieved from http://online.wsj.com /home-page

30. Online book

Pine, R. C. (2004). *Science and the human prospect.* Retrieved from http://home.honolulu.hawaii.edu/~pine/book1-2.html

If access to the book is not free, use "Available from" instead of "Retrieved from."

CITATION MAP 14.3: ARTICLE IN A DATABASE, APA STYLE

Include the following elements when citing an article in a database. If there is no Digital Object Identifier (DOI), use the URL for the journal's home page instead of the URL of the article.

DATABASE RECORD FOR AN ARTICLE

REFERENCES LIST ENTRY FOR AN ARTICLE IN A DATABASE

Poole, D. A., & Lindsay, D. S. (2001). Children's eyewitness reports after exposure to misinformation from parents. *Journal of Experimental Psychology: Applied, 7*(1), 27–50. doi:10.1037//1076-898X.7.1.27

31. Online book chapter

Brady, V. (2006). A flaw in the nation-building process: Negotiating the sacred in our multicultural society. In E. B. Coleman & K. White (Eds.), *Negotiating the sacred: Blasphemy and sacrilege in a multicultural society* (pp. 43–49). Retrieved from http://epress.anu.edu.au/nts _citation.html

32. Blog post

Chatham, C. (2008, August 29). Action without intention: Parietal damage alters attention awareness [Web log post]. Retrieved from http://scienceblogs.com/developingintelligence/2008/08/action _without_intention_parie.php

If you are quoting a comment instead of the original post, place in square brackets *Web log comment.*

33. Lecture notes posted online

Gabaix , X. (2004). *Lecture 14: Happiness* [Lecture notes]. Retrieved from http://ocw.mit.edu/courses/economics/14-13-economics-and -psychology-spring-2004/lecture-notes/

34. Short work from a website

Ennis, R. H. (2002, July 20). *An outline of goals for a critical thinking curriculum and its assessment.* Retrieved from http://faculty.ed.uiuc .edu/rhennis/outlinegoalsctcurassess3.html

When the document is from a large website, such as one sponsored by a university or governmental body, provide the name of the host organization before the URL. Do not include a date with the retrieval information unless the work is likely to change or be updated, as in a wiki for example.

Darling, C. (2002). *Guide to grammar and writing.* Retrieved September 12, 2003, from Capital Community College website: http://cctc2.commnet .edu/grammar/modifiers.htm

CITATION MAP 14.4: SECTION IN A WEB DOCUMENT, APA STYLE

Include the following elements when citing a section in a document you find on the web.

TITLE PAGE OF A WORK FROM A WEBSITE

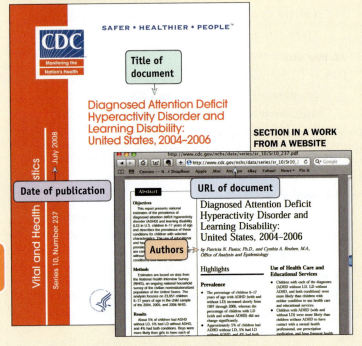

SECTION IN A WORK FROM A WEBSITE

REFERENCES LIST ENTRY FOR A DOCUMENT FROM THE WEB

| Authors | Date of publication (or recent update) | Name of section | Title of document |

Pastor, P. N. and Reuben, C. A. (2008, July). Introduction. In *Diagnosed Attention Deficit Hyperactivity Disorder and Learning Disability: United States, 2004–2006*. Retrieved from http://www.cdc.gov /nchs/data/series/sr_10/sr10_237.pdf

URL of document

American School Counselor Association. (2006). *Position statement: Equity for
all students*. Retrieved from http://asca2.timberlakepublishing.com
/content.asp?contentid=503

When no author is listed, use the name of the organization
hosting the website as the author of the document.

35. E-mail messages and other personal communication

Personal communications such as e-mail messages, letters, interviews, and telephone conversations are not included in the
reference list but should be cited in the text as follows: (S. L.
Johnson, personal communication, September 3, 2013).

36. Online encyclopedia

Dowe, P. (2007). Causal processes. In E. N. Zalta (Ed.), *The Stanford
encyclopedia of philosophy* (Fall 2008 ed.). Retrieved from http://plato
.stanford.edu/archives/sum2007/entries/cognitive-science/

37. Wiki entry

Déjà vu. (n.d.). In *Wikipedia*. Retrieved May 20, 2013, from
http://en.wikipedia.org/wiki/Deja_vu

If no date is provided, use the abbreviation *n.d.*

38. Article in a newsletter

Brady, B. Essential strategies for teaching large classes. (2013, August).
TESOL Connections. Retrieved from http://www.tesol.org/read-and
-publish/newsletters-other-publications/tesol-connections

39. Report online

Yones, M. (n.d.). *Psychology of happiness and unhappiness.* Retrieved
from International Institute of Management website: http://www.iim-edu
.org/executivejournal/index.htm

If the report has a number, mention the number in parentheses after the title: *Title* (Report No. XX).

40. Online government document

Pashler, H., Bain, P., Bottge, B., Graesser, A., Koedinger, K., McDaniel, M., & Metcalfe, J. (2007). *Organizing instruction and study to improve student learning* (NCER 2007–2004). Washington, DC: National Center for Education Research, Institute of Education Sciences, U.S. Department of Education. Retrieved from Institute of Education Sciences website: http://ncer.ed.gov

If no authors had been listed, this entry would have been written as follows:

National Center for Education Research, Institute of Education Sciences. (2007). *Organizing instruction and study to improve student learning* (NCER 2007–2004). Retrieved from http://ncer.ed.gov

41. Online audio and video

Davies, D. (Host). (2010, July 13). A psychiatrist's prescription for his profession [Audio file]. In T. Gross & D. Miller (Executive producers), *Fresh air*. Retrieved from http://www.npr.org/templates/story/story.php?storyId=13

For podcasts, place the main contributor at the beginning of the entry; place in parentheses the contributor's role (producer, director, writer, host, presenter). Place between square brackets the medium (audio file, video file, podcast, webcast).

Gopnik, A. (Presenter). (2009, July 28). Moments of absolute absorption [Video file]. In D. McGee & P. W. Kunhardt (Executive producers), *This emotional life*. Retrieved from http://www.pbs.org/thisemotionallife /perspective/meaning-happiness

OTHER SOURCES

42. Film, video, or DVD

Seidler, D. (Writer), & Hooper, T. (Director). (2011). *The king's speech* [Motion picture]. England: Momentum Pictures.

43. Television series episode

Weiner, M. (Writer), & Hornbacher, S. (Director). (2013). The doorway
[Television series episode]. In M. Weiner (Executive producer), *Mad
men*. New York, NY: AMC.

If referring to the series as a whole, write *Television series* in the
square brackets.

44. Advertisement

RosettaStone [Advertisement]. (2010, July). *National Geographic, 218*(1), 27.

45. Dissertation from a database

Aakre, J. M. (2010). Attributional style in schizophrenia: Associations with
suspiciousness and depressed mood (Doctoral dissertation). Retrieved
from http://www.ohiolink.edu

46. Published interview

Bell, G. (2012). Why people really love technology: An interview with
Genevieve Bell [Interview by A. C. Madrigal]. Retrieved from
http://www.theatlantic.com/

An interview you conducted personally is considered a personal communication. See item 35.

47. Map or chart

Central Intelligence Agency (Cartographer). (2011). China physiography
[Map]. Retrieved from https://www.cia.gov/library/publications
/cia-maps-publications/

48. Work of art

Bates, D. (1995). *Male head IV* [Sculpture]. Fort Worth, TX: Modern Art
Museum of Fort Worth.

Condo, G. (2009). *The fallen butler* [Painting]. New York, NY: Museum of
Modern Art.

49. Photograph

[Photograph of Louise Bieriot]. (1909). Bain Collection. Library of Congress,

   Washington, DC.

If you are using a photograph you have taken yourself, you do
not need to include an entry on your references page.

50. Lecture, speech, or address

The White House, Office of the Press Secretary. (2013, April 23). *Remarks*

   by the president at teacher of the year event. Retrieved from

   http://www.whitehouse.gov/the-press-office/2013/04/23/remarks

   -president-teacher-year-event

14c Sample APA-style paper

The APA recognizes that a paper may have to be modified so
that it adheres to an instructor's requirements. The following
boxes offer tips for preparing a title page, an abstract page, and
the body of a typical student paper. For tips on preparing a
reference list, see **14b**.

TIPS FOR PREPARING THE TITLE PAGE OF AN APA-STYLE PAPER

- The title page includes both the full title of the paper and a shortened version of it. The shortened version, along with a page number, is placed in the header. On the left side of the header, include
  the words "Running head:" (note the colon) and a version of your
  title that consists of no more than fifty characters. Use all uppercase letters for this title. On the right side of the header, insert
  the page number. The title page is page 1 of your paper.

- Place the full title in the upper half of the page, with your name
  below it. You may include your affiliation or a course name or
  number if your instructor requests one. Double-space these lines.

TIPS FOR PREPARING THE ABSTRACT AND THE BODY OF AN APA-STYLE PAPER

- The header for the remaining parts of the paper (including the abstract page, which is page 2) is similar to the header on the title page. It should have the shortened title on the left and the page number on the right. The body of the paper begins on page 3.

- Center the word "Abstract" one inch from the top of the page.

- Unless your instructor provides a word limit, be sure that your abstract is no more than 250 words. For advice on summarizing, see **11f**.

- Double-space throughout the body of the abstract. Do not indent the first line of the abstract.

- Provide the title again on page 3. Center it one inch from the top of the page.

- Use one-inch margins on both the left and right sides of all pages.

- Double-space throughout the body of the paper, indenting each paragraph one-half inch or five to seven spaces.

Running head: SOCIAL STATUS OF AN ART   1

The running head should consist of no more than 50 characters

Use one-inch margins on both sides of the page

The Social Status of an Art:

Historical and Current Trends in Tattooing

Rachel L. Pinter and Sarah M. Cronin

Central Washington University

If required by the instructor, the course name and number replace the institutional affiliation

APA

SOCIAL STATUS OF AN ART   1 inch   1/2 inch   2

Abstract

Current research demonstrates that the social practice of tattooing has changed greatly over the years. Not only have the images chosen for tattoos and the demographic of people getting tattoos changed, but the ideology behind tattooing itself has evolved. This paper first briefly describes the cross-cultural history of the practice. It then examines current social trends in the United States and related ideological issues.

Center the heading

An abstract generally contains between 150 and 250 words

APA

1 inch

The Social Status of an Art: Historical and

Current Trends in Tattooing

Center the title

Tattoos, defined as marks made by inserting pigment into the skin, have existed throughout history in countless cultures. Currently, tattoos are considered popular art forms. They can be seen on men and women from all walks of life in the United States, ranging from a trainer at the local gym to a character on a television show or even a sociology professor. Due to an increase in the popularity of tattooing, studies of tattooing behavior have proliferated as researchers attempt to identify trends. This paper seeks to explore both the history of tattooing and its current practice in the United States.

Use one-inch margins on both sides of the page

The writers' thesis statement forecasts the content of the essay

Tattooing has a long history in most of the world, though its origin is currently unknown. Krcmarik (2003) provides a helpful geographical overview. In Asia, tattooing has existed for thousands of years in Chinese, Japanese, Middle Eastern, and Indian cultures. Evidence of its existence can be seen on artifacts such as 7,000-year-old engravings. In Europe, tattooing flourished during the 19th century, most notably in England. Many of the sailors traveling with Captain James Cook returned with tales of exotic tattooing practices and sometimes with tattoos themselves. The Samoans in the South Pacific are famous for their centuries-old tattooing practice, known as *tatau*—the word from which *tattoo* is said to have originated. The Maori of New Zealand are also well known for their

The writers provide historical and cultural information about tattooing

APA

SOCIAL STATUS OF AN ART   4

hand-carved facial tattoos, known as *Moko* (see Figure 1).

In Africa, tattoos can be found on Egyptian and Nubian mummies, which date back to approximately 2000 BCE. Tattooing is noted in the written accounts of Spanish explorers' encounters with tattooed Mayans in Central America.

Figure 1. A Maori man with a facial tattoo. *Note.* Photo © Tim Graham/ Getty Images.

Finally, in North America, tattooing became popular during the 1900s and has experienced advances and retreats in social acceptance since then. Starting in the 1960s, its popularity rose dramatically.

Clearly, the history of tattooing spans generations and cultures. The practice has gained and lost popularity, often as a result of rather extreme changes in the ideologies supporting or discouraging it. This roller-coaster pattern of acceptance is well demonstrated in the United States. Since the 19th century, the wearing of tattoos has allowed for subculture identification by such persons as sailors, bikers, circus "freak" performers, and prison inmates (DeMello, 1995). As a collective group behavior indicating

SOCIAL STATUS OF AN ART 5

The writers discuss changing perspectives on the appropriate-ness of tattoos

deviant subculture membership, tattooing flourished during this time but remained plagued by negative stereotypes and associations. In the last 10 years, however, the practice has represented a more individualistic yet mainstream means of body adornment. As Figure 2 illustrates, it is not unusual to see a white-collar worker sporting a tattoo.

Figure 2. Tattoos are becoming more common among middle-class professionals. *Note.* Photo © Eric Anthony Photography/Monsoon Images/PhotoLibrary.

Tattooing is now common among both teenagers and older adults, men and women, urbanites and suburbanites, the college-educated and the uneducated, and the rich as well as the poor (Kosut, 2006). Table 1 indicates the wide range of Americans wearing tattoos in 2003 and 2008.

Citation of a work by one author

TABLE 1   PERCENTAGES OF AMERICAN ADULTS WITH ONE
OR MORE TATTOOS

	Year	
Category	2003	2008
All adults	16	14
Region		
East	14	12
Midwest	14	10
South	15	13
West	20	20
Age range		
18–24	13	9
25–29	36	32
30–39	28	25
40–49	14	12
50–64	10	8
65+	7	9
Sex		
Male	16	15
Female	15	13

Note. Adapted from "Three in Ten Americans with a Tattoo Say Having One Makes
Them Feel Sexier," by R. A. Corso, 2008, *Harris Interactive.*

The trend toward acceptance of tattoos may be a result of
how American society views the people who wear them. Earlier,
tattoos were depicted in mainstream print and visual media as
worn by people with low socioeconomic or marginal status; now,
they are considered to be an artful expression among celebrities as
well as educated middle- and upper-class individuals (Kosut, 2006).

SOCIAL STATUS OF AN ART   7

This shift in the symbolic status of tattoos—to a form of self-expression among the social elite rather than deviant expression among the lower classes—has allowed tattoos to be obtained in greater numbers, owing in great part to the importance placed on self-expression in the United States. Even in the workplace, where employees had often been forbidden to display tattoos, employers now "take advantage of the open-mindedness and innovation that younger [tattooed] employees bring into the workplace" (Org, 2003, p. D1).

To clarify a direct quotation from a source, the writers insert a word in square brackets

As the popularity and acceptability of tattoos has increased, tattooing has become part of the greater consumer culture and has thus undergone the process of commercialization that frequently occurs in the United States. Tattoos are now acquired as status symbols, and their prevalence helps to sell tattoo maintenance products, clothing, and skateboards (Kosut, 2006). This introduction into the consumer culture allows tattoos to gain even more popularity; they are now intertwined with mainstream culture.

Researchers have been tracking the popularity of tattoos, though no one seems able to agree on exact numbers (Libbon, 2000). In 2000, MSNBC aired an investigative piece called *Tattoos—Skin Deep*, which cited the tattooing rate at 20% of the population (Rosenbaum, 2000). In 2003, citing a lower number, Harris Interactive reported that 16% of all adults in the United

States have at least one tattoo (Sever, 2003). The actual number of individuals with tattoos is unknown, but most researchers believe the trend has been consistently gaining ground since the 1960s. Statistics on the frequency of tattooing among specific age groups generally show increases (Armstrong, Owen, Roberts, & Koch, 2002; Mayers, Judelson, Moriarty, & Rundell, 2002) although one study (Corso, 2008) showed a slight decrease. However, because of the limitations of the various research designs, more research on a national level is needed to obtain truly representative figures.

Significantly, the increase in acquisition of tattoos has resulted in trends concerning the images and locations of tattoos, which appear to be divided along lines of gender. Many of the tattoo images commonly found on men include, but are not limited to, death themes, various wildlife, military insignia, tribal armbands, and family crests or last names. During the 1980s, cartoon images such as Bugs Bunny and the Tasmanian Devil were also popular for males. Males choose various locations for tattoos, but the most popular male sites are the upper back, back of the calves, and the upper arm, according to tattoo artist Ben Reames (personal communication, March 20, 2008). Conversely, females often obtain tattoos that symbolize traditional femininity, such as flowers, stars, hearts, and butterflies. A noticeable trend for females in the 1980s was the rose tattoo which was often located

The writers list statistics to support a claim

Two citations of articles, both written by four authors, are separated by a semicolon

APA

Citation of an interview with a tattoo artist

SOCIAL STATUS OF AN ART 9

on the breast or ankle. Stars and butterflies now rival the rose in popularity. The ankle continues to be a popular location for females today. Other popular spots for tattoos include the hip, foot (see Figure 3), and lower back. In fact, the lower back experienced a huge surge in popularity during the 1990s (B. Reames, personal communication, July 12, 2007).

Figure 3. Many females who get a tattoo choose to have it on the foot. *Note.* Photo © Color-Blind Images/ Blend Images/Corbis.

The art of tattooing has existed in many culturally determined forms throughout human history, and its current manifestations are as varied as the cultures themselves. However, based on the current literature, the social behavior of tattooing is still quite common in the United States. In fact, Kosut (2006) argues, "New generations of American children are growing up in a cultural landscape that is more tattoo-friendly and tattoo-flooded than any other time in history" (p. 1037). Because today's children see tattoos and tattoo-related products everywhere, usually in neutral or positive situations, they will likely be more accepting of tattoos than earlier generations were. Certainly, the tattooing trend shows no signs of decreasing significantly.

SOCIAL STATUS OF AN ART 10

References

Armstrong, M. L., Owen, D. C., Roberts, A. E., & Koch, J. R. (2002). College students and tattoos: Influence of image, identity, and family. *Journal of Psychosocial Nursing, 40*(10), 20–29.

Corso, R. A. (2008, February 12). *Three in ten Americans with a tattoo say having one makes them feel sexier*. Retrieved from http://www.harrisinteractive.com/Insights/HarrisVault.aspx

DeMello, M. (1995). Not just for bikers anymore: Popular representations of American tattooing. *Journal of Popular Culture, 29*(3), 37–53. Retrieved from http://www.wiley.com/bw/journal.asp?ref=0022-3840

Kosut, M. (2006). An ironic fad: The commodification and consumption of tattoos. *Journal of Popular Culture, 39*(6), 1035–1049. Retrieved from http://www.wiley.com/bw/journal.asp?ref=0022-3840

Krcmarik, K. L. (2003). *History of tattooing*. Retrieved from Michigan State University website: http://www.msu.edu/~krcmari1/individual/history.html

Libbon, R. P. (2000). Dear data dog: Why do so many kids sport tattoos? *American Demographics, 22*(9), 26. Retrieved from http://amiga.adage.com/de

Mayers, L. B., Judelson, D. A., Moriarity, B. W., & Rundell, K. W. (2002). Prevalence of body art (body piercing and tattooing)

1 inch

1/2 inch

Center the heading

Alphabetize the entries according to the author's (or first author's) last name

Indent second and subsequent lines of each entry one-half inch or five spaces

No period follows a URL at the end of an entry

APA

in university undergraduates and incidence of medical complications. *Mayo Clinic Proceedings, 77*, 20–34.

Org, M. (2003, August 28). The tattooed executive. *The Wall Street Journal*. Retrieved from http://online.wsj.com/public/us

Rosenbaum, S. (Executive producer). (2000, August 20). *MSNBC investigates: Tattoos—skin deep* [Television broadcast]. New York, NY: MSNBC.

Sever, J. (2003, October 8). *A third of Americans with tattoos say they make them feel more sexy*. Retrieved from http://www .harrisinteractive.com/Insights/HarrisVault.aspx

Identification
of the type
of medium
is placed
in square
brackets

APA

15 CMS Documentation

The Chicago Manual of Style (CMS), now in its sixteenth edition and published by the University of Chicago Press (2010), provides guidelines for writers, editors, and publishers in history and other subject areas in the arts and humanities. The CMS documentation system uses either footnotes or endnotes and, for most assignments, a bibliography. Each of these citations demonstrates that you have conducted relevant research, credited your sources, and provided the details necessary for your reader to locate your source.

15a CMS note and bibliographic forms

According to CMS style, in-text citations take the form of sequential superscript numbers that refer to **footnotes** (notes at the bottom of each page) or **endnotes** (notes at the end of the text). The information in these notes may be condensed if a bibliography lists all the sources used in the text. The condensed, or short, form for a note includes only the author's last name, the title (sometimes shortened if longer than four words), and the relevant page number(s): Eggers, *Court Reporters*, 312–15.

When a text has no bibliography, the full note form is used for the first citation of each source. For either footnotes or endnotes, place a superscript number in the text wherever documentation of a source is necessary. The number should be as close as possible to whatever it refers to, following most punctuation that appears at the end of the direct quotation or paraphrase but preceding a dash.

TIPS FOR PREPARING FOOTNOTES

- Most word-processing programs will footnote your work automatically. In your software, review the toolbars and menus to locate the tool to allow you to insert a footnote. A superscript number will appear in the cursor's position. A box will also appear at the bottom of your page in which you can insert the requisite information.
- Each note begins with a full-size number followed by a period and a space.
- Indent the first line of a note five spaces.
- Single-space lines within a footnote.
- Double-space between footnotes when more than one appears on a page.
- Use the abbreviation *Ibid.* (not italicized) to indicate that the source cited in an entry is identical to the one in the preceding entry. Include page numbers if they differ from those in the preceding entry: Ibid., 331–32.
- No bibliography is necessary when the footnotes provide complete bibliographic information for all sources.

TIPS FOR PREPARING ENDNOTES

- Place endnotes on a separate page, following the last page of your text and preceding the bibliography (if one is included).
- Center the word *Notes* (not italicized) at the top of the page.
- Use the abbreviation *Ibid.* (not italicized) to indicate that a source cited in an entry is identical to the one in the preceding entry. Include page numbers if they differ from those in the preceding entry: Ibid., 331–32.
- Indent the first line of a note five spaces.
- Single-space within an endnote and leave one blank line between endnotes.
- No bibliography is necessary when the endnotes provide complete bibliographic information for all sources used in the paper.

TIPS FOR PREPARING A BIBLIOGRAPHY

- Start the bibliography on a separate page, following the last page of the body of the text if footnotes are used or following the last page of endnotes.
- Center the word *Bibliography* (not italicized) at the top of your page.
- Alphabetize entries in the bibliography according to the author's last name.
- If a source has more than one author, alphabetize by the last name of the first author.
- For a work without an author, alphabetize the entry according to the first important word in the title.
- To indicate that a source has the same author(s) as in the preceding entry, begin an entry with six hyphens or a three-em dash (———) instead of the name(s) of the author(s). (If you do not know how to create this mark, search for *em dash*, using the Help function of your word processor.)
- Indent the second and subsequent lines of an entry five spaces (that is, use a hanging indent).
- Double-space within entries, as with other parts of your text.

CMS

Directory to CMS Note and Bibliographic Forms

CMS

The following list contains entries for the full note form and the bibliographic form. The short note form is provided only for the first example.

BOOKS

1. Book with one author

Full note form

> 1. Carlo D'Este, *Eisenhower: A Soldier's Life* (New York: Holt, 2002), 417–18.

Provide the author's full name, in normal order, followed by a comma. Italicize the titles of books, magazines, journals, and films. Capitalize all major words. The city of publication, publisher, and date of publication are all within parentheses. Omit the words *Inc.*, *Publishing*, *Publishers*, and *Co.*, but retain the words *Press* and *Books*. You may shorten *University* to *Univ.* as long as you do so consistently.

Short note form

> 1. D'Este, *Eisenhower*, 417–18.

Bibliographic form

D'Este, Carlo. *Eisenhower: A Soldier's Life*. New York: Holt, 2002.

Provide the author's full name, last name first, followed by a comma and the first name. Provide either the full name of the publisher or an abbreviated version. The style chosen must be used consistently throughout the notes and the bibliography. End the entry with a period.

2. Book with two authors

Full note form

> 2. Alice H. Eagly and Linda L. Carli, *Through the Labyrinth: The Truth about How Women Become Leaders* (Boston: Harvard Business School Press, 2007), 28.

Use the word *and* between the authors' names.

Bibliographic form

Eagly, Alice H., and Linda L. Carli. *Through the Labyrinth: The Truth about How Women Become Leaders*. Boston: Harvard Business School Press, 2007.

CITATION MAP 15.1: BOOK, CMS STYLE

Include the following elements when citing a book.

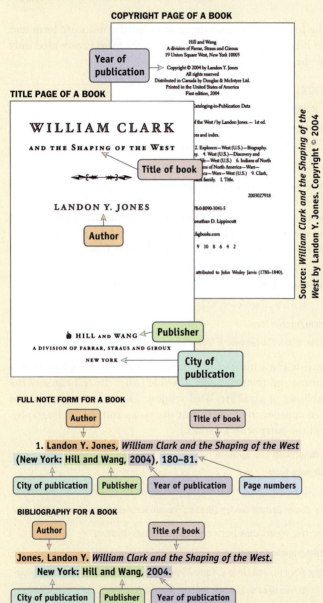

COPYRIGHT PAGE OF A BOOK

Year of publication

Hill and Wang
A division of Farrar, Straus and Giroux
19 Union Square West, New York 10003

Copyright © 2004 by Landon Y. Jones
All rights reserved
Distributed in Canada by Douglas & McIntyre Ltd.
Printed in the United States of America
First edition, 2004

TITLE PAGE OF A BOOK

WILLIAM CLARK
AND THE SHAPING OF THE WEST

Title of book

LANDON Y. JONES

Author

...Cataloging-in-Publication Data

...of the West / by Landon Jones.— 1st ed.

...es and index.

2. Explorers—West (U.S.)—Biography.
...y.   4. West (U.S.)—Discovery and
...fe—West (U.S.)   6. Indians of North
...ns of North America—Wars—
...ca—Wars—West (U.S.)   9. Clark,
...rk family.   I. Title.

2003027918

...78-0-8090-3041-5

...onathan D. Lippincott

...fsgbooks.com

9   10   8   6   4   2

...attributed to John Wesley Jarvis (1780–1840).

Publisher — 🐾 HILL AND WANG
A DIVISION OF FARRAR, STRAUS AND GIROUX
NEW YORK — **City of publication**

Source: *William Clark and the Shaping of the West* by Landon Y. Jones. Copyright © 2004 by Farrar, Straus and Giroux, LLC.

FULL NOTE FORM FOR A BOOK

Author   **Title of book**

1. Landon Y. Jones, *William Clark and the Shaping of the West* (New York: Hill and Wang, 2004), 180–81.

City of publication   **Publisher**   **Year of publication**   **Page numbers**

BIBLIOGRAPHY FOR A BOOK

Author   **Title of book**

Jones, Landon Y. *William Clark and the Shaping of the West.* New York: Hill and Wang, 2004.

City of publication   **Publisher**   **Year of publication**

CMS

198

Invert the first author's name and follow it with a comma, the word *and* (not italicized), and the second author's name in normal order. The second and subsequent lines of an entry are indented five spaces by using the hanging indent in your word processing program.

3. Book with three authors
Full note form

3. Karen A. Foss, Sonja K. Foss, and Cindy L. Griffin, *Feminist Rhetorical Theories* (Thousand Oaks, CA: Sage, 1999).

Bibliographic form

Foss, Karen A., Sonja K. Foss, and Cindy L. Griffin. *Feminist Rhetorical Theories.* Thousand Oaks, CA: Sage, 1999.

Only the first author's name is inverted. If the city of publication is not widely known, include a two-letter state abbreviation.

4. Book with more than three authors
Full note form

4. Mike Palmquist et al., *Transitions: Teaching Writing in Computer-Supported and Traditional Classrooms* (Greenwich, CT: Ablex, 1998), 153.

In a note use the first person's name followed by the phrase *et al.*, which means *and others*. Include all authors' names in the bibliographic form.

Bibliographic form

Palmquist, Mike, Kate Kiefer, James Hartvigsen, and Barbara Goodlew. *Transitions: Teaching Writing in Computer-Supported and Traditional Classrooms.* Greenwich, CT: Ablex, 1998.

5. Multiple works by the same author
In the bibliography, list the works alphabetically by title. After the first work, type six hyphens or a three-em dash in place of the author's name for subsequent entries.

Bibliographic form

Diaz, Junot. *The Brief Wondrous Life of Oscar Wao*. New York: Riverhead
    Books, 2007.

————. *This Is How You Lose Her*. New York: Riverhead Books, 2012.

6. Author not named or unknown
Full note form

6. *Beowulf: A New Verse Translation,* trans. Seamus Heaney (New York:
Farrar, Strauss, and Giroux, 2000), 24.

Bibliography form

Beowulf: A New Verse Translation. Translated by Seamus Heaney. New York:
    Farrar, Strauss, and Giroux, 2000.

7. Book with an editor
Full note form

7. Hanna Schissler, ed., *The Miracle Years* (Princeton, NJ: Princeton
University Press, 2001).

Place the abbreviation *ed.* after the editor's name.

Bibliographic form

Schissler, Hanna, ed. *The Miracle Years*. Princeton, NJ: Princeton University
    Press, 2001.

8. Book with an author and an editor
Full note form

8. Ayn Rand, *The Art of Fiction,* ed. Tore Boeckmann (New York: Plume, 2000).

Use the abbreviation *ed.* for "edited by."

Bibliographic form

Rand, Ayn. *The Art of Fiction*. Edited by Tore Boeckmann. New York: Plume, 2000.

Write out the words *Edited by.*

9. Translated book
Full note form

9. Orhan Pamuk, *Silent House,* trans. Robert Finn (New York: Knopf, 2012).

Use the abbreviation *trans.* for "translated by."

Bibliographic form

Pamuk, Orhan. *Silent House.* Translated by Robert Finn. New York: Knopf, 2012.

Write out the words *Translated by.*

10. Entry in a reference work
Full note form

    10. Robert Cox and Christina R. Foust, "Social Movement Rhetoric," in *The SAGE Handbook of Rhetorical Studies*, ed. Andrea A. Lunsford, Kirt H. Wilson, and Rosa A. Eberly (Thousand Oaks, CA: Sage, 2009), 613.

Bibliographic form

Cox, Robert, and Christina R. Foust. "Social Movement Rhetoric." In *The SAGE Handbook of Rhetorical Studies,* edited by Andrea A. Lunsford, Kirt H. Wilson, and Rosa A. Eberly, 605–27. Thousand Oaks, CA: Sage, 2009.

11. Sacred text
Full note form

    11. John 3:16 (New Revised Standard Version).

    11. Qur'an 7:1–7.

CMS does not include sacred or religious texts in the bibliography.

12. Source quoted in another source
Full note form

    12. Toni Morrison, *Playing in the Dark* (New York: Vintage, 1992), 26, quoted in Jonathan Goldberg, *Willa Cather and Others* (Durham, NC: Duke University Press, 2001), 37.

Bibliographic form

Goldberg, Jonathan. *Willa Cather and Others.* Durham, NC: Duke University Press, 2001.

In the note cite both the original work and the secondary source in which it is quoted. In the bibliography cite the secondary source.

13. Edition after the first
Full note form

13. Edward O. Wilson, *On Human Nature,* 14th ed. (Cambridge: Harvard University Press, 2001).

Bibliographic form

Wilson, Edward O. *On Human Nature.* 14th ed. Cambridge: Harvard University Press, 2001.

14. One volume in a multivolume work
Full note form

14. Thomas Cleary, *Classics of Buddhism and Zen,* vol. 3 (Boston: Shambhala, 2001), 116.

Bibliographic form

Cleary, Thomas. *Classics of Buddhism and Zen.* Vol. 3. Boston: Shambhala, 2001.

15. Government document
Full note form

15. US Bureau of the Census, *Statistical Abstract of the United States,* 120th ed. (Washington, DC, 2001), 16.

Bibliographic form

US Bureau of the Census. *Statistical Abstract of the United States.* 120th ed. Washington, DC, 2001.

16. Selection from an anthology
Full note form

16. Elizabeth Spencer, "The Everlasting Light," in *The Cry of an Occasion,* ed. Richard Bausch (Baton Rouge: Louisiana State University Press, 2001), 171–82.

If you are citing information from a specific page or pages of a book or an article, place the page number(s) at the end of the note.

Bibliographic form

Spencer, Elizabeth. "The Everlasting Light." In *The Cry of an Occasion,*

    edited by Richard Bausch, 171–82. Baton Rouge: Louisiana State

    University Press, 2001.

Use quotation marks to enclose the titles of selections from anthologies. The title is followed by a comma in the note form or by a period in the bibliographic form.

    When only one selection from an anthology is used, inclusive page numbers precede the publication data in the bibliographic entry.

17. Published letter
Full note form

    17. Lincoln to George McClellan, Washington, DC, 13 October 1862, in *This Fiery Trial: The Speeches and Writings of Abraham Lincoln,* ed. William E. Gienapp (New York: Oxford University Press, 2002), 178.

Bibliographic form

Lincoln, Abraham. Abraham Lincoln to George McClellan, Washington, DC,

    13 October 1862. In *This Fiery Trial: The Speeches and Writings of*

    Abraham Lincoln, edited by William E. Gienapp, 178. New York: Oxford

    University Press, 2002.

ARTICLES

18. Article in a journal
Full note form

    18. A. Schedler, "The Menu of Manipulation," *Journal of Democracy* 13, no. 2 (2002): 48.

Use initials for an author's first and middle names only when they are used in the original publication. Include the page number of the specific citation.

Bibliographic form

Schedler, A. "The Menu of Manipulation." *Journal of Democracy* 13, no. 2

    (2002): 36–50.

CITATION MAP 15.2: ARTICLE IN A JOURNAL, CMS STYLE

To cite an article from a journal, include the following elements.

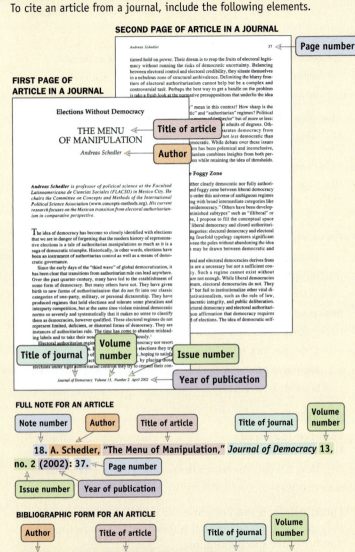

SECOND PAGE OF ARTICLE IN A JOURNAL

Page number

FIRST PAGE OF ARTICLE IN A JOURNAL

Elections Without Democracy

THE MENU OF MANIPULATION — Title of article

Andreas Schedler — Author

Title of journal · Volume number · Issue number

Year of publication

FULL NOTE FOR AN ARTICLE

Note number · Author · Title of article · Title of journal · Volume number

18. A. Schedler, "The Menu of Manipulation," *Journal of Democracy* 13, no. 2 (2002): 37.

Page number · Issue number · Year of publication

BIBLIOGRAPHIC FORM FOR AN ARTICLE

Author · Title of article · Title of journal · Volume number

Schedler, A. "The Menu of Manipulation," *Journal of Democracy* 13, no. 2 (2002): 36–50.

Page numbers · Issue number · Year of publication

In the bibliographic form, include the page span of the article.

19. Article in a magazine
Full note form

19. John O'Sullivan, "The Overskeptics," *National Review,* June 17, 2002, 23.

Bibliographic form

O'Sullivan, John. "The Overskeptics." *National Review,* June 17, 2002, 22–26.

For a magazine published monthly, include only the month and the year, with no comma inserted between them. In a note, mention only the cited page. In the bibliography, include the full page range of the article.

20. Review or book review
Full note form

20. Franny Howes, review of *Out of Athens: The New Ancient Greeks*, by Page duBois, *Rhetoric Society Quarterly* 42, no. 1 (2012), 88.

Bibliographic form

Howes, Franny. Review of *Out of Athens: The New Ancient Greeks*, by Page duBois. *Rhetoric Society Quarterly* 42, no. 1 (2012): 88–90.

21. Newspaper article
Full note form

21. Rick Bragg, "An Oyster and a Way of Life, Both at Risk," *New York Times*, June 15, 2002, national edition, sec. A.

Omit the initial *The* in the newspaper's name. If the city of publication is not part of the name, add it at the beginning (italicized) as part of the name: *St. Paul Pioneer Press.* If the city is not well known or could be confused with another city of the same name, add the state name or abbreviation in parentheses after the city's name. If the paper is a well-known national one, such as the *Wall Street Journal,* it is not necessary to add the city.

Bibliographic form

Bragg, Rick. "An Oyster and a Way of Life, Both at Risk." *New York Times*. June 15, 2002, national edition, sec. A.

If the name of the newspaper and the date of publication are mentioned in your text, no bibliographic entry is needed.

22. Unsigned article in a newspaper
Full note form

22. "Nittany Lions Finish with a Flourish," *Centre Daily Times* (State College, PA), February 26, 2012.

Bibliographic form

Centre Daily Times (State College, PA). "Nittany Lions Finish with a Flourish."
February 26, 2012.

Neither page numbers nor section is required.

ONLINE SOURCES

23. Article from an online journal
Full note form

23. Zina Peterson, "Teaching Margery and Julian in Anthropology-Based Survey Courses," *College English* 68, no. 5 (2006): 481–501, accessed May 5, 2010, doi:10.2307/25472167.

Give the DOI (digital object identifier), a permanent identifying number, when citing electronic sources. If the source does not have a DOI, list the URL (see item 25). If the material is time-sensitive or if your discipline or instructor requires it, include the access date before the DOI or URL.

Bibliographic form

Peterson, Zina. "Teaching Margery and Julian in Anthropology-Based Survey
Courses." *College English* 68, no. 5 (2006): 481–501. Accessed May 5,
2010. doi:10.2307/25472167.

24. Article from a journal database
Full note form

24. Samuel Guy Inman, "The Monroe Doctrine and Hispanic America,"
Hispanic America Historical Review 4, no. 4 (1921): 635, http://www.jstor
.org/stable/2505682.

CITATION MAP 15.3: ARTICLE IN A DATABASE, CMS STYLE

Include the following elements when citing an article in a database.

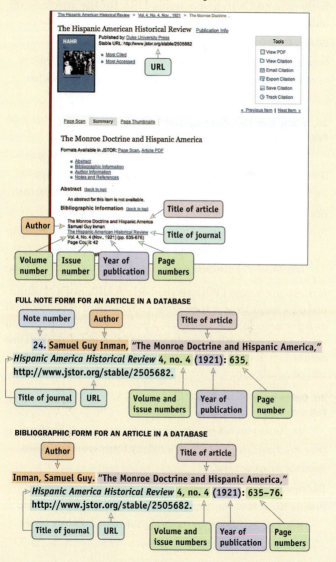

FULL NOTE FORM FOR AN ARTICLE IN A DATABASE

Note number · Author · Title of article

24. Samuel Guy Inman, "The Monroe Doctrine and Hispanic America," *Hispanic America Historical Review* 4, no. 4 (1921): 635, http://www.jstor.org/stable/2505682.

Title of journal · URL · Volume and issue numbers · Year of publication · Page number

BIBLIOGRAPHIC FORM FOR AN ARTICLE IN A DATABASE

Author · Title of article

Inman, Samuel Guy. "The Monroe Doctrine and Hispanic America," *Hispanic America Historical Review* 4, no. 4 (1921): 635–76. http://www.jstor.org/stable/2505682.

Title of journal · URL · Volume and issue numbers · Year of publication · Page numbers

If there is no DOI, give a stable URL for the article in the online database.

Bibliographic form

Inman, Samuel Guy. "The Monroe Doctrine and Hispanic America." *Hispanic America Historical Review* 4, no. 4 (1921): 635–76. http://www.jstor .org/stable/2505682.

25. Article from an online magazine
Full note form

25. Mark Frank, "Judge for Themselves: Why a Supreme Court Ruling on Sentencing Guidelines Puts More Power Back on the Bench," *Time*, January 24, 2005, http://www.time.com/time/magazine/printout/0,8816,1018063,00.html.

Bibliographic form

Frank, Mark. "Judge for Themselves: Why a Supreme Court Ruling on Sentencing Guidelines Puts More Power Back on the Bench." *Time*, January 24, 2005. http://www.time.com/time/magazine/printout/0,8816,1018063,00.html.

If the source has no DOI, cite the URL. A URL or DOI continued on a second line may be broken *after* a colon or double slash or *before* a single slash, a comma, a period, a hyphen, a question mark, a percent symbol, a number sign (#), a tilde (~), or an underline (_). It can be broken either before or after an ampersand (&) or equals sign.

26. Online book
Full note form

26. Marian Hurd McNeely, *The Jumping-off Place*, illus. William Siegel (New York: Longmans, 1929), 28, http://digital.library.upenn.edu/women /mcneely/place/place.html.

Bibliographic form

McNeely, Marian Hurd. *The Jumping-off Place*. Illustrated by William Siegel. New York: Longmans, 1929. http://digitial.library.upenn.edu/women /mcneely/place/place.html.

Include the same information (author, title, city, publisher, year) as for a book. While some online books provide page images of the original book, others do not. If page numbers vary, use a chapter or other section number instead.

27. Electronic book (e-book)
Full note form

27. S. C. Gwynne, *Empire of the Summer Moon* (New York: Scribner, 2010), Kindle edition, chap. 11.

Bibliographic form

Gwynne, S. C. *Empire of the Summer Moon*. New York: Scribner, 2012. Kindle edition.

28. Website
Full note form

28. Jeremy Hylton, The Complete Works of William Shakespeare, *The Tech*, MIT, 1993, http://shakespeare.mit.edu.

Bibliographic form

Hylton, Jeremy. The Complete Works of William Shakespeare. *The Tech*. 1993. http://shakespeare.mit.edu.

Unless no other publication information is available, access dates are not necessary.

29. Work from a website
Full note form

29. Eric Skalac, "BP Well to Stay Sealed after Gulf Spill, Experts Predict," *National Geographic*, last modified April 20, 2011, http://news .nationalgeographic.com/news/Energy/2011/04/110418-oil-spill -anniversary-is-bp-well-sealed/.

Bibliographic form

Skalac, Eric. "BP Well to Stay Sealed after Gulf Spill, Experts Predict." *National Geographic*, last modified April 20, 2011. http://news .nationalgeographic.com/news/Energy/2011/04/110418-oil-spill -anniversary-is-bp-well-sealed/.

CITATION MAP 15.4: WORK FROM A WEBSITE, CMS STYLE

Include the following elements when citing a short work from a website.

FULL NOTE FOR A WORK FROM A WEBSITE

Note number · Author · Title of article · Title of site · URL of website

29. Robin A. Fanslow, "The Migrant Experience," *Voices from the Dustbowl: The Charles L. Todd and Robert Sonkin Migrant Worker Collection,* American Folk Life Center, Library of Congress, last modified April 6, 1998, http://memory.loc.gov/ammem/afctshtml /tsme.html.

Date of publication · Sponsor of site

BIBLIOGRAPHIC FORM FOR A WORK FROM A WEBSITE

Author · Title of article · Title of site · URL of website

Fanslow, Robin A. "The Migrant Experience," *Voices from the Dustbowl: The Charles L. Todd and Robert Sonkin Migrant Worker Collection,* American Folk Life Center, Library of Congress, last modified April 6, 1998, http://memory.loc.gov/ammem/afctshtml /tsme.html.

Date of publication · Sponsor of site

30. Blog entry
Full note form

>30. Megan Slack, "What Is the Sequester?" *The White House Blog*,
February 22, 2013, http://www.whitehouse.gov/blog/2013/02/22/what-sequester.

Bibliographic form

Slack, Megan. "What Is the Sequester?" *The White House Blog*. February 22,

>2013. http://www.whitehouse.gov/blog/2012/02/22/what-sequester.

If *blog* does not appear as part of the name, add it in parentheses after the name. Although all blogs can be cited in notes, only frequently cited blogs appear in the bibliography.

31. E-mail and other personal communication
Full note form

>31. Evan Micheals, e-mail message to James Smith, February 22, 2013.

It is not necessary to list personal communications, such as e-mails, in the bibliography.

32. Podcast
Full note form

>32. Ira Glass, "363: Enforcers," *This American Life*, podcast audio, 57:53,
February 22, 2013, http://www.thisamericanlife.org/play_full.php?play=363.

Bibliographic form

Glass, Ira. "363: Enforcers." *This American Life*. Podcast audio, 57:53. February

>22, 2013. http://www.thisamericanlife.org/play_full.php?play=363.

33. Video or audio
Full note form

>33. Adam Savage, *How Simple Ideas Lead to Scientific Discoveries—
Adam Savage*, video, 7:31, March 13, 2012, https://www.youtube.com
/watch?v+F8UFGu2MgM.

Bibliographic form

Savage, Adam. *How Simple Ideas Lead to Scientific Discoveries—Adam Savage*. Video, 7:31. March 13, 2012. https://www.youtube.com /watch?v+F8UFGu2MgM.

OTHER SOURCES

34. DVD or Blu-ray
Full note form

34. *The Girl with the Dragon Tattoo*, directed by David Fincher (Culver City, CA: Sony Pictures Entertainment, 2011), DVD and Blu-ray.

Bibliographic form

The Girl with the Dragon Tattoo. Directed by David Fincher. Culver City, CA: Sony Pictures Entertainment, 2011. DVD and Blu-ray.

35. Interviews, published and unpublished
Full note form (PUBLISHED)

35. Aldous Huxley, interview by Mike Wallace, *The Mike Wallace Interview: Aldous Huxley (1958-05-18)*, YouTube video, last modified Aug. 1, 2008, http://www.youtube.com/watch?v=KGaYXahbcL4.

Bibliographic form (PUBLISHED)

Huxley, Aldous. Interviewed by Mike Wallace. *The Mike Wallace Interview: Aldous Huxley (1958-05-18)*. YouTube video. Last modified Aug. 1, 2008. http://www.youtube.com/watch?v=KGaYXahbcL4.

Full note form (UNPUBLISHED)

35. John Teodori, interview by James Timothy, November 16, 2007, transcript.

Bibliographic form (UNPUBLISHED)

Unpublished interviews rarely appear in the bibliography, but, if they do, they should include the name of the person being interviewed, the interviewer, the place and date of the interview, and the availability of a transcript or recording.

CMS

36. Sound recording
Full note form

    36. Frédéric Chopin, *Nocturne Op. 9 No. 2*, with Ivan Moravec (piano), recorded in 1966, Nonesuch B000005J03, 1991, compact disc.

Bibliographic form

Chopin, Frédéric. *Nocturne Op. 9 No. 2*. Ivan Moravec (piano). Nonesuch,
    B000005J03, 1991, compact disc. Recorded in 1966.

15b Sample CMS-style paper

The following student paper, a historical research project, addresses an ongoing struggle in South Africa related to electricity usage. Because he included a full bibliography, Cristian Nuñez supplied endnotes written in short form. Only the first pages of his essay, along with portions of his notes and bibliography appear here.

Nuñez   1

Local Politics and National Policy in a Globalized World:

South Africa's Ongoing Electricity Dilemma

Cristian Nuñez

Political Science 87

Professor Stone

December 15, 2010

Since its 1994 inception, the South African democracy has struggled to alleviate national poverty without alienating the global financial community on which it depends. Even though the government's moderate pro-business agenda is intended to reduce poverty, it continues to provide too little support for the nation's poor—an agenda harshly criticized by citizen-advocate groups. One such group is the Soweto Electricity Crisis Committee (SECC), a civic organization advocating free basic utilities for all South Africans, who charges that South Africa's government is not living up to the human rights core of its Constitution, guaranteeing all South Africans access to basic resources.[1] The SECC addresses human rights through its controversial—and illegal—practice of delivering free electricity to South Africa's poorest people.

The Electricity Crisis

Following the 1993 end of apartheid, the majority (African National Congress [ANC]) government swept into power with a mandate to reverse the injustices prevalent in South Africa. Millions of poor nonwhites hoped that affordable housing, modern education, and basic utilities would be expanded in their long-neglected neighborhoods. However, carrying out these goals would prove to be extremely difficult for the new ANC president Nelson Mandela, who had inherited a huge financial crisis from the old National Party regime. To avert a spending crisis of any kind

This introduction establishes the importance of the topic. The thesis statement is the final sentence of the first paragraph

Writer explains how the change from apartheid to democracy inadvertently created additional economic woes for nonwhites in South Africa

Nuñez   3

(one that would devalue South African currency both locally and globally), Mandela's ANC government implemented broad economic reforms in the hope of directing the foreign investment and capital inflows necessary for growing the South African economy.[2]

Figure 1. This township settlement in Soweto typifies the poverty and lack of access to public services for many South African citizens.

CMS

Outlines steps Mandela and the new government took to address the financial problems they had inherited

    One of the economic reforms included the plan to privatize the nation's many parastatals (state-owned enterprises). In preparation for privatization, each parastatal enacted cost-recovery pricing to make itself more competitive and more attractive to foreign investors. Unfortunately for the South African poor, such cost-recovery measures eliminated both subsidized utilities and rent in nonwhite neighborhoods like Soweto, which is located just outside of Johannesburg and has long been a hotbed of revolutionary actions and ideas. In response, a number of civics (community action groups) protested the government's economic reforms, the most brash of them being the SECC.

By 2001, in an effort to remain financially solvent, South Africa's public utility company, the Electricity Supply Commission (Eskom), was disconnecting twenty thousand households a month for not paying their bills. In response, the SECC illegally reconnected more than three thousand Soweto households in a program called "Reconnect the Power."[3] Because no workable solutions to this problem have yet been discovered since those early disconnections, those illegal reconnections remain in place. In 2009, SECC's electricians were reconnecting nearly forty houses per week, resulting in an estimated 60 percent of Soweto residents receiving electricity without charge. For many of the SECC electricians having electric power is a constitutional right, not a luxury. SECC electrician Levy argues that he and the electricians "are giving back what belongs to the people," thereby justifying the SECC's ongoing activism.[4]

The Legacy of Apartheid and Perceptions of Eskom

Although the SECC was established in 2000, the practice of nonpayment for basic needs has a much longer history in South Africa. During apartheid, the ANC urged residents of Soweto and

Nuñez   5

other townships to stop paying their rent and their electricity and water bills (which were often higher than those of households in upper-class white neighborhoods). The boycott the ANC organized was a powerful weapon against apartheid, eventually bankrupting local authorities. Many people retained this stance of resistance following the end of apartheid. "We did not expect this," said Chris Ngcobo, an organizer of the Soweto boycott under apartheid, who now helps oversee an ANC/Eskom project to reverse the culture of nonpayment. "We expected that after the elections people would just pay. But it will not be so easy."[5]

For many residents, nonpayment as protest continued as an intentional act during the Mandela years. During these early post-apartheid years, bill payment was presented as a patriotic gesture in support of the Mandela government.[6] The residents, however, wanted to see improvements first before resuming payment.

The rest of the paper describes the ways in which the SECC has intervened in order to provide electricity to poor, nonwhite South Africans

Nuñez   6

Notes

1. *Countries of the World*.

2. McNeil, "Shedding State Companies."

3. Bond, *Against Global Apartheid*, 170.

4. Fisher, "South Africa Crisis."

5. Daley, "In South Africa."

6. Ibid.

Bibliography

Bond, Patrick. *Against Global Apartheid: South Africa Meets the World Bank, IMF and International Finance.* Cape Town: Univ. of Cape Town Press, 2003.

Chang, Claude V. *Privatisation and Development: Theory, Policy and Evidence.* Hampshire, UK: Ashgate, 2006.

Countries of the World and Their Leaders Yearbook 2011. 2 vols. Detroit: Gale, 2010. http://go.galegroup.com.

Daley, Suzanne. "In South Africa, a Culture of Resistance Dies Hard." *New York Times*, July 19, 1995. http://www.nytimes .com/1995/07/19/world/in-south-africa-a-culture-of -resistance-dies-hard.html.

———. "Seeing Bias in Their Utility Rates, Mixed Race South Africans Riot." *New York Times*, February 7, 1997. http://www.nytimes.com/1997/02/07/world/seeing -bias-in-their-utility-rates-mixed-race-south-africans-riot .html.

Eskom. *Annual Report 1999.* n.d. http://www.eskom.co.za /annreport/main.htm.

Fisher, Jonah. "South Africa Crisis Creates Crusading Electricians." *BBC News*, November 24, 2009. http://news.bbc.co.uk/2 /hi/8376400.stm.

Bibliography begins on a new page

Entries use hanging indent

Two articles by the same author

CMS

Nuñez   8

Kingsnorth, Paul. *One No, Many Yeses*. Sydney: Simon and Schuster,
    2003.

McNeil, Donald G., Jr. "Shedding State Companies, if Sometimes
    Reluctantly." *New York Times*, February 27, 1997.
    http://www.nytimes.com/1997/02/27/business/shedding-
    state-companies-if-sometimes-reluctantly.html.

16 CSE Documentation

The Council of Science Editors (CSE) has established guide-lines for writers in the life and physical sciences: *Scientific Style and Format: The CSE Manual for Authors, Editors, and Publishers*, seventh edition, presents three systems for citing and documenting research sources: the citation-sequence system, the name-year system, and the citation-name system.

16a CSE-style in-text citations

CSE's guidelines for the citation-sequence system, the name-year system, and the citation-name system differ significantly, so be sure to know which you will be expected to use before you get started. Once you know your instructor's preference, follow the guidelines in one of the following boxes as you prepare your in-text references.

TIPS FOR PREPARING CITATION-SEQUENCE IN-TEXT REFERENCES

- Place a superscript number after each mention of a source or each use of material from it. This number corresponds to the number assigned to the source in the end references.

- Be sure to place the number immediately after the material used or the word or phrase indicating the source: Herbert's original method[1] was used.

- Use the same number each time you refer to a source.

- Order the numbers according to the sequence in which sources are introduced: Both Li[1] and Holst[2] have shown . . .

(Continued on page 222)

CSE

TIPS FOR PREPARING CITATION-SEQUENCE IN-TEXT REFERENCES *(Continued)*

- When referring to more than one source, use commas to separate the numbers corresponding to the sources; there is no space after each comma. Use an en dash between two numbers to indicate a sequence of sources: The early studies[1,2,4–7] . . .

TIPS FOR PREPARING NAME-YEAR IN-TEXT REFERENCES

- Place the author's last name and the year of publication in parentheses after the mention of a source: In a more recent study (Karr 2013), these findings were not replicated. Using the author's last name, the reader will be able to find the corresponding entry in the alphabetized reference list.

- Omit the author's name from the parenthetical citation if it appears in the text preceding it: In Karr's study (2013), these findings were not replicated.

- If the source has two authors, use both of their last names: (Phill and Richardson 2013). If there are three or more authors, use the first author's last name and the abbreviation *et al.*: (Drake et al. 2012).

- Use semicolons to separate multiple citations. Order these citations chronologically when the years differ but alphabetically when the years are the same: (Li 2012; Holst 2013) but (Lamont 2012; Li 2012).

TIPS FOR PREPARING CITATION-NAME IN-TEXT REFERENCES

- Arrange your end references alphabetically. Then assign each reference a number. Use the superscript form of this number in the text immediately after the material used or the word or phrase indicating the source: Stress-related illnesses are common among college students.[1]

- Use the same number each time you refer to a source.

- When referring to more than one source, use commas to separate the numbers corresponding to the sources; there is no space after each comma. Use an en dash between two numbers to indicate a sequence of sources: Recent studies of posttraumatic stress disorder[1,2,4–7] . . .

16b CSE-style list of references

On the final page of your paper, list all the sources you have mentioned. The ordering of the entries will depend on which system you have chosen. Both the citation-name system and the name-year system require alphabetical ordering according to the authors' last names; the citation-sequence system requires that the sources be listed in the order they were mentioned in your text.

TIPS FOR PREPARING END REFERENCES

- Center the heading "References" or "Cited References" at the top of the page.

- If you are using the *citation-sequence system*, list the sources in the order in which they were introduced in the text.

- If you are using the *citation-name system*, your end references should be ordered alphabetically according to the first author's last name and then numbered.

- If you are using the *name-year system*, your end references should be ordered alphabetically.

- Entries on citation-sequence and citation-name reference lists differ only in overall organization: citation-sequence references are listed according to the order of occurrence within the text; citation-name references are listed alphabetically. The name-year system differs from both the citation-sequence and citation-name systems only in the placement of the date of publication: the name-year system calls for the date to be placed after the author's name; the citation-sequence and the citation-name systems call for the date to be placed after the publisher's name in entries for books and after the name of the periodical in entries for articles.

- When listing place of publication information, if the city is not well known or could be confused with another city, include an abbreviation for the state or country in parentheses after the name of the city. The name of a country may be spelled out.

The following entries are organized to present the citation-sequence or citation-name system first, followed by entries reflecting the name-year system.

BOOKS

1. Book with one author
Citation-sequence or citation-name system

1. King BJ. How animals grieve. Chicago: University of Chicago Press; 2013.
   193 p.

Begin the entry with the author's last name and his or her first
initial and middle initial (if given). Capitalize only the first
word of the title and any proper nouns or adjectives. Include
the place of publication, the publisher's name, and the year of
publication. Provide the total page count if required, using the
abbreviation *p* for "pages."

Name-year system

King BJ. 2013. How animals grieve. Chicago: University of Chicago Press. 193 p.

2. Book with two or more authors
Citation-sequence or citation-name system

2. Ohanian HC, Ruffini R. Gravitation and spacetime. 3rd ed. Cambridge
   (England): Cambridge University Press; 2013.

Invert the name and initials of all authors, using commas to
separate the names.

Name-year system

Ohanian HC, Ruffini R. 2013. Gravitation and spacetime. 3rd ed. Cambridge
(England): Cambridge University Press.

3. Book with an organization (or organizations) listed as author
Citation-sequence or citation-name system

3. International Organization for Migration. Migration, environment and
   climate change: assessing the evidence. Laczko F, Aghazarm C, editors.
   Geneva (Switzerland): International Organization for Migration; 2009.

The first word of a subtitle is not capitalized unless it is a proper
noun.

Name-year system

[IOM] International Organization for Migration. 2009. Migration, environment and climate change: assessing the evidence. Laczko F, Aghazarm C, editors. Geneva (Switzerland): International Organization for Migration.

4. Book with editor(s)
Citation-sequence or citation-name system

4. Lund B, Hunter P, editors. The microbiological safety of food in healthcare settings. Malden (MA): Blackwell; 2007.

Include the word *editor* or *editors* after the last name.

Name-year system

Lund B, Hunter P, editors. 2007. The microbiological safety of food in healthcare settings. Malden (MA): Blackwell.

5. Section of a book with an editor
Citation-sequence or citation-name system

5. Banich, MT. Hemispheric specialization and cognition. In: Whitaker HA, editor. Concise encyclopedia of brain and language. Oxford (England): Elsevier; 2010. p. 224–230.

Name-year system

Banich, MT. 2010. Hemispheric specialization and cognition. In: Whitaker HA, editor. Concise encyclopedia of brain and language. Oxford (England): Elsevier. p. 224–230.

6. Chapter or part of an edited book
Citation-sequence or citation-name system

6. Martin DJ. Social data. In: Wilson J, Fotheringham AS, editors. The handbook of geographic information science. Malden (MA): Blackwell; 2008. p. 35–48.

Name-year system

Martin DJ. 2008. Social data. In: Wilson J, Fotheringham AS, editors. The handbook of geographic information science. Malden (MA): Blackwell. p. 35–48.

7. Paper or abstract in conference proceedings
Citation-sequence or citation-name system

7. Barge, RA. Using standards to support human factors engineering. In: Anderson M, editor. Contemporary ergonomics and human factors 2013: proceedings of the International Conference on Ergonomics and Human Factors; 2013 Apr 15–18, Cambridge, England. Croydon (England): Taylor & Francis; 2013. p. 135–137.

Name-year system

Barge, RA. 2013. Using standards to support human factors engineering. In: Anderson M, editor. Contemporary ergonomics and human factors 2013: proceedings of the International Conference on Ergonomics and Human Factors; 2013 Apr 15–18; Cambridge, England. Croydon (England): Taylor & Francis. p. 135–137.

ARTICLES

8. Article in a scholarly journal
Citation-sequence or citation-name system

8. Kao-Kniffin J, Freyre DS, Balser TC. Increased methane emissions from an invasive wetland plant under elevated carbon dioxide levels. Appl Soil Ecol. 2011;48(3):309–312.

Place a period after the abbreviated name of the journal (abbreviations can be found online by searching for "CSE journal abbreviations"). Next, list the year of publication, the volume number, and the issue number. Place a semicolon between the year of publication and the volume number. Put the issue number in parentheses. Note that there are no spaces separating the year, the volume number, and the issue number. Page numbers should be expressed as a range.

Name-year system

Kao-Kniffin J, Freyre DS, Balser TC. 2011. Increased methane emissions from an invasive wetland plant under elevated carbon dioxide levels. Appl Soil Ecol. 48(3):309–312.

C S E

CITATION MAP 16.1: ARTICLE IN A JOURNAL, CSE STYLE

Include the following elements when citing an article from a journal.

FIRST PAGE OF A JOURNAL ARTICLE

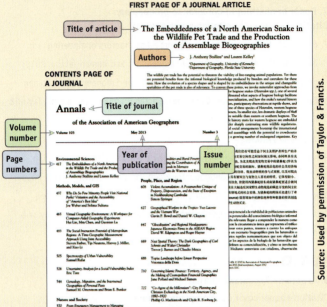

CONTENTS PAGE OF A JOURNAL

Title of article

Authors

Title of journal

Volume number

Page numbers

Year of publication

Issue number

CITATION-SEQUENCE OR CITATION-NAME FORMAT

Authors   Title of article

8. Stallins JA, Kelley L. The embeddedness of a North American snake in the wildlife pet trade and the production of assemblage biogeographies. Ann Assoc Am Geogr. 2013;103(3):417–436.

Title of journal   Year of publication   Volume and issue numbers   Page numbers

NAME-YEAR FORMAT

Authors   Year of publication   Title of article

Stallins JA, Kelley L. 2013. The embeddedness of a North American snake in the wildlife pet trade and the production of assemblage biogeographies. Ann Assoc Am Geogr. 103(3):417–436.

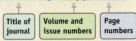

Title of journal   Volume and issue numbers   Page numbers

9. Article in a weekly journal
Citation-sequence or citation-name system

9. Mishra SK, Hoon MA. The cells and circuitry for itch responses in mice. Science. 2013 May 24:968–971.

Name-year system

Mishra SK, Hoon MA. 2013 May 24. The cells and circuitry for itch responses in mice. Science. 968–971.

10. Article in a magazine
Citation-sequence or citation-name system

10. McKibben B. Carbon's new math. Natl Geogr. 2007;212(4):33–37.

List the volume and issue numbers when available.

Name-year system

McKibben B. 2007. Carbon's new math. Natl Geogr. 212(4):33–37.

11. Article in a newspaper
Citation-sequence or citation-name system

11. O'Connor A. Heart attack risk linked to time spent in traffic. New York Times. 2004 Oct 26;Sect. F:9 (col. 4).

Include the section letter, page number, and column number.

Name-year system

O'Connor A. 2004 Oct 26. Heart attack risk linked to time spent in traffic. New York Times. Sect. F:9 (col. 4).

ONLINE SOURCES

12. Online book
Citation-sequence or citation-name system

12. Institute of Medicine, Committee on the Effect of Climate Change on Indoor Air Quality and Public Health. Climate change, the indoor environment, and health [Internet]. Washington (DC): National Academy Press; 2011 [cited 2013 May 26]. Available from: http://www.nap.edu/catalog.php?record_id=13115

Place the word *Internet* in brackets after the title of the book or journal. Give the date of access in brackets after the date of publication. Provide the full URL unless it is excessively long, in which case give the URL for the home page only.

Name-year system

Institute of Medicine, Committee on the Effect of Climate Change on Indoor Air Quality and Public Health. 2011. Climate change, the indoor environment, and health [Internet]. Washington (DC): National Academy Press; [cited 2013 May 26]. Available from: http://www.nap.edu/catalog.php?record_id=13115

13. Article in an online journal
Citation-sequence or citation-name system

13. Miller MR, White A, Boots M. Host life span and the evolution of resistance characteristics. Evol [Internet]. 2007 [cited 2007 Oct 31]; 61(1):2–14. Available from: http://www.blackwell-synergy.com/doi/full/ 10.1111/j.1558–5646.2007.00001.x

Name-year system

Miller MR, White A, Boots M. 2007. Host life span and the evolution of resistance characteristics. Evol [Internet]. [cited 2007 Oct 31]; 61(1):2–14. Available from: http://www.blackwell-synergy.com/doi/full/10.1111/ j.1558–5646.2007.00001.x

14. Article in a database
Citation-sequence or citation-name system

14. Stave G, Darcey DJ. Prevention of laboratory animal allergy in the United States. J Occup Environ Med [Internet]. 2012 [cited 2013 May 17]; 54(5):558–563. Academic Search Complete. Ipswich (MA): EBSCO. Available from: http://web.ebscohost.com. Document No.: 75239696.

Because CSE does not provide specific guidelines for citing an article retrieved from a database, this entry follows the guidelines for citing an online journal and a database.

CITATION MAP 16.2: ARTICLE IN A DATABASE, CSE STYLE

Include the following elements when citing an article in a database.

RECORD FOR AN ARTICLE IN A DATABASE

END OF DATABASE RECORD

CITATION-SEQUENCE OR CITATION-NAME FORMAT

NAME-YEAR FORMAT

C
S
E

Name-year system

Stave G, Darcey DJ. 2012. Prevention of laboratory animal allergy in the United States. J Occup Environ Med [Internet]. [cited 2013 May 17]; 54(5):558–563. Academic Search Complete. Ipswich (MA): EBSCO. Available from: http://web.ebscohost.com. Document No.: 75239696.

15. Article in an online magazine
Citation-sequence or citation-name system

15. Shermer M. Weirdonomics and quirkology: how the curious science of the oddities of everyday life yields new insights. Sci Am [Internet]. 2007 [cited 2007 Nov 1]; 1297(5):45. Available from: http://www.sciam.com/issue.cfm after clicking on the article link.

Name-year system

Shermer M. 2007. Weirdonomics and quirkology: how the curious science of the oddities of everyday life yields new insights. Sci Am [Internet]. [cited 2007 Nov 1]; 1297(5):45. Available from: http://www.sciam.com/issue.cfm after clicking on the article link.

16. Article in an online newspaper
Citation-sequence or citation-name system

16. Singer N. Making ads that whisper to the brain. New York Times [Internet]. Online version. 2010 Nov 13 [cited 2010 Nov 29]; [1 p.]. Available from: http://www.nytimes.com/2010/11/14/business/14stream.html?ref=health

Name-year system

Singer N. 2010 Nov 13. Making ads that whisper to the brain. New York Times [Internet]. Online version. [cited 2010 Nov 29]; [1 p.]. Available from: http://www.nytimes.com/2010/11/14/business/14stream.html?ref=health

17. Website
Citation-sequence or citation-name system

17. Southern California Earthquake Data Center [Internet]. Pasadena (CA): Caltech; c2013 [updated 2013 Jan 31; cited 2013 Jun 3]. Available from: http://www.data.scec.org/

Name-year system

Southern California Earthquake Data Center [Internet]. c2013. Pasadena (CA): Caltech; [updated 2013 Jan 31; cited 2013 Jun 3]. Available from: http://www.data.scec.org/

18. Short work from a website
Citation-sequence or citation-name system

18. National Wind Institute [Internet]. Lubbock (TX): Texas Tech University; c2013. The Enhanced Fujita scale; 2011 Aug 4 [cited 2013 Jun 3]; [13 paragraphs]. Available from: http://www.spc.noaa.gov/efscale/

Be sure to include both the copyright date for the site and the publication date for the short work.

Name-year system

National Wind Institute [Internet]. c2013. Lubbock (TX): Texas Tech University. The Enhanced Fujita scale; 2011 Aug 4 [cited 2013 Jun 3]; [13 paragraphs]. Available from: http://www.spc.noaa.gov/efscale/

19. Report from a government agency
Citation-sequence or citation-name system

19. Centers for Disease Control and Prevention, Department of Health and Human Services. Fourth National Report on Human Exposure to Environmental Chemicals, 2009 [Internet]. Atlanta (GA): Centers for Disease Control and Prevention; 2009 [cited 2010 Dec 10]. Available from: http://www.cdc.gov/exposurereport/pdf/FourthReport.pdf

Name-year system

Centers for Disease Control and Prevention, Department of Health and Human Services. 2009. Fourth National Report on Human Exposure to Environmental Chemicals, 2009 [Internet]. Atlanta (GA): Centers for Disease Control and Prevention; [cited 2010 Dec 10]. Available from: http://www.cdc.gov/exposurereport/pdf/FourthReport.pdf

20. Online video
Citation-sequence or citation-name system

20. Cresci C, Mullinkosson B, Price-Waldman S. Among giants [video on the
    Internet]. [place unknown]: Rainhouse Cinema; 2011 [cited 2013
    May 26]. Available from: http://rainhousecinema.com/films/

Name-year system

Cresci C, Mullinkosson B, Price-Waldman S. 2011. Among giants [video on
the Internet]. [place unknown]: Rainhouse Cinema; [cited 2013 May 26].
Available from: http://rainhousecinema.com/films/

16c | Sample CSE-style paper

Writing assignments in the natural sciences range from literature reviews to laboratory reports. Kayla Berg, whose research
paper follows, was asked to review the causes and impacts of a
natural disaster for a geology course. Kayla applied the guidelines in the CSE manual in formatting her paper. However,
those guidelines do not cover all features of undergraduate
papers, and Kayla's title page was formatted according to her
instructor's directions. Kayla used the CSE name-year system
to cite and document her sources.

CSE

Thailand Tsunami

Kayla Berg

Geology 380: Environmental Geology

November 5, 2009

1

Abstract

In 2004, an earthquake off the coast of Sumatra caused a tsunami that struck the coasts of several countries, causing not only a great deal of human suffering but also much environmental damage. This paper reports on various types of damage caused by the tsunami and the safety precautions that have been put into place to avoid similar destruction in the future.

Page header includes short form of title and page number

The writer establishes her authority by providing background information from reputable sources

Thailand Tsunami   2

Introduction

In December 2004, an earthquake with a magnitude of 9.0 occurred about 250 km off the west coast of Sumatra (in Indonesia) (Figure 1). The epicenter of the earthquake was located in the Indian Ocean at 3.3°N and 95.9°E. (Lukkunprasit and Ruangrassamee 2008).

This earthquake caused a series of tsunami waves that struck the coasts of Thailand, Indonesia, Sri Lanka, India, Somalia, Madagascar, Kenya, Tanzania, Malaysia, Myanmar, and Bangladesh (At-a-glance 2005). These waves had a negative impact on these areas. They caused damage to groundwater, wells, ecosystems,

Figure 1. Epicenter of the earthquake and the areas affected by the tsunami (© GraphicMaps.com)

mangrove trees, coral reefs, and buildings (Szczucinski et al. 2006). This paper investigates the damage caused by this tsunami, commonly known as the Thailand Tsunami.

The thesis states the purpose of the paper

Causes and Consequences of the Tsunami

Plate Tectonics

Tsunamis are commonly generated by earthquakes that arise in subduction zones. These earthquakes are created when one plate subducts beneath (descends under) another plate and becomes stuck as a result of friction. The motion of the subducting plate causes distortion of the overriding plate, which results in an accumulation of energy. At some point, the energy built up in the overriding plate is released, causing the plates to unlock. When the plates unlock, the bottom plate continues to move downward while the top plate snaps upward. The amount the seafloor moves as a result of movement of the upper plate determines the size of the tsunami that will be created (Geist et al. 2006).

The writer explains how tsunamis are created

Cause of the 2004 Tsunami

Off the coast of Sumatra in the Indian Ocean, the India Plate and the Eurasia Plate meet to form a subduction zone (Geist et al. 2006). In this zone, the India Plate, because it is denser, subducts beneath the Eurasia Plate. It is believed that on the day of the tsunami, the Eurasia Plate moved upward a small amount at first and then jumped violently. When this occurred, a magnitude 9.0 earthquake occurred and caused the seafloor to rise 8 m in

Section headings indicate the hierarchy of information

CSE

some areas and a tsunami to form. When the earthquake happened, waves formed on the surface of the water. These waves were seen by satellite and looked no bigger than 1 m high. However, when the waves reached the coast of Sumatra about 2 hours later, they were about 30 m in height (Geist et al. 2006).

Loss of Life and Property

More than 1 million people were displaced because of the tsunami's environmental impact, and more than 285,000 people were killed. The greatest loss of human life occurred along the coast of Sumatra. In addition, the tsunami caused over $10 billion worth of damage to houses, buildings, and farms (Szczucinski et al. 2006). Buildings have been reconstructed and improved since the disaster. To help protect houses from future tsunamis, openings have been built to create a path for the water to flow through. Low sea walls have also been created. These will reduce the force of the waves before they hit the shoreline (Lukkunprasit and Ruangrassamee 2008).

Environmental Impacts

Erosion

In the countries affected by the tsunami, major coastal erosion occurred. The two main causes of the erosion were wave scour and subsidence. Wave scour is caused when waves hit the coast with enough force to carry sediment displaced by the wave back out to sea. Subsidence is a decrease in elevation of the land, generally caused by the depletion of water that underlies the area

In this section and the following sections, the writer discusses the types of harm caused by the tsunami

Thailand Tsunami   5

that subsided. In some areas along the coast, human activity such
as cast mining had already caused the ground to subside. Therefore,
when the waves hit the coast, the depressions were filled with
salty water. This water sat in the depressions and contaminated the
groundwater. In areas with flat beaches, there was a large amount
of wave scour and erosion. The areas with flatter coastal regions
also experienced inundation by seawater that extended between
340 m and 560 m inland. Along coasts with steep rocky cliff faces,
the water was not able to travel inland more than 100 m (Figure 2).

Figure 2. Points along the coast affected by the tsunami. Graphs A
through G show inundation and run-up amounts. The vertical axis
shows the height in meters the water attained above the average
sea level. The horizontal axis shows the distance in meters the
water traveled inland from the shoreline (Szczucinski et al. 2006).

Captions
help readers
understand
graphs

Reefs and dunes also prevented run-up in some areas. If coral reefs or dunes are present, less run-up occurs because the reefs or dunes reduce the force of the waves (Szczucinski et al. 2006).

Tsunami Deposits

Most erosion occurred within 50 m of the shoreline. Within this high erosion area, no tsunami deposits could be found. However, beyond 50 m inland, tsunami deposits have been found. These deposits were composed of sand and marine sediments consisting of shells, corals, and microorganisms (Szczucinski et al. 2006). The thickness of these deposits varied based on the amount of run-up, the vegetation, the topography, and other obstructions. The average thickness of the tsunami deposits was 8 cm. However, in some places, the deposits were 52 cm thick and completely covered some of the vegetation. Figure 3 shows a typical tsunami deposit that occurred in an inundation zone. The bottom layer is the original layer of soil; on top of this layer is the tsunami deposit with layers of coarse sand and fine sand (Szczucinski et al. 2006). Large amounts of salt and heavy metals were found in the tsunami deposits. Of great concern were the deposits that included potassium, sodium, copper, lead, and zinc, substances that could reach toxic levels in crops (Szczucinski et al. 2006). In addition, small amounts of mercury sulfide were discovered in the seawater in the depressions that were due to cast mining in the area. Because it is highly toxic, mercury sulfide can pose a threat to

Thailand Tsunami   7

Figure 3. Cross section of a typical tsunami deposit (Szczucinski et al. 2006)

humans and other organisms. It can also leak into the groundwater system and pollute drinking water (Boszke and Astel 2007).

Salinity

The high salinity of the ocean water in the tsunami and of the tsunami deposits greatly affected groundwater and inland surfaces. Over time, the salt in tsunami deposits seeped into the soil and eventually into the groundwater, thus polluting it. The amount of pollution depended on the extent of inundation in an area. Groundwater and wells were also polluted by fecal bacteria

Following CSE style, the writer uses abbreviations for units of measurement

cse

that leaked into the soil when septic systems were damaged by the tsunami (Szczucinski et al. 2006).

Ecosystems

Ecosystems were greatly affected by the tsunami. Coral reefs were destroyed, damaged, or moved. The closer the reefs were to the shoreline, the more they were affected by wave impact and backwash. Another part of the ecosystem that was destroyed was the sea grass beds, which are important sources of income for local fisherman and fishing companies. The beds were buried under sand from inland erosion and backwash (Szczucinski et al. 2006).

Vegetation

Mangrove trees located close to the shoreline were completely destroyed, while mangrove trees further inland experienced little to no damage. When the high-energy wave hit the mangroves close to the shoreline, it had a devastating effect because they have not evolved to withstand such conditions. Even though mangrove trees near the coast were destroyed, they helped protect vast areas of land from great damage. In areas where these trees were abundant, the amount of damage done by the water was greatly reduced (Yanagisawa et al. 2009). Many other types of trees were pulled out of the ground by the force of the wave (Szczucinski et al. 2006).

Other vegetation was affected by the salinity of the ocean water in the wave and the large amounts of tsunami deposits. Plants either withered from the intake of the salty water or died because they were buried under the tsunami deposits.

Conclusion

The amount of damage that different areas received was determined by multiple factors. For example, the bathymetry (the depth of water along the shoreline) and the morphology of the shoreline affected the amount of force the tsunami had when it hit the coast. If an area had offshore coral reefs or coastal mangroves, the amount of erosion and damage inland was often reduced. However, within 50 days of the tsunami, ecosystems in areas like Thailand were already beginning to heal and to rebuild themselves, and about 4 months after the event, water, animals, and sea grass, which had been depleted, were beginning to return to their original quantities (Szczucinski et al. 2006). Scientists have been able to study damage in different areas and determine factors that increase or decrease it.

By studying this tsunami, scientists have become able to predict which areas are prone to tsunami effects. They have also gained information that helps them predict the orientation of tsunami waves, where they will go and how far they will travel inland (Geist et al. 2006). Early prediction, along with the construction of seawalls and the improvement of houses, should lessen the impact of any future tsunami in the area devastated by the Thailand Tsunami.

The writer describes what was learned from studying the effects of the tsunami

CSE

10   Thailand Tsunami

References

Entries are single spaced with an extra line between entries

At-a-glance: countries hit. 2005 Dec 22. BBC News [Internet]. [cited 2011 Jan 9]; [1 p.]. Available from: http://news.bbc.co.uk/2/hi/4126019.stm

Boszke, L, Astel A. 2007. Fractionation of mercury in sediments from coastal zone inundated by tsunami and in freshwater sediments from the rivers. J Environ Sci Health. 42(7):847–858.

Each entry aligns at left margin

Geist, EL, Titov, VV, Synolakis, CE. 2006. Tsunami: wave of change. Sci Am. 294(1):56–63.

Lukkunprasit P, Ruangrassamee, A. 2008. Building damage in Thailand in the 2004 Indian Ocean tsunami and clues for tsunami-resistant design. IES J. 1(1Pt A: Civ & Struct Eng.):17–30.

Szczucinski W, Chaimanee N, Niedzielski G, Rachlewicz G, Saisuttichai D, Tepsuwan T, Lorenc S, Siepak J. 2006. Environmental and geological impacts of the 26 December 2004 tsunami in coastal zone of Thailand—overview of short- and long-term effects. Pol J of Environ Stud. 15(5):793–810.

Yanagisawa H, Koshimura S, Goto K, Miyagi T, Imamura F, Ruangrassamee A, Tanavud C. 2009. Damage to mangrove forest by 2004 tsunami at Pakarang Cape and Namkem, Thailand. Pol J of Environ Stud. 18(1):35–42.

G

GRAMMAR

17 Sentence Essentials

When you think of the word *grammar*, you might also think of the word *rule*—a regulation you must obey. But *rule* has another meaning: "a statement of what should be done to gain some benefit," as in *An important rule to follow when exercising is to drink plenty of water.* Grammar rules provide you with beneficial advice on how to achieve success as a writer. Because grammar rules describe how language is commonly or conventionally used, to follow grammar rules simply means to write in a way that is considered appropriate by a specific set of readers. This chapter covers concepts of grammar that will help you understand how to write clear, convincing, and conventional sentences.

17a Parts of speech

When you look up a word in the dictionary, you will often find it followed by one or more of these labels: *adj.*, *adv.*, *conj.*, *interj.*, *n.*, *prep.*, *pron.*, and *v.* (or *vb.*). These are the abbreviations for the traditional eight parts of speech: *adjective*, *adverb*, *conjunction*, *interjection*, *noun*, *preposition*, *pronoun*, and *verb*.

(1) Verbs

Verbs that indicate action (*walk, drive, study*) are called **action verbs**. Verbs that express being or experiencing are called **linking verbs**, which link a subject to a subject complement; they include *be, seem,* and *become* and the sensory verbs *look, taste, smell, feel,* and *sound.* Both action verbs and linking verbs are frequently accompanied by **auxiliary** or **helping verbs**, which come before the main verb and add shades of meaning, such as information about time (*will* study this afternoon), ability (*can* study), or obligation (*must* study).

THINKING RHETORICALLY
VERBS

Decide which of the following sentences evokes a clearer image:

➤ The team captain **was** absolutely ecstatic.
➤ Grinning broadly, the team captain **shot** both her arms into the air.

You probably chose the sentence with the action verb *shot* rather than the sentence with *was*. When their goal is vibrant imagery, successful writers avoid using the verb *be* in any of its forms (*am, is, are, was, were,* or *been*). Instead, they use vivid action verbs.

(2) Nouns

Nouns usually name people, places, things, and ideas. **Proper nouns** are specific names: *Bill Gates, Redmond, Microsoft Corporation.* **Common nouns** refer to any member of a class or category: *person, city, company.* There are three types of common nouns.

- **Count nouns** refer to people, places, things, and ideas that can be counted. They have singular and plural forms: *boy, boys; car, cars; concept, concepts.*
- **Noncount nouns** refer to things or ideas that cannot be counted: *furniture, information.*
- **Collective nouns** are nouns that refer to groups and that can be either singular or plural, depending on the context of the sentence: *The **committee** published its report* [singular]. *The **committee** disagree about their duties* [plural].

> **THINKING RHETORICALLY**
> **NOUNS**
>
> Nouns like *entertainment* and *nutrition* that refer to concepts are called **abstract nouns**. In contrast, nouns like *guitar* and *apple* that refer to things perceivable by the senses are called **concrete nouns**. When your rhetorical situation calls for the use of abstractions, balance them with tangible details conveyed through concrete nouns.

(3) Pronouns

Most pronouns (*it*, *he*, *she*, *they*, and many others) replace **antecedents**—nouns or noun phrases that have already been mentioned.

➤ My parents bought the cheap, decrepit house because **they** thought **it** had charm.

A pronoun and its antecedent may be found either in the same sentence or in separate, though usually adjacent, sentences.

➤ The students collaborated on a research project last year. **They** even presented their findings at a national conference.

The pronouns in the preceding examples are **personal pronouns**. For a discussion of other types of pronouns, see chapter **21**.

(4) Adjectives

Adjectives most commonly modify nouns: *spicy* food, *special* price. Sometimes they modify pronouns: *blue* ones, anyone *thin*. Adjectives usually answer one of these questions: Which one? What kind of . . . ? How many? What color or size or shape (and so on)? Although adjectives usually precede the nouns they modify, they occasionally follow them: *enough* time, time *enough*. Adjectives may also follow linking verbs such as *be, seem,* and *become*:

The moon is **full** tonight.   He seems **shy**.

Articles, *a, an,* and *the,* are also used before nouns. The article *a* is used before a consonant sound (**a** yard, **a** university, **a** VIP); *an* is used before a vowel sound (**an** apple, **an** hour, **an** NFL team).

MULTILINGUAL WRITERS
ARTICLE USAGE

English has two types of articles: indefinite and definite. The **indefinite articles** *a* and *an* indicate that a singular noun is used in a general way, as when you introduce the noun for the first time or when you define a word.

➤ Pluto is **a** dwarf planet.

➤ There has been **a** controversy over the classification of Pluto.

➤ **A** planet is a celestial body orbiting a star such as our sun.

The **definite article**, *the,* is used before a noun that has already been introduced or when a reference is obvious. *The* is also used before a noun that is related in form or meaning to a word previously mentioned.

➤ Scientists distinguish between planets and dwarf planets. One of **the** dwarf planets in our solar system is Pluto.

➤ Scientists are not sure how to classify some celestial bodies. **The** classification of Pluto proved to be controversial.

The definite article also appears before a noun considered unique, such as *moon, universe,* and *sky*.

➤ **The** moon is full tonight.

(5) Adverbs

Adverbs most frequently modify verbs. They provide information about time, manner, place, and frequency, thus answering one of these questions: When? How? Where? How often?

➤ The conference <u>starts</u> **tomorrow**. [time]

➤ I **rapidly** <u>calculated</u> the cost. [manner]

➤ We <u>met</u> **here**. [place]

➤ They **often** <u>work</u> late on Thursdays. [frequency]

Adverbs that modify verbs can often move from one position in a sentence to another.

➤ He **carefully** removed the radio collar.

➤ He removed the radio collar **carefully**.

Adverbs also modify adjectives and other adverbs by intensifying or otherwise qualifying the meanings of those words.

➤ I was **extremely** <u>curious</u>. [modifying an adjective]

➤ The team played **surprisingly** <u>well</u>. [modifying an adverb]

THINKING RHETORICALLY
ADVERBS

What do the adverbs add to the following sentences?

➤ The scientist **delicately** places the slide under the microscope.
➤ "You're late," he whispered **vehemently**.
➤ She is **wistfully** hopeful.

Adverbs can help you portray an action, indicate how someone is speaking, and add detail to a description.

(6) Prepositions

A **preposition** is a word that combines with a noun and any of its modifiers to provide additional detail—often answering one of these questions: Where? When?

➤ **In** the early afternoon, we walked **through** our old neighborhood. [answers the questions *When?* and *Where?*]

A preposition may also combine with a pronoun.

➤ We walked **through** it.

A grammar rule that has caused much controversy over the years is the one that advises against ending a sentence with a preposition. Most professional writers now follow this rule only when they adopt a formal tone. If their rhetorical situation calls for an informal tone, they will not hesitate to place a preposition at the end of a sentence.

➤ He found friends **on** whom he could depend. [formal]

➤ He found friends he could depend **on**. [informal]

SOME COMMON PREPOSITIONS				
about	behind	for	of	to
above	between	from	on	toward
after	by	in	out	under
as	despite	into	past	until
at	during	like	since	up
before	except	near	through	with

Phrasal prepositions consist of more than one word.

➤ **Except for** the last day, it was a wonderful trip.

SOME COMMON PHRASAL PREPOSITIONS		
according to	due to	in spite of
as for	except for	instead of
because of	in addition to	with regard to

(7) Conjunctions

Conjunctions are connectors; they fall into four categories: coordinating, correlative, subordinating, and adverbial. A **coordinating conjunction** connects similar words or groups of words; that is, it generally links a word to a word, a phrase to a phrase (**17d**), or a clause to a clause (**17e**). There are seven coordinating conjunctions. Use the made-up word *fanboys* to help you remember them.

F	A	N	B	O	Y	S
for	and	nor	but	or	yet	so

➤ tired **yet** excited [*Yet* joins two words and signals contrast.]

➤ in the boat **or** on the pier [*Or* joins two phrases and marks them as alternatives.]

➤ We did not share a language, **but** somehow we communicated. [*But* joins two independent clauses and signals contrast.]

In the example sentence above, *but* links two independent clauses and thus is preceded by a comma. A coordinating conjunction such as *but* may also link independent clauses that stand alone as sentences.

> The momentum in the direction of globalization seems too powerful to buck, the economic logic unmatchable. **But** in a region where jobs are draining away, and where an ethic of self-reliance remains a dim, vestigial, but honored memory, it seems at least an outside possibility.   —BILL MCKIBBEN, "Small World"

A **correlative conjunction** (or **correlative**) consists of two parts. The most common correlatives are *both . . . and, either . . . or, neither . . . nor,* and *not only . . . but also.*

➤ **Not only** did they run ten miles, **but** they **also** swam twenty laps. [*Not only . . . but also* joins two independent clauses and signals addition.]

Generally, a correlative conjunction links similar structures. The following sentence has been revised because the correlative conjunction was linking a phrase to a clause.

> Not only ~~saving~~ *did he save* the lives of the accident victims, **but** he **also** prevented many spinal injuries.

A **subordinating conjunction** introduces a dependent clause (**17e**). It also carries a specific meaning; for example, it may indicate cause, concession, condition, purpose, or time. A dependent clause that begins a sentence is followed by a comma.

> **Unless** the project receives funding, the research will stop. [*Unless* signals a condition.]

> She studied Spanish **when** she worked in Costa Rica. [*When* signals time.]

SUBORDINATING CONJUNCTIONS			
after	before	once	unless
although	even if	since	until
as if	even though	so that	when
as though	if	than	whether
because	in that	though	while

Adverbial conjunctions—such as *however, nevertheless, then,* and *therefore*—link independent clauses (**17e**). These conjunctions, also called **conjunctive adverbs**, signal relationships such as cause, condition, and contrast. Adverbial conjunctions are set off by commas. An independent clause preceding an adverbial conjunction may end in a semicolon or a period.

> The senator thought the plan was reasonable**; however,** the voters did not.

> The senator thought the plan was reasonable**. However,** the voters did not.

➤ The senator thought the plan was reasonable. The voters, **however,** did not.

➤ The senator thought the plan was reasonable. The voters did not, **however**.

ADVERBIAL CONJUNCTIONS			
also	indeed	moreover	still
finally	instead	nevertheless	then
furthermore	likewise	nonetheless	therefore
however	meanwhile	otherwise	thus

(8) Interjections

Interjections most commonly express an emotion such as surprise or dread. Interjections that come before a sentence end in a period or an exclamation point.

➤ **Oh.** Now I understand.

➤ **Wow!** Your design is astounding.

Interjections that begin or interrupt a sentence are set off by commas.

➤ **Hey,** what are you doing?

➤ The solution, **alas,** was not as simple as I had hoped it would be.

EXERCISE 17.1

Identify the part of speech for each word in the sentences below.

1. Hey, are you a fan of both anime and manga?

2. If you are, you should join the University Anime and Manga Club.

3. Every Tuesday at noon, we watch current anime or swap favorite manga.

4. Memberships are free; however, donations are always welcome.

5. Whenever you have time, you can simply look for us in the Student Union.

17b Subjects and predicates

A sentence consists of two parts:

SUBJECT + PREDICATE

The **subject** is generally someone or something that either performs an action or is described. The **predicate** expresses the action initiated by the subject or gives information about the subject.

> The <u>landlord</u> + <u>renovated</u> the apartment.
> [The subject performs an action; the predicate expresses the action.]
>
> <u>They</u> + <u>had sounded</u> reasonable.
> [The subject is described; the predicate gives information about the subject.]

The central components of the subject and the predicate are often called the **simple subject** (the main noun or pronoun) and the **simple predicate** (the main verb and any auxiliary verbs). They are underlined in the examples above.

Compound subjects and **compound predicates** include a connecting word (conjunction) such as *and, or,* or *but.*

➤ <u>Republicans</u> **and** <u>Democrats</u> are debating this issue. [compound subject]

➤ The candidate <u>stated his views on abortion</u> **but** <u>did not discuss stem-cell research</u>. [compound predicate]

17c Complements

Complements are parts of the predicate required by the verb to make a sentence complete. A complement is generally a pronoun, a noun, or a noun with modifiers.

> The committee chair introduced —
> - **her**. [pronoun]
> - **Sylvia Holbrook**. [noun]
> - **the new but well-known member**. [noun with modifiers]

There are four different complements: direct objects, indirect objects, subject complements, and object complements.

The **direct object** either receives the action of the verb or shows the result of the action.

➤ Steve McQueen drove **a Ford Mustang** in the movie *Bullitt*.

➤ I. M. Pei designed **the East Building of the National Gallery**.

Indirect objects typically name the person(s) receiving or benefiting from the action indicated by the verb. Verbs that often take indirect objects include *buy, give, lend, sell, send,* and *write*.

$$\overset{v}{\text{gave}} \quad \overset{io}{\text{the new employees}} \quad \overset{do}{\text{computers}}$$

➤ The supervisor gave **the new employees** computers.
[*To whom* were the computers given?]

$$\overset{v}{\text{wrote}} \quad \overset{io}{\text{them}} \quad \overset{do}{\text{recommendation letters}}$$

➤ She wrote **them** recommendation letters.
[*For whom* were the recommendation letters written?]

The **subject complement** follows a linking verb. The most common linking verb is *be* (*am, is, are, was, were, been*). Other linking verbs are *become, seem,* and *appear* and the sensory verbs *feel, look, smell, sound,* and *taste*. A subject complement can be a pronoun, a noun, or a noun with modifiers. It can also be an adjective.

> The winner was ⎯
>
>   **you**. [pronoun]
>
>   **Harry Solano**. [noun]
>
>   **the lucky <u>person</u> with the highest score**.
>   [noun with modifiers]
>
>   **ecstatic**. [adjective]

The **object complement** helps complete the meaning of a verb such as *call, elect, make, name,* or *paint.* The object complement can be a noun or an adjective, along with any modifiers.

> Reporters called the rookie **the best <u>player</u>**. [noun with modifiers]

> The strike left the fans **somewhat <u>disappointed</u>**. [adjective with modifier]

EXERCISE 17.2

Identify the subject and the predicate in each sentence. Then, looking at just the predicate, identify the type of complement the sentence contains.

1. A naturalist gave <u>us</u> <u>a short lecture on the Cascade Mountains</u>.

2. He showed <u>slides of mountain lakes and heather meadows</u>.

3. Douglas fir predominates in the Cascade forests.

4. Mountaineers and artists consider <u>the North Cascades</u> <u>the most dramatic mountains in the range</u>.

5. Timberlines are <u>low</u> because of the short growing season.

6. Many volcanoes are in the Cascades.

7. Mt. Rainier is <u>the highest volcano in the range</u>.

8. Many visitors to this area hike <u>the Pacific Crest Trail</u>.

9. My friend lent <u>me</u> <u>his map of the trail</u>.

10. The trail begins in southern California, passes through Oregon and Washington, and ends in British Columbia.

17d | Phrases

A **phrase** is a sequence of grammatically related words without a subject, a predicate, or both. A phrase is categorized according to its most important word.

(1) Noun phrases

A noun phrase consists of a main noun and its modifiers. It can serve as a subject or as a complement. It can also be the object of a preposition such as *in, of, on, at,* or *to.*

➤ **The heavy frost** killed **many fruit trees**. [subject and direct object]

➤ **My cousin** is **an organic farmer**. [subject and subject complement]

➤ **His farm** is in **eastern Oregon**. [subject and object of the preposition *in*]

MULTILINGUAL WRITERS
NUMBER AGREEMENT IN NOUN PHRASES

Some words must agree in number with the nouns they precede. The words *a, an, this,* and *that* are used before singular nouns; *some, few, these, those,* and *many* are used before plural nouns.

➤ **an/that** opportunity [singular noun]

➤ **some/few/those** opportunities [plural noun]

The words *less* and *much* precede nouns representing abstract concepts or masses that cannot be counted (noncount nouns).

➤ **less** freedom, **much** water [noncount nouns]

(2) Verb phrases

A verb is essential to the predicate of a sentence. It generally expresses action or a state of being. Besides a main verb, a **verb phrase** includes one or more **auxiliary verbs**, sometimes called *helping verbs*, such as *be*, *have*, *do*, *will*, and *should*.

➤ The passengers **have deplaned**. [auxiliary verb + main verb]

(3) Verbal phrases

A **verbal phrase** differs from a verb phrase in that the verb form in a verbal phrase serves as a noun or a modifier rather than as a verb.

➤ He <u>was **reading**</u> the story aloud. [*Reading* is part of the verb phrase *was reading*.]

➤ **Reading** is fundamental to academic success. [*Reading* serves as a noun. COMPARE: **It** is fundamental to academic success.]

➤ The student **reading** aloud is an education major. [*Reading aloud* modifies *the student*.]

Verbal phrases are divided into three types: gerund phrases, participial phrases, and infinitive phrases.

Gerund phrases include a verb form ending in *-ing*. A gerund phrase serves as a noun, usually functioning as the subject or object in a sentence.

➤ <u>**Writing** a **bestseller**</u> was her only goal. [subject]

➤ My neighbor enjoys <u>**writing** about **distant places**</u>. [object]

Because gerund phrases act as nouns, pronouns can replace them.

That was her only goal.　　　My neighbor enjoys **it**.

THINKING RHETORICALLY

GERUNDS

What is the difference between the following sentences?

➤ They bundle products together, which often results in higher consumer costs.

➤ Bundling products together often results in higher consumer costs.

In the first sentence, the actor, *they*, is the focus. In the second sentence, the action of the gerund phrase, *bundling products together*, is the focus. As you revise, ask yourself whether you want to emphasize actors or actions.

Participial phrases include either a present participle (a verb form ending in *-ing*) or a past participle (a verb form ending in *-ed* for regular verbs or another form for irregular verbs). Participial phrases function as modifiers.

➤ **Fearing a drought**, the farmers used less irrigation water.

➤ All the farmers in the area, **plagued by drought**, used less irrigation water.

➤ Farmers conserved water, **fearing a drought in late summer**.

Remember that gerund and participial phrases differ in function. A gerund phrase functions as a noun; a participial phrase functions as a modifier.

➤ **Working together** can spur creativity. [gerund phrase]

➤ **Working together**, the students designed their own software. [participial phrase]

A present participle (-*ing* form) cannot function alone as the main verb in a sentence. It must be accompanied by a form of *be* (*am, is, are, was,* or *were*).

➤ They *are* **thinking** about the future.
          ^

THINKING RHETORICALLY
PARTICIPIAL PHRASES

If some of your sentences sound monotonous or choppy, try combining them by using participial phrases.

➤ *Crowded along the city streets, fans celebrated*
   ~~Fans crowded along the city streets. They were celebrating~~
   ^
   their team's first state championship.

Infinitive phrases serve as nouns or as modifiers. The form of the infinitive is distinct—the infinitive marker *to* followed by the base form of the verb.

➤ The company intends **to hire** **twenty new employees**. [noun]

➤ We discussed his plan **to use** **a new packing process**. [modifier of the noun *plan*]

➤ **To attract** **customers**, the company changed its advertising strategy. [modifier of the verb *changed*]

Some instructors advise against putting words between the infinitive marker *to* and the base form of the verb.

➤ *Under the circumstances, the*
   ~~The~~ jury was unable to, ~~under the circumstances,~~ convict the
   ^
   defendant.

This is good advice to remember if the intervening words create a cumbersome sentence. However, most writers today recognize that a single word splitting an infinitive can provide emphasis.

➤ He did not expect to actually publish his work.

MULTILINGUAL WRITERS

VERBS FOLLOWED BY GERUNDS AND/OR INFINITIVES

Some verbs in English can be followed by a gerund, some can be followed by an infinitive, and some can be followed by either.

Followed by a Gerund

admit   avoid   consider   deny   dislike   enjoy   finish

➤ She **enjoys playing** the piano.

Followed by an Infinitive

agree   decide   deserve   hope   need   plan   promise   seem

➤ She **promised to play** the piano for us.

Followed by Either a Gerund or an Infinitive

begin   continue   like   prefer   remember   stop   try

➤ She **likes to play** the piano.   ➤ She **likes playing** the piano.

Although either a gerund phrase or an infinitive phrase can follow these verbs, the resulting sentences may differ in meaning.

➤ We **stopped discussing** the plan. [The discussion has ended.]

➤ We **stopped to discuss** the plan. [The discussion has not yet started.]

(4) Prepositional phrases

Prepositional phrases provide information about time, place, cause, manner, and so on. They can also answer one of these questions: Which one? What kind of . . . ?

➤ **With great feeling**, Martin Luther King expressed his dream **of freedom**.

[*With great feeling* describes the way the speech was delivered, and *of freedom* specifies the kind of dream.]

➤ King delivered his most famous speech **at a demonstration in Washington, DC**.

[Both *at a demonstration* and *in Washington, DC* provide information about place.]

A prepositional phrase consists of a **preposition** (a word such as *at*, *of*, or *in*) and a pronoun, noun, or noun phrase (called the **object of the preposition**). A prepositional phrase modifies another element in the sentence.

➤ Everyone **in class** went to the play. [modifier of the pronoun *everyone*]

➤ Some students met the professor **after** the play. [modifier of the verb *met*]

(5) Appositives

An **appositive** is most often a noun or a noun phrase that refers to the same person, place, thing, or idea as a preceding noun or noun phrase but in different words. When the appositive simply specifies the referent, no commas are used.

➤ Cormac McCarthy's novel ***The Road*** won a Pulitzer Prize. [specifies which of McCarthy's books won the award]

When the appositive provides extra details, commas set it off.

➤ *The Road*, **a novel by Cormac McCarthy,** won a Pulitzer Prize. [provides an extra detail about the book]

(6) Absolute phrases

An **absolute phrase** is usually a noun phrase modified by a prepositional phrase, an adjective phrase, or a participial phrase.

➤ **Her guitar in the front seat**, she pulled away from the curb.

➤ **More vaccine having arrived**, the staff scheduled its distribution.

The first absolute phrase provides details; the second expresses cause.

EXERCISE 17.3

Label the underlined phrases in the following sentences as noun phrases, verb phrases, prepositional phrases, or verbal phrases. For verbal phrases, specify the type: gerund, participial, or infinitive. When a long phrase includes a short phrase, identify just the long phrase. Finally, identify any appositive phrases or absolute phrases in the sentences.

1. <u>After the Second World War</u>, <u>fifty-one countries</u> formed <u>the United Nations, an international organization dedicated to peace, tolerance, and cooperation</u>.

2. <u>The Charter of the United Nations was written in 1945</u>.

3. <u>According to this charter</u>, the United Nations <u>may address</u> a wide range <u>of issues</u>.

4. <u>The United Nations</u> devotes most of its energies to <u>protecting human rights</u>, <u>maintaining peace</u>, and <u>encouraging social development</u>.

5. <u>To reach its goals</u>, the United Nations depends on funding <u>from its member states</u>.

6. <u>Its blue flag easily recognized everywhere</u>, the United Nations now includes <u>193 member states</u>.

7. <u>Symbolizing peace</u>, the emblem <u>on the flag</u> is a map <u>enclosed by olive branches</u>.

17e   **Clauses**

(1) Independent clauses

A **clause** is a group of related words that contains a subject and a predicate. An **independent clause**, sometimes called a *main clause*, has the same grammatical structure as a simple sentence: both contain a subject and a predicate.

➤ The students earned high grades.

An independent clause can stand alone as a complete sentence. Other clauses can be added to independent clauses to form longer, more detailed sentences.

(2) Dependent clauses

A **dependent clause** also has a subject and a predicate. However, it cannot stand alone as a complete sentence because of the word introducing it—usually a relative pronoun or a subordinating conjunction.

➤ The athlete **who placed first** grew up in Argentina. [relative pronoun]

➤ She received the gold medal **because she performed flawlessly**. [subordinating conjunction]

   Noun clauses are dependent clauses that serve as subjects or objects. They are introduced by *if*, *that*, or a *wh-* word such as *why*, *what*, or *when*. To decide whether a clause is a noun clause, try replacing it with a pronoun such as *it* or *this*.

➤ **What the witness said** may not be true. [subject]

➤ We do not understand **why they did it**. [direct object]

When no misunderstanding would result, the word *that* can be omitted from the beginning of a clause.

➤ The scientist said **she was moving to Australia**. [*that* omitted]

However, *that* should always be retained when there are two noun clauses.

➤ The scientist said **that she was moving to Australia** and **that her research team was planning to accompany her**. [*that* retained in both noun clauses]

An **adjectival clause**, or **relative clause**, follows a pronoun, noun, or noun phrase and answers one of these questions: Which one? What kind of . . . ? Such clauses, which nearly always follow the words they modify, usually begin with a **relative pronoun** (*who, whom, that, which,* or *whose*) but sometimes start with a **relative adverb** (*when, where,* or *why*).

➤ Nobody likes news reports **that pry into someone's private life**. [answers the question *What kind of news reports?*]

➤ Students **who have good study habits** begin their research early. [answers the question *Which students?*]

A relative pronoun can be omitted as long as the meaning of the sentence is still clear.

➤ Mother Teresa was someone **the whole world admired**. [*Whom,* the direct object of the clause, has been omitted: the whole world admired *whom.*]

➤ She was someone **who cared more about serving than being served**. [*Who* cannot be omitted because it is the subject of the clause.]

An **adverbial clause** usually answers one of the following questions: Where? When? Why? How? How frequently? In what manner? Adverbial clauses are introduced by subordinating conjunctions such as *because, although,* and *when.*

➤ **When the need arises**, the company hires new writers. [answers the question *How frequently does the company hire new writers?*]

➤ She acted **as though she cared only about herself**. [answers the question *How did she act?*]

THINKING RHETORICALLY
ADVERBIAL CLAUSES

In an adverbial clause that refers to time or establishes a fact, both the subject and any form of the verb *be* can be omitted. Using such **elliptical constructions** will make your writing more concise.

➤ **Though tired**, they continued to study for the exam.
  [COMPARE: **Though they were tired**, they continued to study for the exam.]

Be sure that the omitted subject of an elliptical clause is the same as the subject of the independent clause. Otherwise, revise either the adverbial clause or the main clause.

➤ While *I was* reviewing your report, a few questions occurred to me.

OR

➤ While reviewing your report, *I thought of* a few questions ~~occurred to me~~.

EXERCISE 17.4

1. Identify the dependent clauses in the following paragraph.

2. Identify the underlined words as coordinating, correlative, subordinating, or adverbial conjunctions.

[1]If you live by the sword, you might die by the sword. [2]<u>However</u>, <u>if</u> you make your living by swallowing swords, you will not necessarily die by swallowing swords. [3]At least, this is the conclusion Brian Witcombe and Dan Meyer reached <u>after</u> they surveyed forty-six professional sword swallowers. [4](Brian Witcombe is a radiologist, <u>and</u> Dan Meyer is a famous sword swallower.) [5]Some of those surveyed mentioned <u>that</u> they had experienced <u>either</u> "sword throats" <u>or</u> chest pains, <u>and</u> others who let their swords drop to their stomachs described perforation of their innards, <u>but</u> the researchers could find no listing of a sword-swallowing mortality in the medical studies they reviewed. [6]The researchers did not inquire into the reasons for swallowing swords in the first place.

CHECKLIST FOR USING A GRAMMAR CHECKER

Most word-processing programs have features that help writers identify grammar errors as well as problems with usage and style, but these grammar checkers have significant limitations. A grammar checker will usually identify certain errors.

- fused sentences, sometimes called run-on sentences (chapter **19**)
- wordy or overly long sentences (chapter **30**)
- missing apostrophes in contractions (**33b**)

However, a grammar checker can easily miss many kinds of errors.

- sentence fragments (chapter **18**)
- dangling or misplaced modifiers (chapter **22**)
- problems with pronoun-antecedent agreement (chapter **21**)
- errors in subject-verb agreement (**20f**)
- misused or missing commas (chapter **31**)

Because these omissions can weaken your credibility as a writer, you should never rely solely on a grammar checker to find them. Furthermore, grammar checkers can mark as wrong some words or phrases that you have chosen deliberately.

Used carefully, a grammar checker can be a helpful tool, but keep the following advice in mind.

- Use a grammar checker only in addition to your own editing and proofreading.
- Always evaluate any sentences flagged by a grammar checker to determine whether there is, in fact, a problem.
- Adjust the settings on your grammar checker to look for specific types of errors. If you are using Microsoft Word, select Tools; then select either Spelling and Grammar or Options to customize your settings.
- Carefully review the revisions proposed by a grammar checker before accepting them. Sometimes the proposed revisions create new errors.

18 Sentence Fragments

As its name suggests, a **sentence fragment** is only a piece of a sentence; it is not complete.

18a Recognizing sentence fragments

A sentence is considered a fragment when it is incomplete in one of three ways. It is missing a subject *or* a verb, it is missing both, or it is a dependent clause. Most fragments can be attached to adjacent sentences.

MISSING VERB Alternative medical treatment may include hypnosis. ——— *the* ^The placement of a patient into a sleeplike state.

MISSING SUBJECT Derived from a word meaning "nervous sleep.," ^*hypnotism* Hypnotism actually refers to a type of focused attention.

NO SUBJECT OR VERB *Contrary to popular belief, the* ^The hypnotic state differs from sleep. ~~Contrary to popular belief.~~

DEPENDENT CLAUSE Most people can be hypnotized easily. ~~Although~~ *, although* the depth of the trance for each person varies.

18b Phrases as sentence fragments

A phrase is a group of words without a subject and/or predicate. When punctuated as a sentence (that is, with a period or other end punctuation), it becomes a fragment. To revise a phrase fragment, you can often attach it to a nearby sentence.

VERBAL PHRASE AS A FRAGMENT

➤ Early humans valued color. *, creating* **Creating permanent colors with natural pigments**.

PREPOSITIONAL PHRASE AS A FRAGMENT

➤ For years, the Scottish have dyed sweaters with soot. *, originally* **Originally from the chimneys of peat-burning stoves**.

APPOSITIVE PHRASE AS A FRAGMENT

➤ During the Renaissance, one of the most highly valued pigments was ultramarine. *—an* **An extract from lapis lazuli**.

ABSOLUTE PHRASE AS A FRAGMENT

➤ The deciduous trees of New England are known for their brilliant autumn color. *, sugar* **Sugar maples dazzling tourists with their orange and red leaves**.

Instead of attaching a fragment to a nearby sentence, you can sometimes recast the fragment as a complete sentence.

FRAGMENT   Humans painted themselves for a variety of purposes. **To attract a mate, to hide themselves from game or predators, or to signal aggression**.

REVISION   Humans used color for a variety of purposes. For
example, they painted themselves to attract a mate,
to hide themselves from game or predators, or to
signal aggression.

18c Dependent clauses as sentence fragments

A dependent clause is a group of words with both a subject and
a predicate, but because it begins with a subordinating conjunction or a relative pronoun, it cannot stand alone as a sentence.

➤ More than two thousand people were aboard the *Titanic*. *, which* ~~Which~~
was the largest ocean liner in 1912.

➤ The iceberg was no surprise. *because* ~~Because~~ **the *Titanic*'s wireless**
operators had received reports of ice in the area.

You can also recast the fragment as a complete sentence by
removing the subordinating conjunction or relative pronoun
and supplying any missing elements.

➤ The iceberg was no surprise. The *Titanic*'s wireless operators
had received reports of ice in the area.

THINKING RHETORICALLY
FRAGMENTS

When used judiciously, fragments—like short sentences—
emphasize ideas or add surprise. However, fragments are generally permitted only when the rhetorical situation allows the use
of a casual tone.

> **May. When the earth's Northern Hemisphere awakens from**
> **winter's sleep and all of nature bristles with the energies of**
> **new life.** My work has kept me indoors for months now. I'm
> not sure I'll ever get used to it.
>
> —KEN CAREY, *Flat Rock Journal: A Day in the Ozark Mountains*

EXERCISE 18.1

Follow the guidelines in this chapter to locate and revise the fragments in the following paragraph. If you find it necessary, make other improvements as well. Be prepared to explain your revisions.

[1]One of the most popular rides at any county fair or amusement park is the Ferris wheel. [2]The original Ferris wheel, designed by George Washington Gale Ferris, Jr., for a national exposition in 1893. [3]Rose to a height of 264 feet. [4]And accommodated 2,140 passengers. [5]Ferris's goal was to build something that would surpass in effect the Eiffel Tower. [6]Which was constructed just a few years earlier. [7]Though Ferris's plans were not immediately accepted. [8]Once they were, and the wheel opened to the public, it became an immediate success. [9]At times carrying thirty-eight thousand passengers a day. [10]Since the nineteenth century. [11]Engineers have designed taller and taller Ferris wheels. [12]The 541-foot Singapore Flyer holds the record, but the Beijing Great Wheel, currently under construction. [13]Will be over a hundred feet taller.

19 Comma Splices and Fused Sentences

A **comma splice**, or **comma fault**, refers to the incorrect use of a comma between two independent clauses (a clause including a subject and predicate that can stand alone as a complete sentence).

➤ Most stockholders favored the merger, *but* the management did not.

A **fused sentence**, or **run-on sentence**, consists of two independent clauses run together without any punctuation at all.

➤ The first section of the proposal was approved ⌃ the budget will *; however,* have to be resubmitted.

To revise a comma splice or a fused sentence, include appropriate punctuation and any necessary connecting words.

19a Locating comma splices and fused sentences

You can find comma splices and fused sentences by remembering that they commonly occur in certain contexts.

- With transitional words and phrases such as *however,* *therefore,* and *for example*

COMMA SPLICE   The director is unable to meet you this week ⌃ however ⌃ next week she has time on Tuesday. *;* *,*

- When an explanation or an example is given in the second sentence

FUSED SENTENCE   The cultural center has a new collection of spear points ⌃ many of them were donated by a *. Many* retired anthropologist.

- When a positive clause follows a negative clause, or vice versa

COMMA SPLICE   A World Cup victory is not just an everyday sporting event, it ⌃ is a national celebration. *. It*

- When the subject of the second clause is a pronoun whose antecedent is in the preceding clause

FUSED SENTENCE   Lake Baikal is located in southern Russia ⌃ it *. It* is 394 miles long. [The pronoun *it* refers to Lake Baikal.]

19b Revising comma splices and fused sentences

If you find comma splices or fused sentences in your writing, try one of the following methods to revise them.

(1) Link independent clauses with a comma and a coordinating conjunction

By linking clauses with a comma and a coordinating conjunction (*and*, *but*, *or*, *nor*, *for*, *so*, or *yet*), you signal the relationship between the clauses.

> **FUSED SENTENCE** The diplomats will end their discussion on Friday *,and* they will submit their final decision on Monday.

> **COMMA SPLICE** Some diplomats applauded the treaty, *but* others opposed it vehemently.

(2) Link independent clauses with a semicolon or a colon or separate them with a period

When you link independent clauses with a semicolon, the semicolon usually indicates addition or contrast. When you link clauses with a colon, the second clause serves as an explanation or an elaboration of the first. A period indicates that each clause is a complete sentence, distinct from surrounding sentences.

> **COMMA SPLICE** Our division's reports are posted on our web page**;** hard copies are available by request.

> **COMMA SPLICE** Our division's reports are posted on our web page**.** Hard copies are available by request.

> **FUSED SENTENCE** Our mission statement is simple**:** we aim to provide good athletic gear at affordable prices.

(3) Recast an independent clause as a dependent clause or as a phrase

A dependent clause includes a subordinating conjunction such as *although* or *because*, which indicates how the dependent and independent clauses are related (in a cause-and-effect relationship, for example). A prepositional phrase includes a preposition such as *in*, *on*, or *because of* that may also signal a relationship directly. Verbal, appositive, and absolute phrases suggest relationships less directly because they do not include connecting words.

COMMA SPLICE *Because the* ~~The~~ wind had blown down power lines, the whole city was without electricity for several hours. [dependent clause]

COMMA SPLICE *Because of the downed* ~~The wind had blown down~~ power lines, the whole city was without electricity for several hours. [prepositional phrase]

COMMA SPLICE *The wind having* ~~The wind had~~ blown down power lines, the whole city was without electricity for several hours. [absolute phrase]

(4) Integrate one clause into the other

When you integrate clauses, you will generally retain the important details but omit or change some words.

FUSED SENTENCE The proposal covers all *the points except assessment procedures.* ~~but one point it does not describe how the project will be assessed.~~

(5) Use transitional words or phrases to link independent clauses

Another way to revise fused sentences and comma splices is to use transitional words and phrases such as *however*, *on the contrary*, and *in the meantime*.

FUSED SENTENCE Sexual harassment is not an issue for just
women *. After all,* men can be sexually harassed too.
^

COMMA SPLICE The word *status* refers to relative position within
a group *; however,* it is often used to indicate only posi-
^
tions of prestige.

19c   Divided quotations

When dividing quotations with signal phrases such as *he said*
or *she asked*, use a period between independent clauses.

COMMA SPLICE "Beauty brings copies of itself into being,"
states Elaine Scarry, *. "It* makes us draw it,
^
take photographs of it, or describe it to other
people."

Both parts of the quotation are complete sentences, so the
signal phrase is attached to the first, and the sentence is punctuated with a period.

EXERCISE 19.1

Revise each comma splice or fused sentence in the following paragraph. Some sentences may not need revision.

[1]In *The Politics of Happiness*, Derek Bok, former president of Harvard University, discusses recent findings that researchers studying well-being have reported. [2]He mentions, for example, research showing that measurements of happiness in the United States have not risen much in the last fifty years, people are responding to survey questions about their levels of happiness in much the same way as they did in 1960. [3]Even though average incomes have grown, levels of happiness have not. [4]Bok believes that people become accustomed to higher standards of living they do not realize how quickly they adapt and so do not become happier. [5]Bok recognizes that not everyone's income has increased but notes that, strangely enough, the disparity between rich and poor has not caused increased dissatisfaction among the poor, he cites further studies showing that citizens in countries with costly welfare programs are not necessarily happier than citizens in countries with welfare programs that are not as generous. [6]Because of these studies, Bok suggests that our government not focus on economic growth alone as an indicator of well-being but that it instead take into account current research on what makes people happy. [7]This discussion "is bound to contribute to the evolution of society and the refinement of its values," he explains, "that alone will be an accomplishment of enduring importance to humankind" (212).

Verbs

Choosing verbs to convey your message precisely is the first step toward writing clear sentences.

20a Verb forms

Regular verbs have four forms: a base form, an *-s* form (third-person singular in the present tense), an *-ing* form (present participle), and an *-ed* form (past participle).

VERB FORMS OF REGULAR VERBS

Base Form	-s Form (Present Tense, Third Person, Singular)	-ing Form (Present Participle)	-ed Form (Past Form or Past Participle)
work	works	working	worked
watch	watches	watching	watched
apply	applies	applying	applied
stop	stops	stopping	stopped

CAUTION

When verbs are followed by words with similar sounds, you may find their endings (-s or -ed) difficult to hear. In addition, these verb endings may seem unfamiliar because your dialect does not have them. Nonetheless, you should use -s and -ed when you write for an audience that expects you to include these endings.

> ➤ She ~~seem~~ *seems* satisfied with the report.

> ➤ We were ~~suppose~~ *supposed* to receive the results yesterday.

Irregular verbs are not as predictable as regular verbs. The past form and the past participle seldom carry the *-ed* suffix. Most irregular verbs, such as *write*, have forms similar to some of those for regular verbs: base form (*write*), *-s* form (*writes*), and *-ing* form (*writing*). However, the past form (*wrote*) and the past participle (*written*) differ from the regular forms.

VERB FORMS OF COMMON IRREGULAR VERBS

Base Form	Past Form	Past Participle
arise	arose	arisen
awake	awaked, awoke	awaked, awoken
be	was/were	been
begin	began	begun
break	broke	broken
bring	brought	brought
buy	bought	bought
choose	chose	chosen
come	came	come
dive	dived, dove	dived
do	did	done
dream	dreamed, dreamt	dreamed, dreamt
drink	drank	drunk
drive	drove	driven
eat	ate	eaten
forget	forgot	forgotten
forgive	forgave	forgiven
get	got	gotten, got
give	gave	given
go	went	gone
hang (suspend)	hung	hung
keep	kept	kept
know	knew	known

(continues on page 280)

(continued)	**VERB FORMS OF COMMON IRREGULAR VERBS**	
lay (to place)	laid	laid
lead	led	led
lie (to recline)	lay	lain
lose	lost	lost
pay	paid	paid
prove	proved	proved, proven
rise	rose	risen
say	said	said
see	saw	seen
set	set	set
sink	sank	sunk
sit	sat	sat
sneak	snuck, sneaked	snuck, sneaked
speak	spoke	spoken
stand	stood	stood
steal	stole	stolen
swim	swam	swum
take	took	taken
tell	told	told
throw	threw	thrown
wear	wore	worn
write	wrote	written

MULTILINGUAL WRITERS
OMISSION OF FORMS OF *BE* IN OTHER LANGUAGES

Forms of the verb *be* can be omitted in some languages. In English, however, they are necessary.

➤ Sentence without an auxiliary verb: The population *is* growing.

➤ Sentence without a linking verb: It *is* quite large.

A **prepositional verb** is a frequently occurring combination of a verb and a preposition. *Rely on, think about, look like,* and *ask for* are all prepositional verbs. A **phrasal verb** is a combination of a verb and a particle such as *up, out,* or *on.* A **particle** resembles an adverb or a preposition, but it is so closely associated with a verb that together they form a unit of meaning. *Carry out, make up, take on,* and *turn out* are common phrasal verbs. Notice that each one has a meaning that can be expressed in a single word: *do, form, accept,* and *attend.*

MULTILINGUAL WRITERS
PHRASAL VERBS

Definitions of phrasal verbs are sometimes difficult to determine. For example, *find out* means "to discover." If you are unsure of the definition of a phrasal verb, look it up. Phrasal verbs are often listed at the end of an entry for a common verb such as *do, make, take, turn,* or *find.*

The **auxiliary verbs** *be, do,* and *have* combine with main verbs, both regular and irregular.

be	*am, is, are, was, were surprised*
	am, is, are, was, were writing
do	*does, do, did call*
	doesn't, don't, didn't spend
have	*has, have, had prepared*
	has, have, had read

Another type of auxiliary verb is called a **modal auxiliary**. There are nine modal auxiliaries: *can, could, may, might, must, shall, should, will,* and *would.*

COMMON MEANINGS OF MODAL AUXILIARIES

Meaning	Modal Auxiliary	+	Main Verb	Example
Ability	can, could		afford	They *can afford* to buy a small house.
Certainty	will		leave	We *will leave* tomorrow.
Obligation	must		return	You *must return* your books soon.
Advice	should		talk	He *should talk* with his counselor.
Permission	may		use	You *may use* the computers in the library.

CAUTION

When a modal auxiliary occurs with the auxiliary *have* (*must have forgotten*, *should have known*), *have* frequently sounds like the word *of*. When you proofread, be sure that modal auxiliaries are not followed by *of*.

➤ They **could ~~of~~ taken** another route.
         have

Most modal verbs have more than one meaning. *Could* sometimes refers to ability (***I could** swim a mile when I was sixteen*). However, *could* can also refer to possibility (*Something good **could** happen*).

EXERCISE 20.1

Revise the following sentences. Explain any changes you make.

1. Any expedition into the wilderness suffer its share of mishaps.
2. The Lewis and Clark Expedition began in May 1804 and end in September 1806.
3. Fate must of smiled on Meriwether Lewis and William Clark, for there were no fatalities under their leadership.

4. Lewis and Clark lead the expedition from St. Louis to the Pacific Ocean and back.

5. By 1805, the Corps of Discovery, as the expedition was call, included thirty-three members.

6. The Corps might of lost all maps and specimens had Sacajawea, a Native American woman, not fish them from the Missouri River.

20b Verb tenses

Verb tenses provide information about time. For example, the tense of a verb may indicate that an action took place in the past or that an action is ongoing. Verb tenses are labeled as present, past, or future; they are also labeled as simple, progressive, perfect, or perfect progressive. The following chart shows how these labels apply to the tenses of *walk*.

Some of the tenses have more than one form because they depend on the person and number of the subject. **Person** refers to the role of the subject. First person (*I, we*) indicates that the subject of the verb is the writer or writers. Second person (*you*) indicates that the subject is the audience. Third person (*he, she, it, they*) indicates that the subject is someone or something other than the writer or audience. **Number** indicates whether the subject is one (*I, he, she, it, you*-singular) or more than one (*we, they, you*-plural).

VERB TENSES

	Present	Past	Future
Simple	I/you/we/they **walk** He/she/it **walks**	**walked**	**will walk**
Progressive	I **am walking** You/we/they **are walking** He/she/it **is walking**	I/he/she/it **was walking** You/we/they **are walking**	**will be walking**

(continues on page 284)

(continued)	VERB TENSES		
	Present	Past	Future
Perfect	I/you/we/they **have walked** He/she/it **has walked**	**had walked**	**will have walked**
Perfect progressive	I/you/we/they **have been walking** He/she/it **has been walking**	**had been walking**	**will have been walking**

MULTILINGUAL WRITERS
VERBS NOT USED IN THE PROGRESSIVE FORM

Some verbs that do not express actions but rather mental states, emotions, conditions, or relationships are not used in the progressive form. These verbs include *believe, belong, contain, cost, know, own, prefer,* and *want.*

▶ The book ~~is containing~~ *contains* many Central American folktales.

20c Verb tense consistency

By using verb tenses consistently, you help your readers understand when the actions or events you are describing took place. Every verb tense has two parts: time frame and aspect. *Time frame* refers to whether the tense is present, past, or future. *Aspect* refers to whether it is simple, progressive, perfect, or perfect progressive. (See the chart in **20b**.) Consistency in the time frame of verbs, though not necessarily in their aspect, ensures that sentences reporting a sequence of events link together logically. In the following paragraph, notice that the time frame remains in the past, but the aspect may be either simple, perfect, or progressive.

At that point, Kubrick **had finished** *Dr. Strangelove.* [*past perfect*]

Working independently, he **started** his science-fiction masterpiece, [*simple past*]

2001: A Space Odyssey with much of Hollywood unaware that he **was working** in a new genre. [*past progressive*]

If you do need to shift to another time frame, you can use a time marker.

now, then, today, yesterday

in two years, during the 1920s

after you finish, before we left

➤ The Minnesota State Fair **attracts** thousands of visitors each day. **Last year**, the average daily attendance **exceeded** [*simple present* / *time marker* / *simple past*]

100,000.

You may be able to change time frames without including time markers when you wish (1) to explain or support a general statement with information about the past, (2) to compare and contrast two different time periods, or (3) to comment on a topic.

➤ Thomas Jefferson, author of the Declaration of Independence, **is** considered one of our country's most brilliant citizens. His achievements **were** many, as **were** his interests. [The second sentence provides evidence from the past to support the claim in the first sentence.]

Before you turn in your final draft, check your verb tenses to ensure that they are logical and consistent. Revise any that are not.

➤ The white wedding dress <u>comes</u> *came* into fashion when Queen
Victoria wore a white gown at her wedding to Prince Albert of
Saxe. Soon after, brides who could afford them bought stylish
white dresses for their weddings. Brides of modest means,
however, <u>continue</u> *continued* to choose dresses they could wear more
than once.

EXERCISE 20.2

Revise the following paragraph so that it contains no unnecessary
shifts in verb tense.

I **had** already **been walking** for a half hour in the semidark-
ness of Amsterdam's early-morning streets when I **came** to a red
light. I **am** in a hurry to get to the train station and no cars **were**
out yet, so I **cross** over the cobblestones, passing a man waiting
for the light to change. I never **look** back when he **scolds** me for
breaking the law. I **had** a train to catch. I **was** going to Widnau,
in Switzerland, to see Aunt Marie. I **have** not **seen** her since I **was**
in second grade.

20d Voice

Voice indicates the relationship between a verb and its subject.
When a verb is in the **active voice**, the subject is generally a
person or thing performing an action. When a verb is in the
passive voice, the subject is usually the *receiver* of the action.

ACTIVE   Jen Wilson **wrote** the essay.

PASSIVE   The essay **was written** by Jen Wilson.

Some passive sentences do not include a *by* phrase because the
actor is unknown or unimportant.

➤ Jen Wilson's essay **was published** in the student newspaper.

The terms *active* and *passive* can sometimes cause confusion. As grammatical terms, they do not refer to the difference between action and inaction—running vs. napping. The best way to decide whether a sentence is in the passive voice is to examine its verb phrase.

(1) Verbs in the passive voice

The verb phrase in a sentence written in the passive voice consists of a form of the auxiliary verb *be* (*am, is, are, was, were, been*) and a past participle. Depending on the verb tense, other auxiliaries such as *have, will,* and *should* may appear as well. The following sentences include common forms of *call* in the passive voice.

➤ The meeting *is called* to order. [simple present]

➤ The recruits *were called* to duty. [simple past]

➤ The council *is being called* to act on the proposal. [present progressive]

➤ Ms. Jones *has been called* to jury twice already. [present perfect]

Generally, sentences that do not include both a form of the auxiliary verb *be* and a past participle are in the active voice.

(2) Choosing between the active and passive voice

To use the active voice for emphasizing an actor and an action, first make the actor the subject of the sentence; then choose verbs that will help your readers see what the actor is doing.

➤ A group of students **planned** the graduation ceremony.

Use the passive voice when you want to stress the recipient of the action, rather than the actor, or when the actor's identity is unimportant or unknown.

➤ Tuition increases **were discussed** at the board meeting.

Writers of scientific prose often use the passive voice to high-light the experiment rather than the experimenter, as in this excerpt from a student lab report:

> First, the slides **were placed** on a compound microscope under low power, a 40× magnification level. The end of the root tip **was located**; then the cells immediately behind the root cap **were examined**.

EXERCISE 20.3

Identify the voice in each sentence as active or passive.

1. In a *National Geographic* report, Tom O'Neill describes the discovery of ancient art in Guatemala.

2. Archaeologist William Saturno recently discovered the oldest known Maya mural.

3. The mural was found in a tunnel used by looters.

4. The tunnel was actually a small room attached to a pyramid.

5. The mural was dated to about 150 years before the beginning of the Maya Classic period.

6. The mural's colors were documented and photographed.

20e   Mood

The **mood** of a verb expresses the writer's attitude toward the factuality of what is being expressed. The **indicative mood** is used for statements and questions regarding fact or opinion. The **imperative mood** is used to give commands or directions. The **subjunctive mood** is used to state requirements, make requests, and express wishes.

INDICATIVE	We will be on time.
IMPERATIVE	Be on time!
SUBJUNCTIVE	The director insists that we be on time.

The subjunctive mood is also used to signal hypothetical situations (situations that are not real or not currently true: *If I* **were** *president, I'd protect national parks.*).

Verb forms in the subjunctive mood serve a variety of functions. The **present subjunctive** is the base form of the verb. It is used to express necessity.

➤ The doctor recommended that he **go** on a diet. [active voice]

➤ We demanded that you **be reimbursed**. [passive voice]

The **past subjunctive** has the same form as the simple past (for example, *had, offered, found,* or *wrote*). However, the past subjunctive form of *be* is *were* for all subjects, regardless of person or number. This form is used to present hypothetical situations.

➤ If they **offered** me the job, I would take it. [active voice]

➤ Even if he **were promoted,** he would not change his mind. [passive voice]

The **perfect subjunctive** verb has the same form as the past perfect tense: *had* + past participle. The perfect subjunctive signals that a statement is not factual.

➤ I wish I **had known** about the scholarship competition. [active voice]

➤ If she **had been awarded** the scholarship, she would have quit her part-time job. [passive voice]

TIPS FOR USING THE SUBJUNCTIVE

- In clauses beginning with *as if* and *as though*, use the past subjunctive or the perfect subjunctive:

  ➤ He acts as if he *were* **was** the owner.

  ➤ She looked at me as though she *had* **heard** this story before.

(Continued on page 290)

> ### TIPS FOR USING THE SUBJUNCTIVE *(Continued)*

- In nonfactual dependent clauses beginning with *if*, use the past subjunctive or the perfect subjunctive. Avoid using *would have* in the *if* clause.

  >   *were*
  > ➤ If I ~~was~~ rich, I would buy a yacht.

  >   *had*
  > ➤ If the driver ~~would have~~ checked his rearview mirror, the accident would not have happened.

- In dependent clauses following verbs that express wishes, use the past subjunctive or the perfect subjunctive.

  >   *were*
  > ➤ I wish I ~~was~~ taller.

  >   *had*
  > ➤ My brother wishes he studied harder years ago.

- In *that* clauses expressing suggestions or demands, following verbs such as *ask, insist,* or *recommend,* use the base form of the verb in the *that* clause.

  >   *be*
  > ➤ The director asks that fans ~~are~~ patient for the next film in the popular series.

EXERCISE 20.4

Use subjunctive verb forms to revise the following sentences.

1. The planners of Apollo 13 acted as if the number 13 was a lucky number.

2. Superstitious people think that if NASA changed the number of the mission, the astronauts would have had a safer journey.

3. They also believe that if the lunar landing would have been scheduled for a day other than Friday the Thirteenth, the crew would not have encountered any problems.

4. The crew used the lunar module as though it was a lifeboat.

5. After the successful splashdown, NASA administrators required that an investigative board was established.

6. If NASA ever plans a space mission on Friday the Thirteenth again, the public would object.

20f Subject-verb agreement

To say that a verb *agrees* with a subject means that the form of the verb (*-s* form or base form) is appropriate for the subject. For example, if the subject refers to one person or thing (*an athlete*, *a computer*), the *-s* form of the verb (*runs*) is appropriate. If the subject refers to more than one person or thing (*athletes*, *computers*), the base form of the verb (*run*) is appropriate. Notice in the following examples that the singular third-person subjects in the first line take a singular verb (*-s* form) and all the other subjects take the base form.

He, she, it, Joe, a student	has, looks, writes
I, you, we, they, the Browns, the students	have, look, write

The verb *be* does not follow this pattern. It has three different present-tense forms and two different past-tense forms.

I	am/was
He, she, it, Joe, a student	is/was
You, we, they, the Browns, the students	are/were

(1) Words between the subject and the verb

When phrases such as the following occur between the subject and the verb, they do not affect the number of the subject or the form of the verb.

| along with | in addition to | not to mention |
| as well as | including | together with |

➤ Her **salary**, <u>together with</u> tips, **is** just enough to live on.

➤ **Tips**, <u>together with</u> her salary, **are** just enough to live on.

(2) Subjects joined by *and*

A compound subject (two nouns joined by *and*) that refers to a single person or thing takes a singular verb.

➤ The **founder <u>and</u> president** of the art association **was** elected to the board of the museum.

(3) Subjects joined by *or* or *nor*

When singular subjects are linked by *or*, *either . . . or*, or *neither . . . nor*, the verb is singular as well.

➤ The **provost <u>or</u>** the **dean** usually **presides** at the meeting.

➤ <u>**Either**</u> his **accountant <u>or</u>** his **lawyer has** the will.

If the linked subjects differ in number, the verb agrees with the subject closer to the verb.

➤ Neither the basket nor the **apples were** expensive. [plural]

➤ Neither the apples nor the **basket was** expensive. [singular]

(4) Inverted order

In most sentences, the subject precedes the verb.

➤ The large **cities** of the Northeast **were** the hardest hit by the winter storms.

The subject and verb can sometimes be inverted for emphasis; however, they must still agree.

➤ The hardest hit by the winter storms **were** the large **cities** of the Northeast.

When *there* begins a sentence, the subject and verb are always inverted; the verb still agrees with the subject, which follows it.

>   *v*   *s*
> There **are** several **cities** in need of federal aid.

(5) Clauses with relative pronouns

In an adjectival (relative) clause, the subject is generally a relative pronoun (*that, who,* or *which*). To determine whether the relative pronoun is singular or plural, you must find its antecedent (the word or words it refers to). When the antecedent is singular, the relative pronoun is singular; when the antecedent is plural, the relative pronoun is plural. In essence, the verb in the adjectival clause agrees with the antecedent.

>   *sing ant*   *sing v*
> **The person <u>who</u> reviews** proposals is out of town this week.

>   *pl ant*   *pl v*
> The director met with the **students <u>who</u> are** studying abroad next quarter.

>   *pl ant*   *pl v*
> The Starion is one of the new **models <u>that</u> include** a DVD player as standard equipment.

(6) Indefinite pronouns

The indefinite pronouns *each, either, everybody, everyone,* and *anyone* are considered singular and so require singular verb forms.

> <u>**Either**</u> of them **is willing** to lead the discussion.

> <u>**Everybody**</u> in our apartment building **has** a parking place.

All, any, some, none, half, and *most* can be either singular or plural, depending on whether they refer to a unit or quantity (singular) or to individuals (plural).

>   *sing v*
> My sister collects antique **jewelry**; <u>**some**</u> of it **is** quite valuable.

➤ My sister collects comic **books**; <u>some</u> *pl v* **are** quite valuable.

When an indefinite pronoun is followed by a prepositional phrase beginning with the preposition *of*, the verb agrees in number with the object of the preposition.

➤ **None** of *pl obj* **those** *pl v* **are** spoiled.

➤ **None** of the *sing obj* **food** *sing v* **is** spoiled.

(7) Collective nouns and measurement words

Collective nouns and measurement words require singular verbs when they refer to groups or units. They require plural verbs when they refer to individuals or parts.

SINGULAR (REGARDED AS A GROUP OR UNIT)	PLURAL (REGARDED AS INDIVIDUALS OR PARTS)
The **majority rules**.	The **majority** of us **are** in favor.
Ten million gallons of oil **is** more than enough.	**Ten million gallons** of oil **were spilled**.

(8) Words ending in -s

Titles of works that are plural in form (for example, *Star Wars* and *Dombey and Son*) are treated as singular because they refer to a single book, movie, recording, or other work.

➤ *The Hunger Games* **is** one of the films she discussed in her paper.

Some nouns ending in -*s* are singular: *linguistics, news,* and *Niagara Falls.*

➤ The **news is** encouraging.

Nouns such as *athletics, politics,* and *electronics* can be either singular or plural, depending on their meanings.

| SINGULAR | **Statistics is** an interesting subject. |
| PLURAL | **Statistics are** often misleading. |

(9) Subjects and subject complements

Some sentences may have a singular subject and a plural subject complement, or vice versa. In either case, the verb agrees with the subject.

➤ Her primary **concern is** rising health-care costs.

➤ **Croissants are** the bakery's specialty.

THINKING RHETORICALLY

AGREEMENT OF RELATED SINGULAR AND PLURAL NOUNS

When a sentence has two or more nouns that are related, use either the singular form or the plural form consistently.

➤ The **student** raised her **hand**. The **students** raised their **hands**.

Occasionally, you may have to use a singular noun to retain an idiomatic expression or to avoid ambiguity.

➤ **They** kept their **word**.

(10) Subjects beginning with *what*

When *what* may be understood as "the thing that," the verb in the main clause is singular.

➤ What we need **is** a new policy. [*The thing that* we need is a new policy.]

If *what* is understood as "the things that," the verb in the main clause is plural.

➤ What we need **are** new guidelines. [*The things that* we need are new guidelines.]

EXERCISE 20.5

Choose the correct form of the verb in parentheses.

1. There (is/are) at least two good reasons for changing motor oil: risk of contamination and danger of additive depletion.

2. Reasons for not changing the oil (include/includes) the cost to the driver and the inconvenience of the chore.

3. What I want to know (is/are) the number of miles I can drive before I have to change my oil.

4. My older brother says three thousand miles (is/are) not long enough.

5. Each of the car manuals I consulted (recommends/recommend) five-thousand-mile intervals.

6. Neither the automakers nor the oil station attendants (know/knows) how I drive.

---

21   Pronouns

When you use pronouns effectively, you add clarity and coherence to your writing.

21a   Recognizing pronouns

A **pronoun** is commonly defined as a word that refers to a noun or noun phrase already mentioned—its **antecedent**.

➤ <u>John</u> said **he** would guide the trip.

➤ <u>The participant with the most experience</u> said **he** would guide
the trip.

Most pronouns refer to nouns, but some such as *this*, *that*, *my*,
and *their* come before nouns.

➤ **This** <u>man</u> is our guide.   **My** <u>map</u> is over there.

Pronouns are categorized as personal, reflexive/intensive, relative, interrogative, demonstrative, or indefinite.

(1) Personal pronouns

Personal pronouns are like nouns: they refer to people, places,
things, ideas, and so on.

SINGULAR	I, me, you, he, him, she, her, it
PLURAL	we, us, you, they, them

(2) Possessive pronouns

Possessive pronouns are personal pronouns that indicate ownership and similar relationships.

SINGULAR	my, mine, your, yours, his, her, hers, its
PLURAL	our, ours, your, yours, their, theirs

Avoid confusing possessive forms with common contractions:
it's (*it is*), *they're* (*they are*), and *who's* (*who is*).

(3) Reflexive/intensive pronouns

Reflexive pronouns direct the action back to the subject (*I saw
myself*); intensive pronouns are used for emphasis (*I myself
questioned the judge*).

SINGULAR	myself, yourself, himself, herself, itself
PLURAL	ourselves, yourselves, themselves

Avoid using a reflexive pronoun as a subject.

➤ Ms. Palmquist and ⌃*myself* discussed our concern with the senator.

Hisself, themself, and *theirselves* are inappropriate in academic or professional writing. Instead, use *himself* and *themselves.*

(4) Relative pronouns

An adjectival clause (or relative clause) ordinarily begins with a relative pronoun: *who, whom, which, that,* or *whose.* To provide a link between this type of dependent clause and the main clause, the relative pronoun corresponds to a word or words in the main clause called the **antecedent**.

➤ The students talked to **a reporter who** had just returned from overseas.

Who, whose, and *whom* ordinarily refer to people; *which* refers to things; *that* refers to things and, in some contexts, people. The possessive *whose* (used in place of the awkward *of which*) usually refers to people but sometimes refers to things.

Knowing the difference between an essential clause and a nonessential clause will help you decide whether to use *which* or *that.* A clause that a reader needs in order to identify the antecedent correctly is an **essential clause**.

➤ **The person who presented the award** was last year's winner.

If the essential clause were omitted from this sentence, the reader would not know which person was last year's winner.

A **nonessential clause** is *not* needed for correct identification of the antecedent and is thus set off by commas. A nonessential clause often follows a proper noun (a specific name).

➤ **Andrea Bowen, who presented the award,** was last year's winner.

If the nonessential clause were removed from this sentence, the reader would still know the identity of last year's winner.

According to a traditional grammar rule, *that* is used in essential adjectival clauses, and *which* is used in nonessential adjectival clauses.

➤ I need a job **that** pays well.

➤ For years, I have had the same job, **which** pays well enough.

However, some professional writers use *which* in essential clauses. Nonetheless, if you are following APA guidelines, use *which* only in nonessential clauses.

(5) Interrogative pronouns

The interrogative pronouns *what*, *which*, *who*, *whom*, and *whose* are question words.

➤ **Who** won the award?   **Whom** did you see?

(6) Demonstrative pronouns

The demonstrative pronouns *this* and *these* indicate that someone or something is close by in time, space, or thought. *That* and *those* signal remoteness.

➤ **These** issues will be addressed in the next section.

➤ He envied **those** people who could live simply.

(7) Indefinite pronouns

Indefinite pronouns usually do not refer to specific persons, objects, ideas, or events.

anyone	anybody	anything
everyone	everybody	everything
someone	somebody	something
no one	nobody	nothing
each	either	neither

Indefinite pronouns do not refer to an antecedent. In fact, some indefinite pronouns *serve* as antecedents.

➤ **Someone** forgot **her** purse.

21b | Pronoun case

To understand the uses of pronouns, you must first be able to recognize person and number. **Person** indicates whether a pronoun refers to the writer (**first person**), to the reader (**second person**), or to another person, place, thing, or idea (**third person**). **Number** reveals whether a pronoun is singular or plural.

Case refers to the form a pronoun takes to indicate its relationship to other words in a sentence. There are three cases relevant to understanding pronouns: subjective, objective, and possessive (also called genitive).

➤ **He** [subjective] wants **his** [possessive] legislators to help **him** [objective].

CASE:	Subjective		Objective		Possessive	
NUMBER:	Singular	Plural	Singular	Plural	Singular	Plural
First person	I	we	me	us	my, mine	our, ours
Second person	you	you	you	you	your, yours	your, yours
Third person	he, she, it	they	him, her, it	them	his, her, hers, its	their, theirs

(1) Pronouns in the subjective case

A pronoun that is the subject of a sentence is in the **subjective case**. To determine which pronoun form is correct in a compound subject (a noun and a pronoun joined by *and*), say the sentence using the pronoun alone, omitting the noun. For the following sentence, notice that "*Me* solved the problem" seems strange, but "*I* solved the problem" is fine.

> ~~Me and~~ Marisa *and I* solved the problem.

Place the pronoun *I* last in the sequence. If the compound subject contains two pronouns, test each one by itself.

> *He* ~~Him~~ and I joined the club in July.

Pronouns following a *be* verb (*am, is, are, was, were, been*) should also be in the subjective case.

> The first to arrive were Kevin and ~~me~~ *I*.

MULTILINGUAL WRITERS
NOUN OR PRONOUN AS SUBJECT

In some languages, a noun in the subject position may be followed by a pronoun. In Standardized English, though, such a pronoun should be omitted.

> My roommate ~~he~~ works in the library for three hours a week.

(2) Pronouns in the objective case

Whenever a pronoun follows an action verb or a preposition, it takes the **objective case**.

The whole staff admired **him**. [direct object]

The staff sent **him** a card. [indirect object]

The staff depended on **him**. [object of a preposition]

Pronouns joined by *and* or *or* are also in the objective case when they follow a verb or preposition.

> They will appoint you or ~~I~~ *me*. [direct objects]

> They lent Tom and ~~I~~ *me* money for tuition. [indirect objects]

> Jan sat between my brother and ~~I~~ *me*. [objects of the preposition]

To determine whether to use the subjective or objective case, remember to say the sentence with just the pronoun. Notice that "They will appoint *I*" does not sound right.

(3) Possessive forms

Pronouns in the **possessive case** can be divided into two groups based on whether they are followed by nouns. *My*, *your*, *his*, *her*, *its*, *our*, and *their* are all followed by nouns; *mine*, *yours*, *his*, *hers*, *ours*, and *theirs* are not. (Note that *his* is in both groups.)

➤ **Their** budget is higher than **ours**. [*Their* is followed by a noun; *ours* is not.]

(4) Appositive pronouns

Appositive pronouns are in the same case as the nouns they rename.

➤ Our group—Becky, Lee, and ~~me~~ *I*—argued for the new policy. [subjective]

➤ My grandmother gave her old art books to her grandchildren— Josh, Evan, Kayla, and ~~I~~ *me*. [objective]

(5) *Who/whoever and whom/whomever*

To choose between *who* and *whom* or between *whoever* and *whomever*, you must first determine whether the word is functioning as a subject or an object. A pronoun functioning as the subject takes the subjective case.

➤ **Who** won the award? [COMPARE: **She** won the award.]

➤ The teachers knew **who** won the award.

➤ The student **who** won the award was quite surprised.

➤ **Whoever** won the award deserved it.

When the pronoun is an object, use *whom* or *whomever*.

➤ **Whom** did they hire? [COMPARE: They hired **him**.]

➤ I do not know **whom** they hired.

➤ The student **whom** they hired graduated in May.

➤ **Whomever** they hired will have to work hard this year.

Whom may be omitted in sentences when no misunderstanding would result.

➤ The friend he relied on moved away. [*Whom* has been omitted after *friend*.]

(6) Pronouns with infinitives and gerunds

A pronoun grouped with an infinitive (*to* + the base form of a verb) takes the objective case.

➤ The director wanted **me** to help **him**.

A gerund (*-ing* verb form functioning as a noun) is preceded by a possessive pronoun.

➤ I appreciated **his** helping Denise. [COMPARE: I appreciated **Mike's** helping Denise.]

Notice that a possessive pronoun is used before a gerund but not before a present participle (*-ing* verb form functioning as an adjective).

➤ I saw **him** helping Luke.

(7) Pronouns in elliptical constructions

The words *as* and *than* frequently introduce **elliptical constructions**—clauses in which the writer has intentionally omitted words. To check whether you have used the correct case in an elliptical construction, read the written sentence aloud, inserting any words that have been omitted from it.

➤ She admires Clarice as much as **I**. [subjective case]
Read aloud: She admires Clarice as much as *I do*.

➤ She admires Clarice more than **me**. [objective case]

Read aloud: She admires Clarice more than *she admires me.*

EXERCISE 21.1

Revise the following paragraph, using appropriate pronouns. Some sentences may not require editing.

¹When me and my brother were in middle school, we formed a band with our friends Jason and Andrew. ²My grandmother had given Jake a guitar and I a drum kit for Christmas. ³We practiced either alone or together for the rest of the winter. ⁴Then, in the spring, we met up with Jason, who we had known for years. ⁵Him and his cousin Andrew, whom we later called Android, were excited to join me and Jake. ⁶Jason already had a guitar, and Andrew could sing. ⁷After we played together one afternoon, we decided to call ourself *The Crash.* ⁸Jason and Andrew came over to our house to jam whenever they're parents let them—which was most of the time. ⁹Our parents did not mind our noise at all. ¹⁰My dad said us playing reminded him of his own teenage garage band.

EXERCISE 21.2

Correct the pronoun errors in the following sentences. Not all sentences have errors.

1. The board of directors has asked you and I to conduct a customer survey.

2. They also recommended us hiring someone with extensive experience in statistical analysis.

3. Whomever understands statistics should take the lead on this project.

4. Although the board asked me to be in charge, I would like you to recruit and interview candidates.

5. The directors recognize your expertise and will surely approve of you taking the lead.

21c   Pronoun-antecedent agreement

A pronoun and its antecedent (the word or word group to which it refers) agree in number (both are singular or both are plural).

➤ The **supervisor** said **he** would help.
[Both antecedent and pronoun are singular.]

➤ My **colleagues** said **they** would help.
[Both antecedent and pronoun are plural.]

MULTILINGUAL WRITERS
POSSESSIVE PRONOUNS

A possessive pronoun (*his*, *her*, *its*, *their*, *my*, *our*, or *your*), also called a **possessive determiner**, agrees with its antecedent, not with the noun it precedes.

➤ Ken Carlson brought ~~her~~ *his* young daughter to the office today.
[The possessive pronoun *his* agrees with the antecedent, *Ken Carlson*, not with the following noun, *daughter*.]

(1) Indefinite pronouns

An indefinite pronoun such as *everyone*, *someone*, or *anybody* takes a singular verb form.

➤ Everyone **has** [not *have*] the right to an opinion.

Difficulties arise, however, because words like *everyone* and *everybody* seem to refer to more than one person even though they take a singular verb. Thus, the definition of grammatical number and our everyday notion of number conflict. In conversation and informal writing, a plural pronoun (*they*, *them*, or *their*) is often used with the singular *everyone*. Nonetheless, when you write for an audience that expects you to follow traditional grammar rules, make sure to use a third-person singular pronoun.

➤ Everyone has the combination to ~~their~~ *his or her* private locker.

You can avoid the awkwardness of using *his* or *her* by using an article instead, making both the antecedent and the possessive pronoun plural, or rewriting the sentence using the passive voice (the *be* auxiliary + the past participle).

➤ Everyone has the combination to **a** private locker. [article]

➤ **Students** have combinations to **their** private lockers. [plural antecedent and plural possessive pronoun]

➤ The combination to a private locker **is issued** to everyone. [passive voice]

(2) Two antecedents joined by *or* or *nor*

If a singular and a plural antecedent are joined by *or* or *nor*, place the plural antecedent second and use a plural pronoun.

➤ Either the senator **or** her <u>assistants</u> will explain how <u>they</u> devised the plan for tax reform.

➤ Neither the president **nor** the <u>senators</u> stated that <u>they</u> would support the proposal.

(3) Collective nouns

When an antecedent is a collective noun such as *team, faculty,* or *committee,* determine whether you intend the noun to be understood as singular or plural. Then, make sure that the pronoun agrees in number with the noun.

➤ The choir decided that ^*it* ~~they~~ would tour during the winter.
[Because the choir decided as a group, *choir* should be considered singular.]

➤ The committee may disagree on methods, but ^*they* ~~it~~ must agree on basic aims.
[Because the committee members are behaving as individuals, *committee* is regarded as plural.]

EXERCISE 21.3

Revise the following sentences so that pronouns and antecedents agree. Some verb forms will have to change as well.

1. A researcher relies on a number of principles to help them make ethical decisions.

2. Everyone should have the right to participate in a study only if they feel comfortable doing so.

3. A team of researchers should provide its volunteers with consent forms, in which they describe to the volunteers the procedures and risks involved in participation.

4. Every participant should be guaranteed that the information they provide will remain confidential.

5. Institutions of higher education require that a researcher address ethical issues in their proposals.

21d   Clear pronoun reference

The meaning of each pronoun in a sentence should be immediately obvious. In the following sentence, the pronoun *he* clearly refers to the antecedent, *Jack*.

➤ **Jack** has collected shells since **he** was eight years old.

(1) Ambiguous pronoun reference

Revise sentences in which a pronoun can refer to either of two antecedents.

➤ Anna told her sister ~~that she had~~ to call home.

(2) Remote pronoun reference

To help readers understand your meaning, place relative pronouns as close to their antecedents as possible.

➤ The **poem** *that was originally written in 1945* has been published in a new book. ~~**that** was~~ ~~originally written in 1945.~~

[A poem, not a book, was first published in 1945.]

Notice, however, that a relative pronoun does not always have to follow its antecedent directly. In the following example, there is no risk of misunderstanding.

➤ We slowly began to notice <u>changes</u> in our lives **that** we had never expected.

(3) Broad pronoun reference

Pronouns such as *it*, *this*, *that*, and *which* sometimes refer to the sense of a whole clause, sentence, or paragraph.

➤ Large corporations may seem stronger than individuals, but **that** is not true. [*That* refers to the sense of the whole first clause.]

In academic situations, revise sentences that do not have specific antecedents.

➤ When class attendance is compulsory, some students feel that education is being forced on them. This *perception* is unwarranted. [In the original sentence, *this* had no clear antecedent.]

(4) Implied reference

Express an idea explicitly rather than merely implying it.

➤ My father is a music teacher. *Teaching music* It is a profession that requires much patience. [In the original sentence, *it* had no expressed antecedent.]

Be especially careful to provide clear antecedents when referring to the work or possessions of others. The following sentence requires revision because *she* can refer to someone other than Jen Norton, who could be an editor instead of an author.

➤ In ~~Jen Norton's~~ *her* new book, *Jen Norton* she argues for election reform.

(5) The use of *it* without an antecedent

The expletive *it* does not have a specific antecedent. Instead, it is used to postpone, and thus give emphasis to, the subject of a sentence. If a sentence that begins with this expletive is wordy or awkward, replace *it* with the postponed subject.

➤ ~~It was~~ *Trying to repair the car* ~~no use trying to repair the~~ ~~car.~~ *useless.*

EXERCISE 21.4

Edit the following sentences to make all references clear.

1. A singer, songwriter, and human rights activist, it is no wonder that Joan Baez is one of today's most inspirational public figures.

2. Baez's father worked for the United Nations Education, Scientific and Cultural Organization (UNESCO), which meant that as a young girl, she lived in many different countries.

3. Though you might find it hard to believe, Baez recorded her first album when she was only nineteen years old.

4. Baez had a younger sister, Mimi Fariña, who was also a singer-songwriter; sometimes she joined her on tour.

5. In 2011, at a general meeting of the human-rights organization Amnesty International, they gave Baez a special award for her inspirational activism.

21e Pronoun consistency

Whenever you write, you must establish your point of view (perspective). Your point of view will be evident in the pronouns you choose. *I* or *we* indicates a first-person point of view, which is appropriate for writing that includes personal views or experiences. If you decide to address the reader as *you*, you are adopting a second-person point of view. However, because a second-person point of view is rare in academic writing, avoid using *you* unless you need to address the reader. If you select the pronouns *he, she, it, one,* and *they,* you are writing with a third-person point of view. The third-person point of view is the most common point of view in academic writing.

Although you may find it necessary to use different points of view, especially if you are comparing or contrasting other people's views with your own, be careful not to confuse readers by shifting perspective unnecessarily.

To an observer, a sleeping person appears passive, unrespon-

sive, and essentially isolated from the rest of the world and its

barrage of stimuli. While it is true that ~~you are~~ unaware of most *[someone asleep is]*

surrounding noises ~~when you are asleep, our~~ brain is far from *[, that person's]*

inactive. In fact, the brain can be as active during sleep as it

is ~~when you are awake.~~ When ~~our brains are~~ asleep, the rate *[in a waking state]* *[it is]*

and type of electrical activity change.

EXERCISE 21.5

Revise the following paragraph so that there are no unnecessary shifts in point of view.

[1]Many car owners used to complain about deceptive fuel-economy ratings. [2]The issue was ignored until our gas prices started to rise dramatically. [3]Because of increased pressure from consumer organizations, the United States Environmental Protection Agency now takes into account factors such as quick acceleration, changing road grades, and the use of air conditioning, so the new ratings should reflect your real-world driving conditions. [4]Nonetheless, the ratings can never be exact because we all have different driving habits.

21f Use of first-person and second-person pronouns

Using *I* is appropriate when you are writing about personal experience. In academic and professional writing, the use of the first-person singular pronoun is also a clear way to distinguish your own views from those of others. However, if you frequently repeat *I feel* or *I think*, your readers may suspect that you do not understand much beyond your own experience.

We, the first-person plural pronoun, is trickier to use correctly. When you use it, make sure that your audience can tell which individuals are included in this plural reference. For example, if you are completing a course assignment, does *we* mean you and the instructor, you and your fellow students, or some other group (such as all Americans)? Because you may inadvertently use *we* in an early draft to refer to more than one group of people, as you edit, check to see that you have used this pronoun consistently.

If you address readers directly, you will undoubtedly use the second-person pronoun *you* (as we, the authors of this handbook, have done). There is some disagreement, though, over whether to permit the use of the indefinite *you* to mean "a person" or "people in general." If your instructor tells you to avoid using the indefinite *you*, recast your sentences. For example, use *one* instead of *you*.

➤ Even in huge, anonymous cities, ~~you find~~ *one finds* community spirit.

If the use of *one* is too formal, try changing the word order or using different words.

➤ Community spirit is found even in huge, anonymous cities.

EXERCISE 21.6

Revise the following paragraph to eliminate the use of the first- and second-person pronouns.

¹In my opinion, some animals should be as free as we are. ²For example, I think orangutans, African elephants, and Atlantic bottlenose dolphins should roam freely rather than be held in captivity. ³We should neither exhibit them in zoos nor use them for medical research. ⁴If you study animals such as these, you will see that, like us, they show emotions, self-awareness, and intention. ⁵You might even find that some use language to communicate. ⁶It is clear to me that they have the right to freedom.

22   Modifiers

Modifiers are words, phrases, or clauses that modify; that is, they qualify or limit the meaning of other words. When used effectively, modifiers enliven writing with details and enhance its coherence.

22a   Recognizing modifiers

You can distinguish an adjective from an adverb by determining what type of word is modified. **Adjectives** modify nouns and pronouns; **adverbs** modify verbs, adjectives, and other adverbs.

ADJECTIVES	ADVERBS
She looked **curious**.	She looked at me **curiously**.
[modifies pronoun]	[modifies verb]
productive meeting	**highly** productive meeting
[modifies noun]	[modifies adjective]
a **quick** lunch	**very** quickly
[modifies noun]	[modifies adverb]

In addition, consider the form of the modifier. Many adjectives end with one of these suffixes: *-able, -al, -ful, -ic, -ish, -less,* or *-y.*

> accept**able** rent**al** event**ful** angel**ic** sheep**ish** effort**less** sleep**y**

Present participles (verb + *-ing*) and past participles (verb + *-ed*) can also be used as adjectives.

> a **determining** factor   a **determined** effort

Be sure to include the *-ed* ending of a past participle.

> ➤ Please see the ~~enclose~~ enclosed documents for more details.

MULTILINGUAL WRITERS
ADJECTIVE SUFFIXES IN OTHER LANGUAGES

In some languages, adjectives and nouns agree in number. In Spanish, for example, when a noun is plural, the adjective is plural as well: *vistas claras.* In English, however, adjectives do not have a plural form: *clear views.*

The easiest type of adverb to identify is the adverb of manner. It is formed by adding *-ly* to an adjective.

> care**fully**   unpleasant**ly**   silent**ly**

Although you may not hear the *-ly* ending when you speak, be sure to include it when you write.

➤ They bought only ~~local~~ grown vegetables. *locally*

However, not all words ending in *-ly* are adverbs. Certain adjectives related to nouns also end in *-ly* (*friend*, *friendly*; *hour*, *hourly*). In addition, not all adverbs end in *-ly*. Adverbs that indicate time or place (*today*, *tomorrow*, *here*, and *there*) do not have the *-ly* ending. A few words—for example, *fast*, *right*, and *well*—can function as either adjectives or adverbs.

➤ They like **fast** cars. [adjective]

➤ They ran **fast** enough to catch the bus. [adverb]

(1) Modifiers of linking verbs and action verbs

An adjective used after a sensory linking verb (*look*, *smell*, *taste*, *sound*, or *feel*) modifies the subject of the sentence. A common error is to use an adverb after this type of verb.

➤ I felt ~~badly~~ about missing the rally. [The adjective *bad* modifies *I*.] *bad*

However, when *look*, *smell*, *taste*, *sound*, or *feel* is used as an action verb, it can be modified by an adverb.

➤ She looked **angrily** at the referee. [The adverb *angrily* modifies *looked*.]
   BUT She looked **angry**. [The adjective *angry* modifies *she*.]

Good is an adjective and so is not used with action verbs.

➤ The whole team played ~~good~~. *well*

EXERCISE 22.1

Revise the following sentences to include adjectives and adverbs considered conventional in academic writing.

1. Relaxation techniques have been developed for people who feel uncomfortably in some way.

2. Meditation is one technique that is real helpful in relieving stress.

3. People searching for relief from tension have found that a breathing meditation works good.

4. They sit quiet and concentrate on both inhaling and exhaling.

5. They concentrate on breathing deep.

(2) Nouns as modifiers

Adjectives and adverbs are the most common modifiers, but nouns can also be modifiers (***movie*** *critic*, ***reference*** *manual*). A string of noun modifiers can be cumbersome. The following example shows how a sentence with too many noun modifiers can be revised.

➤ The ~~Friday afternoon~~ Student Affairs Committee meeting has been postponed. *scheduled for Friday afternoon*

(3) Phrases and clauses as modifiers

Participial phrases, prepositional phrases, and some infinitive phrases are modifiers.

➤ **Growing in popularity every year,** mountain bikes now dominate the market. [participial phrase]

➤ Mountain bikes first became popular **in the 1980s**. [prepositional phrase]

➤ Some people use mountain bikes **to commute to work**. [infinitive phrase]

Adjectival and adverbial clauses are both modifiers.

➤ BMX bicycles have frames **that are relatively small**. [adjectival clause]

➤ **Although mountain bikes are designed for off-road use**, many people use them on city streets. [adverbial clause]

22b   Comparatives and superlatives

Many adjectives and adverbs have three forms. The **positive form** is the word you would look for in a dictionary. The **comparative form**, which either ends in *-er* or is preceded by *more* or *less*, compares two elements. The **superlative form**, which either ends in *-est* or is preceded by *most* or *least*, compares three or more elements:

POSITIVE	COMPARATIVE	SUPERLATIVE
hard	harder	hardest
deserving	more/less deserving	most/least deserving

(1) Complete and logical comparisons

When using the comparative form of an adjective or an adverb, be sure to indicate what two elements you are comparing.

➤ A diesel engine is **heavier**/ _than a gas engine._

Occasionally, the second element in a comparison is implied.

➤ She wrote **two** papers; the instructor gave her a **better** grade on the second [paper].

A comparison should also be logical. The following example illogically compares *population* and *Wabasha*.

➤ The **population** of Winona is larger than _that of_ **Wabasha**.

(2) Double comparatives or superlatives

Use either an ending or a preceding qualifier, not both, to form a comparative or superlative.

➤ The first bridge is ~~more~~ **narrower** than the second.

➤ The ~~most~~ **narrowest** bridge is in the northern part of the state.

Comparative and superlative forms of modifiers that have absolute meanings, such as *a more perfect society* and *the most unique campus*, are rarely used in academic writing.

EXERCISE 22.2

Provide the comparative or superlative form of each modifier.

1. Amphibians can be divided into three groups. Frogs and toads are in the (common) group.

2. Because they do not have to maintain a specific body temperature, amphibians eat (frequently) than mammals do.

3. Reptiles may look like amphibians, but their skin is (dry).

4. During the Devonian period, the (close) ancestors of amphibians were fish with fins that looked like legs.

22c **Double negatives**

The term **double negative** refers to the use of two negative words to express a single negation. Consider revising any sentences that include *not* and another negative word such as *no, nothing, nobody, hardly, barely,* or *scarcely.*

➤ He did**n't** keep ~~no~~ ^any^ records.

➤ I could**n't** ~~hardly~~ quit in the middle of the job.

MULTILINGUAL WRITERS

NEGATION IN OTHER LANGUAGES

The use of two negative words in one sentence is common in languages such as Spanish:

➤ Yo **no** compre nada. ["I didn't buy anything."]

If your native language allows this type of negation, be sure to revise any double negatives you find in your academic and professional writing.

22d **Placement of modifiers**

Effective placement of modifiers will improve the clarity and coherence of your sentences. A **misplaced modifier** obscures the meaning of a sentence.

(1) Placing modifiers near the words they modify

Readers expect phrases and clauses to modify the nearest grammatical element.

➤ ~~Crouched and ugly, the~~ *The* young boy gasped at the *crouched and ugly* phantom moving across the stage. [The repositioned modifiers *crouched* and *ugly* describe the phantom, not the boy.]

(2) Using limiting modifiers

Place the limiting modifiers *almost, even, hardly, just,* and *only* before the words or word groups they modify. Altering placement can alter meaning.

➤ The committee can **only** nominate two members for the position. [The committee cannot *appoint* the two members to the position.]

➤ The committee can nominate **only** two members for the position. [The committee cannot nominate more than two members.]

➤ **Only** the committee can nominate two members for the position. [No person or group other than the committee can nominate members.]

(3) Revising squinting modifiers

A **squinting modifier** can be interpreted as modifying either what precedes it or what follows it. To avoid such lack of clarity, you can reposition the modifier, add punctuation, or revise the entire sentence.

SQUINTING

Even though Erikson lists some advantages **overall** his vision of a successful business is faulty.

REVISED

Even though Erikson lists some **overall** advantages**,** his vision of a successful business is faulty. [modifier repositioned; punctuation added]

REVISED

Erikson lists some advantages**; however, overall,** his vision of a successful business is faulty. [sentence revised]

EXERCISE 22.3

Improve the clarity of the following sentences by moving the modifiers.

1. Alfred Joseph Hitchcock was born the son of a poultry dealer in London.

2. Hitchcock was only identified with thrillers after making his third movie, *The Lodger.*

3. Hitchcock's most famous movies revolved around psychological improbabilities that are still discussed by movie critics today.

(Continued on page 320)

(Continued)

4. Although his movies are known for suspense sometimes moviegoers also remember Hitchcock's droll sense of humor.

5. Hitchcock just did not direct movie thrillers; he also produced two television series.

6. Originally a British citizen, Queen Elizabeth II knighted Alfred Hitchcock in 1980.

22e   Dangling modifiers

Dangling modifiers do not clearly modify anything in the rest of the sentence. If a sentence begins with an introductory modifier, be sure that what follows—namely, the subject of the sentence—is actually being modified.

➤ Lying on the beach, *we found that* time became irrelevant. [Time cannot lie on a beach.]

➤ When *you are* exercising strenuously, it is important to drink plenty of water. [subject added to the modifier; "it" is not exercising]

Although you will most frequently find a dangling modifier at the beginning of a sentence, you may sometimes find one at the end of a sentence.

➤ Adequate lighting is important *for anyone* ~~when~~ studying. [Lighting cannot study.]

EXERCISE 22.4

Revise any misplaced or dangling modifiers.

1. Climbing a mountain, fitness becomes all-important.

2. In determining an appropriate challenge, considering safety precautions is necessary.

3. Even when expecting sunny weather, rain gear should be packed.

4. Although adding extra weight, climbers should not leave home without a first-aid kit.

5. By taking pains at the beginning of a trip, agony can be averted at the end of a trip.

S
EFFECTIVE SENTENCES

23 Sentence Unity

Effective academic and professional writing is composed of sentences that are consistent, clear, and complete.

23a Choosing and arranging details

Well-chosen details (of time, location, or cause) add interest and credibility to your writing.

MISSING IMPORTANT DETAIL   An astrophysicist from the Harvard-Smithsonian Center has predicted a galactic storm.

WITH DETAIL ADDED   An astrophysicist from the Harvard-Smithsonian Center has predicted **that** a galactic storm **will occur within the next ten million years**.

The added detail about time clarifies the sentence and helps readers accept the information. Every word and every detail you use should contribute to your central thought, as in the following excerpt:

> I was accustomed to hear remarks about my beauty; but now, for the first time, I became conscious of it and recognized it. I noticed the ivory whiteness of my skin, the beauty of my mouth, the size and liquid darkness of my eyes, and how the long, black lashes that fringed and shaded them produced an effect that was strangely fascinating even to me.
>
> —JAMES WELDON JOHNSON, *The Autobiography of an Ex-Colored Man*

23b Revising mixed metaphors

When you use language that evokes images, make sure that the images are meaningfully related. Revise sentences that create **mixed metaphors**—combinations of images that do not make sense together—by replacing words that evoke conflicting images.

➤ As he climbed the corporate ladder, he *incurred a large* ~~sank into a sea of~~ debt.

The odd image of a man hanging onto a ladder as it disappears into the water can easily be revised with the removal of one conflicting image.

23c Revising mixed constructions

A sentence that begins with one kind of grammatical structure and shifts to another is a **mixed construction**.

➤ *Practicing* ~~By practicing~~ a new language daily will help you become proficient. [*Practicing* (a gerund phrase) replaces a prepositional phrase, *By practicing*, which cannot serve as the subject of the verb *will help*.]

➤ *Her scholarship award* ~~Although she won a scholarship~~ does not give her the right to skip classes. [*Although she won a scholarship* (an adverbial clause) cannot serve as the subject. The editing makes the noun phrase *Her scholarship award* the subject.]

You can revise a mixed construction by changing the subject or using the beginning of the current sentence as a modifier and adding a new subject after it.

➤ Although she won a scholarship, **she** does not have the right to skip classes.

| **23d** | **Relating sentence parts** |

When the subject of a sentence is described as being or doing the logically impossible, the sentence has **faulty predication**. Similarly, mismatches between a verb and its complement can obscure meaning.

(1) Mismatch between subject and verb

A sentence's subject and verb must create a meaningful idea.

| MISMATCH | The absence of detail screams out at the reader. [An *absence* cannot scream.] |
| REVISION | The reader immediately notices the absence of detail. |

When a form of the verb *be* joins two parts of a sentence, these two parts should be logically related.

➤ ~~The importance of free speech~~ is essential to a democracy.
 ^*Free speech*
 [*Importance* cannot be essential.]

(2) Mismatch of verbs and complements

A verb and its complement should fit together meaningfully. To make sure that a relative pronoun in the object position is connected logically to a verb, replace the pronoun with its antecedent. Then check that the verb and object have a logical connection.

MISMATCH	The inspiration <u>that the author created</u> touched young writers. [*The inspiration* is the antecedent for *that*. "The author created the inspiration" does not make sense.]
TEST	The author created the inspiration. [Not logical]
REVISION	The author inspired young writers.

Verbs used to report the words of others appear in signal phrases and are followed by specific types of complements. A few common verbs and their complements are listed below.

VERBS FOR SIGNAL PHRASES AND THEIR COMPLEMENTS

Verb + *that* **noun clause**

agree	claim	report	suggest
argue	demonstrate	state	think

➤ The researcher <u>reported</u> that the weather patterns had changed.

Verb + noun phrase + *that* **noun clause**

convince	remind	tell

➤ He <u>told</u> the reporters that he was planning to resign.

Verb + *wh-* **noun clause**

demonstrate	discuss	report	suggest
describe	explain	state	wonder

➤ She <u>described</u> what had happened.

EXERCISE 23.1

Revise the following sentences so that each verb is followed by a conventional complement. When you use reporting verbs before clauses, be sure the clauses follow one of these patterns.

1. The scholarship committee wondered that applications should follow criteria.

2. President Obama argued the spending cuts.

3. The two groups agreed how the problem could be solved.

4. Brown and Edwards described that improvements had been made to the old building.

5. They told that such a catastrophe could happen.

> ### 23e   Avoiding *is when, is where,* and *reason . . . is because* constructions

Some common structures in our spoken language are considered faulty in academic writing because of their mismatched sentence parts.

(1) Mismatches in definitions

In a definition, the term being defined should be followed by a noun or a noun phrase, not an adverbial clause. Avoid using *is when* or *is where.*

➤ *Ecology* is ~~when you~~ study the relationships among living organisms and between living organisms and their environment.

the ... *of* (insertions)

➤ *Exploitative competition* is ~~where~~ two or more organisms ~~vie~~ for a limited resource such as food.

the contest between ... *vying* (insertions)

(2) Mismatch of *reason* with *is because*

In academic writing, avoid the construction the *reason . . . is because.* The word *because* means "for the reason that." Saying "the reason is for the reason that" is redundant.

➤ The ~~reason the~~ old train station was closed ~~is~~ because it had fallen into disrepair.

> ### 23f   Including necessary words

Take care to include all necessary small words such as articles, prepositions, verbs, and conjunctions.

➤ Graduation will take place in *the* Bryce Jordan Center.

When a sentence has a compound verb (two verbs linked by a conjunction), you may need to supply a preposition for each verb.

➤ He neither **believes** *in* nor **approves of** exercise. [The verb *believes* does not work with *of.*]

All verbs, both auxiliary and main, should be included to make sentences complete.

➤ Voter turnout has never *been* and will never be 100 percent.

When a sentence consists of two short clauses and the verb in both clauses is the same, the verb in the second clause can be omitted.

➤ The wind **was** fierce and the thunder [was] deafening.

Include the word *that* before a clause when it makes the sentence easier to read.

➤ The paleontologists discovered *that* the fossil provided a link between the dinosaur and the modern bird.

That should always be retained when a sentence has two parallel clauses.

➤ The graph indicated **that the population had increased** but **that the number of homeowners had not**.

23g Completing comparisons

A comparison has two parts: someone or something is compared to someone or something else. Comparisons should include all necessary words to make the comparison complete.

➤ His first novel was better *than the one just published*.

➤ Your GRE scores are more important *than your internship experience*.

Complete comparisons must also be logical so that the meaning is clear.

UNCLEAR Her test scores are higher than the other students.

Are the *scores* being compared to *students*?

CLEAR	Her test scores are higher than **those of** the other students.
CLEAR	Her test scores are higher than the other **students' scores**.

23h Completing intensifiers

In speech, the intensifiers *so*, *such*, and *too* are used to mean "very," "unusually," or "extremely."

➤ That movie was **so** funny.

In academic and professional writing, however, the intensifiers *so*, *such*, and *too* require a completing phrase or clause.

➤ Child custody is **too** complex an issue **to cover in one class discussion**.

EXERCISE 23.2

Revise each of the following sentences to make them clear and complete.

1. Ralph McQuarrie sketched designs for R2D2 and Darth Vader, including his mask. Iain McCaig wanted to create something scarier for *The Phantom Menace*.

2. He drew generic male face with metal teeth and long red ribbons of hair falling in front of it.

3. He designed a face that looked as though it been flayed.

4. The evil visage of Darth Maul was so horrible. To balance the effect, McCaig added elegant black feathers.

24 Subordination and Coordination

Subordination and coordination indicate relationships between ideas and add variety to sentences.

24a Using subordination effectively

Using subordination allows you to clarify the relationships among the ideas in a sentence. Subordinate grammatical structures (dependent clauses, phrases, even single words) cannot stand alone; they are attached to or embedded in an independent (or main) clause.

(1) Subordinating conjunctions

A **subordinating conjunction** specifies the relationship between a dependent clause and an independent clause. For example, it might signal a causal relationship.

➤ Our team won the swim meet **because** **the members inspire one another**.

Some Frequently Used Subordinating Conjunctions

Cause	*because*
Concession	*although, even though*
Condition	*if, unless*
Effect	*so that*
Sequence	*before, after*
Time	*when*

By using subordinating conjunctions, you can combine short sentences and indicate how they are related.

> *After we*   *, we*
> We spent all day Saturday studying. We went to hear Kofi
> Annan at Schwab Auditorium.

(2) Relative pronouns

Dependent clauses can begin with a **relative pronoun** (*who, whom, which, that,* or *whose*).

> The Roman temple has a portico **that opens to the morning sun.**

> Steven Spielberg produced and directed a film about Abraham
> *, which quickly won many awards, including the Oscar for best actor*
> Lincoln. [Adding a dependent clause (beginning with the relative
>
> pronoun *which*) embeds details into the sentence without sacri-
>
> ficing conciseness.]

CAUTION

A relative clause beginning with *which* can modify a specific word or phrase—or refer to an entire independent clause. Take care to make your reference explicit.

> *As*   *he will have*
> ~~He is~~ a top graduate of our prestigious business school, ~~which should~~
> ~~guarantee him~~ many interviews.

24b Using coordination effectively

Coordinate means "being of equal rank." Use coordination to link elements that have the same grammatical form. For example, they may be two words that are both adjectives, two phrases that are both prepositional, or two clauses that are both independent.

    a **stunning** and **satisfying** conclusion [adjectives]

    in the attic or **in the basement** [prepositional phrases]

    The company was losing money, yet **the employees suspected nothing**. [independent or main clauses]

To indicate the relationship between coordinate words, phrases, or clauses, choose an appropriate coordinating conjunction.

Coordinating Conjunctions

Addition	*and*
Alternative	*or, not*
Cause	*for*
Contrast	*but, yet*
Result	*so*

➤ The hike to the top of Angels Landing has countless
switchbacks. ~~It also has~~ *and* dangerous drop-offs. [Using

coordination helps avoid unnecessary repetition.]

You can also link two independent clauses with a semicolon, a semicolon and an adverbial conjunction (such as *however* or *nevertheless*), or a colon. Each connection indicates a specific relationship between the two clauses.

➤ Hikers follow the path; climbers scale the cliff wall.

The careful punctuation of two independent clauses will help you avoid comma splices and fused sentences (chapter **19**).

MULTILINGUAL WRITERS
CHOOSING CONJUNCTIONS

In English, use either a coordinating conjunction or a subordinating conjunction (but not both) to signal a connection between clauses.

➤ **Because** he had a headache, ~~so~~ he went to the health center.

➤ *He*
  Because had a headache, **so** he went to the health center.

EXERCISE 24.1

Using subordination and coordination, revise the sentences in the following paragraph so that they emphasize the ideas you think are important.

[1]The Lummi tribe lives in the Northwest. [2]The Lummis have a belief about sorrow and loss. [3]They believe that grief is a burden. [4]According to their culture, this burden should not be carried alone. [5]After the terrorist attack on the World Trade Center, the Lummis wanted to help shoulder the burden of grief felt by others. [6]Some of the Lummis carve totem poles. [7]These carvers crafted a healing totem pole. [8]They gave this pole to the citizens of New York. [9]Many of the citizens of New York had family members who were killed in the terrorist attacks. [10]The Lummis do not believe that the pole itself heals. [11]Rather, they believe that healing comes from the prayers and songs said over it. [12]For them, healing is not the responsibility of a single person. [13]They believe that it is the responsibility of the community.

24c Avoiding faulty or excessive subordination and coordination

(1) Choosing precise conjunctions

Because subordinating conjunctions specify a relationship between ideas, choose them carefully.

> *Because*
> ➤ ^As time was running out, I randomly filled in the remaining circles on the exam sheet. [The use of *as* is distracting because it can mean either "because" or "while."]

Your choice of coordinating conjunction should also convey your meaning precisely.

➤ The rain continued to fall, ~~and~~ the concert was canceled. [To
indicate a cause-and-consequence relationship, *so* is more
precise than *and*, which indicates that the rain and concert are
equally significant.]

so (above the crossed-out "and")

(2) Excessive subordination and coordination

Subordination and coordination are less effective when overused. In the following sentence, two dependent clauses compete for the reader's focus.

INEFFECTIVE SUBORDINATION
Although researchers used to believe that ancient Egyptians
were the first to domesticate cats, they now think that cats may
have provided company for humans five thousand years earlier
because the intact skeleton of a cat has been discovered in a
Neolithic village on Cyprus.

The revision is clearer than the original sentence because it elim-
inates one of the dependent clauses.

REVISED
Although researchers used to believe that ancient Egyptians
were the first to domesticate cats, they now think that cats may
have provided company for humans five thousand years earlier.
They base their revised estimate on the discovery of an intact
cat skeleton in a Neolithic village on Cyprus.

Overuse of coordination results in a rambling sentence that is
difficult to follow.

INEFFECTIVE COORDINATION	The lake was surrounded by forest, and it was large and clean, so it looked refreshing.
REVISED	Surrounded by forest, the large, clean lake looked refreshing.

EXERCISE 24.2

Revise the following sentences to eliminate faulty or excessive coordination and subordination.

1. Duct tape was invented for the U.S. military during World War II to keep the moisture out of ammunition cases because it was strong and waterproof.

2. Duct tape was originally called "duck tape" as it was waterproof and ducks are like that too and because it was made of cotton duck, which is a durable, tightly woven material.

3. When the war was over, house builders used duck tape to connect ductwork together, and the builders started to refer to duck tape as "duct tape" and eventually the color of the tape changed from the green that was used during the war to silver, which matched the ducts.

4. Many new colorful forms of duct tape are available, although they are more expensive and less practical than standard silver.

25 Parallelism

Parallelism is the use of grammatically equivalent structures to clarify meaning and to emphasize ideas. Two or more elements are considered parallel when they have similar grammatical forms—when, for example, all are nouns or all are prepositional phrases.

25a Using coordinating conjunctions

Parallel elements are frequently joined by a **coordinating conjunction** (*and, but, or, yet, so, nor,* or *for*).

➤ The new teacher is both <u>determined</u> **and** <u>dedicated</u>.

➤ Her goals include <u>publicizing student and faculty research</u>, <u>increasing research funding</u>, **and** <u>improving research facilities</u>.

➤ He said <u>that we would conduct a similar project</u> **but** <u>that we would likely get different results</u>.

25b Repeating words and grammatical forms for paired ideas

Parallel structures allow you to pair ideas and create connections in sentences. By repeating a preposition, the infinitive marker *to*, or the introductory word of a clause, you can create parallel structures that are clear, succinct, and emphatic.

➤ She wanted her audience **to remember** the protest song and *to understand* ^ ~~be understanding of~~ its origin.

➤ The team vowed **that** they would support each other, **that** they would play their best, and *that* ^ they would win the tournament.

Repeating a pattern emphasizes the relationship of ideas. The following example includes the *-ing* form (present participle) of two different verbs.

➤ Many Detroit homeowners are selling their houses or *remodeling* ^ ~~should remodel~~ to enhance value.

Two or three structures joined by *and*, *but*, or *or* should be parallel, as in the following sentence.

➤ Mortgage rates *rise,* ^ ~~are rising~~, and building codes change, but the real estate market remains strong.

THINKING RHETORICALLY
PARALLELISM

Parallel elements make your writing easy and pleasurable to read. But consider breaking from the parallel pattern to emphasize a point. For example, to describe a friend, you could start with two adjectives and then switch to a noun phrase.

➤ My friend Alison is **kind**, **modest**, and **the smartest mathematician in the state**.

25c Creating parallelism in lists, headings, and outlines

Each item in a list or formal outline should be parallel (**2c**). Headings in any document should be in parallel form whenever possible (**7a**).

➤ People all around me are **buying**, **remodeling**, or **selling** their houses.

➤ In his speech, the president charged his generation with lofty goals: (1) reigniting economic growth, (2) restoring the American dream, and (3) ~~to make sure~~ *putting* government *to* works for average citizens.

25d Using correlative conjunctions

Correlative conjunctions (or **correlatives**) are pairs of words that link other words, phrases, or clauses, including *both . . . and, either . . . or, neither . . . nor, not only . . . but also,* and *whether . . . or.* Always use the same grammatical structures following each conjunction in the pair.

➤ **Whether** <u>at home</u> **or** <u>at school</u>, he is always busy.

His team practices not only

➤ ~~Not only practicing~~ at 6 a.m. during the week, but ~~his team~~
also ~~scrimmages~~ on Sunday afternoons. [The editing makes the
elements after the correlative conjunctions *not only . . . but also*
parallel.]

EXERCISE 25.1

Rewrite the following sentences to create parallel structures.

1. Helen was praised by the vice president, and her administrative
   assistant admired her.

2. When she hired new employees for her department, she looked
   for applicants who were accomplished, able to work hard, and
   able to speak clearly.

3. At meetings, Helen was always prepared, participating actively
   yet politely, and generated innovative responses to department
   concerns.

4. In her annual report, she wrote that her most important
   achievements were attracting new majors and scholarship
   donations were higher.

5. When asked about her leadership style, Helen said that she
   preferred collaborating with others rather than to work alone in
   her office.

6. Whether in the department's meetings or conventions, Helen
   prepared her remarks in advance.

26 Emphasis

In any piece of writing, some of your ideas are more important than others. You can use emphasis to make those ideas stand out.

26a Placing words and using punctuation

In every sentence some words receive more emphasis than others. In general, the major stress of any sentence comes at the end or toward the end of a sentence. When you read aloud the brief sentence *We discussed the film*, you will likely stress *film*. Take advantage of this tendency by finishing a sentence with the most important information—usually an idea that is new to the reader.

➤ *Some viewers* ~~The film's stop-motion animation was~~ raved about *the film's stop-motion animation.* ~~by many viewers.~~

To ensure that readers focus on the end of the sentence, use an occasional colon or dash to set off the information (**32b, 35d**).

➤ The everyday episodes of online cruelty added together became what he was warned about**:** bullying.

26b Ordering ideas from least to most important

By arranging your ideas in **climactic order**—from least important to most important—you build up suspense. In the following example, the writer places the reasons to avoid the online model of Facebook in order of increasing importance:

➤ A growing wave of Internet start-ups seeks to avoid the Facebook model that draws users online, consumes all their free time, and addicts them to an alternative to real life.

26c Repeating important words

Repetition used deliberately emphasizes key words or ideas (**25b**).

We **forget** all too soon the things we thought we could never **forget**. We **forget** the loves and betrayals alike, **forget** what we whispered and what we screamed, **forget** who we are.

—JOAN DIDION, "On Keeping a Notebook"

26d Inverting word order

Most sentences begin with a subject and end with a predicate (**27c**). When you move words out of their normal order, you draw attention to them. Notice the inverted word order in the second sentence of the following passage.

[1]The Library Committee met with the City Council on several occasions to persuade them to fund the building of a library annex. [2]So successful were their efforts that a new wing will be added by next year. [3]This wing will contain archival materials that were previously stored in the basement.

The modifier *so successful* appears at the beginning of the sentence, rather than in its normal position, after the verb: Their efforts were *so successful* that . . . . The inverted word order emphasizes the committee's accomplishment.

MULTILINGUAL WRITERS
INVERTING WORD ORDER

Although most English sentences take the form of subject-verb-object, more interesting ones involve inversions of various types. Sometimes the main verb in the form of a participle is placed at the beginning of the sentence. The subject and the auxiliary verb(s) are then inverted.

➤ **Carved** into the bench **were someone's initials**.

    [COMPARE: Someone's initials were carved into the bench.]

An adjective may also begin a sentence. In this type of sentence, the subject and the linking verb are inverted.

➤ **Crucial** to our success **was the dedication of our employees**.

    [COMPARE: The dedication of our employees was crucial to our success.]

26e Using an occasional short sentence

In a paragraph of long or complicated sentences, a short sentence works well for emphasis, especially when it appears immediately after an especially long sentence.

➤ After organizing the kitchen, buying the groceries, slicing the vegetables, mowing the lawn, weeding the garden, hanging the decorations, and setting up the grill, I was ready to have a good time when my guests arrived. **Then the phone rang**.

Take care not to use too many short sentences; the overall effect is choppy (**27a**).

EXERCISE 26.1

Use the strategy in parentheses to add emphasis in the following sentences. You may add or delete words as necessary.

1. (climactic order) In the 1960 Olympics, Wilma Rudolph tied the world record in the 100-meter race, she tied the record in the 400-meter relay, she won the hearts of fans from around the world, and she broke the record in the 200-meter race.

2. (inversion) Rudolph's Olympic achievement is impressive, but her victory over a crippling disease is even more spectacular.

3. (occasional short sentence) Rudolph was born prematurely, weighing only four and one-half pounds. As a child, she suffered from double pneumonia, scarlet fever, and then polio.

4. (inversion) Her siblings' willingness to help was essential to her recovery, as were her mother's vigilant care and her own determination.

5. (climactic order) Rudolph set a scoring record in basketball, she set the standard for future track and field stars, and she set an Olympic record in track.

27   Variety

A variety of sentence types and lengths makes your writing lively and distinctive.

27a   Varying sentence length and form

Avoid the choppy effect of a series of short sentences by combining some of them into longer sentences. You can combine sentences by using coordinating conjunctions (such as *and*, *but*, and *or*) to show a connection.

➤ Minneapolis ~~is one of~~ the Twin Cities. ~~St. Paul is the other.~~ ~~They~~
   _{and St. Paul are called}   _{, but}   _{they}
   differ in many ways.

You can also combine sentences using subordinating conjunctions (such as *because*, *although*, and *when*) or relative pronouns (such as *who*, *that*, and *which*).

➤ _{Although legislation}
   ~~Legislation~~ on space tourism has not been passed. ~~Plans~~ for
                                                          _{, plans}
   a commercial rocket service are going forward anyway. [Adding
   although creates a dependent clause and clarifies the logical
   relationship between ideas.]

➤ Today, lawmakers discussed some new legislation. ~~This legislation~~
                                                     _{that}
   would promote the safety of rocket passengers. [The editing puts
   emphasis on the first clause. The relative pronoun *that* introduces a description of the legislation.]

27b Varying sentence openings

Many writers begin their sentences with a subject. Although this pattern is common, relying on it too heavily—especially in too many sentences in a row—can make writing sound dull. Experiment with the following alternatives for beginning your sentences.

BEGINNING WITH AN ADVERB

➤ *Immediately, the* ~~The~~ dentist stopped drilling ~~immediately~~ and asked me how I was doing.

BEGINNING WITH A PHRASE

➤ *Reflecting* *the reporter* ~~The reporter, reflecting~~ on the election, understood clearly how the incumbent defeated the challenger. [participial phrase]

➤ **A town of historic interest**, Santa Fe also has many art galleries. [appositive phrase]

BEGINNING WITH A TRANSITIONAL EXPRESSION

In each of the following examples, the transitional expression shows the relationship between the ideas in the pair of sentences.

➤ Many restaurants close within a few years of opening. **But** others, which offer good food at reasonable prices, become well established.

➤ Independently owned restaurants struggle to get started for a number of reasons. **First of all**, they have to compete against successful restaurant chains.

BEGINNING WITH A DEPENDENT CLAUSE

➤ When I was twelve years old, I started making movies. [COMPARE: I started making movies when I was twelve years old.]

27c   Using cumulative and periodic sentences

In a cumulative sentence, the idea expressed in the independent clause comes first, followed by supporting ideas and details.

➤ **The day was hot for June,** a pale sun burning in a cloudless sky, wilting the last of the irises, the rhododendron blossoms drooping.
—ADAM HASLETT, "Devotion"

In a **periodic sentence**, however, the independent clause comes last, emphasized just before the period.

➤ Because the scar resulting from the burn is typically much larger than the original lesion, allowing for less intricacy, **the designs tend to be much simpler than those used in tattoos**.
—NINA JABLONSKI, *Skin: A Natural History*

Both of these types of sentences can be effective. Because cumulative sentences are more common, however, the less common periodic sentence tends to provide emphasis.

27d   Using questions, exclamations, and commands

You can vary the sentences in a paragraph by introducing an occasional question, exclamation, or command.

QUESTION

It can be uncomfortable for a boy to watch the frenzied, uninhibited enthusiasm of girl fans screaming for their idols, whether it's Sinatra, the Beatles, or Michael Jackson. That is partly jealousy too—*who wouldn't want to be the one who inspires girls to make that kind of noise?* But it's also partly because we envy that enthusiasm.
—ROB SHEFFIELD, *Talking to Girls about Duran Duran*

You can either answer the question or let readers answer it for themselves, in which case it is called a **rhetorical question**.

EXCLAMATION

But at other moments, the classroom is so lifeless or painful or confused—and I so powerless to do anything about it—that my claim to be a teacher seems a transparent sham. Then the enemy is everywhere: in those students from some alien planet, in the subject I thought I knew, and in the personal pathology that keeps me earning my living this way. *What a fool I was to imagine that I had mastered this occult art—harder to divine than tea leaves and impossible for mortals to do even passably well!*

—PARKER PALMER, *The Courage to Teach*

COMMAND

Now I stare and stare at people shamelessly. *Stare.* It's the way to educate your eye.

—WALKER EVANS, *Unclassified*

In this case, a one-word command, "Stare," provides variety.

EXERCISE 27.1

Use the strategy in parentheses to revise the following sentences for variety. You may want to combine, invert, shorten, or lengthen some of the sentences. Add or delete words as needed to provide clarification, relationships, and emphasis.

1. (combine) The civil rights activist and the conservative pundit appear to have little in common. They both take pleasure in addressing audiences.

2. (combine) Their ideologies could not be more different. Both see the Bible as a moral foundation. The well-being of the United States should be reconstructed from that biblical foundation.

3. (begin with an adverb and combine) Both liberal and conservative activists argue that their agenda is best for America's future. Neither group mentions the power and potential of working together.

EXERCISE 27.2

Rewrite each sentence so that it does not begin with a subject.

1. (begin with a phrase) John Spilsbury was an engraver and mapmaker from London who made the first jigsaw puzzle in about 1760.

2. (begin with a transitional expression) He pasted a map onto a piece of wood and used a fine-bladed saw to cut around the borders of the countries.

3. (begin with an adverb) The jigsaw puzzle was first an educational toy and has been a mainstay in households all over the world ever since its invention.

4. (begin with a phrase) The original puzzles were quite expensive because the wooden pieces were cut by hand.

5. (begin with an adverb) Most puzzles are made of cardboard today.

6. (periodic sentence) Lee's passion became mountain biking after he recovered, built up his strength, and gained self-confidence.

7. (cumulative sentence) He received donations and help from the community. His neighbors walked his two dogs. His coworkers brought precooked meals for the week.

8. (change one sentence to a question) There are multiple activities that can help survivors of traumatic brain injury toward recovery. Advocates believe that reviewing and practicing conversation and people skills are both essential to success.

L

EFFECTIVE LANGUAGE

28 Good Usage

Using the right words at the right time can make the difference between having your ideas taken seriously and seeing them brushed aside. The right words make your writing easy and pleasurable to read; they achieve a clear style that your audience understands and is appropriate for the occasion. Sentences that are ornate—including flowery or fancy language—may not be understood by a broad audience.

ORNATE   The majority believes that achievement derives primarily from the diligent pursuit of allocated tasks.

CLEAR   Most people believe that success results from hard work.

28a Appropriate word choice

You may find yourself writing for an audience that you know will welcome slang and colloquial expressions or for a specialized audience who will immediately understand technical jargon. Otherwise, the following advice can help you determine which words to use and which to avoid. A good dictionary will also help you. Words labeled *dialect, slang, colloquial, nonstandard,* or *unconventional* are generally inappropriate for academic and professional writing. If a word has no label, you can safely assume that it can be used in writing for school or work.

(1) Slang

Slang covers a wide range of words or expressions that are considered casual or fashionable by people in a particular age group, locality, or profession. Although such phrases are used in conversation or in writing intended to mimic conversation, they are usually out of place in academic or professional writing.

(2) Conversational (or colloquial) words

Words labeled *colloquial* in a dictionary are fine for casual conversation and for written dialogues or personal essays on a light topic. Such words are sometimes used for special effect in academic writing, but you should usually replace them with more appropriate words. For example, conversational words such as *dumb* and *kid around* could be replaced by *illogical* and *tease*.

(3) Regionalisms

Regionalisms—such as *poke* for "bag" and *sweeper* for "vacuum cleaner"—can make essay writing lively and distinctive, but they are often considered too informal for most academic and professional writing.

(4) Technical words or jargon

When writing for a diverse audience, an effective writer will not refer to the need for bifocals as *presbyopia*. However, technical language is appropriate when the audience can understand it (as when one physician writes to another about tachycardia) or when the audience (a heart patient, for example) would benefit by learning the terms in question.

28b Inclusive language

By choosing words that are inclusive rather than exclusive, you invite readers into your writing. Prejudiced or derogatory language about skin color, cultural-ethnic background, body size or shape, physical or mental ability, or sexual orientation has no place in academic or professional writing; using it undermines your authority and credibility.

(1) Nonsexist language

Effective writers show equal respect for males and females. For example, they avoid using *man* to refer to people in general because they understand that the word excludes women.

> *Achievements [OR Human achievements]*
> **Man's** ~~achievements~~ in science are impressive.

> *Spouses*
> ~~The~~ **wives** of the university's administrators always meet on
> the Friday afternoon before a football game.

TIPS FOR AVOIDING SEXIST LANGUAGE

When reviewing drafts, revise the following types of sexist language.

- **Generic *he/his*.** Revise by changing *he* to *he or she*, using a
  plural form, or rewriting the sentence.

  > *Doctors*   *their*
  > A ~~doctor~~ should listen to ~~his~~ patients.

  > By listening to patients, **doctors** obtain important diagnostic
  > information. [elimination of *his* by revising the sentence]

- **Terms such as *mankind*.** Replace terms such as *mankind* or
  those with *-ess*, *-ix*, or *-man* endings (*stewardess*, *chairman*) with
  gender-neutral terms.

  > *all working people*
  > Labor laws benefit ~~the common man~~.

- **Stereotypical gender roles**. Use gender-neutral terms.

  > *University pilots*   *their flight plans*
  > Each ~~university pilot~~ must supply ~~his flight plan~~ before takeoff.

- **Inconsistent use of titles.** Use titles or full names, but do so
  consistently.

  > *Peter and Mary Holmes*
  > ~~Mr. Holmes and his wife, Mary,~~ took a long trip to China.
  > [title removed]

- **Unstated gender assumption.** Avoid stereotypical language and
  assumptions.

  > *Have*   *parents*
  > ~~Ask~~ your ~~mother to~~ make your costume for the school pageant.

EXERCISE 28.1

Revise the following sentences to eliminate sexist language.

1. The men's and ladies' teams volunteered to raise money for new athletic uniforms.

2. Mothers should read to their small children.

3. Some fans admired the actress because of her movies; others praised her daring as an aviatrix.

4. For six years, he worked as a mailman in a small town.

(2) Nonracist language

Rarely is it necessary to identify anyone's race or ethnicity in academic or professional writing except, for example, if you are writing a demographic report, an argument against existing racial inequities, or a historical account of a particular event involving ethnic groups. Determining which terms a particular group prefers can be difficult because preferences sometimes vary within a group and change over time. One conventional way to refer to Americans of a specific descent is to include an adjective before the word *American*: *African American*, *Asian American*, *European American*, *Latin American*, *Mexican American*, *Native American*. In addition to *African American* and *European American*, *Black* (or *black*) and *White* (or *white*) have long been used. People of Spanish-speaking descent may prefer *Chicano/Chicana*, *Hispanic*, *Latino/Latina*, *Puerto Rican*, or other terms. Members of cultures that are indigenous to North America may prefer a specific name such as *Cherokee* or *Haida*, though some also accept *American Indian*, *indigenous peoples*, or *Native Peoples*.

(3) Writing about any difference respectfully

If a writing assignment requires you to distinguish people based on age, physical or mental ability, geographical area, religion, or sexual orientation, show respect to the human beings you discuss by using the terms they prefer.

(a) Referring to age   Although some people object to the term *senior citizen*, a better alternative has not emerged. When used respectfully, the term refers to a person who has reached the age of retirement (but may not have decided to retire) and is eligible for certain privileges granted by society. However, if you know your audience would object to the term *senior citizen*, find out which alternative is preferred.

(b) Referring to disability or illness   A current recommendation for referring to disabilities and illnesses is "to put the person first." Place focus on the individual rather than on the limitation: *persons with disabilities* is preferred over *disabled persons*, *the teenager with autism* rather than *that autistic*. You can find out whether such person-first expressions are preferred by noting whether they are used in the articles and books (or by the people) you consult.

(c) Referring to geographical areas   Certain geographical terms need to be used with special care. Though most frequently used to refer to people from the United States, the term *American* may also refer to people from Canada, Mexico, and Central or South America. If your audience may be confused by this term, use *people from the United States* or *U.S. citizens* instead.

The term *Arab* refers to people who speak Arabic. If you cannot use specific terms such as *Iraqi* or *Saudi Arabian*, be sure you know that a country's people speak Arabic and not another language. Iranians, for example, are not Arabs because they speak Farsi.

(d) Referring to religion   Reference to a person's religion should be made only if it is relevant. Because religions have both conservative and liberal followers, be careful not to make generalizations about political stances.

(e) Referring to sexual orientation   If your purpose for writing makes it necessary to identify sexual orientation, choose terms used by the people you are discussing. For instance, *LGBTQ* includes preferred terms for all the people who are not firmly heterosexual: lesbian, gay, bisexual, transgender, or questioning.

29 Precise Word Choice

By choosing the right word and putting it in the right place, you can communicate exactly what you mean and make your writing memorable to your intended audience.

29a Accurate and precise word choice

(1) Denotations and connotations

Denotations are definitions of words, such as those that appear in dictionaries. For example, the noun *beach* denotes a sandy or pebbly shore. Select words whose denotations convey your point exactly.

➤ Many of Sofia Coppola's films are ~~obsessed~~ _fascinated_ with celebrity. [Because *obsessed* can mean "an unhealthy interest" its use is imprecise.]

Connotations are the associations evoked by a word. The context in which a word appears affects the associations it evokes. In a report on shoreline management, *beach* has scientific and geographic connotations; in a fashion magazine, this word is associated with bathing suits, sunglasses, and sunscreen. The challenge for writers is to choose the words that are most likely to spark the appropriate connotations in their readers' minds.

➤ Mr. Kreuger's ~~relentlessness~~ ^{persistence} has earned praise from his supervisors.

[*Relentlessness*, a quality with negative connotations, is unlikely to be praised.]

(2) Providing readers with helpful details

A **general word** is all-inclusive, indefinite, and sweeping in scope. A **specific word** is precise, definite, and limited in scope.

General	Specific	More Specific/Concrete
food	fast food	cheeseburger
place	city	Atlanta

An **abstract word** refers to a concept or idea, a quality or trait, or anything else that cannot be touched, heard, or seen. A **concrete word** signifies a particular object, a specific action, or anything that can be touched, heard, or seen.

ABSTRACT   democracy, evil, strength, charity

CONCRETE   mosquito, hammer, plastic, fog

As you select words, be as specific and concrete as you can. Ask yourself questions about what you want to say: Exactly who? Exactly what? Exactly when? Exactly where? Exactly how? In the following example, notice what a difference concrete words can make in expressing an idea and how adding details can expand or develop it.

VAGUE	She has kept no reminders of performing in her youth.
SPECIFIC	She has kept no sequined costume, no photographs, no fliers or posters from that part of her youth.

—LOUISE ERDRICH, "The Leap"

(3) Figurative language

Figurative language is the use of words in an imaginative rather than a literal sense. Similes and metaphors are the chief **figures of speech**. A **simile** is a comparison of dissimilar things that includes *like* or *as*. A **metaphor** is an implied comparison of dissimilar things, without *like* or *as*.

> **SIMILE**
>
> He was **like a piece of rare and delicate china which was always being saved from breaking and finally fell**.
>
> —ALICE WALKER, "To Hell with Dying"

> **METAPHOR**
>
> His **money was a sharp pair of scissors** that snipped rapidly through tangles of red tape.
>
> —HISAYE YAMAMOTO, "The Brown House"

29b   Clichés and euphemisms

When forced or overused, certain expressions lose their impact. For example, the expressions *bite the dust*, *breath of fresh air*, and *smooth as silk* were once striking and thus effective. Excessive use, though, has drained them of their original force and made them **clichés**. Newer expressions such as *put a spin on something* and *think outside the box* have also lost their vitality because of overuse. Nonetheless, clichés are so much a part of the language that nearly every writer uses them from time to time. But effective writers often give a fresh twist to an old saying.

I seek a narrative, a fiction, to order days like the one I spent several years ago, on a gray June day in Chicago, when I took a roller-coaster ride on the bell curve of my experience.

—GAYLE PEMBERTON, "The Zen of Bigger Thomas"

[Notice how much more effective this expression is than a reference to "being on an emotional roller coaster."]

Sometimes writers coin new expressions called **euphemisms** to substitute for words that have coarse or unpleasant connotations. To avoid the word *dying*, for example, a writer might say that someone is *passing on*. However, euphemisms sometimes obscure facts. Euphemisms such as *revenue enhancement* for *tax hike* and *pre-owned* for *used* are considered insincere or deceitful. And a euphemism such as *ethnic cleansing* is a frightening camouflage for actual *genocide*.

EXERCISE 29.1

Replace the following overused expressions with carefully chosen words. Then use the replacements in sentences.

1. all ears

2. back to the drawing board

3. take a breather

4. mail it in

29c | Idioms and collocations

Idioms are fixed expressions whose meanings cannot be entirely determined by knowing the meanings of their parts—*pull weight, turn on a dime, put a sock in it*. **Collocations** are common combinations of words (*strong coffee, fast plane*). Unlike idioms, they have meanings that *can* be determined by knowing the meanings of their parts—*depend on, fond of, little while, right now*. Regardless of whether you are using an idiom or a collocation, if you make even a small inadvertent change to the expected wording, you may distract or confuse your readers.

➤ She bought two ~~blocks~~ *bars* of soap.

➤ They had ~~an invested~~ *a vested* interest in the project.

As you edit your writing, keep an eye out for idioms or collocations that might not be worded correctly. Then check a dictionary or the **Glossary of Usage** at the end of the book to ensure that your usage is appropriate. Writers sometimes have trouble with the following collocations, all of which contain prepositions.

CHOOSING THE RIGHT PREPOSITION

Instead of	Use
according **with**	according **to** the source
accused **for**	accused **of** the crime
based **off of**	based **on** the novel
in accordance **to**	in accordance **with** policy
independent **to**	independent **of** his family
happened **on**	happened **by** accident
superior **than**	superior **to** others

29d Clear definitions

When words have more than one meaning, establish which meaning you have in mind in a particular piece of writing. A definition can set the terms of the discussion.

➤ In this essay, I use the word *communism* **in the Marxist sense of social organization based on the holding of all property in common**.

A **formal definition** first states the term to be defined, then puts it into a class, and finally differentiates it from other members of that class.

➤ A *phosphene* [term] is **a luminous visual image** [class] that **results from applying pressure to the eyeball** [differentiation].

A synonym or examples can easily clarify the meaning of a term.

➤ *Machismo*, **confidence with an attitude**, can be a pose rather than a reality.

➤ Many homophones **(such as *be* and *bee*, *in* and *inn*, or *see* and *sea*)** are not spelling problems.

30 Conciseness

Effective writers convey their thoughts clearly and efficiently, choosing each word wisely, making sure their readers understand.

30a Eliminating wordiness and other redundancies

After writing a first draft, review your sentences to make sure that they contain only the words necessary to make your point.

(1) Redundancy

Restating a key point in different words can help readers understand it. But if you rephrase readily understood terms, your work will suffer from **redundancy**—repetition for no good reason.

➤ Ballerinas auditioned ~~in the tryouts~~ for *The Nutcracker*.

works as a farrier
➤ Mr. Hickey ~~is currently employed~~ at Blue Meadow Farms~~, where he works as a farrier.~~

MULTILINGUAL WRITERS
USING RELATIVE PRONOUNS

Review your sentences to make sure that no clause includes both a personal pronoun (*I, me, he, him, she, her, it*) and a relative pronoun (*who, that, which*) referring to the same antecedent.

➤ The drug **that** we were testing ~~it~~ has not been approved by the Food and Drug Administration.

➤ The professor who directs the emphasis ~~she~~ likes to meet with students.

---

(2) Unnecessary words and wordy phrases

As you edit a draft, delete words that add no meaning to adjacent words and shorten wordy expressions.

If
➤ ~~In the event that~~ taxes are raised, ~~expect complaints on the part of the voters.~~ *voters will complain.*

Students without access to their cars
➤ ~~In my humble opinion, the fact that~~ students are forbidden ~~from bringing cars to campus is one feature of my belief that they~~ will not drink and drive.

In addition, watch for vague words such as *area, aspect, factor, feature, kind, situation, thing,* and *type.* They may signal wordiness.

Effective
➤ ~~In an employment situation, effective~~ communication is essential at work.

REPLACEMENTS FOR WORDY EXPRESSIONS

Instead of	Use
at this moment (point) in time	now, today
due to the fact that	because
for the purpose of	for
it is clear (obvious) that	clearly (obviously)
without a doubt	undoubtedly
in the final analysis	finally
in my opinion	[can be omitted]
in today's society	today

USELESS WORDS IN COMMON PHRASES

yellow [in color]   connect [up together]
at 9:45 a.m. [in the morning]   [really and truly] fearless
[basic] essentials   circular [in shape]
[make an] estimate   large [in size]

(3) *There are* and *it is*

There or *it* may function as an **expletive**—a word that signals that the subject of the sentence will follow the verb, usually a form of *be*. Writers use expletives to emphasize words that would not be emphasized in the typical subject-verb order.

➤ Three children were playing in the yard. [typical order]

➤ There were three children playing in the yard. [use of expletive]

However, if you find that you have drafted several sentences that begin with expletives, revise a few of them.

➤ ~~There were hundreds~~ of fans crowding onto the field.
   Hundreds   *were*

➤ ~~It~~ was frightening ~~to join the crowd.~~
   Joining the crowd   .

(4) Relative pronouns

The relative pronouns *who*, *which*, or *that* can frequently be deleted without affecting the meaning of a sentence. If one of these pronouns is followed by a form of the verb *be* (*am, is, are, was, were*), you can often omit the pronoun and some-times the verb as well.

➤ The change ~~that~~ the young senator proposed yesterday angered most legislators.

➤ Bromo, ~~which is~~ Java's highest mountain, towers above its neighbors.

30b Using elliptical constructions

An **elliptical construction** is one that deliberately omits words that can be understood from the context.

➤ Speed is the goal for some swimmers, endurance ~~is the goal~~ for others, and relaxation ~~is the goal~~ for still others.

Sometimes, as an aid to clarity, commas mark omissions in elliptical constructions.

➤ My family functioned like a baseball team: my mom was the coach; my brother, the pitcher; and my sister, the shortstop. [Use semicolons to separate items with internal commas.]

EXERCISE 30.1

Rewrite the sentences below to eliminate wordiness.

1. He submitted in an application letter and résumé for every job advertised.

2. Prior to the time of the ceremony, he had not received an award.

3. The library is located in the vicinity of the post office.

4. The fans who were watching television made a lot of noise.

5. Compulsory attendance in all English classes is required.

6. It is important to register early.

P

PUNCTUATION

31 The Comma

Pauses are often signaled by commas, but pauses are not a reliable guide for comma placement. Commas are often called for where speakers do not pause, and speakers may pause when no comma is necessary. Better guidance for using commas comes from some basic principles for comma usage.

31a Joining clauses with coordinating conjunctions

Use a comma before a coordinating conjunction (*and*, *but*, *for*, *nor*, *or*, *so*, or *yet*) to join independent clauses.

➤ George H. W. Bush served as president from 1989 to 1993**,** **and** his son George W. Bush served from 2001 to 2009.

➤ Presidents Andrew Johnson and Lyndon Johnson shared the same last name**,** **but** they were not related.

Without the conjunctions, the sentences above would be considered comma splices; without both the conjunctions and the commas, the sentences would be considered fused sentences (see chapter **19**).

When clauses are short, commas may be omitted.

➤ His grandson ran for president but his son did not.

EXERCISE 31.1

Insert commas where needed.

1. When people get goose bumps, they may be reacting to a sudden drop in the temperature or they may be responding to a strong emotion.

2. In general, people notice goose bumps on their forearms but some people also report having goose bumps on their legs.

3. When a goose is plucked, its flesh protrudes and these protrusions are what goose bumps supposedly resemble but the technical term for goose bumps is *piloerection.*

4. The German and Italian languages also have words that refer to goose flesh but French and Spanish translations refer to hens.

5. Many people report that they get goose bumps when they hear about heroic behavior yet it is not uncommon for people to have a similar response to beauty in nature or art.

6. Not only humans experience piloerection but other mammals do as well.

31b Setting off introductory words, phrases, or clauses

Place a comma after a word, phrase, or clause that comes before the main clause of a sentence.

➤ **Clearly,** the project deserves additional funding.

➤ **Despite a downturn in the national economy,** the number of students enrolled in this university has increased.

➤ **Because many students cannot afford tuition,** they find part-time jobs or apply for loans.

A comma may be omitted after a short introduction as long as the sentence is still clear.

➤ **In 2013** the enrollment at the university increased.

Insert necessary commas in the following paragraph. Explain why each comma is needed. Some sentences may not require commas.

[1]If you had to describe sound would you call it a wave? [2]Although sound cannot be seen people have described it this way for a long time. [3]In fact the Greek philosopher Aristotle believed that sound traveling through air was like waves in the sea. [4]Envisioning waves in the air he hypothesized that sound would not be able to pass through a vacuum because there would be no air to transmit it. [5]Aristotle's hypothesis was not tested until nearly two thousand years later. [6]In 1654 Otto von Guericke found that he could not hear a bell ringing inside the vacuum he had created. [7]Thus Guericke established the necessity of air for sound transmission. [8]However although most sound reaches us through the air it travels faster through liquids and solids.

31c   Separating elements in a series

A comma appears after each item in a series except the last one.

➤ Ethics are based on **moral, social,** or **cultural values**. [words]

➤ The company's code of ethics encourages **seeking criticism of work, correcting mistakes,** and **acknowledging the contributions of everyone**. [phrases]

Following a tradition in print and online journalism, some writers omit the comma between the final two items in a series. But omitting the comma can lead to confusion, and including it is never wrong.

THINKING RHETORICALLY
COMMAS AND CONJUNCTIONS IN A SERIES

How do the following sentences differ?

➤ We discussed them all: life**,** liberty**, and** the pursuit of happiness.

➤ We discussed them all: life **and** liberty **and** the pursuit of happiness.

➤ We discussed them all: life**,** liberty**,** the pursuit of happiness.

The first sentence follows conventional guidelines; that is, a comma and a conjunction precede the last element in the series. The less conventional second and third sentences do more than convey information. Having two conjunctions and no commas, the second sentence slows down the pace of the reading, causing stress to be placed on each of the three elements in the series. In contrast, the third sentence, with commas but no conjunctions, speeds up the reading, as if to suggest that the rights listed do not need to be stressed because they are so familiar. To get a sense of how your sentences will be read and understood, try reading them aloud to yourself.

31d | **Separating coordinate adjectives**

Two or more adjectives that precede the same noun are called **coordinate adjectives**. To test whether adjectives are coordinate, either interchange them or put *and* between them. If the altered version of the phrase is acceptable, the adjectives are coordinate and should be separated by a comma.

➤ Crossing the **rushing, shallow** creek, I slipped off a rock and fell into the water. [COMPARE: a rushing and shallow creek OR a shallow, rushing creek]

The adjectives in the following sentence are not separated by a comma. Notice that they cannot be interchanged or joined by *and*.

➤ Sitting in the water, I saw an **old wooden** bridge. [NOT a wooden old bridge OR an old and wooden bridge]

31e   Setting off nonessential elements

Words, phrases, and clauses are considered nonessential when the information they convey is unnecessary for identifying who or what is being described or discussed. All nonessential elements should be set off by commas. No commas are used when the information answers the question *Which?*

ESSENTIAL WORD	The mountaineer **Walter Harper** was the first to summit Denali. [Which mountaineer? Walter Harper—no commas are needed]
NONESSENTIAL WORD	The first mountaineer to summit Denali**,** **Walter Harper,** was an Alaska Native. [Which first mountaineer? does not make sense—commas are needed]
ESSENTIAL PHRASE	The mountain **towering above us** brought to mind our abandoned plan for climbing it. [Which mountain? the one towering above us—no commas are needed]
NONESSENTIAL PHRASE	Denali**,** **towering above us,** brought to mind our abandoned plan for climbing it. [Which Denali? does not make sense—commas are needed]

ESSENTIAL CLAUSE	They climbed a mountain **that is over fifteen thousand feet high**. [Which mountain? one that is over fifteen thousand feet high—no comma is needed]
NONESSENTIAL CLAUSE	They climbed Denali**,** **which is over fifteen thousand feet high**. [Which Denali? does not make sense—a comma is needed]

31f Setting off transitions, parenthetical expressions, and contrasted elements

Commas customarily set off transitional expressions such as *for example*, *that is*, *however*, and *namely*.

➤ Travelers**,** **for example,** must be prepared for the unexpected.

Because they generally indicate little or no pause in reading, transitional expressions such as *also*, *too*, *at least*, and *thus* need not be set off by commas.

➤ Traveling to exotic places **thus** requires planning.

Use commas to set off parenthetical elements, such as words or phrases that provide commentary you wish to stress.

➤ Over the past year, my flights have**,** **miraculously,** been on time.

Commas set off sentence elements in which words such as *never* and *unlike* express contrast.

➤ A planet**,** unlike a star**,** reflects rather than generates light.

EXERCISE 31.3

Set off nonessential elements with commas.

1. Maine Coons long-haired cats with bushy tails are known for their size.

2. The largest cat on record for example was forty-eight inches long.

3. These animals which are extremely gentle despite their large size often weigh twenty pounds.

4. Most Maine Coons have exceptionally high intelligence for cats which enables them to recognize language and even to open doors.

5. Unlike most cats Maine Coons will play fetch with their owners.

6. According to a legend later proven to be false Maine Coons are descendants from Turkish Angora cats owned by Marie Antoinette.

31g   Setting off dates, place names, and elements in an address

Use commas to make dates, place names, and addresses easy to read.

➤ Martha left for Peru on **Wednesday, February 12, 2013,** and returned on March 12.

➤ **Nashville, Tennessee,** is the largest country-and-western music center in the United States.

➤ I had to write to **Ms. Melanie Hobson, Hobson Computing, 2873 Central Avenue, Orange Park, FL 32065**. [No comma is used between the state abbreviation and the zip code.]

31h Setting off quotations

Many sentences containing direct quotations also contain signal phrases (or attributive tags) such as *The author claims* or *According to the author*. Whether they appear at the beginning, in the middle, or at the end of a sentence, signal phrases should be set off with commas.

➤ According to Jacques Barzun, "It is a false analogy with science that makes one think latest is best."

➤ "It is a false analogy with science," claims Jacques Barzun, "that makes one think latest is best."

➤ "It is a false analogy with science that makes one think latest is best," claims Jacques Barzun.

31i Unnecessary commas

Commas are not used between the following elements.

SUBJECT AND VERB	**Rain** at frequent intervals **produces** mosquitoes.
TWO VERBS THAT AGREE WITH THE SAME SUBJECT	I **read** the comments carefully and then **started** my revision.
REPORTING VERB AND *THAT*	The author **noted** that the results of the study were not conclusive.
CONJUNCTION AND SUBJECT	We worked very hard on her campaign for state representative, **but** the **incumbent** was too strong to defeat in the northern districts.
***SUCH AS* OR *LIKE* AND THE EXAMPLE THAT FOLLOWS**	Many university applicants take entrance exams **such as** the ACT or the SAT.
ESSENTIAL ELEMENT AND THE REST OF THE SENTENCE	Everyone **who has a mortgage** is required to have fire insurance.

MONTH OR HOLIDAY AND YEAR	The class reunion is tentatively planned for June 2018.
	The last time she saw them was on Thanksgiving Day 2010.
EXCLAMATION POINT OR QUESTION MARK AND CLOSING QUOTATION MARKS	"Dave, stop. Stop, will you? Stop, Dave. Will you stop?" implores the supercomputer HAL in *2001: A Space Odyssey*.

EXERCISE 31.4

Revise the following sentences, inserting commas where they are needed and deleting commas when they are unnecessary.

1. Alvar Nuñez Cabeza de Vaca unlike most other Spanish conquistadors came to perceive Native Americans as equals.

2. On February 15, 1527 Cabeza de Vaca was appointed to an expedition, headed for the mainland of North America.

3. The expedition landed near what is now Tampa Bay, Florida sometime in March, 1528.

4. Devastated by misfortune the expedition dwindled rapidly.

5. Cabeza de Vaca and three other members however survived.

6. His endurance now tested Cabeza de Vaca lived as a trader and healer among Native Americans of the Rio Grande Basin learning from them and eventually speaking on their behalf to the Spanish crown.

32 The Semicolon and the Colon

The semicolon and the colon both mark boundaries within a sentence and indicate how ideas are linked. They are not interchangeable, however.

32a The semicolon

The semicolon most frequently connects two independent clauses, but it can be used for other purposes as well.

(1) Connecting independent clauses

A semicolon placed between two independent clauses indicates that they are closely related. The second of the two clauses generally supports or contrasts with the first.

➤ For many cooks, basil is a key ingredient; it appears in recipes worldwide. [support]

➤ Sweet basil is used in many Mediterranean dishes; Thai basil is used in Asian and East Indian recipes. [contrast]

Sometimes, a transitional expression such as *for example* (**3d(2)**) or an adverbial conjunction such as *however* (**17a(7)**) accompanies a semicolon and further establishes the relationship between the ideas.

➤ Basil is omnipresent in the cuisine of some countries; **for example,** Italians use basil in salads, soups, and many vegetable dishes.

➤ The culinary uses of basil are well known; **however,** this herb also has medicinal uses.

A comma is usually inserted after a transitional expression, though it can be omitted if doing so will not lead to a misreading.

(2) Separating elements that contain commas

In a series of phrases or clauses that contain commas, semicolons indicate where each phrase or clause ends and the next begins.

➤ To survive, mountain lions need a large area in which to range**;** a steady supply of deer, skunks, raccoons, foxes, and opossums**;** and the opportunity to find a mate, establish a den, and raise a litter.

Semicolons do not set off phrases or dependent clauses. Use commas for this purpose.

➤ We consulted Alinka Kibukian**;,** the local horticulturalist.
                                  ∧

➤ Our trees survived**;,** even though we live in a harsh climate.
                        ∧

EXERCISE 32.1

Revise the following sentences, using semicolons to separate independent clauses or elements that contain internal commas.

1. Soccer is a game played by two opposing teams on a rectangular field, each team tries to knock a ball, roughly twenty-eight inches in circumference, through the opponent's goal.

2. The game is called *soccer* only in Canada and the United States, elsewhere it is known as *football*.

3. Generally, a team consists of eleven players: defenders (or fullbacks), who defend the goal by trying to win control of the ball, midfielders (or halfbacks), who play both defense and offense, attackers (or forwards), whose primary responsibility is scoring goals; and a goalkeeper (or goalie), who guards the goal.

4. In amateur matches, players can be substituted frequently, however, in professional matches, the number of substitutions is limited.

32b   The colon

A colon calls attention to what follows. It also separates titles from subtitles. The colon also has special uses in business correspondence and scriptural or bibliographic references.

(1) Directing attention to an explanation, a summary, or a quotation

When a colon appears between two independent clauses, it signals that the second clause will explain or expand on the first.

➤ No one expected the game to end as it did: after seven extra innings, the favored team collapsed.

A colon is also used after an independent clause to introduce a direct quotation.

➤ Marcel Proust explained the importance of mindfulness: "The true journey of discovery consists not in seeking new landscapes but in having fresh eyes."

CAUTION

Style manuals differ with regard to the use of an uppercase or a lowercase letter to begin an independent clause following a colon.

MLA The first letter should be lowercase unless (1) it begins a word that is normally capitalized, (2) the independent clause is a quotation, or (3) the clause expresses a rule or principle.

APA The first letter should be uppercase.

CMS The first letter should be lowercase unless (1) it begins a word that is normally capitalized, (2) the independent clause is a quotation, or (3) two or more related sentences follow the colon.

(2) Signaling that a list follows

A colon can be used to introduce a list. Note that an independent clause precedes the list.

➤ The website provides statistics for three states**:** Washington, Oregon, and Idaho.

Avoid placing a colon between a verb and its complement or after the words *including* and *such as*.

➤ The website provides statistics for many states including⊘ Washington, Oregon, and Idaho.

➤ The website provides statistics on topics such as⊘population and education.

(3) Separating a title and a subtitle

Use a colon between a work's title and its subtitle.

*Collapse***:** *How Societies Choose to Fail or Succeed*

(4) Specialized uses in business correspondence

A colon follows the salutation of a business letter and any notations.

Dear Dr. Horner**:**   Enc**:**

A colon introduces the headings in a memo.

To**:**   From**:**   Subject**:**   Date**:**

(5) Separating elements in time, bibliographic, or scriptural references

Colons are used in bibliographies to separate the city and publisher and in numbers to indicate hours and minutes.

Boston**:** Wadsworth   4**:**15 p.m.

Colons are often used between numbers in scriptural references.

Psalms 3**:**5   Gen. 1**:**1

However, MLA requires the use of periods instead of colons.

Psalms 3.5   Gen. 1.1

EXERCISE 32.2

Insert colons where they are needed in the following sentences.

1. Before we discuss marketing, let's define the behavior of consumers consumer behavior is the process individuals go through as they select, buy, or use products or services to satisfy their needs and desires.

2. The process consists of six stages recognizing a need or desire, finding information, evaluating options, deciding to purchase, purchasing, and assessing purchases.

3. When evaluating alternatives, a house hunter might use some of the following criteria price, location, size, age, style, and landscaping design.

4. The post-purchase assessment has one of two basic results satisfaction or dissatisfaction with the product or service.

---

33   The Apostrophe

Apostrophes serve a number of purposes. For example, you can use them to show that someone owns something (*my neighbor's television*), that someone has a specific relationship with someone else (*my neighbor's children*), or that someone has produced or created something (*my neighbor's recipe*). Apostrophes are also used in contractions (*can't, don't*) and in certain plural forms (*x's* and *y's*).

33a   Indicating ownership and other relationships

An apostrophe, often followed by an *s*, signals the **possessive case** of nouns. Possessive nouns are used to express a variety of meanings.

OWNERSHIP	**Fumi's** computer, the **photographer's** camera
ORIGIN	**Einstein's** ideas, the **student's** decision
HUMAN RELATIONSHIPS	**Linda's** sister, the **employee's** supervisor
POSSESSION OF PHYSICAL OR PSYCHOLOGICAL TRAITS	**Mona Lisa's** smile, the **team's** spirit
ASSOCIATION BETWEEN ABSTRACTIONS AND ATTRIBUTES	**democracy's** success, **tyranny's** influence
IDENTIFICATION OF DOCUMENTS	**driver's** license, **bachelor's** degree
IDENTIFICATION OF THINGS OR DAYS NAMED AFTER PEOPLE	**St. John's** Cathedral, **Valentine's** Day
SPECIFICATION OF AMOUNTS	a **day's** wages, an **hour's** delay

(1) Singular nouns, indefinite pronouns, abbreviations, and acronyms

Add an apostrophe and an *s* to indicate the possessive case of singular nouns, indefinite pronouns such as *everyone* and *nobody* (**21a(7)**), abbreviations, and acronyms.

the dean**'s** office [noun]

Yeats**'s** poems [noun]

anyone**'s** computer [indefinite pronoun]

the NFL**'s** reputation [abbreviation]

OPEC**'s** price increase [acronym]

Walter Bryan Jr.**'s** letter [abbreviation]

When a singular proper noun ends in *s*, you will have to consult the style guide for your discipline. The *MLA Handbook for Writers of Research Papers* recommends always using *'s* (*Illinois's legislature* and *Dickens's novels*). CMS allows exceptions to this rule. An apostrophe without an *s* may be acceptable when a singular common noun ends in *s* (*physics' contribution*) and when the name of a place or an organization ends in *s* but refers to a single entity (*United States' foreign aid*).

Possessive pronouns (*my, mine, our, ours, your, yours, his, her, hers, its, their, theirs,* and *whose*) are not written with apostrophes.

➤ The committee concluded **its** discussion.

(2) Plural nouns ending in *s*

Add only an apostrophe to indicate the possessive case of plural nouns that end in *s*.

➤ the boys' game   the babies' toys   the Joneses' house

Plural nouns that do not end in *s* need both an apostrophe and an *s*.

➤ men's lives   women's health   children's projects

CAUTION

An apostrophe is not needed to make a noun plural. To make most nouns plural, add *s* or *es*. Add an apostrophe only to signal ownership, origin, and other similar relationships.

➤ The ~~protesters'~~ met in front of the conference center.
  ^protesters

➤ The protesters' meeting was on Wednesday.

To form the plural of a family name, use *s* or *es*, not an apostrophe.

➤ The ~~Johnson's~~ participated in the study.
  ^Johnsons

  [COMPARE: The Johnsons' participation in the study was crucial.]

(3) To show collaboration or joint ownership

An apostrophe and an *s* follow the second of two singular nouns. Just an apostrophe follows the second of two plural nouns that already ends in *s*.

➤ the carpenter and the **plumber's** decision [They made the decision collaboratively.]

➤ the Becks and the **Lopezes'** cabin [They own one cabin jointly.]

(4) To show separate ownership or individual contributions

Each plural noun is followed by an apostrophe; each singular noun is followed by *'s*.

➤ the **Becks'** and the **Lopezes'** cars [Each family owns a car.]

➤ the **carpenter's** and the **plumber's** proposals [They each made a proposal.]

(5) Compound nouns

An apostrophe and an *s* follow the last word of a compound noun.

➤ my brother-in-**law's** friends, the attorney **general's** statements [singular]

➤ my brothers-in-**law's** friends, the attorneys **general's** statements [plural]

To avoid awkward constructions such as the last two, consider using a prepositional phrase beginning with *of* instead: *the statements of the attorneys general.*

(6) Nouns preceding gerunds

Depending on its number, a noun that precedes a gerund takes either an apostrophe and an *s* or just an apostrophe.

➤ Lucy**'s having** to be there seemed unnecessary. [singular noun preceding gerund]

➤ The family appreciated the lawyers' **handling** of the matter. [plural noun preceding gerund]

Sometimes you may find it difficult to distinguish between a gerund and a participle. A good way to tell the difference is to note whether the emphasis is on an action or on a person. In a sentence containing a gerund, the emphasis is on the action; in a sentence containing a participle, the emphasis is on the person.

➤ The completion of the project depends on **Tim's providing** the illustrations. [gerund]

➤ I heard **Tim discussing** his plans. [participle]

(7) Names of products and geographical locations

Follow an organization's preference for its name or the name of a product; follow local conventions for a geographical location.

Consumers Union	Actors' Equity	Taster's Choice
Devil's Island	Devils Tower	Lands' End

EXERCISE 33.1

Following the pattern of the example, change the modifier after each noun to a possessive form that precedes the noun.

EXAMPLE

proposals made by the committee   *the committee's proposals*

1. the holiday celebrating the birthdays of Washington and Lincoln

2. a drive lasting an hour

3. the position taken by HMOs

4. the report given by the eyewitness

5. the generosity of the Lees

6. a new book coauthored by Pat and Alan

7. the weights of the children

8. the spying done by the neighbor

33b **Marking omissions in contractions**

Apostrophes mark omissions in contractions.

they're [they are]   who's [who is]

it's [it is]   you're [you are]

Apostrophes also mark omissions in numbers and in words mimicking speech.

class of '14 [class of 2014]

y'all [you all]   singin' [singing]

CAUTION

Be careful not to confuse possessive pronouns (such as *its, their, whose, your*) with contractions (*it's, they're, who's, you're*). Whenever you write a contraction, you should be able to substitute the complete words for it without changing the meaning.

POSSESSIVE PRONOUN	CONTRACTION
Its motor is small.	**It's** [It is] a small motor.
Whose turn is it?	**Who's** [Who is] representing us?

33c **Forming certain plurals**

These plurals are generally formed by adding *s* only:

1990s   fours and fives   YWCAs

two *and*s   the three *R*s   PhDs

Lowercase letters are made plural by adding both an apostrophe and an *s*: *p*'s and *q*'s. MLA differs from this style in recommending the use of apostrophes for the plurals of uppercase letters (four A's) as well as lowercase letters (the *x*'s and *y*'s in an equation). Note that letters used as letters, rather than as grades or abbreviations, are italicized (**38b**).

EXERCISE 33.2

Insert apostrophes where needed, delete them when unnecessary, and correct any misspellings.

1. Who's responsibility was it?

2. Hansons book was published in the early 1920s.

3. NPRs fund drive begins in five days'.

4. Few students' enrolled during the academic year 13–14.

5. They're were more maybes than nos in the survey results.

6. They hired a rock n roll band for they're engagement party.

7. Only three of the proposals are still being considered: your's, our's, and the Craigs.

8. Youll have to include the ISBNs of the books' your going to purchase.

---

34 Quotation Marks

Quotation marks indicate that the words between them were first written or spoken by someone else or that they are the title of a short work.

34a Direct quotations

Double quotation marks set off direct quotations. Single quotation marks enclose a quotation within a quotation.

(1) Direct quotations

Double quotation marks enclose only quotations, not expressions such as *she said* or *he replied.* When a sentence ends with quoted material, place the period inside the quotation marks.

➤ "I believe that we learn by practice," writes Martha Graham. "Whether it means to learn to dance by practicing dancing or to learn to live by practicing living, the principles are the same."

When using direct quotations, reproduce all quoted material exactly as it appears in the original.

(2) Quotations within quotations

Use single quotation marks for any quotation embedded in another quotation.

➤ According to Anita Erickson, "when the narrator says, 'I have the right to my own opinion,' he means that he has the right to his own delusion" (22).

However, if the embedded quotation appears in a block quotation, use double quotation marks. (Note that double quotation marks are not used to mark the beginning and end of a block quotation.)

> Anita Erickson claims that the narrator uses the word *opinion* deceptively:
>> Later in the chapter, when the narrator says, "I have the right to my own opinion," he means that he has the right to his own delusion. Although it is tempting to believe that the narrator is making decisions based on a rational belief system, his behavior suggests that he is more interested in deception. (22)

(3) Dialogue

When creating a dialogue, enclose in quotation marks what each person says. Begin a new paragraph whenever the speaker changes.

Farmer looked up, smiling, and in a chirpy-sounding voice he said, "But that feeling has the disadvantage of being . . ." He paused a beat. "Wrong."

"Well," I retorted, "it depends on how you look at it."

—TRACY KIDDER, *Mountains Beyond Mountains*

When quoting more than one paragraph by a single speaker, put quotation marks at the beginning of each paragraph but only at the end of the last paragraph.

(4) Short excerpts of poetry included within a sentence

When quoting fewer than four lines of poetry, enclose them in quotation marks.

➤ After watching a whale swim playfully, the speaker in "Visitation" asks, "What did you think, that joy / was some slight thing?"

34b Titles of short works

Quotation marks enclose the title of a short work, such as a story, an essay, or a song. The title of a larger work, such as a book, play, website, film, television program, magazine, or newspaper, should be italicized.

SHORT STORIES	"The Lottery"	"The Fall of the House of Usher"
ESSAYS	"Walden"	"Play-by-Play"
ARTICLES	"Small World"	"Arabia's Empty Quarter"
BOOK CHAPTERS	"Rain"	"Cutting a Dash"
SHORT POEMS	"Orion"	"Mending Wall"
SONGS	"Lazy River"	"The Star-Spangled Banner"
TV EPISODES	"Show Down!"	"The Last Time"

Use single quotation marks for a title within a longer title that is enclosed in double quotation marks.

"Irony in 'The Sick Rose'" [article about a poem]

34c | **With other punctuation marks**

To decide whether to place another punctuation mark inside or outside quotation marks, note whether the punctuation mark is part of the quotation or part of the surrounding text.

(1) With commas and periods

When your sentence starts with an expression such as *she said* or *he replied*, use a comma to separate it from the quotation (**31h**). Place a period inside the closing quotation marks.

➤ She replied, "There's more than one way to slice a pie."

If your sentence starts with the quotation instead, place a comma inside the closing quotation marks.

➤ "There's more than one way to slice a pie," she replied.

When quoting material from a source, provide the relevant page number(s).

➤ According to Diane Ackerman, "Love is a demanding sport involving all the muscle groups, including the brain" (86).

> **CAUTION**
>
> Do not put a comma after *that* when it precedes a quotation.
>
> ➤ Diane Ackerman claims that "[l]ove is a demanding sport involving all the muscle groups, including the brain" (86).

(2) With semicolons and colons

Place semicolons and colons outside quotation marks.

➤ His favorite song was "Cyprus Avenue"; mine was "Astral Weeks."

➤ Stereotypical themes can be easily found in "The Last One": love, lust, and revenge.

(3) With question marks, exclamation points, and dashes

If the direct quotation includes a question mark, an exclamation point, or a dash, place that punctuation *inside* the closing quotation marks.

➤ Jeremy asked, "What is truth?"

➤ Gordon shouted, "Congratulations!"

➤ Laura said, "Let me tell—" just as Dan walked into the room.

Use just one question mark inside the quotation marks when a question ends with a quoted question.

➤ Why does the protagonist ask, "Where are we headed?"

If the punctuation is not part of the quoted material, place it *outside* the closing quotation marks.

➤ Who wrote "The Figure a Sentence Makes"?

EXERCISE 34.1

Revise sentences in which quotation marks are used incorrectly and insert quotation marks where they are needed. Do not alter sentences that are written correctly. (The numbers in parentheses are page numbers, placed according to MLA guidelines.)

1. Have you read Nicholas Negroponte's essay Creating a Culture of Ideas?

2. Negroponte starts his article with a problem: Innovation is inefficient (2).

3. However, he also believes that "without innovation we are doomed—by boredom and monotony—to decline" (2).

4. The biggest challenge in stimulating a creative culture, asserts Negroponte, is finding ways to encourage multiple points of view (2).

5. Negroponte suggests that new ideas are created by 'providing a good educational system, encouraging different viewpoints, and fostering collaboration' (3).

(Continued on page 390)

EXERCISE 34.1   *(Continued)*

6. According to the author, "More than ever before, in the new "new economy," research and innovation will need to be housed in those places where there are parallel agendas and multiple means of support" (3).

34d   Misused quotation marks

Avoid using quotation marks to enclose **indirect quotations**, material that restates or reports someone's words. Paraphrases and summaries generally include indirect quotations.

➤ Concluding his review of the album, Wilson said that "he was confounded by its mixed messages."

Quotation marks are also not used around words to add emphasis or to call attention to slang or other colloquial expressions. Instead, take the time to choose suitable words.

➤ Funny clips from late night talk shows often "go viral" *spread through social-networking sites* the next day.

35 The Period and Other Punctuation Marks

To indicate the end of a sentence, you can use one of three punctuation marks: the period, the question mark, or the exclamation point. Other punctuation marks are used within sentences—along with commas, semicolons, and colons—for such purposes as setting off elements or marking omissions. This chapter covers the use of dashes, parentheses, square brackets, ellipsis points, and slashes.

Use one space after a period, a question mark, or an exclamation point. MLA and APA guidelines suggest that leaving two spaces after end punctuation is acceptable. However, both style manuals present sample papers that have single spaces after concluding punctuation marks.

35a   The period

(1) At the end of a sentence

Use a period at the end of a sentence.

➤ Many adults in the United States are overfed yet undernourished.

In addition, place a period at the end of an instruction or recommendation.

➤ Eat plenty of fruits and vegetables.

(2) After some abbreviations

    Dr.   Jr.   a.m.   p.m.   vs.   etc.   et al.

Only one period follows an abbreviation that ends a sentence.

➤ The tour begins at 1:00 p.m.

35b The question mark

Place a question mark after a direct question.

➤ How does the atomic clock work? Who invented this clock?

➤ The question asked at the meeting was, how does the clock work?

Use a period after an indirect question (a question embedded in a statement).

➤ The article answers the question of how the clock was developed?•

MULTILINGUAL WRITERS
INDIRECT QUESTIONS

In English, the subject and verb in indirect questions are not inverted as they would be in the related direct question.

➤ We do not know when ~~will~~ the meeting *will* end.
  [COMPARE: When will the meeting end?]

Place a question mark after each question in a series of related questions, even when they are not full sentences.

➤ Can the atomic clock be used in cell phones? Word processors? Car navigation systems?

35c The exclamation point

An exclamation point often marks the end of a sentence, but its primary purpose is rhetorical—to create emphasis.

➤ Whoa! What a game!

Use the exclamation point sparingly so that you do not diminish its value. If you do not intend to signal strong emotion, place a comma after an interjection and a period at the end of the sentence.

➤ Well, no one seriously expected this victory.

35d The dash

A dash marks a break in thought or tone, sets off a nonessential element for emphasis or clarity, or follows an introductory list or series. To create a dash (also called an em dash), type two hyphens with no spaces between, before, or after them.

(1) Marking a break in the normal flow of a sentence

➤ I was awed by the almost superhuman effort Stonehenge represents—but who wouldn't be?

(2) Setting off a nonessential element

Use a dash or a pair of dashes to set off extra comments or details.

➤ Dr. Kruger's specialty is mycology—the study of fungi.

➤ The Grandview Trail—steep and unmaintained—is tough even for experienced hikers.

(3) Following an introductory list or series

After the dash, the main part of the sentence sums up the meaning of the list.

➤ Eager, determined to succeed, and scared to death—all of these describe how I felt on the first day at work.

THINKING RHETORICALLY
DASHES AND PARENTHESES

Dashes and parentheses are both used to set off part of a sentence, but they differ in the amount of emphasis they signal. Whereas dashes call attention to the material that is set off, parentheses usually deemphasize such material.

➤ Her grandfather—born during the Great Depression—was appointed to the Securities and Exchange Commission.

➤ Her grandfather (born in 1930) was appointed to the Securities and Exchange Commission.

35e   **Parentheses**

Use parentheses to set off information that is not closely related to the main point of a sentence or paragraph but that provides an interesting detail, an explanation, or an illustration.

> The 5-foot-2-inch dynamo ("I act tall," she says) has piloted her career with dazzling audacity.
>
> —ANNE STOCKWELL, "Salma Hayek"

In addition, place parentheses around an acronym or an abbreviation when introducing it after its full form.

➤ The Search for Extraterrestrial Intelligence (SETI) uses the Very Large Array (VLA) outside Socorro, New Mexico, to scan the sky.

If you use numbers or letters in a list within a sentence, set them off by placing them within parentheses.

➤ Your application should include (1) a current résumé, (2) a statement of purpose, and (3) two letters of recommendation.

THINKING RHETORICALLY

COMMAS, DASHES, AND COLONS

Although a comma, a dash, or a colon may be followed by an explanation, an example, or an illustration, the impact varies.

➤ He never failed to mention what was most important to him**,** the bottom line.

➤ He never failed to mention what was most important to him—the bottom line.

➤ He never failed to mention what was most important to him**:** the bottom line.

The comma, one of the most common punctuation marks, barely draws attention to what follows it. The dash, in contrast, signals a longer pause and so places more emphasis on the information that follows. The colon is more direct and formal than either of the other two punctuation marks.

35f Square brackets

Square brackets set off additions or alterations used to clarify direct quotations.

➤ "They [hyperlinks] are what turn the Web from a library of pages into a web" (Weinberger 170).
[Adding *hyperlinks* in brackets specifies what is meant by *They* in the quotation.]

➤ David Weinberger claims that "[t]he Web has blown documents apart" (xi).

To avoid the awkwardness of using brackets in this way, you may be able to quote only part of a sentence so that no change in capitalization is needed.

➤ David Weinberger claims that the Web "breaks the traditional publishing model" (x).

Use brackets to set off material that is itself set within parentheses.

➤ People frequently provide personal information online. (See, for example, David Weinberger's *Small Pieces Loosely Joined* [Cambridge: Perseus, 2002].)

35g | **Ellipsis points**

Ellipsis points, three equally spaced periods, indicate an omission from a quoted passage or a reflective pause or hesitation.

(1) Marking an omission from a quoted passage

ORIGINAL
More than 2,000 languages, or about 30 percent of all the world's languages, are spoken in Africa by just less than 12 percent of the world's total population.

—PETER K. AUSTIN, *One Thousand Languages*

OMISSION FROM THE MIDDLE OF THE SENTENCE
Austin (2008) states that over "2,000 languages . . . are spoken in Africa by just less than 12 percent of the world's total population."

Note that ellipsis points are not used to indicate an omission from the beginning of the quotation.

To indicate omitted words from the end of a quotation, put a space between the last word and the ellipsis points. Then add the end punctuation mark (a period, a question mark, or an exclamation point). If the quoted material is followed by a parenthetical source or page reference, the end punctuation comes after the second parenthesis.

OMISSION FROM THE END OF THE SENTENCE
Austin states that "over 2,000 languages, or about 30 percent of all the world's languages, are spoken in Africa . . . " (220).

To signal the omission of a sentence or more (even a paragraph or more), place an end punctuation mark before the ellipsis points, with one space before and after the ellipsis points.

OMISSION OF A SENTENCE OR MORE
According to Peter K. Austin, "Languages are endangered across North Africa. . . . Morocco has nine indigenous languages, with five endangered, and two nearly extinct."

(2) Indicating an unfinished sentence or marking a pause

Use ellipsis points to indicate that you are intentionally leaving a sentence incomplete or to signal a reflective pause.

➤ Keith saw four menacing youths coming toward him . . . and ran.

35h The slash

A slash between words, as in *and/or* and *he/she*, indicates that either word is applicable in the given context. There are no spaces before and after a slash used in this way. Because extensive use of the slash can make writing choppy, use it judiciously. (If you are following APA or MLA guidelines, avoid using *he/she*, *him/her*, and so on.)

When quoting poetry, use the slash to mark line divisions and include a space before and after the slash.

➤ Wallace Stevens refers to the listener who, "nothing himself, beholds / Nothing that is not there and the nothing that is."

EXERCISE 35.1

Add punctuation as indicated in square brackets.

1. The United Nations Educational, Scientific and Cultural Organization UNESCO was established in 1945. [parentheses]

2. Encouraging cultural diversity, fostering intercultural discussions, and promoting peace these are just a few of UNESCO's goals. [dash]

3. The organization routinely responds to global concerns such as the HIV AIDS epidemic. [slash]

4. According to a recent policy statement, the "Millennium Summit of Heads of States New York, September 2010 recognized the value of cultural diversity for the enrichment of humankind . . ." (UNESCO 4). [square brackets]

M

MECHANICS

36 Spelling and the Hyphen

Proofreading for spelling mistakes is essential as you near the end of the writing process. Your teachers, employers, or supervisors will expect you to submit polished work.

TIPS FOR USING A SPELL CHECKER

The spell checker is a wonderful invention, though you must use it with care.

- Proofread your work carefully, even if you are using a spell checker. Spell checkers will not catch all typos, such as *form* instead of *from*.

- Double-check words you frequently misspell. If you often misspell homophones such as *there/their* (**36b**), check for these words after using the spell checker.

- If a spell checker regularly flags a word that is not in its dictionary but that is spelled correctly (such as a proper noun, specialized term, or foreign word), add that word to the dictionary.

- Use a dictionary to look up unfamiliar words that are highlighted by the spell checker. Evaluate the alternative words or spellings the spell checker provides, because some of them may change the meaning of your sentence.

- Do not automatically accept changes the spell checker suggests. Reject any offers the spell checker makes to correct all instances of a particular error.

36a Spelling and pronunciation

Many words in English are not spelled the way they are pronounced, so pronunciation is not a reliable guide to correct spelling. Here are a few words typically misspelled because they include unpronounced letters:

condem*n*   foreign   lab*o*ratory   mus*c*le   solem*n*

Here are a few that include letters that are often not heard in rapid speech:

can*d*idate   diff*e*rent   gover*n*ment   sep*a*rate   lib*r*ary   Feb*r*uary

You can teach yourself the correct spellings of words by pronouncing them to yourself the way they are spelled, that is, by pronouncing each letter mentally so that you "hear" even silent letters.

CAUTION

The words *and*, *have*, and *than* are often not stressed in speech and are thus frequently misspelled.

➤ They would rather ^*have* of written two papers ^*than* then taken midterm ^*and* an final exams.

36b   Words that sound alike

Words that sound alike but are spelled differently (*aid/aide*, *principle/principal*) are frequently confused. Consult the **Glossary of Usage** for help with many of these commonly confused words. Also troublesome are two-word sequences that carry different meanings depending on whether they are written as one word or as two separate words.

Everyday life was grueling.

They do not fight **anymore**.

She attended class **every day**.

They could not find **any more** evidence.

Other examples include *awhile/a while*, *everyone/every one*, *maybe/may be*, and *sometime/some time*.

Singular nouns ending in *-nce* and plural nouns ending in *-nts* are also easily confused.

Assistance is available.   I have two **assistants**.

His **patience** wore thin.   Some **patients** waited for hours.

Be sure to include an apostrophe in contractions but not in possessive pronouns. (Before including contractions, find out whether your assignment permits their use.)

CONTRACTIONS   it's, you're, there's, who's

POSSESSIVES   its, your, theirs, whose

36c   Prefixes and suffixes

When a prefix is added to a base word (often called the **root**), the spelling of the base word is unaffected.

necessary, **un**necessary   moral, **im**moral

However, adding a suffix to the end of a base word often changes the spelling.

(1) Dropping or retaining a final e

- If a suffix begins with a vowel, the final *e* of the base word is dropped: bride, brid**al**; come, com**ing**. However, to keep the /s/ sound of *ce* or the /j/ sound of *ge*, retain the final *e* before *-able* or *-ous*: notice**able**, courage**ous**.
- If a suffix begins with a consonant, the final *e* of the base word is retained: entire, entire**ly**; rude, rude**ness**. Some exceptions are *argument*, *ninth*, *truly*, and *wholly*.

(2) Doubling a final consonant

- If a consonant ends a one-syllable word with a single vowel or ends a stressed syllable with a single vowel, double the final consonant: stop, sto**pped**; omit, omi**tted**.

- If there are two vowels before the consonant, the consonant is not doubled: remain, remain**ed**, remain**ing**.
- If the final syllable is not stressed, the consonant is not doubled: edit, edit**ed**, edit**ing**; comment, comment**ed**, comment**ing**.

(3) Changing or retaining a final y

- Change a final *y* following a consonant to *i* when adding a suffix (except *-ing*): lazy, laz**ily**; defy, def**ied**, BUT defy**ing**.
- Retain the final *y* when it follows a vowel: gray, gray**ish**; stay, stay**s**, stay**ed**; obey, obey**s**, obey**ed**.
- Some verb forms are irregular and thus can cause difficulties. For a list of irregular verbs, see pages 279-280.

(4) Retaining a final *l*

The letter *l* at the end of a word is retained when *ly* is added.

cool, coo**lly**   formal, forma**lly**   real, rea**lly**   usual, usua**lly**

EXERCISE 36.1

Add the specified suffix to the words that follow it.

Example

-ly: late, casual, psychological
    lately casually psychologically

1. *-ing*: put, admit, write, use, try, play

2. *-able*: desire, read, trace, knowledge

3. *-ly*: true, sincere, normal, general

---

(5) Forming plurals

- Add *es* to most nouns ending in *s*, *z*, *ch*, *sh*, or *x*: box, box**es**.

- If a noun ends in a consonant and *y*, change the *y* to *i* and add *es*: company, compan**ies**; ninety, ninet**ies**.
- If a noun ends in a consonant and *o*, add *es*: hero, hero**es**. Note that sometimes just *s* is added (photo, photo**s**) and other times either *s* or *es* can be added (motto**s**, motto**es**).
- Certain nouns have irregular plural forms: woman, wom**en**; child, child**ren**; foot, f**ee**t.
- Add *s* to most proper nouns: the Kennedy**s**. Add *es* to most proper nouns ending in *s*, *z*, *ch*, *sh*, or *x*: the Jones**es**.

Words borrowed from Latin or Greek generally form their plurals as they did in the original language.

SINGULAR

criterion   alumnus, alumna   analysis   datum   species

PLURAL

criter**ia**   alumn**i**, alumn**ae**   analys**es**   dat**a**   species

Sometimes two different forms are acceptable: the plural form of *syllabus* is either *syllabuses* or *syllabi*.

36d Confusion of *ei* and *ie*

An old rhyme will help you remember the order of letters in most words containing *e* and *i*:

Put *i* before *e*
Except after *c*
Or when sounded like *a*
As in *neighbor* and *weigh*.

Words with *i* before *e*: bel**ie**ve, ch**ie**f, pr**ie**st, y**ie**ld

Words with *e* before *i*, after *c*: conc**ei**t, perc**ei**ve, rec**ei**ve

Words with *ei* sounding like *a* in *cake*: **ei**ght, r**ei**n, th**ei**r, h**ei**r

Words that are exceptions to the rules in the rhyme include *either*, *neither*, *species*, *foreign*, and *weird*.

36e Hyphens

Hyphens link two or more words functioning as a single word and separate word parts to clarify meaning. They also have many conventional uses in numbers, fractions, and measurements.

(1) Linking two or more words

If two or more words serve as a single adjective before a noun, they should be hyphenated. If the words follow the noun, they are not hyphenated.

> You submitted an **up-to-date** report.

> The report was **up to date**.

When the second word in a hyphenated expression is omitted, the first word is still followed by a hyphen.

> They discussed both **private-** and **public-sector** partnerships.

A hyphen is not used after adverbs ending in *ly* (*poorly planned event*).

(2) Other uses of hyphens

A hyphen is also used after certain prefixes and in certain numbers.

BETWEEN REPEATED LETTERS	anti-intellectual
FOR CLARITY	re-sign (NOT resign) the petition
AFTER *SELF-* OR *EX-*	self-esteem, ex-wife
BEFORE CAPITALIZED WORDS	un-American, non-Mexican
IN NUMBERS TWENTY-ONE THROUGH NINETY-NINE	one hundred thirty-two
IN FRACTIONS	three-fourths, one-half

When you form a compound modifier that includes a number and a unit of measurement, place a hyphen between them: *two-year-old boy*.

EXERCISE 36.2

Convert the following word groups into hyphenated compounds.

Example

a movie lasting two hours   *a two-hour movie*

1. a supervisor who is well liked
2. a television screen that is forty-eight inches across
3. a highway with eight lanes
4. a painting from the seventeenth century
5. a chemist who won the Nobel Prize
6. a virus that is food borne

37 Capitals

Capital letters draw attention to significant details—for example, the beginnings of sentences or the names of particular people, places, and products.

37a Proper nouns

Proper nouns are capitalized, even when they are used as modifiers (*Mexico*, *Mexican government*). Words such as *college*, *company*, *park*, and *street* are capitalized only if they are part of a name (*a university* but *Oregon State University*).

The following names and titles should be capitalized: personal names, including titles; names of deities, religions, religious followers, and sacred works; names of awards, products, and companies; names of countries, ethnic or cultural groups, and languages; names of bridges, buildings, monuments, and geographical features or regions; names of universities and specific courses; names of days of the week, months, and holidays (but not seasons); names of historical documents, periods, and events; names of political parties and government agencies; and military terms.

CAPITALIZED	NOT CAPITALIZED
Noam Chomsky, Chomskyan	a linguist, a theoretical perspective
Uncle Rory	my uncle
President Lincoln	the president of the United States
God (a name)	a god
Bible, Koran, Talmud	sacred works
Academy Award	an award
Nike, Nike Free	a company, a running shoe
Japan, Japanese	a country, a language
Empire State Building	a building
Grand Canyon	a canyon
the West	a western state
Howard University	a university
Biology 101	a biology course
Fourth of July	a holiday
May	a month
Bill of Rights	a historical document
Renaissance	the sixteenth century
Great Depression	a recession
Democratic Party	democratic process
Internal Revenue Service	a government agency
Gulf War	a war
U.S. Army	an army

37b   Titles and subtitles

The first and last words in titles and subtitles are capitalized, as are major words—that is, all words other than articles (*a*, *an*, and *the*), coordinating conjunctions (*and*, *but*, *for*, *nor*, *or*, *so*, and *yet*), prepositions (such as *in*, *on*, and *of*), and the infinitive marker *to*.

> *Dictation: A Quartet*

> "To Be a Student or Not to Be a Student"

> "Stop-and-Go Signals"

The American Psychological Association (APA) has two sets of guidelines: one for titles in the body of a paper and one for titles on a reference list. In the body of the paper, all words that have more than four letters are capitalized. On the reference list, only the first word of the title and proper nouns are capitalized.

> *Southwestern Pottery from Anasazi to Zuni* [MLA]

> *Southwestern Pottery From Anasazi to Zuni* [APA, body of paper]

> *Southwestern pottery from Anasazi to Zuni* [APA, reference list]

37c   Beginning a sentence

The first letter of a sentence begins with a capital letter, but there are certain types of sentences that deserve special note.

(1) A quoted sentence

Capitalize only the first word in a quoted sentence, even if you interrupt the sentence with commentary.

> ➤ When asked to name the books she found most influential, Nadine Gordimer responded, "In general, the works that mean most to one—change one's thinking and therefore maybe one's life—are those read in youth."

➤ "**O**ddly," states Ved Mehta, "**l**ike my earliest memories, the books that made the greatest impression on me were the ones I encountered as a small child."

(2) A freestanding parenthetical sentence

Capitalize the first word of a freestanding sentence inside parentheses.

➤ The recordings used in the study were made in the 1980s. (**T**itles of the recordings can be found in the appendix.)

If the sentence inside the parentheses occurs within a sentence of your own, the first word should not be capitalized.

➤ The recordings used in the study were made in the 1980s (**t**itles of the recordings can be found in the appendix).

(3) An independent clause following a colon

Lowercase the first letter of an independent clause (a clause with a subject and a predicate) following a colon.

➤ The ear thermometer is used quite frequently now: **t**his type of thermometer records a temperature more accurately than a glass thermometer.

However, if two or more independent clauses (or sentences) follow the colon, capitalize the first word of each clause.

➤ Two new thermometers have replaced the old thermometers filled with mercury: **T**he digital thermometer uses a heat sensor to determine body temperature. **T**he ear thermometer is actually an infrared thermometer that detects the temperature of the eardrum.

The APA manual recommends capitalizing the first word of *any* independent clause following a colon. The MLA manual advises capitalizing the first word only when the independent clause that follows is a rule or principle.

➤ Think of fever as a symptom, not as an illness: **I**t is the body's response to infection. [APA]

➤ He has two basic rules for healthy living: **E**at sensibly and exercise strenuously at least three times a week. [APA and MLA]

(4) An abbreviated question

Capitalize the first words of all abbreviated questions.

➤ How do researchers distinguish the legal codes for families? For individuals? For genetic research?

37d   Computer keys, menu items, and icon names

Capitalize each word in the names of specific computer keys, menu items, and icons.

➤ For more information, select Clinical Trials from the Research menu.

EXERCISE 37.1

Edit the capitalization errors in the following paragraph. Be prepared to explain any changes that you make.

[1]Swimmer michael phelps holds the record as the most decorated olympian. [2]By the end of the 2012 olympics in london, england, he had earned twenty-two medals (The previous record holder had eighteen). [3]In the 2008 summer olympic games in beijing, china, phelps finished first eight times. [4]Afterwards, with a bonus he was given by the sports company speedo, phelps established a Foundation to promote healthy lifestyles and the sport of swimming, especially among children. [5]According to phelps, the swimming pool provided a place for him "To have fun, stay healthy, set goals, work hard and gain confidence."

38 Italics

Italics indicate that a word or a group of words is being used in a special way, for example, to indicate titles or foreign words.

38a Titles of works published or produced separately

Italics indicate the title of a work published or produced as a whole rather than as part of a larger work. A newspaper, for example, is a separate work, but an editorial in a newspaper is not; thus, the title of the newspaper is italicized, and the title of the editorial is enclosed in quotation marks.

The titles of the following kinds of separate works are italicized:

BOOKS	*The Round House*	*Far from the Tree*
MAGAZINES	*Wired*	*National Geographic*
NEWSPAPERS	*USA Today*	*Wall Street Journal*
PLAYS, FILMS	*Photograph 51*	*Argo*
TELEVISION SHOWS	*American Idol*	*Mad Men*
RADIO SHOWS	*Morning Edition*	*Fresh Air*
RECORDINGS	*Kind of Blue*	*Stronger*
WORKS OF ART	*American Gothic*	*David*
LONG POEMS	*Paradise Lost*	*The Divine Comedy*
PAMPHLETS	*Saving Energy*	*Tips for Gardeners*

According to MLA and CMS guidelines, an initial *the* in a newspaper or periodical title is not italicized when mentioned in a sentence.

➤ The story was published in the *New York Times*.

When an italicized title includes the title of a separate work within it, the embedded title is not italicized.

Modern Interpretations of Paradise Lost

The following titles are *not* italicized.

HISTORICAL DOCUMENTS	Bill of Rights, U.S. Constitution, Declaration of Independence
RELIGIOUS TEXTS	Bible, Koran, Torah, Book of Genesis
WEBSITES	Google, Reuters

However, if you are following MLA guidelines, italicize the names of websites.

38b Other uses of italics

Use italics for foreign words; genus and species names; legal cases; names of ships, submarines, aircraft, and spacecraft; words, letters, or figures referred to as such; and emphasized words.

FOREIGN WORD	*fútbol*
GENUS AND SPECIES	*Homo sapiens*
LEGAL CASE	*Miranda v. Arizona*
NAME OF SHIP, AIRCRAFT, OR SPACECRAFT	USS *Enterprise*, *Enola Gay*, *Atlantis*
REFERENCE TO WORD	The word *love* is hard to define.
REFERENCE TO LETTER OR FIGURE	The number *2* and the letter *Z* often look similar.
EMPHASIZED WORD	These *are* the right files.

38c Words not italicized

Italics are not used for a reference to a legal case by an unofficial name.

➤ All the major networks covered the O. J. Simpson trial.

But do italicize the shortened name of a well-known legal case.

➤ The Supreme Court decision in *Brown* forced racial integration of schools.

Italics are also not used for the names of trains, the models of vehicles, and the trade names of aircraft.

Orient Express   Ford Mustang   Boeing 787

EXERCISE 38.1

Identify words that require italics in the following sentences.

1. To celebrate an early book of poetry by James Joyce, Chamber Music, the Frye Art Museum exhibited paintings from its permanent collection to accompany Joyce's poems.

2. The website Frye Art Museum features three of the paintings that were on display: The Birch Grove, Lady Curzon, and The Duel.

3. In an article published in Seattle Weekly, Brian Miller interviewed curator Scott Lawrimore.

4. Another exhibit at the Frye featured paintings, such as Sorrow and No. 21, commissioned to accompany music inspired by Joyce's poetry.

5. The songs can be found on an anthology album, also called Chamber Music, released in 2008.

6. Interactive is a key word for describing this exhibit, as there were also shelves of artifacts for people to examine.

39   Abbreviations and Numbers

An **abbreviation** is a shortened version of a word or phrase: *assn.* (association), *dept.* (department), *et al.* (*et alii*, or "and others"). An **acronym** is a special form of abbreviation formed by combining the initial letters and/or syllables of a series of words: *AIDS* (**a**cquired **i**mmune **d**eficiency **s**yndrome), *sonar* (**so**und **na**vigation **r**anging).

39a   Abbreviations of names or titles

If a person's name commonly appears with initials before the last name, follow each initial with a period and a space.

J. R. R. Tolkien   J. K. Rowling

When initials are used for an entire name, no spaces or periods are used.

MLK   LBJ

Certain abbreviations are used before and/or after a person's name.

Ms. Gretel Lopez   **Mrs.** Marcus

Kim Beck, **MD**   Samuel Levy **Jr.**

Dr. Redshaw   **Sen.** McCain

Prof. Elizabeth Chang   Lee Evans, **PhD**

Gen. David Petraeus   **Rev.** Talitha Arnold

Academic, government, military, and other titles are generally spelled out, especially when only a last name is used.

Professor Hood   President Obama   General Dunwoody

39b Addresses in correspondence

The names of states and words such as *Street*, *Road*, and *Company* are written out when they appear in formal writing and in letters, including in the address at the top of the page. However, they are abbreviated when used in the address on an envelope.

Derson Manufacturing Co.
200 Madison St.
Watertown, MN 55388

When addressing correspondence within the United States, use the two-letter state abbreviations established by the U.S. Postal Service.

39c Acceptable abbreviations in academic and professional writing

Some abbreviations have become so familiar that they are considered acceptable substitutes for full words (*math*, *exam*, *lab*). If you are unsure of whether an abbreviation is appropriate, spell out the word.

➤ The film ~~prof.~~ *professor* worked on a documentary about Walt Disney.

(1) Abbreviations for special purposes

Words such as *volume*, *chapter*, and *page* are abbreviated (*vol.*, *ch.*, and *p.*) in bibliographies and in citations of research sources, but they are written out within sentences.

(2) Abbreviations for time periods and zones

82 BC ("before Christ") OR 82 BCE ("before the common era")

AD 95 (*anno Domini*) OR 95 CE ("common era")

7:40 a.m. (*ante meridiem*)   10:00 p.m. (*post meridiem*)

4:52 EST (Eastern Standard Time)

(3) The abbreviation for the United States (U.S. or US) as an adjective

the U.S. Navy, the US economy

[COMPARE: They moved to the United States in 1990.]

The abbreviation *U.S.* or *US* should be used only as an adjective. When using *United States* as a noun, spell it out. MLA lists *US* as the preferred abbreviated form, and APA uses *U.S.*

(4) Some abbreviations for Latin expressions

Certain abbreviations for Latin expressions are common in academic writing.

cf. [compare]   et al. [and others]   i.e. [that is]

e.g. [for example]   etc. [and so forth]   vs. OR v. [versus]

39d Acronyms

Introduce an acronym by placing it in parentheses after the group of words it stands for.

➤ The Federal Emergency Management Administration (FEMA) was criticized by many after Hurricane Katrina.

MULTILINGUAL WRITERS

USING ARTICLES WITH ABBREVIATIONS, ACRONYMS, OR NUMBERS

When you use an abbreviation, an acronym, or a number, you sometimes need an indefinite article. Choose *a* or *an* based on the pronunciation of the initial sound of the abbreviation, acronym, or number: use *a* before a consonant sound and *an* before a vowel sound.

➤ **an IBM** computer [*IBM* begins with a vowel sound.]

➤ **a NASA** engineer [*NASA* begins with a consonant sound.]

➤ **a 1964** Mustang [*1964* begins with a consonant sound.]

39e Spelling out numbers

Depending on their uses, numbers are treated in different ways. MLA recommends spelling out numbers that are expressed in one or two words (*nine, ninety-one, nine hundred, nine million*). A numeral is used for any other number (*9½, 9.9, 999*), unless it begins a sentence.

➤ The register recorded 164 names.

APA advises spelling out only numbers below ten. Both MLA and APA recommend using words rather than numerals at the beginning of a sentence.

➤ One hundred sixty-four names were recorded in the register.

When numbers or amounts refer to the same entities throughout a passage, use numerals when any of the numbers would be more than two words long if spelled out.

➤ Only 5 of the 134 delegates attended the final meeting. The remaining 129 delegates will be informed by e-mail.

39f | Common uses of numerals

Numerals are typically used for the following:

TIMES OF DAY	9:30 p.m.
DATES	September 11, 2001, OR 11 September 2001, OR 9/11
DECADES	1999 to 2003 OR 1999–2003
ADDRESSES	25 Arrow Drive, Apartment 1
IDENTIFICATION OF PROPER NOUNS	Edward III Highway 61
PARTS OF BOOKS AND PLAYS	chapter 1, page 15 act 2, scene 1 OR Act II, Scene I
DECIMALS	a 2.5 average
PERCENTS	12 percent

When monetary amounts are mentioned frequently, they can be expressed with numerals and symbols: $20.00, 99¢, or $0.99.

EXERCISE 39.1

Edit the following sentences to correct the usage of abbreviations and numbers.

1. In 1817, construction on the Erie Canal was started in Rome, NY.
2. The original canal was 363 mi. long, running between Albany and Buffalo.
3. Pres. Thomas Jefferson refused to use fed. funds for the canal.
4. DeWitt Clinton, United States senator from NY, found support for the construction of the canal in the state legislature.
5. In 2000, the United States Congress established the Erie Canalway National Heritage Corridor.
6. The Corridor is over 500 miles long and runs through 23 counties of upstate New York.

40 Writing about Literature

When you write about literature, you discuss such literary elements as plot, characters, and setting, but you also establish a rhetorical opportunity for writing, explore and focus your subject, formulate a purposeful thesis statement that is supported by reference to the literary work itself, address an audience, and arrange your thoughts in the most effective way. In short, when you write about literature, you respond rhetorically.

40a Literature and its genres

Works of literature can be divided into categories, or **genres**. A genre is identified by its particular features or conventions. Some genres are timeless and universal (drama and poetry, for instance); others are context-specific and develop within a specific culture (the graphic novel, for instance, is a fairly recent cultural phenomenon). Even when genres overlap (for example, some poems are referred to as prose poems, and Shakespeare's plays are written in verse), the identifiable features of each genre are still evident.

Some of the most widely studied literary genres are fiction, drama, and poetry, though many forms of nonfiction (including personal essays and memoirs, literacy narratives, and manifestos) are studied in literature courses. All imaginative literature can be characterized as fictional, but the term *fiction* is applied specifically to novels and short stories. Drama differs from all other imaginative literature in one specific way: it is meant to be performed. Poetry shares the components of both fiction and drama, but it is primarily characterized by extensive use of connotative language, imagery, allusions, figures of speech, symbols, sound, meter, and rhythm.

40b Rhetorical reading and literary interpretation

The most successful writing about literature starts with rhetorical or active reading. Therefore, as you read, examine your own reactions. Are you amused, moved, or confused? Which characters interest you? Are you able to follow the plot? Does the work remind you of any experience of your own or other works you have read? Does it introduce you to a different historical or geographical setting, or do you encounter a familiar setting and cast of characters? These first impressions can provide the seeds from which strong essays will grow, especially when they are later modified as you consider the work further.

(1) Your personal response to reading literature

When reflecting on your response to some element in a work of literature, consider how your reading might be shaped by the factors that define who you are. After all, what you bring to the page is important. If you find yourself responding positively or negatively to a character, a plot twist, or the setting in a novel or play, you might ask yourself whether this response has anything to do with your psychological makeup, political beliefs, gender, sexual orientation, cultural-ethnic group, social class, religion, or geographic location. Thinking about what you bring to a work of literature helps you focus on a rhetorical opportunity for writing and may suggest a theoretical approach to use as framework for your interpretation.

(2) Developing your topic using evidence in the text

If you are choosing your own topic, your first step is to reflect on your personal response as you formulate a tentative thesis statement. Next, consider what specific evidence from the text will best explain and support your interpretation and thesis statement.

Most readers (including your instructor) will be interested in what *you* think, so you need to discover a way to demonstrate your originality by focusing on a topic you can develop adequately and then applying one or more rhetorical methods (**3c**). You might explain why you consider a character heroic. Or you might demonstrate how the repeated appearance of an object throughout a story serves as a reminder of a particular idea or theme.

(3) Researching what other readers have said about a literary work

You will undoubtedly anchor your essay in your own interpretation, but you will enrich that interpretation with the sometimes conflicting responses of others, from literary experts to classmates. Although it is tempting to lean heavily on the interpretations of scholarly experts, you should use them in the same way you use other outsides sources: to enrich your own interpretation and support your own points. No matter what outside sources you tap, be sure to give credit to them by citing them (**13a–c**).

To locate scholarly material on a specific writer, work, or literary theory, you can start by consulting your library's resources. Your library's catalog and certain reference books are the best starting points (**9b–e**). For instance, *The MLA International Bibliography*, an index of books and articles about literature, is an essential resource for literary studies. Works such as *Contemporary Authors*, *The Oxford Companion to English Literature*, and *The New Princeton Handbook of Poetic Terms* can be useful when you are beginning your research or when you have encountered terms you need to clarify.

(4) Types of literary interpretation

Writing about a literary work requires you to focus on the work itself and to demonstrate that you have read it carefully—a process known as **close reading**. Close reading allows you to offer an **interpretation**, an explanation of what you see in a work.

When your interpretation explains the contribution of one feature of a literary work (such as the setting or main character) to the work's overall meaning, it is called an **analysis**.

Explication, usually used only with poetry, is an interpretation that attempts to explain every element in a literary work. When explicating Gwendolyn Brooks's "We Real Cool," a writer might note the repetition of the word *we*, which reinforces the brotherhood of these young men who left school to participate in the poem's catalog of nonschool activities: "lurk late," "sing sin," "thin gin," "jazz June," and "die soon."

An **evaluation** of a literary work gauges how successfully the author communicates meaning to readers. The most common types of evaluation are book, theater, and film reviews. Like any other interpretation, an evaluation is a type of argument in which a writer uses both positive and negative evaluative statements that are supported by textual evidence.

40c Vocabulary for discussing literature

Like all specialized fields, literature has its own vocabulary, which describes the various features of literary texts and the concepts of literary analysis. As you learn this vocabulary, you will learn more than just a list of terms: you will study how to understand, interpret, and write about literature.

(1) Characters

The **characters** are the humans or humanlike personalities (aliens, robots, animals, and other creatures) who carry the plot forward. One of these characters is usually considered the main character, called the **protagonist**, who is in external conflict with another character or an institution or in internal conflict with himself or herself. This conflict usually reveals the **theme**, or the central idea of the work.

You need to understand the characters in any work you read, so pay close attention to their appearance, their language, and their actions. You also need to pay attention to what the narrator or other characters say about them and how the other characters treat and react to them.

The cast of City Lights Theater Company of San Jose's 2011 production of *August: Osage County*, photo by Kit Wilder.

Figure 40.1. Attending to how characters talk about and treat one another helps you interpret the work as a whole.

(2) Imagery

The imagery in a piece of literature is conveyed by **descriptive language**, or words that describe a sensory experience. In the following passage from "The Ring of Time," a literary essay by E. B. White, notice the sensory images and the repetition White uses to hammer home Florida's dampness.

> On many days, the dampness of the air pervades all life, all living. Matches refuse to strike. The towel, hung to dry, grows wetter by the hour. The newspaper, with its headlines about integration, wilts in your hand and falls limply into the coffee and egg. Envelopes seal themselves. Postage stamps mate with one another as shamelessly as grasshoppers. But most of the time the days are models of beauty and wonder and comfort, with the kind sea stroking the back of the warm sand. At evening there are great flights of birds over the sea, where the light lingers; the gulls, the pelicans, the terns,

the herons stay aloft for half an hour after land birds have gone to roost. They hold their ancient formations, wheel and fish over the Pass, enjoying the last of day like children playing outdoors after suppertime.

—E. B. WHITE, "The Ring of Time"

The damp towel, wilting newspaper, sticky envelopes and postage stamps—these images convey the heavy dampness of the locale.

(3) Narrator

The **narrator** of a literary work tells the story. The voice doing the telling can seem to be that of the author's **persona** (a fictional construction not to be confused with the author), a specific character (or one of several characters who are taking turns telling the story), or an all-knowing presence (referred to as an **omniscient narrator**) that transcends both characters and author alike. Whatever the type of voice, the narrator's tone reveals his or her attitude toward events and characters and even, in some circumstances, toward readers.

(4) Plot

The **plot** is what happens in the story, the sequence of events (the narrative)—and more. The plot establishes how events are patterned or related in terms of conflict and resolution. Narrative answers "What comes next?" and plot answers "Why?" Consider this example describing the novel *Jane Eyre*:

NARRATIVE	A young English woman becomes a tutor for a lively French girl, Adèle.
PLOT	When a young English woman is hired to tutor Adèle, the tutor finds herself falling in love with Rochester, Adèle's father, who is still married to Bertha, the mad woman in the attic.

Plot usually begins with a conflict, an unstable situation that sets events in motion (for instance, the state of tension between the rich Rochester and Jane, the poor tutor). In what is called the **exposition**, the author introduces the characters, setting, and background—the elements that not only constitute the unstable situation but also relate to the events that follow. The subsequent series of events leads to the **climax** (or **turning point**). What follows is **falling action** (or **dénouement**) that leads to a resolution of the conflict and a stable situation, though not necessarily a happy ending.

By permission of Oxford University Press.

Figure 40.2. In the beloved story of *Jane Eyre*, a poor orphan struggles her way into the world of learning, work, and, finally, love.

(5) Setting

Setting involves place—not just the physical setting, but also the social setting (the morals, manners, and customs of the characters). Setting also involves time—not only historical time, but also the length of time covered by the narrative. Setting includes **atmosphere**, or the emotional response to the situation, often shared by the reader with the characters. Being aware of the features of the setting will help you better understand the story, whether it is written as fiction, drama, or poetry.

(6) Theme

The main idea of a literary work is its **theme**. To test whether your idea is central to the work in question, check to see if the idea is supported by the setting, plot, characters, and images. If so, it can be considered the work's theme. The most prominent literary themes arise out of external or internal conflict: character versus character, character versus herself or himself, character versus nature, or character versus society.

When you believe you have identified the theme, state it as a sentence—and be precise. A theme conveys a specific idea; it should not be confused with a topic.

TOPIC	an orphan becomes successful
VAGUE THEME	a mistreated orphan can marry a rich man
SPECIFIC THEME	*Jane Eyre* reveals the conflict between a brilliant but poor girl and a society that expects to suppress her longing for an education and a home of her own.

CHECKLIST FOR INTERPRETING A LITERARY WORK

- From whose point of view is the story told?
- Who is the protagonist? How is his or her character developed?
- With whom or what is the protagonist in conflict?
- How are the other characters depicted and distinguished through dialogue?
- What is the theme of the work? How does the author use setting, plot, characters, and symbols to establish that theme?

40d Approaches to interpreting literature

An interpretation of a literary work can be shaped by your personal response to what you have read, by the views of other readers, whom you wish to support or challenge, or by a specific type of literary theory.

Literary theory, the scholarly discussion of how the nature and function of literature can be determined, ranges from approaches that focus almost exclusively on the text itself (its language and structure) to approaches that show how the text relates to author, reader, language, society, culture, economics, or history. Familiarity with literary theory enriches your reading of literature as well as your understanding of the books and essays about literature that you will discover when you do research.

(1) Reader-response theory

According to **reader-response theory**, readers construct meaning as they read and interact with the elements within a text, with each reader bringing something different (intellectual values and life experiences) to the text on every reading. Thus, meaning is not fixed *on* the page but rather depends on what each reader brings *to* the page. Furthermore, the same reader can have different responses to the same literary work when rereading it after a number of years: a father of teenagers might find Gwendolyn Brooks's poem "We Real Cool" more disturbing than it had seemed when he first read it in high school. Although a reader-response approach to literature encourages diverse interpretations, you cannot simply say, "Well, that's what this work means to me" or "That's my interpretation." You must demonstrate to your audience how each element of the work supports your interpretation.

(2) Feminist and gender-based literary theories

The significance of sex, gender, or sexual orientation within a particular social context is the interpretive focus of **feminist** and **gender-based literary theories**. These theories enable a reader to analyze the ways in which a work (through its characters, theme, or plot) promotes or challenges the prevailing intellectual or cultural assumptions of its day with regard to issues related to gender and sexuality, such as patriarchy and compulsory heterosexuality. For instance, Edith Wharton's *The Age of Innocence* compares two upper-class nineteenth-century women in terms of the specific social pressures that shaped and constricted their lives and loves. A feminist critic might emphasize the oppression of these women and the repression of their sexuality. Using a gender-based approach, another critic might focus on both women's financial dependence on men.

(3) Race-based literary theory

A useful form of race-based literary criticism, **critical-race theory** (including **African American literary criticism**) focuses on the significance of race relations within a specific historical and social setting to explain the experience and literary production of any people whose history is characterized by political, social, and psychological oppression. Not only does this theoretical approach seek out previously neglected literary works, but it also illuminates the ways in which race, ethnicity, and the imbalance of power inform many works. Zora Neale Hurston's *Their Eyes Were Watching God*, Rudolfo Anaya's *Bless Me, Ultima*, and Frederick Douglass's *Narrative*, which demonstrate how racism affects the characters' lives, have taken on considerable cultural value in the last twenty years. Closely associated with critical-race theory is **postcolonial theory**, which takes into account the relationship of the colonized with the colonizer and the challenge a text can direct at the dominant powers at a particular time and place, asserting a drive toward the liberation of oppressed social groups. Joseph Conrad's *Heart of Darkness*, Jean Rhys's *Wide Sargasso Sea*, Daniel Defoe's *Robinson Crusoe*, and E. M. Forster's *A Passage to India* can all be read productively through the lens of postcolonial theory.

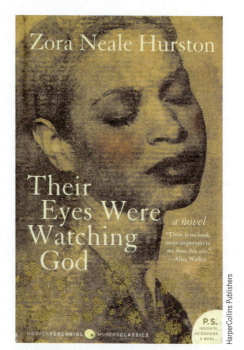

Figure 40.3. In *Their Eyes Were Watching God*, a mature and complex black woman recounts her life in three acts, based on her relationships with three very different men.

(4) Text-based literary theory

Text-based literary theory demands concentration on the piece of literature itself, and only the use of specific examples from the text validates an interpretation. A close reading of the work is essential with this approach. And nothing more than what is contained within the text itself—not information about the author's life, culture, or society—is needed to understand and appreciate the text's unchanging meaning. Readers may change, but the meaning of the text does not.

(5) Context-based literary theory

Context-based literary theory considers the historical period during which a work was written and the cultural and economic patterns that prevailed during that period. For example, recognizing that Willa Cather published *My Ántonia* during World War I can help account for the darker side of that novel about European immigrants' harsh life in the American West. Critics who use a context-based and class-based approach known as **cultural studies** consider how a literary work interacts with economic conditions, socioeconomic classes, and other cultural artifacts (such as songs or fashion) from the period in which it was written.

40e Conventions for writing about literature

Writing about literature involves adhering to several conventions.

(1) Using first person

When writing an analysis of a piece of literature, you may use the first-person singular pronoun, *I*.

➤ Although some critics believe Rudolfo Anaya's novel to be about witchcraft, I think it is about the power of belief.

By using *I*, you indicate that you are presenting your opinion about a work. When you propose or argue for a particular belief or interpretation, you must support it with specific evidence from the text itself.

(2) Using present tense

Use the present tense when discussing a literary work or reporting how others have interpreted the work you are discussing (**11c**).

➤ In "A Good Man Is Hard to Find," the grandmother reaches out to touch her killer just before he pulls the trigger.

➤ As Toni Morrison demonstrates in her analysis of the American literary tradition, black Americans continue to play a vital role.

(3) Documenting sources

When writing about a work, cite the version of the work you are discussing by using the MLA format for listing works cited (chapter **13**). When you use a works-cited list, you must indicate specific references whenever you introduce a line or passage. According to MLA style, information on the author (and perhaps the text, too) should appear either in the setup or along with the specific location in parentheses directly after the quotation (**11c**). A period, a semicolon, or a comma should follow the parentheses. Quotations from short stories, novels, and creative nonfiction are identified by the author's name and page number.

➤ "A man planning to spend money on me was an experience rare enough to feel odd" (Gordon 19).

Quotations from poems are referred to by line number with the author's name or text included if not mentioned before.

➤ "O Rose, thou are sick!" (Blake 1).

Some instructors may prefer that you follow an alternate system using notes for documentation (described in an earlier edition of the *MLA Handbook* but no longer included in the seventh edition). In this notes system, you acknowledge the first quotation from a work by using a superscript number and then providing an explanatory note on a separate page at the end of your paper.

TEXT

. . . as Toni Morrison states (127).[1]

OR

. . . tendency to misread texts by African American writers (Morrison 127).[1]

NOTE

1. Toni Morrison, *Playing in the Dark: Whiteness and the Literary Imagination* (New York: Vintage, 1992). All subsequent references to this work will be identified with page numbers in parentheses within the text.

If you use this note form, you do not need to repeat the bibliographic information in a separate entry or include the author's name in subsequent parenthetical references to page numbers. Check with your instructor about the format expected from you.

(4) Quoting poetry

When quoting from poems and plays written in verse, type quotations involving three or fewer lines in the text and insert a slash with a space on each side to separate the lines (**35h**). Quotations from plays require act, scene, and line numbers.

➤ Christina Rossetti opens her poem "Uphill" with a two-line question and answer: "Does the road wind uphill all the way? / Yes, to the very end" (1-2).

Quotations of more than three lines should be indented one inch from the left-hand margin and double-spaced. Do not use slashes at the ends of lines and make sure to follow the original text for line breaks, special indenting, or spacing. For this type of block quotation, place your citation outside the final punctuation mark.

To signal the omission of a full line or more in quoted poetry that is set off from text, use spaced periods covering the length of either the line above it or the omitted line.

The yellow fog that rubs its back upon the window-panes,

. . . .

Curled once about the house, and fell asleep.

—T. S. ELIOT, "The Love Song of J. Alfred Prufrock"

(5) Referring to authors' names

Use the full name of the author of a work in your first reference and only the last name in all subsequent references. For instance, refer to "Charlotte Brontë" or "Willa Cather" the first time, and after that, use "Brontë" or "Cather." Never refer to a female author differently than you do a male author. For example, use "Robert Browning and Elizabeth Barrett Browning" or "Browning and Barrett Browning" (not "Browning and Mrs. Browning" or "Browning and Elizabeth").

40f | Sample literary interpretation

In the following essay, undergraduate English major Jessi Hank analyzes Willa Cather's novel *My Ántonia*, focusing on the cultural power of gender roles.

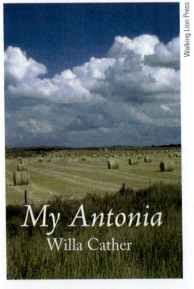

Walking Lion Press

Figure 40.4. In *My Ántonia*, a young man remembers a beautiful, vigorous young woman who rose above society's expectations, despite her poverty and hardships.

Hank 1

Jessi Hank

Dr. Jaap

English 490

27 October 2012

Defying Mainstream Gender Roles from a Child's Perspective

My Ántonia, set in Nebraska at the turn of the twentieth

century, is a novel about a young man, Jim Burden, and his much-

admired friend, Ántonia. An orphan, Jim takes the train from his

home in Virginia to the plains of Nebraska, where he lives with

his loving grandparents, is educated, and eventually makes his

way to Harvard Law School. On the other hand, Ántonia, newly

arrived from Bohemia, endures a series of hardships that directly

connect to being poor and female. Although Jim narrates this

novel, the point of view is Cather's and one of critique. Through

the eyes of the gender-privileged Jim, Cather's readers experience a

chronological story of opportunities, restrictions, and punishments

directly associated with whether a person is male or female.

Cather is not blatant or harsh in her criticism; instead, she

simply uses a male narrator to tell the story. A female narrator

might need to comment on the inequity of gendered roles and

expectations, to experience them herself, but Jim-as-narrator offers

his recollections of childhood memories that provide the story

with a sense of juvenile honesty. For Jim, unbiased by age and

**First lines
name the
novel, provide
overview, and
demonstrate
understanding**

**Thesis states
main point of
the essay**

**Writer uses
literary
present tense
to describe
the action in
the novel**

Quotation from a secondary source

experience, societal norms are just the way things are. And through Jim, Cather can tell of "the world and other women, including her own female characters, from a male point of view" (Lambert 676).

Besides using a male narrator to expose these inequities, Cather also uses historical details. She critiques society's conception of women and their capabilities through her descriptions of women's physical labor at the turn of the twentieth century. At that time, most women (all but the very wealthy) were expected to perform such traditional "women's" work, as housework, gardening, childcare, and the care of small animals.

Writer uses past tense to describe historical background and beliefs

Ántonia and the other female characters attend to such work, but Ántonia distinguishes herself by making time to finish her work and take English lessons from Jim. But then her loving father, depressed with the grim life he and his family live in America, commits suicide. One of Ántonia's two brothers is capable of taking over the farming but needs her to work beside him, which she does, exclaiming, "I can work like mans now" (Cather 80). Thus, after her father's death, Ántonia begins to do her women's work as well as men's hard manual labor. She wears her father's boots and hat over her too-small dress and rolled-up sleeves as she plows, plants, harvests, and threshes. Because she is poor and because she is a girl (not valued as much as her older brother, Ambrosch), she can no longer make any time to take English lessons.

Hank 3

Girls-as-exploited-hard-workers is another gender-related idea Cather explores in her novel, with Ántonia as Cather's example. Ántonia's brother, Ambrosch, realizes that he can make even more money if he hires his sister out as a farm hand, a prerogative older males had at the time. So Ántonia works on farm after farm, cutting, threshing, and binding wheat. When the ladies in town hear about Ántonia's fate, they decide to intercede, in the only way women could do. Mrs. Harling, the Burdens' neighbor, hires Ántonia as a housemaid, claiming that she "can bring something out of that girl" (Cather 99). Mrs. Harling has high hopes and no doubts about Ántonia's ability to work, learn new things, and become more ladylike. Jim tells of admiring these hired girls, mostly uneducated, poor immigrant girls, who have no alternative but to work hard for money to pull their families out of debt (Cather 128). These hard-working girls "had no alternative but to go into service"; thus, there is a sense of desperation in their quest for work and keeping that work. But there is also a sense of pride in that work, as these young women unselfishly "were always helping to pay" for things that the family needed back home (Cather 128). Features of the novel that we might normally consider feminine (interest in pretty clothes, music, and social life) are limited to the lives of the richer city girls, whom Jim seems to pity for having nothing purposeful or profitable to do with their time (Yukman 96).

> Writer uses a topic sentence to set up her interpretation

Hank 4

In addition to the conventional conception of what females were physically capable (and incapable) of doing, there is a question of what society expects of women in this novel. Despite the very real physical demands on working-class girls, the female characters are, nonetheless, expected to be meek, dainty, and enclosed, staying "indoors in winter because of the cold, and in summer because of the heat" (Cather 128). Jim even goes so far as to say that "girls who had to walk more than half a mile to school were pitied" (Cather 127), though through his telling of the story we learn that Ántonia loves working in the fields, feels connected to the land, and wants to make the most of her hardworking life, just like her father. And it is also through Jim's eyes that readers can experience the social-class discrimination of the hired, country girls, who "were considered a menace to the gendered social order" because they took pride in their work and did not sit idly around as was expected of [females]" (Cather 129). This idea of the proper young woman indicates that society was overly protective of women from "good," rich families, who were expected to be more like ornaments on a mantel than functional members of society. In almost every way, the hard-working Ántonia challenges those expectations of inequality. She blatantly declares that she "like(s) to be like a man," with regard to her physical working capabilities and to the pride she takes in her hard work (Cather 80, 89). But when her vigor

and enthusiasm extend to dancing, Ántonia finds herself in trouble.
She soon leaves the more protective Harlings to work for Mr. Cutter,
the money-lender (Cather 133). Eventually, Ántonia finds herself
pregnant, engaged, and yet abandoned. Even though she is referred
to as "poor Ántonia," she seems "proud of the baby," whose picture
she has taken and framed by the town photographer (Cather 195).
Obviously, there was a societal schism between expectations for
and the actual capabilities of women.

> Details from the novel support interpretation

Cather criticizes gender roles in other ways as well. The over-
masculinization of the male characters Ambrosch and Mr. Cutter
focuses attention on society's expectations of men. Ambrosch holds
high expectations for his family's economic status, especially
after his father's death (Cather 87). The locals talk about the ways
Mr. Cutter mistreats and cheats everyone, both in his financial
dealings and his marriage. The depiction of these men is harsh,
with Ambrosch hiring out his sister for additional physical labor
and with Cutter hatching a plan to rape her. When his plan goes
awry, he is so upset that he murders his wife and kills himself.
These portrayals of hard males create a striking juxtaposition
between societal expectations for males and those for females.

Cather also employs juxtaposition to reveal the societal
roles and expectations of men and women both in the city and
the country. Jim's preference for the girls who like to work hard

amplifies Cather's challenge to the negative connotation associated with hard-working women. Also, Ántonia's blatant disregard for what society expects of her (to be ashamed, somber, discouraged) allows Cather to challenge stereotypical perceptions of women and their capacities at the time. Even if her representation of gender roles is considered somewhat unfair, even formulaic, Cather is, nevertheless, able to criticize society by carefully pinpointing and addressing rigid conventions within Midwestern society in the early part of the twentieth century.

Hank 7

Works Cited

Cather, Willa. *My Ántonia*. 1918. Boston: Houghton, 1988. Print.

Lambert, Deborah G. "The Defeat of a Hero: Autonomy and

Sexuality in *My Ántonia*." *American Literature* 53.4 (1982):

676-90. *JSTOR.* Web. 25 Oct. 2012.

Yukman, Claudia. "Frontier Relationships in Willa Cather's *My*

Ántonia." *Pacific Coast Philology* 23.1/2 (1988): 94-105.

JSTOR. Web. 25 Oct. 2012.

41 Writing in the Social Sciences

The **social sciences** include such disciplines as psychology, anthropology, sociology, political science, and economics. Researchers in these disciplines study how humans behave as members of groups—families, peer groups, ethnic communities, political parties, and many others. The goal of research in the social sciences is to examine and explain behavior occurring under a particular set of circumstances. For example, Danielle Dezell, the student whose report is featured later in this chapter, investigated whether students depend on gender stereotypes to assign status to certain occupations. Typical assignments in the social sciences are library research projects, case studies, and laboratory or field reports.

41a Audience, purpose, and the research question

The first step toward completing a writing assignment for a course in the social sciences is to determine your audience and purpose. Your audience will always include your instructor, but it could include students in your class and sometimes people outside your class. Identifying your audience will help you decide how much background information to present, how much technical language to include, and what types of reasoning and sources to use.

Once you know what your purpose is and to whom you are writing, you can craft a research question that will help you find sources, evaluate them, and use them responsibly. Here are some examples of types of research questions that could be posed about the topic of community service performed by students:

Question about causes or purposes

What reasons do students give for performing community service?

Question about consequences

What do students believe they have learned through their community service?

Question about process

How do instructors help students get involved in community service?

Question about definitions or categories

What does community service entail?

Question about values

What values do instructors hope to cultivate by encouraging students to perform community service?

41b Evidence, sources, and reasoning

Researchers in the social sciences study the behavior of humans and other animals. To make accurate observations of their subjects' activities, these researchers either design controlled laboratory experiments or conduct field research. Interviews and surveys are the two most common techniques for gathering data in the field, although observations are also widely used. Both laboratory experiments and field research yield data that social-science researchers can use as evidence to make statements (or claims) about the behavior of humans and other animals.

Researchers in the social sciences distinguish between quantitative studies and qualitative studies. **Quantitative studies**, such as laboratory experiments and surveys, yield data that can be presented in numerical form, as statistics. Using statistical data and formulas, researchers show how likely it is for a behavior to occur or to have certain consequences. If you decide to undertake a quantitative study, you should turn your research question into a **hypothesis**, an objective prediction of what the results of your experiment or survey will be. The results of your study will either prove or disprove your hypothesis. Be prepared to provide possible explanations for either outcome.

Hypotheses are best formed after a sustained period of observation and preliminary research. When presenting her hypothesis about gender stereotypes and occupational status, Danielle Dezell states her prediction in the context of existing research.

> Although studies have not correlated participant gender and occupational status (Parker et al., 1989), Teig and Susskind (2008) found that occupational gender did correlate with occupational status. The current study expects to find that people's ranking of occupational status correlates with the stereotyped gender of the occupation.

Researchers who perform **qualitative studies**, such as observations and interviews, are interested in interpreting behavior by first watching, listening to, or interacting with individuals or a group. If you decide to conduct a qualitative study, you will not reason *from* a hypothesis but will reason *to* a hypothesis. You will observe a phenomenon and note what you see or hear. Then, instead of reporting numbers as evidence, you will provide detailed descriptions and discuss their significance.

Researchers in the social sciences recognize that some studies have both quantitative and qualitative features. They also expect to use both primary and secondary sources in many of their research projects. Primary sources consist of data derived from experiments, observations, surveys, or interviews.

Secondary sources are articles or case studies written about a research topic.

41c   Conventions of language and organization

(1) Style guidelines

Most of the social sciences follow the guidelines presented in the *Publication Manual of the American Psychological Association*, Sixth Edition. This manual stresses the importance of writing prose that is clear, concise, unbiased, and well organized. The following specific tips can help you write in the style recommended by the manual.

TIPS FOR PREPARING A PAPER IN THE SOCIAL SCIENCES

- Use the active voice as often as possible, although the passive voice may be acceptable for describing research method(s).

- Choose verb tenses carefully. Use the present tense to discuss results and report conclusions (as in "The findings suggest . . ."). Reserve the past tense for referring to specific events in the past and for describing your procedures (as in "Each participant signed a consent form . . .").

- Use a first-person pronoun rather than referring to yourself or to any coauthor(s) and yourself in the third person.

  We
  ➤ ~~The experimenters~~ retested each participant after a rest period.

- Clarify cumbersome phrases by placing the main noun first.

  method for testing
  ➤ the literacy ~~testing method~~

---

(2) Organization

Assignments in the social sciences will generally require you to (1) state a research question, thesis, or hypothesis; (2) discuss research that has already been published about your topic; (3) describe your research method; and (4) present your conclusions or results.

To organize the information they are presenting, writers in the social sciences use tables and graphs, which provide data in formats that aid interpretation, as well as headings, which are designed to signal levels of importance. Danielle Dezell includes a table to display her results (see page **457**). If you decide to use a table to display your data, be sure to refer to the table by number (for example, Table 1) and explain the significance of the information it provides. Without a brief discussion of the table, your readers may have difficulty understanding why you included it.

Graphs provide a visual representation of data. Danielle uses line graphs to highlight her comparison of gender stereotypes and perceptions of occupational status (see page **459**). Graphs are labeled as numbered figures. Like tables, they should be discussed in the text.

(3) Reference list

At the end of any assignment you complete for a course in the social sciences, you should include a list of all the sources you used. See **14b** for guidelines for preparing a list of references and see sample lists of references on pages **191–192** and **461**.

41d Examples of writing in the social sciences

(1) Library research report

Library research reports are written by both students and professionals. The purpose of such reports is to bring together several related sources on a specific topic in order to examine that topic closely. Writing such a report will require you to read a number of sources and then summarize, critique, and synthesize those sources. Library research reports generally include the following elements.

- statement of the research question or thesis
- presentation of background information, using sources
- discussion of major findings presented in the sources
- application of those findings to the specific research question
- conclusions
- references

An excerpt from a library research report is shown in figure 41.1. In the report's introduction, authors Matthew Gervais and David Sloan Wilson present background information for their study. Notice that the authors maintain a neutral stance that conveys an impression of impartiality, although they clearly and strongly state their point of view.

(2) Case study

A case study is a qualitative project that requires a researcher to describe a particular participant or group of participants. The researcher refrains from making generalizations about the participant(s) in the study and instead focuses on the behavior of the participant(s). After describing the behavior, the researcher usually suggests a solution to the problem faced by the participant(s). Most case studies include the following information.

- an introduction to the participant(s)
- a description of the problem
- observations
- a presentation of strategies to solve the problem

First paragraph presents
past studies on the topic

Next paragraph discusses
gaps in the research

INTRODUCTION

Laughter and humor were accorded high evolutionary significance by Darwin (1872) and have received increasing attention from biologists and psychologists during the last 30 years. This attention has resulted in myriad empirical advances and has left laughter and humor well characterized on multiple proximate levels (see Provine 2000; Vaid 2002; Bachorowski and Owren 2003; van Hooff and Preuschoft 2003; Wild, Rodden et al. 2003). Laudably, this research has spawned a number of hypotheses attempting to explain the ultimate evolutionary origins of laughter and humor (e.g., Eibl-Eibesfeldt 1989; Weisfeld 1994; Pinker 1997; Ramachandran 1998; Harris 1999; Miller 2000; Provine 2000; Owren and Bachorowski 2001; Caron 2002; Howe 2002; Jung 2003; Storey 2003). Nevertheless, the scientific study of laughter and humor is still in its infancy relative to other comparable subjects in emotions and communication research.

Many empirical questions about laughter and humor remain unanswered or neglected. For example, most researchers (e.g., Provine 2000; Owren and Bachorowski 2003; Vettin and Todt 2004) have failed to make the important distinction between Duchenne (stimulus-driven and emotionally valenced) and non-Duchenne (self-generated and emotionless) laughter (Keltner and Bonanno 1997; see also Wild, Rodden et al. 2003). While laughter has recently been found to occur most frequently during casual conversation and not following deliberate humor (Provine 1993; LaGreca et al. 1996; Vettin and Todt 2004), researchers have yet to question whether such conversational laughter is different in kind from that following humor. This oversight might well be the root cause of the widespread confusion concerning the diversity of forms and functions that characterizes laughter today (Keltner and Bonanno 1997).

Figure 41.1. An excerpt from the introduction of a library research report.

Figure 41.2 is an excerpt from a case study, one of many that can be found on the website *Improving Provision for Disabled Psychology Students.*

Bill is a . . . psychology student with dyslexia. In addition to difficulties with arithmetic and organisational skills, he has particular problems with short-term memory. . . .

He has always found psychology a fascinating subject. Though he doesn't feel that his impairment directed his decision to study psychology, he suggests that it may be one reason why he was interested in "how the mind works."

Bill finds that he has to work harder than most people to achieve the same level of performance. Since reading takes him a long time, he has found it difficult to keep up with all the allocated work necessary for the degree and feels overwhelmed by the sheer volume and rate of work he has to get through. The biggest barrier he has to overcome is only having a period of one week to submit some of his laboratory reports: "I can't even get the reading for lab reports done in the week we have to complete reports, never mind getting the actual report written up!"

In terms of more positive experiences, he has found it particularly beneficial when lecturers put their lecture slides on the web before classes, giving him adequate time to print them out and thus enabling him to make notes on the printed-out slide during the lecture. This saves him from having to take so many notes, and allows him time to take in the material that is being taught.

Figure 41.2. An excerpt from a case study posted online.

41e   Sample laboratory report

Social science students and professionals often conduct research in a laboratory or in the field (that is, in a natural setting). Reports based on this type of research contain standard sections: introduction, method, results, and discussion. An example is Danielle Dezell's laboratory report on gender stereotypes and occupations. Written according to the style guidelines of the American Psychological Association (APA), her report includes all the standard sections. Because Danielle asked fellow students to participate in her study, she was required to submit a proposal for her study and a consent form to the institutional review board at her university for approval.

Although Danielle collaborated with Cameron Dooley and Elaine Acosta on the experiment described in the report, she wrote the report on her own.

Gender Stereotypes and Perceptions of Occupational Status

Among University Students

Danielle Dezell

Central Washington University

Abstract

Introduces the purpose of the study

This study investigated whether the gender of participants affected their view of certain occupations and whether the gender typically associated with an occupation affected participants' ranking of the status of that occupation. Participants were asked (1) to write a response to a prompt designed to elicit gender-specific pronouns and (2) to rate the status of one of three occupations typically associated with a gender. The results were compared to see whether the interaction between participant gender and stereotypical occupational gender influenced the perception of the status of the occupation and to discover whether participant gender influenced the perception of occupational gender.

Gender Stereotypes and Perceptions of Occupational Status

Among University Students

Occupational gender stereotypes are important to examine for their possible influence not only on a person's occupational choice but also on perceptions of status associated with occupations. When university-age students consider possible careers, they often choose one based on their own gender and on the stereotypical gender assigned to an occupation (Evans & Diekman, 2009). They may also choose an occupation according to the status they believe it to have. An investigation into gender stereotypes about occupations is a first step in limiting their influence on students' career choices.

Gender stereotypes begin in early childhood, when children see how society views certain professions. These societal influences can have long-term effects on how children may stereotype various occupations (Firestone, Harris, & Lambert, 1999). Several studies using school-age children as participants have examined the strength of these early stereotypes. Miller and Hayward (2006) showed that participants often preferred occupations that were stereotyped to their own gender (i.e., boys preferred stereotypically male jobs, and girls preferred stereotypically female jobs). Another study conducted by Teig and Susskind (2008) looked at both status and stereotypes. When participants were asked to rate the status of

Establishes the importance of the report

Provides readers with necessary information and demonstrates credibility by discussing work of other researchers

GENDER STEREOTYPES AND PERCEPTIONS   4

jobs, the researchers found that out of the 18 highest ranked jobs,
only 3 were classified as feminine. Of all the occupations, 27.8%
of masculine occupations had a high status ranking, while 15.4%
of feminine occupations had a high status ranking. Participants in
this study classified both *librarian* and *elementary school teacher*
as stereotypically feminine occupations. The researchers found
that there was a significant correlation between the gender of the
participant and how he or she ranked the status of an occupation.
However, the researchers pointed out that as girls grew older,
their tendency to stereotype lessened. Boys, though, continued
to carry gender stereotypes into adulthood. Miller and Hayward
(2006) noted that men generally prefer occupations traditionally
performed by men.

Refers to previous studies and synthesizes their findings

In a study whose participants were college-age students,
Shinar (1975) looked at how the participants rated the masculinity
and femininity of various occupations on a 1-to-7 Likert scale
(1 being *masculine* and 7 being *feminine*). The study showed
that both men and women held gender stereotypes about certain
occupations. The participants rated *miner* as a fully masculine job
(mean rating of 1.000) and *manicurist* as a mostly feminine job
(mean rating of 6.667). Shinar also reported that *head librarian*
had a mean rating of 5.583, *high school teacher* a mean rating of
4.000, and *carpenter* a mean rating of 1.667. What is interesting is
that Shinar showed that both women and men demonstrated

GENDER STEREOTYPES AND PERCEPTIONS   5

gender stereotyping, whereas, over 30 years later, Seguino (2007)
and Miller and Hayward (2006) found that men had much stronger
stereotypes than women. Miller and Hayward also suggested that
women grow out of a stereotyping mindset by age 18.

Although certain occupations clearly seem to be gender
stereotyped, occupational status is not always related to gender.
Parker, Chan, and Saper (1989) found that there was no significant
correlation between participant gender and occupational status
ratings. It might be tempting to believe that jobs associated with
masculinity would be ranked as having higher social status, but
these researchers showed that the status of many traditionally
masculine jobs (e.g., *heavy equipment operator*) was considered
low. This finding is especially interesting because it suggests that
when people choose an occupation, they might rely more on the
perception of the gender associated with an occupation than on
the perception of status.

One way to test how people stereotype a job according to
gender is to ask them to assign a pronoun to a certain occupation.
This simple test provides insight into how gender stereotypes of
occupations work and whether males or females are more likely
to hold such stereotypes. A study looking at the gender people
attributed to different gender-neutral characters introduced in a
dialogue script found that both men and women were more likely to
assume that a character was male. The same study also found that

> Contributes to the scholarly conversation on gender stereotypes

men and women had equal biases toward gender assumptions

(Merritt & Kok, 1995). In a similar study, participants were asked

to attribute a gender to various stuffed animals. Both children

and adults used the male pronoun to describe stuffed animals that

were gender-neutral (Lambdin, Greer, Jibotian, Wood, & Hamilton,

2003).

After reporting the work of other researchers in previous paragraphs, the writer introduces her hypothesis

    This study aims to discover both whether participants

stereotype certain occupations as being either male or female

and whether participants rate the status of an occupation based

on whether the occupation has historically been a masculine,

feminine, or gender-neutral occupation. The findings of previous

studies suggest that both males and females do stereotype certain

occupations. Although studies have not correlated participant

gender and occupational status (Parker et al., 1989), Teig and

Susskind (2008) found that occupational gender did correlate with

occupational status. The current study expects to find that people's

ranking of occupational status correlates with the stereotyped

gender of the occupation.

Method

Information on methodology helps readers decide whether the researcher's findings are reliable and valid

Participants

    A total of eight groups participated in the study. Numbers

of participants in each group varied. Overall, there were 40

participants, 11 males and 29 females. All participants were

students at Central Washington University and were 19 years old

GENDER STEREOTYPES AND PERCEPTIONS   7

or older. The participants were all volunteers and were randomly assigned to one of three experimental conditions.

Materials

The materials for each experimental condition were a sheet of paper that presented one of three different writing prompts and asked for four pieces of demographic information. A script from which the researcher read was also used. Each writing prompt was a scenario about an employee of a school who had a problem; however, the employee's occupation in each prompt differed. The occupations and their associated gender stereotypes were as follows: *librarian* (female), *woodshop teacher* (male), and *high school teacher* (gender neutral). The occupations were chosen based on the percentage of females employed in each occupation, according to statistics from the Bureau of Labor Statistics (Bureau of Labor Statistics, 2010). The statistics showed that *high school teacher* was the most gender-neutral occupation (54.9% female). The occupation *librarian* was found to be gender segregated toward females (81.8% female). There were no statistics for *woodshop teacher*, though there were statistics for *carpenter* (1.6% female). Because most carpenters are male, it is quite likely that most people would stereotype the occupation of woodshop teacher as male. A focus on jobs that were all in a school environment prevented the creation of confounds based on the status of a work environment.

The writing prompts excluded any language that might allow the participant to infer the gender of the person in the prompt (e.g., no pronouns were used). A 5-point Likert scale was used to measure how participants rated the status of an occupation. Each of the three prompt sheets used identical wording in the directions, prompts, Likert scale, and demographic items (i.e., gender, age, class standing, and major); the only difference among the prompts was the occupation used.

Procedure

Each group of participants had two administrators. The study took approximately 15 minutes. One administrator passed out consent forms, collected them, and then distributed the prompts, while the other administrator read the appropriate directions from the script. Once the participants had the prompt, they were given 10 minutes to complete the story. After the administrators collected the stories, participants were debriefed and provided with the opportunity to ask questions.

Results

Uses statistics to report results

The descriptive statistics can be found in Table 1. A two-way between-subjects ANOVA with $\alpha = .05$ showed that the interaction between participant gender and occupation in the prompts was not significant, $F(2, 34) = .88$, $p > .05$. Of the two main effects, only gender was significant, $F(1, 34) = .001$, $p < .05$. However, occupation had a nonsignificant main effect, $F(2, 34) = .052$, $p > .05$. The

TABLE 1 *DESCRIPTIVE STATISTICS*

Gender of Participant	Occupation in Prompt	Mean	Std. Deviation	N
F	Librarian	2.75	.452	12
	High School Teacher	2.75	.463	8
	Woodshop Teacher	2.56	.527	9
	Total	2.69	.471	29
M	Librarian	5.00	.545	1
	High School Teacher	3.20	1.304	5
	Woodshop Teacher	3.20	.837	5
	Total	3.36	1.120	11
Total	Librarian	2.92	.760	13
	High School Teacher	2.92	.862	13
	Woodshop Teacher	2.79	.699	14
	Total	2.88	.757	40

averages of means are graphed in Figure 1. The homogeneity of variance test was significant, $F(5, 34) = .003$, $p < .05$. The first chi-square test, which was run on the interaction between participant gender and type of pronoun used by the participant in responding to the prompt, had a Pearson's correlation of .267, which is not significant. The second chi-square test between occupation in the prompt and pronoun type had a Pearson's correlation of .000.

Discussion

The results of the study showed that there was no interaction between the status ranking of an occupation and the gender stereotyping of that occupation. This is contrary to the findings of Teig and Susskind (2008), who found that the gender stereotype of an

Statistics reported in previous section explained in this section occupation affects the rating of its status. However, it is similar to the findings of Parker et al. (1989), who showed that the gender of a participant had no bearing on occupational status. All three occupations were ranked on average as having medium status (mean of 2.875). *Librarian* had a mean status of 2.92; *high school teacher*, a mean status of 2.92; and *woodshop teacher*, a mean status of 2.79. While there may not be a significant difference, the mean status ranking is lowest for *woodshop teacher*, which agrees with the finding of Parker et al. (1989) that manual labor jobs were rated as having a lower status. Neither part of this study's hypothesis was supported by the results. Levene's test of homogeneity of variance had a significant outcome, indicating that the groups were unequal and the result is not due to random sampling.

The results from the gender-stereotyping tests were more intriguing. There was a significant correlation between the occupation mentioned in the prompt and the type of pronoun chosen by the participant to respond to the prompt (feminine, masculine, or neutral). Participants did stereotype the occupations, but what is interesting is that females used gender-specific pronouns much more than males did. When writing their stories about the various occupations, male participants used gender-neutral pronouns 72% of the time, whereas female participants used gender-neutral pronouns only 41% of the time. These findings are contrary to those of Merritt and Kok (1995), who found that when participants

Compares
results
with those
of other
researchers

GENDER STEREOTYPES AND PERCEPTIONS   11

Figure 1. Means for main effects.

are presented with unspecified characters, they generally designate the gender as male. The findings of this study also contradict the occupational-stereotype findings of Shinar (1975), who stated that men use stereotypes more than women, and of Miller and Hayward (2006), who reported that females tend to use fewer stereotypes once they are enrolled in college.

Writer acknowledges some limitations of the study

One of the biggest limitations of the study was that there were so few participants, especially men. Data elicited from a larger number of male participants would have provided a more accurate picture of how men view occupational stereotypes. The prompts could also have been worded better. Because of the awkward wording of the prompts, participants had a good idea of what the study was looking for and so may have adjusted their responses. Another limitation is that there were only three occupations. Including a greater number of occupations would have made it possible to state conclusions about gender stereotypes more firmly. Future studies should include not only more occupations but also occupations that obviously have different statuses. This study chose occupations that were all in the same environment in order to avoid confounds; however, if there were many different types of occupations from a variety of environments, participants might not be able to determine as easily the researcher's intent. Despite these limitations, this study suggests that people are starting to have fewer assumptions about the relation between gender and occupation.

GENDER STEREOTYPES AND PERCEPTIONS   13

References

Bureau of Labor Statistics. (2010). *Household data: Annual averages*

[Data file]. Retrieved from http://www.bls.gov/cps/cpsaat11

Evans, C., & Diekman, A. (2009). On motivated role selection:

Gender beliefs, distant goals, and career interest. *Psychology*

of Women Quarterly, 33(2), 235–249. doi:10.1111/j.1471-

6402.2009.01493.x

Firestone, J., Harris, R., & Lambert, L. (1999). Gender role

ideology and the gender based differences in earnings.

Journal of Family and Economic Issues, 20(2), 191–215.

doi:10.1023/A:1022158811154

Lambdin, J. R., Greer, K. M., Jibotian, K. S., Wood, K. R., &

Hamilton, M. C. (2003). The animal = male hypothesis:

Children's and adult's beliefs about the sex of non-sex-

specific stuffed animals. *Sex Roles, 48*(11/12), 471–482.

doi:10.1023/A:1023567010708

Merritt, R. D., & Kok, C. J. (1995). Attribution of gender to a

gender-unspecified individual: An evaluation of the people =

male hypothesis. *Sex Roles, 33*(3/4), 145–157. doi:10.1007/

BF01544608

Miller, L., & Hayward, R. (2006). New jobs, old occupational

stereotypes: Gender and jobs in the new economy. *Journal of*

GENDER STEREOTYPES AND PERCEPTIONS   14

> *Education & Work, 19*(1), 67–93. doi:10.1080/
>
> 13639080500523000

Parker, H., Chan, F., & Saper, B. (1989). Occupational

> representativeness and prestige rating: Some observations.
>
> *Journal of Employment Counseling, 26*(3), 117–131. Retrieved
>
> from http://www.employmentcounseling.org

Seguino, S. (2007). Plus ça change? Evidence on global trends in

> gender norms and stereotypes. *Feminist Economics, 13*(2),
>
> 1–28. doi:10.1080/13545700601184880

Shinar, E. (1975). Sexual stereotypes of occupations. *Journal of*

> *Vocational Behavior, 7*(1), 99–111. Retrieved from
>
> http://www.sciencedirect.com/science/journal/00018791

Teig, S., & Susskind, J. (2008). Truck driver or nurse? The impact

> of gender roles and occupational status on children's
>
> occupational preferences. *Sex Roles, 58*(11/12), 848–863.
>
> doi:10.1007 /s11199-008-9410-x

42 Writing in the Humanities

The humanities include disciplines such as philosophy, art history, history, foreign languages, religion, comparative literature, cultural studies, women's and gender studies, and English. Scholars in the humanities study the artifacts of human culture (artwork, novels, plays, architecture, musical compositions and forms, philosophical treatises, and handicrafts, as well as popular media) to better understand the wide variety of human experience, both past and present.

In courses in the humanities, you will write in a variety of ways and for various purposes; it is therefore important to analyze your rhetorical situation before you begin drafting.

42a Audience, purpose, and the research question

Before writing for a humanities course, determine your rhetorical opportunity, audience, and purpose. Thinking about your rhetorical opportunity (what you are writing in response to, and why) will help you shape your research question, narrow your purpose, and identify your audience. Knowing who your audience comprises helps you determine how much background information on your topic to provide, how technical your language should be, and what kinds of evidence will be most persuasive.

Most researchers in the humanities write to convey a particular interpretation of a cultural artifact to a specific audience or to inform readers about the history of a particular event, individual, artifact, or social movement. They may also write to evaluate a work of art or a performance. Once you have determined your purpose for writing, you can develop a research question that will help you focus your research, find and evaluate sources, and use those sources responsibly. Research questions in the humanities often focus on texts or cultural products. The following are some potential questions that scholars in the humanities might ask about the experience of African Americans during the civil rights movement:

Questions about causes or purposes

What events stimulated the Montgomery bus boycott during the civil rights movement?

Questions about consequences

How did singer and actor Harry Belefonte contribute to the success of the civil rights movement?

Questions about process

What did civil rights workers do to gain national attention for their cause?

Questions about definitions or categories

What kinds of protest tactics did different African American leaders, such as Martin Luther King and Malcolm X, advocate during the civil rights movement?

Questions about values

What does the struggle for equal rights for African Americans reveal about the values of white Americans during the 1960s?

42b Evidence, sources, and reasoning

The aim of writers in the humanities is to understand human experiences by observing and interpreting cultural artifacts; therefore, most claims in the humanities are not put forth as statements of absolute fact. Instead, researchers in the humanities often seek to demonstrate the validity of their interpretations through detailed analyses of texts, relying on textual evidence, logical reasoning, and the work of other scholars in a particular field to present a compelling argument for an interpretation. After considering the available evidence, researchers in the humanities advance a claim, or **thesis**, that expresses their interpretation of the artwork, performance, or some other object or event.

(1) Using primary sources

Most researchers in the humanities begin their studies by working directly with a **primary source**, which can be a person, an object, or a text. For art historians, this primary source might be a drawing, a painting, or a sculpture, which they analyze in terms of the formal qualities of the work (line, color, shape, texture, composition, and so forth) and elements that have symbolic importance. They then write an explanation of how these features work together to create meaning in the work. For instance, in his *Early Netherlandish Painting*, art historian Erwin Panofsky performs a critical analysis of Jan van Eyck's *Arnolfini Portrait*, arguing that the elaborate details of the scene, such as the dog (representing fidelity), the two additional figures reflected in a mirror on the wall who may have served as witnesses, and van Eyck's signature on the wall indicate that the scene documents a wedding. More recently, art historians have challenged this interpretation: in her article, "'In the Name of God and Profit': Jan van Eyck's *Arnolfini Portrait*," Margaret Carroll argues that the painting does not portray a wedding; rather it is an important document that gives the wife power of attorney. And in "The Arnolfini Double Portrait: A Simple Solution," Margaret Koster suggests that the painting memorializes Arnolfini's deceased wife. Each of these interpretations draws on formal and stylistic evidence from the painting itself as well as on knowledge of the cultural context in which it was created.

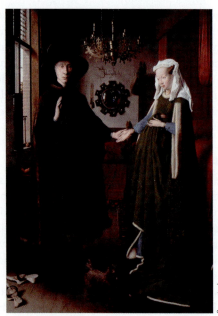

Superstock

Figure 42.1. Jan van Eyck's *Arnolfini Portrait*, from the fifteenth century, has been the subject of many analyses by art historians.

For historians, primary sources include letters, government documents, newspapers, pamphlets, and other materials produced during a particular time period about some person, group, or event. For example, in her biography of nineteenth-century Paiute activist Sarah Winnemucca, Sally Zanjani uses letters written by Winnemucca, transcriptions of her public speeches, newspaper accounts of her activities, photographs, diaries, and other firsthand accounts to reconstruct Winnemucca's personal life and motivations. Like other historians, Zanjani analyzes these sources by comparing what they say, evaluating the reliability of their creators, and then generating her own interpretation of the information they present.

(2) Using secondary sources

Researchers in the humanities also use **secondary sources**, or works written by other scholars on their topic, to understand what these scholars think about the topic and to help establish the social and historical context for the topic. For instance, Zanjani refers to earlier biographies of Winnemucca and then demonstrates how her own work offers new evidence about Winnemucca's life. Zanjani also relies on other historians for historical context that was not explicitly discussed in her primary sources, such as information about nineteenth-century American Indian reservations, government military policies regarding Native Americans, and so forth.

42c Conventions of language and organization

(1) Following conventions of style

When writing in the humanities, you will use language and formatting as prescribed by the style manual of the particular discipline. Some writers in the humanities, particularly those writing about languages and literature, use MLA style (chapter **13**). Other writers in the humanities, including historians and art historians, follow conventions outlined in *The Chicago Manual of Style* (CMS), Sixteenth Edition (chapter **15**), or in Kate Turabian's *A Manual for Writers of Research Papers, Theses, and Dissertations*, Eighth Edition, which is based on CMS style.

Unlike writers in the sciences, often claiming objectivity in their writing, most writers in the humanities recognize that an interpretation is colored by the perspective of the person expressing it. Thus, writers in the humanities often acknowledge their own position on a topic, especially if it has a clear effect on their interpretation. In particular, many writers in the humanities use the first-person pronoun *I* when describing the results of their research. Writers in the humanities also use the active voice, which focuses readers' attention on the agent performing the action (**20d**).

(2) Organizing information according to specific conventions

Research papers in the humanities include a thesis statement that indicates the author's position on the topic (**2b**), evidence that supports the thesis statement, and a conclusion that restates the major claim and explains why the topic is important. (Specific formats for organizing papers in the humanities are discussed in the next section.)

Headings can help you organize your writing. Most short humanities papers do not require headings, but for longer papers, Turabian's style manual suggests the following heading levels.

First-Level Heading

- First-level headings are centered and boldfaced (or italicized), with major words capitalized.

Second-Level Heading

- Second-level headings are centered and not boldfaced (or italicized), with major words capitalized.

Third-Level Heading

- Third-level headings are flush with the left margin and boldfaced (or italicized), with major words capitalized.

(3) Including a bibliography

Include any sources you have used for your project in a bibliography at the end of the paper (**15a**). A bibliography not only demonstrates that you have done sufficient research but also allows your readers to obtain any of the sources that interest them.

42d Examples of writing in the humanities

(1) Historical research paper

Researchers in the humanities write historical research papers to reconstruct past events or eras or to profile individuals. To explain or interpret some feature of the past, most historians use a combination of primary sources (newspapers, diaries, cookbooks, medical guides, and so forth, published at the time of the event or during the lifetime of the person) and secondary sources (writings by later historians about the event or person or about the primary sources). A historical research paper allows you to place your interpretation in the context of others that have been offered, using some sources to support your interpretation and others to refute the alternative interpretations.

The introduction to a historical research paper explains the importance of the topic and provides the thesis. Following the introduction and thesis, the body of the paper provides evidence from both primary and secondary sources to support the thesis. Finally, the conclusion to a historical research paper should reconsider the major claim of the paper in terms of its overall significance and implications for research, teaching, practice, and so forth.

(2) Critical review

Students in humanities courses, as well as professional writers, are often asked to write reviews of various creative works, including films, literary works, art exhibitions, musical performances, theatrical performances, and dance performances. The purpose of a critical review is to evaluate the quality of the work for an audience that wants to know what the work is about and whether it would be worthwhile to experience themselves. Accordingly, when you write a critical review, begin with a brief introduction to the work (the title and the artist, composer, or director as well as the location where the work can be seen or heard) and some kind of evaluative statement, or thesis, that gives readers your general opinion of the work. Following this introduction, provide a brief description of the work that helps readers unfamiliar with it to understand the review. As you evaluate the strengths and weaknesses of the work, be sure to provide examples from it to support your evaluation. Finally, most reviews conclude with a summary statement that drives home the final evaluation of the work. (See a sample critical review in **42e**.)

(3) Critical analysis

Many researchers in the humanities write critical analyses in which they argue for a specific interpretation of the work under examination, with an aim toward deepening an audience's appreciation of that work. If your assignment is to write a critical analysis, your instructor is likely interested in assessing both your understanding of the work and your ability to think critically about it. Critical analyses usually focus on formal, stylistic, or symbolic features of a work and explain how these elements work together to create meaning. (See **42b** for more information on using evidence in critical analysis.) Such analyses sometimes explore the ways in which class, gender, or racial relationships are expressed in a work.

Most critical analyses include the following sections.

- **Introduction.** The introduction provides a brief historical context for the work. It may also explain why the work ought to be reexamined—perhaps scholars have overlooked the work's significance or have not considered other possible meanings of the work. At the end of the introduction, the thesis, a clearly focused claim, states the writer's interpretation of the work.
- **Body.** The body of the analysis provides the evidence—the formal, stylistic, symbolic, or contextual details that support the writer's interpretation. Many analyses also address differing interpretations of the work, explaining why the writer's interpretation is more convincing. This section can be organized in a number of ways: through comparison and contrast of data or artifacts; or with a chronological, thematic, or emphatic (from less to more familiar or from less to more contestable) arrangement.

- **Conclusion.** The conclusion should review the thesis as well as the most important evidence supporting the writer's interpretation. Frequently, the conclusion also addresses implications; in other words, the writer explains to readers why his or her interpretation is so important, what effect the work may have had on other works or the cultural context, or what the writer's interpretation may mean to readers today.

42e Sample critical review

In the following theatrical review, student Matthew Marusak makes an argument for his negative review of a production of Tennessee Williams's play *Suddenly Last Summer*.

1

Not So *Suddenly Last Summer*

Matthew Marusak

Theatre 464

Professor Headrick

March 15, 2012

Writer uses a format based on Turabian's style manual for the title and header

I began to nod off halfway through Carla Gugino's ardent, over-the-top, twenty-minute monologue at the end of Tennessee Williams's *Suddenly Last Summer* (Roundabout at Laura Pels Theatre, Harold and Miriam Steinberg Center for Theatre; 4 November 2011). It's not that there is anything inherently wrong with the material: Williams's stark, deeply ambiguous play about the dangers of sexual repression, denial, and deception remains as potent as ever. Rather, Roundabout's production turns an urgent and emotionally explosive work into an uncomfortably dull, embarrassingly archaic exercise in trying an audience's patience.

Writer introduces the performance and gives a brief evaluation of the production

In theory, any revival of this play should be utterly and wholly riveting. In its production at the Laura Pels Theatre, however, something has gone inexplicably awry. Violet Venable (an imposing Blythe Danner) is a wealthy widow—mannered and shrouded in a contradictory haze of unrelenting misery and dreamy-eyed idealism—suffering from the great loss of her son, Sebastian (discussed but never seen), who perished under a veil of

Describes the basic plot of the play for readers

2

mystery the previous summer. As her story unfolds, Mrs. Venable
does her best to cloud Sebastian's implicit homosexuality and the
events surrounding his death by praising him as a great artist—the

way she wants him
to be remembered.
Mrs. Venable sends
the sophisticated
yet suspicious
Dr. Cukrowicz
(a debonair Gale
Harold) to evaluate
her niece, Catharine
Holly (a woefully
miscast Carla

Gale Harold and Carla Gugino perform in
Tennessee Williams's play *Suddenly Last
Summer*. (Photo © Joan Marcus.)

Gugino), who, having allegedly witnessed Sebastian's death,
was sent away to a psychiatric hospital after her experience. The
decision is made to perform a lobotomy on the young woman at
the wishes of her clandestinely cruel, manipulative aunt. Only
under the influence of a powerful truth serum does Catharine
finally reveal the shocking circumstances of her cousin's death.

    Suddenly Last Summer is a staggering achievement of drama;
but this revival, directed with a heavy hand by Mark Brokaw, has

*Writer provides
both positive
and negative
features of the
production as
he continues
his evaluation*

no life. Noteworthy, though, is Santo Loquasto's dazzling set design. Sebastian's magical greenhouse garden is wonderfully staged, and scenes in the interior of the house are simply elegant. Loquasto's costume design is also impressive, while Peter Golub's original score is by turns lovely and haunting. A baffling technical aspect, however, is David Weiner's lighting design, which seems both inappropriate from scene to scene and peculiarly inconsistent.

Unfortunately, there are problems with the cast as well. Blythe Danner, while giving a respectable performance, is not nearly as good as she could have been. She speaks in a distracting, maddeningly uneven dialect and gives the character far more nervous tics than are necessary. Lost is the nuance of the character, as is her caustic wit (as seen in Katharine Hepburn's superior portrayal in the 1959 film version). Danner's polished poise works for the character in many ways, but too often she seems overly rehearsed. Moreover, Carla Gugino should never have been cast as Catharine. She has neither the presence nor the charm to pull off the role convincingly, and Catharine's fiery passion is lost in what seems to be little more than a bid for a Tony nomination in the monologue. Rounding out the leads is Gale Harold, who does his best with the play's most underwritten role, making Dr. Cukrowicz at once both charismatic and calculating.

4

Roundabout's revival of *Suddenly Last Summer,* while technically robust, leaves its audience exhausted and bored, suspended in a time capsule of clashing theatrical ideologies. Everyone involved tries too hard to make an impression, instead of allowing genuine talent and Williams's wonderful material to speak for themselves. I cannot rightfully recommend this production, though it might be worth seeing for Gale Harold alone. He's an underrated, underutilized actor, and his authenticity is an unadulterated pleasure to watch.

Conclusion summarizes the major strengths and weaknesses of the production and indicates why the weaknesses outweigh the strengths

43 Writing in the Natural Sciences

The **natural sciences** include mathematics, the biological sciences (biology, botany, and zoology), the physical sciences (chemistry and physics), and the earth sciences (geology and astronomy). They also include **applied sciences** such as medicine and allied health studies, engineering, and computer science. The natural sciences are problem-solving disciplines that report or analyze results derived from meticulous observation and experimentation. Writing assignments you can expect to receive in natural science courses include literature reviews, field reports, and laboratory reports.

43a Audience, purpose, and the research question

Before you start working on a writing assignment for a course in the natural sciences, consult with your instructor as you determine your audience and your purpose. Your instructor will always be one of your readers, but he or she may ask you to share your work with other readers as well. By knowing who constitutes your audience(s), you will be able to gauge how much background information is adequate, how much technical language is appropriate, and what types of evidence and reasoning are necessary.

After you have determined your purpose and audience, formulate a research question that will guide you to sources and help you to use them responsibly. The following example research questions focus on global warming.

Question about cause

What causes global warming?

Question about consequences

What are the effects of global warming?

Question about process

How can global warming be stopped?

Question about definitions or categories

What types of greenhouse gases are responsible for global warming?

Question about values

What are a scientist's responsibilities concerning the public in the face of global warming?

Research questions in the sciences are often narrowed to enable precise measurements.

Question about length, distance, frequency, and so on

How far has Mendenhall Glacier receded each year for the past decade, and do the values show any trend?

Question about comparisons and correlations

How are emission intensities related to the total amount of emissions?

43b Evidence, sources, and reasoning

Researchers in the natural sciences attempt to quantify phenomena in the world around them. They look for **empirical evidence**—facts that can be measured or tested—to support their claims. Most of their investigations, then, are set up as experiments. If you conduct an experiment for a course in the natural sciences, you will be expected to start with a **hypothesis**, a prediction that serves as a basis for experimentation. To test the hypothesis, you will follow a procedure—one designed by yourself, established in another study, or specified by your instructor. The results of your experiment will either validate your hypothesis or show it to be in error. This systematic way of proceeding from a hypothesis to verifiable results is called the **scientific method**. Consisting of six steps, this method helps ensure the objectivity and accuracy of experimental findings.

THE SCIENTIFIC METHOD

1. *State a problem.* When you recognize and then state a problem, you establish your rhetorical opportunity (the reason for your writing).

2. *Collect evidence.* Close observation is the key technique for collecting evidence. Be sure to record all details as accurately as you can. Alternatively, you may read the reports of other researchers who have addressed a problem similar to yours. If you draw on observations or experiments, you are using primary sources; if you use scientific articles and statistical charts, you are using secondary sources.

3. *Form a hypothesis.* A hypothesis is a tentative claim, or prediction, about the phenomenon you are studying.

4. *Test the hypothesis.* Although you will have conducted some research before formulating the hypothesis, you continue that research through additional observation or experimentation.

5. *Analyze the results.* Look at your results in light of your hypothesis. Attempt to find patterns, categories, or other relationships.

6. *State the conclusion.* If you have validated your hypothesis, explain why it accounts for *all* of your data. If your hypothesis is disproved, suggest revisions to it or offer a new one.

Reports based on the six steps of the scientific method are **quantitative studies**, because their results are presented as numerical data. Another type of study performed by scientists, especially those working in the field, is a **qualitative study**. The data in qualitative studies are produced through observation and analysis of natural phenomena. It is not uncommon, however, for studies to have both quantitative and qualitative features.

Regardless of the type of study they perform, scientists depend on previous research to place their work in context. They draw from both primary sources (experiments, observations, surveys, and so on) and secondary sources (books and articles already published on a topic).

43c Conventions of language and organization

(1) Style guidelines

The conventions that most writers in the sciences follow are presented in a manual titled *Scientific Style and Format*, Seventh Edition, compiled by the Council of Science Editors (CSE). However, you may sometimes be asked to use another manual, such as that published by the American Chemical Society, the American Institute of Physics, the American Mathematical Society, the American Medical Association, or the United States Geological Society. Before starting any writing project, check with your instructor to see which style manual you should use.

The CSE manual says that effective scientific prose has the qualities of accuracy, clarity, conciseness, and fluency. The following tips can help you write in the style recommended by the manual.

> **TIPS FOR PREPARING A PAPER IN THE NATURAL SCIENCES**
>
> - Select words that convey meaning precisely.
> - Avoid gender bias.
> - If two different wordings are possible, choose the more succinct alternative.
> - Clarify cumbersome noun phrases by placing modifiers after the main noun.
>
>   ➤ the frequency ~~measuring system~~
>
>   *system for measuring*
>
> - When using an introductory participial phrase, be sure that it modifies the subject of the sentence. Participial phrases that begin with *based on* are particularly troublesome, so double-check to make sure that such a phrase modifies the subject.
>
>   ➤ Based on the promising results, the new medication
>
>   *decision to approve*
>
>   ~~was approved.~~
>
>   *seemed reasonable.*

(2) Organization

The most common writing assignments in the natural sciences are various types of reports—literature reviews, field reports, and laboratory reports. The next section describes the specific formats for these reports.

All scientific reports include headings and often subheadings to help readers find and understand information. Writers in the natural sciences also use tables and figures (such as graphs, drawings, and maps) to organize information. Essential for presenting numerical data, tables should be numbered and titled. Each table should be introduced in the text so that readers will understand its purpose. Alyssa Jergens, the student whose field report is featured later in this chapter, includes two tables: one to summarize her data and one to report the results of a statistical test (**43e**). She introduces her first table in this way: "Data from our observational study can be found in Table 1 and Figure 2." Alyssa also uses two figures in her report. The first is a diagram depicting the method used for recording data. The second provides a visual representation of the data in the corresponding table. Like tables, figures should be numbered, titled, and introduced in the text. For an example of a map used as a figure, see Kayla Berg's paper on the tsunami that hit Thailand in 2004 (**16c**).

(3) Reference lists

CSE provides three options for citing sources and listing them at the end of a paper: the citation-sequence system, the citation-name system, and the name-year system. See **16b** for specific guidelines for creating a reference list.

43d Examples of writing in the natural sciences

(1) Literature review

A **literature review** is essentially an evaluative overview of research directly related to a specific topic. It focuses on both strengths and weaknesses of previous research—in methodology or interpretation—with the goal of establishing what steps need to be taken to advance research on the topic. A literature review may be assigned as part of a longer paper, in which case the information it contains appears in the introductory section. In her study of agate formation, student Michelle Tebbe included the following paragraphs, which provide, respectively, a historical account of research on her topic and a review of relevant current studies.

Scientific interest in agate dates back at least to the 18th century when Collini (1776) contemplated the source of silica for agate formation and suggested a mechanism for producing repetitive banding. In the mid-19th century,

(Continued on page 482)

(Continued)

Noeggerath (1849) hypothesized that the repetitive banding of agate is indicative of natural, external (to the agate-bearing cavity), rhythmic processes such as bedrock leaching of silica by a fluid that enters into cavities via infiltration canals, forming agate after many separate infiltrations. Other processes such as variation in water-table height (Bauer 1904) and alternating wet-dry seasons (Linck and Heinz 1930) have been credited as responsible for rhythmic infilling of cavities by silica-rich solutions.

These now traditional ideas on agate formation imply fluid-rock interaction at low temperatures (<250 °C). Empirical support for low formation temperatures comes from several published studies. Based on hydrogen and oxygen isotope data, Fallick et al. (1985) estimated the temperature of formation of Devonian and Tertiary basalt-hosted Scottish agate to be approximately 50 °C. Using the same methods, Harris (1989) inferred the temperature of formation for basalt-hosted agate from Namibia to be approximately 120 °C. Lueth and Goodell (2005) performed fluid-inclusion analyses for agate from the Paraná Basalts, Rio do Sul, Brazil, and inferred the temperature of formation to be <50 °C for darker-colored samples and 140–180 °C for lighter-colored samples.

(2) Field report

Field work is research done in a natural environment rather than in a laboratory. Examples of field work range from recording beach erosion to studying avalanche patterns. To record their observations and analyses, researchers working in the field write **field reports**. These reports consist mainly of description and analysis, which may be presented together or in separate sections (**43e**). A field report sometimes includes a reference list of sources mentioned in the text.

(3) Laboratory report

The most common writing assignment in the natural sciences is a **laboratory report**. The purpose of a lab report is to describe an experiment, including the results obtained, so that other researchers understand the procedure used and the conclusions drawn. When writing a lab report, you should explain the purpose of your research, recount the procedure you followed, and discuss your results. The format of this type of report follows the steps of the scientific method by starting with a problem and a hypothesis and concluding with a statement proving, modifying, or disproving the hypothesis.

- The **abstract** states the problem and summarizes the results. (You may not have to include an abstract if your report is short or if your instructor does not require it.)
- The **introduction** states the research question or hypothesis clearly and concisely, explains the scientific basis for the study, and provides brief background material on the subject of the study and the techniques to be used. The introduction usually includes citations referring to relevant sources.
- The **methods and materials** section is a narrative that describes how the experiment was conducted. It lists the materials that were used, identifies where the experiment was conducted, and describes the procedures that were followed. (Your lab notes should help you remember what you did.) Anyone who wants to repeat your work should be able to do so by following the steps described in this section.
- **Results** are reported by describing (but not interpreting) major findings and supporting them with properly labeled tables or graphs showing the empirical data.
- The **discussion** section includes an analysis of the results and an explanation of their relevance to the goals of the study. This section also reports any problems encountered and offers suggestions for further testing of the results.

- **References** are listed at the end of the report. The list includes only works that are referred to in the report. The comprehensiveness and the accuracy of this list allow readers to evaluate the quality of the report and put it into a relevant context.

43e Sample field report

Alyssa Jergens wrote the following field report for a biology course. Her assignment was to form and test a hypothesis on the density and positioning of lichen growth on tree trunks. She worked as a member of a research group, but all the members wrote their own reports. Following the guidelines she was given by her instructor, Alyssa describes the observational study in the Methods section and analyzes the findings in the Results section.

1

Lichen Distribution on Tree Trunks

Alyssa Jergens

General Biology I

October 1, 2009

Method

Our group formulated the hypothesis that lichens grow
more densely on higher parts of tree trunks than on lower parts
of tree trunks. Our null hypothesis was as follows: there will be
no difference in lichen density at various heights on tree trunks.
Our hypothesis on lichen density led us to predict that the largest
clusters of lichens would be found predominately on higher
portions of tree trunks.

We conducted our study by sampling 20 trees in a designated
area of the Central Washington University campus. Each tree trunk
was divided into three sections based on height: from ground level
to 0.5 m above the ground; from 0.5 m to 1.0 m above the ground;
and from 1.0 m to 1.5 m above the ground. Data were recorded on
a diagram (Figure 1). To the right in the diagram are the height
ranges of the sections of tree trunks. The tick marks indicate how
many trees had most of their lichens in that section of trunk.

Writer
describes the
observational
research

2

1.0–1.5 m

0.5–1.0 m

0.0–0.5 m

Diagram used for data collection presented in Method section

Figure 1. Method for recording lichen density

Results

Findings presented in Results section

    Our observations of lichen growth revealed that lichens are more commonly found on the lower parts of tree trunks. Data from our observational study can be found in Table 1 and Figure 2. Note that 15 of 20 trees had the densest lichen growth on the lowest section of the trunk (ground level to 0.5 m above the ground).

TABLE 1.   SUMMARY OF DATA

Section of tree trunk	0.0–0.5 m	0.5–1.0 m	1.0–1.5 m
Number of trees with highest lichen density in given trunk section	15	3	2

3

Figure 2. Association of trunk height with lichen distribution

To ensure that the pattern of lichen growth we found was not random, we performed a chi-square test. The observed number, f_o, was determined by counting the total number of trees having the most lichens in each height division. The expected number, f_e, was calculated by taking the total number of trees observed (20) and dividing it by the total number of height divisions (3), to arrive at an expected value of 6.67. The chi-square test results are summarized in Table 2; the calculated value is 15.69.

The critical value for the chi-square test given to us in class was 5.99. Our calculated chi-square value, 15.69, is greater than the critical value. Therefore, because the data from this observational study do not exhibit a random pattern, it can be concluded that a nonrandom pattern is present. The results of

Bar graph provides a visual representation of the data

Explains the statistical test that was used to ensure that the results were not random

Concluding paragraph acknowledges that the findings did not support the original hypothesis the chi-square test show that our null hypothesis can be refuted. Although a pattern does exist in the sample of trees we observed, it was not the result we hypothesized. Our hypothesis stated that lichens would grow more densely on the upper portions of tree trunks rather than on the lower portions. Contrary to our expectations, our data and the results of the chi-square test indicate that lichens grow more densely on the lower portions of tree trunks than on the upper portions.

TABLE 2. RESULTS OF CHI-SQUARE TEST

	Observed number (f_o)	Expected number (f_e)	$f_o - f_e$	$(f_o - f_e)^2$	$\dfrac{(f_o - f_e)}{(f_e)}$
0.0–0.5 m	15	6.67	8.33	69.39	10.40
0.5–1.0 m	3	6.67	–3.67	13.47	2.02
1.0–1.5 m	2	6.67	–4.67	21.81	3.27
Total	20	20			15.69

44 Writing in Business

Business writing includes many genres, ranging from application letters and résumés to reports designed to improve sales. Whether you are trying to get a job or preparing a report for a supervisor, you will benefit from writing clearly and concisely, choosing a tone appropriate for your audience.

44a Conventions of language and organization

In any business environment, you will face both anticipated and unexpected deadlines. The following strategies for effective business communication will help you produce comprehensive, concise, and well-organized documents on time.

> **STRATEGIES FOR EFFECTIVE BUSINESS COMMUNICATION**
>
> **Be direct.**
> - State the purpose of your document in your opening paragraph.
> - Write straightforward sentences that your audience will find easy to understand.
> - Use technical language only when writing for a specialized audience.
>
> **Be concise.**
> - Include only necessary details.
> - Use numbers, bullets, or descriptive headings that guide readers to information.
>
> *(Continued on page 490)*

STRATEGIES FOR EFFECTIVE BUSINESS COMMUNICATION   *(Continued)*

- Use graphs, tables, and other visual elements that convey information succinctly.

Use conventional formatting.

- Follow the standard formats that have been established within a business or industry or use the formats outlined in this chapter.

- Avoid informal language unless you know that a casual tone is acceptable.

- Edit and proofread your documents carefully.

44b Business letters

Though business letters serve a variety of purposes, they all generally follow a standard block format: each element is aligned flush with the left margin (set at one inch), with single spacing between lines and double spacing between paragraphs and standard elements.

ELEMENTS OF A STANDARD BUSINESS LETTER

- **Return address.** If you are not required to use stationery with a letterhead, type your address one inch from the top of the paper.

- **Date.** If you are using letterhead stationery, type the date one or two lines below the letterhead's last line. Otherwise, type the date beneath your return address.

- **Recipient's name and address.** Provide the full name and address of the recipient. If you do not know the person's name, try to find it by checking the company's website or phoning the company. If you cannot find the recipient's name, use an appropriate title such as *Personnel Director* or *Customer Service Manager*.

ELEMENTS OF A STANDARD BUSINESS LETTER

- **Greeting.** The conventional greeting is *Dear* followed by the recipient's name and a colon. If you and the recipient use first names to address each other, use the person's first name. Otherwise, use *Mr.*, *Ms.*, *Mrs.*, or *Miss* and the last name. (Choose *Ms.* when you do not know a woman's preference.) Avoid the sexist *Dear Sir, Dear Gentlemen,* or *Dear Madam* and the stilted *To Whom It May Concern* or *Dear Sir or Madam*.

- **Body of the letter.** Most business letters fit on a single sheet of paper. If your letter must continue on a second page, include the recipient's last name, the date, and the page number in three single-spaced lines at the top left on the second page.

- **Closing.** Close your letter with an expression such as *Sincerely* or *Cordially* followed by a comma.

- **Signature.** Type your full name four lines below the closing. Then, in the space above your typed name, sign your full name, using blue or black ink. If you have addressed the recipient by his or her first name, sign just your first name.

- **Additional information.** If you are enclosing extra material such as a résumé, type the word *Enclosure* or the abbreviation *Encl.* two lines below your name. You may also note the number of enclosures or the identity of the document(s): for example, *Enclosures (3)* or *Encl.: 2013 Annual Year-End Report*. If you would like the recipient to know the names of people receiving copies of the letter, use the abbreviation *cc* (for "carbon copy") and a colon followed by the other recipients' names. Place this element on the line directly below the enclosure line or, if there is no enclosure, two lines below your name.

The sample **letter of inquiry** (a letter intended to elicit information) in figure 44.1 illustrates the parts of a typical business letter.

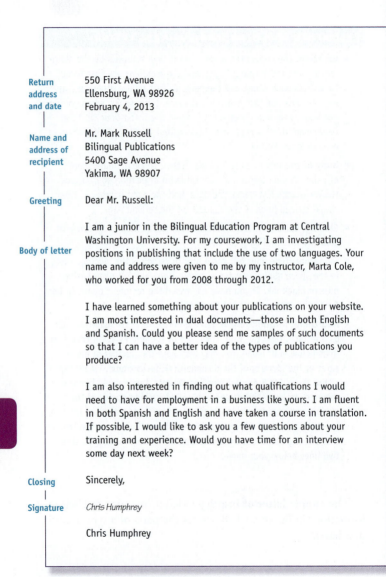

Return address and date

550 First Avenue
Ellensburg, WA 98926
February 4, 2013

Name and address of recipient

Mr. Mark Russell
Bilingual Publications
5400 Sage Avenue
Yakima, WA 98907

Greeting

Dear Mr. Russell:

Body of letter

I am a junior in the Bilingual Education Program at Central Washington University. For my coursework, I am investigating positions in publishing that include the use of two languages. Your name and address were given to me by my instructor, Marta Cole, who worked for you from 2008 through 2012.

I have learned something about your publications on your website. I am most interested in dual documents—those in both English and Spanish. Could you please send me samples of such documents so that I can have a better idea of the types of publications you produce?

I am also interested in finding out what qualifications I would need to have for employment in a business like yours. I am fluent in both Spanish and English and have taken a course in translation. If possible, I would like to ask you a few questions about your training and experience. Would you have time for an interview some day next week?

Closing

Sincerely,

Signature

Chris Humphrey

Chris Humphrey

Figure 44.1. A sample letter of inquiry.

44c Business memos and e-mails

A **memo** (short for *memorandum*) is a brief, single-topic document sent within a business to announce a meeting, explain an event or situation, set a schedule, or request information or action (see figure 44.2). E-mail messages are also used for these purposes as well as for external communication with clients, prospective employees, or people at other companies. The basic guidelines for writing memos also apply to e-mail messages.

Because it is circulated internally, a memo is usually less formal than a letter. Nonetheless, it should still be direct and concise: a memo should be no longer than a page, and an e-mail

To: Intellectual Properties Committee
From: Leo Renfrow, Chair of Intellectual Properties Committee   **Heading**
Date: March 15, 2012
Subject: Review of Policy Statement

At the end of our last meeting, we decided to have our policy
statement reviewed by someone outside our university. Clark   **Body of**
Beech, chair of the Intellectual Properties Committee at Lincoln   **memo**
College, agreed to help us. Overall, as his review shows, the format
of our policy statement is sound. Dr. Beech believes that some of
the content should be further developed, however. It appears that
we have used some ambiguous terms and included some conditions
that would not hold up in court.

Early next week, my assistant will deliver a copy of Dr. Beech's
review to each of you. Please look it over before our next meeting,
on March 29. If you have any questions or comments before then,
please call me at ext. 1540. I look forward to seeing all of you at
the meeting.

Figure 44.2. A sample business memo.

no longer than a screen. A conversational tone is acceptable for an internal message to a coworker, but a more formal tone is required for an e-mail or memo to a supervisor, for example. Also use caution with the information you include in business e-mail and remember that the content of e-mail can easily be forwarded by others, and most employers have access to messages written by employees.

The guidelines for formatting these kinds of documents, are fairly standard, but a particular company or organization may establish its own format.

ELEMENTS OF A STANDARD BUSINESS MEMO OR E-MAIL

- **Heading.** On four consecutive lines, type *To* followed by a colon and the name(s) of the recipient(s), *From* followed by a colon and your name and title (if appropriate), *Date* followed by a colon and the date, and *Subject* followed by a colon and a few words identifying the memo's subject. (The abbreviation *Re*, for "regarding," is sometimes used instead of *Subject*.) This information should be single-spaced. If you are sending copies to individuals whose names are not included in the *To* line, place those names on a new line beginning with *cc* ("carbon copy") and a colon. Most e-mail software supplies these header lines on any new message.

- **Body.** Use the block format, single-spacing lines within each paragraph and double-spacing between paragraphs. Double-space between the heading and the body of the memo. Open your memo or e-mail with the most important information and establish how it affects your audience. Use your conclusion to establish goodwill.

- **Signature.** It is not strictly necessary to sign a memo or e-mail because your name is in the heading. Some writers, however, do sign their names, often with a polite closing such as *Sincerely* or *Best wishes*. One way to enhance the professional tone of your messages is to use an e-mail signature—a set of information that identifies you and your institution.

44d Résumés

A **résumé** emphasizes a person's job qualifications by highlighting relevant experience and abilities. Writing an impressive résumé requires smart choices about what to include, what to accentuate, and what to exclude altogether. Your résumé is, in effect, going to someone's office for a job interview, so make sure it is dressed for success. Effective résumés are brief, so try to design your résumé to fit on a single page. Use high-quality paper (preferably white or off-white) and a laser printer. Choose a standard format and a traditional typeface, applying them consistently throughout. Use boldface or italic type only for headings. Resist the impulse to make the design unnecessarily complicated: when in doubt, opt for simplicity.

Remember that an employer receives many résumés and so may not spend much time reading yours. Along with its accompanying letter of application, a résumé should command attention and establish a positive first impression—immediately. To make sure your qualifications stand out, place them in conventional places and use clear headings and sufficient spacing. Your résumé may be organized chronologically (from most to least recent) or functionally (according to your skill sets). Résumés generally include the elements listed in the box on page 497.

Joe Delaney's résumé (figure 44.3) highlights his educational background first, then mentions his computer skills, extracurricular activities, and work experience.

Joseph F. Delaney III
138 Main Street, Apt. 10D
Cityville, PA 16800
(555) 544-9988   JoeDel4@psu.edu

OBJECTIVE   To obtain a position in project and risk management

EDUCATION
Pennsylvania State University, University Park, PA, 2009–2013
Majors: IST BS (Information Context Option), Psychology BS
Dean's List: Summer 2010, Fall 2011, and Spring 2013
Cumulative GPA: 3.60
Relevant Classes:
- Project Management in Technology—learned to apply basic concepts of project management to the information sciences
- Database Management—managed a project team that applied MySql, PHP, and HTML in completing Rabble Mosaic Creator, described at www.schoolproject.psu.edu/~100

COMPUTER AND TECHNICAL SKILLS
- MySql, PHP, GD Library, C++, Java
- TCP/IP, network security, LANs and WANs
- HTML, XML, and project and risk management

CLUBS/ACTIVITIES
IST Student Government:
- Regular participation in the student government's Academic Committee
- Student resource for the IST Student Executive Board
IST Academic Committee:
- Participated in regularly scheduled meetings with the dean, Henry C. Foley, and the professor in charge, John Yen
- Worked with the administration to address students' problems

WORK EXPERIENCE
Penn State Pollock Library, University Park, PA, May–July 2012
- Assisted patrons of the library in using computers, printers, and the Internet via a wireless network using VPN
- Coordinated computers in my designated area and assisted with defragmenting, rebooting, reformatting, charging, and normal maintenance of laptops

HONORS
- 2011 scholarship student in the College of IST; recipient of the Cingular Wireless Trustee Scholarship
- Pollock Library 2012 student employee of the year

Figure 44.3. Sample résumé.

ELEMENTS OF A RÉSUMÉ

- **Name, address, phone number(s), and e-mail address**
- **Career objective(s).** Mention short-term goals and jobs or positions for which you are applying.
- **Educational background.** List your degrees or diplomas, special honors, participation in advanced programs, relevant coursework, and your grade point average (if it is impressive generally or in your major).
- **Work experience.** Include all your jobs (paying, volunteer, and internships, as well as military service). List dates, places of employment, and job titles, describing your duties with active verbs that emphasize your initiative and your sense of responsibility.
- **Extracurricular activities.** List your extracurricular activities if they relate directly to the position for which you are applying or demonstrate distinctive leadership, athletic, or artistic abilities.
- **References.** Do not include the names and addresses of references (people who have agreed to speak or write on your behalf). Instead, take a list of references to interviews. The list should include their names and addresses as well as their telephone numbers or e-mail addresses.

44e Letters of application

Writing a **letter of application**, or **cover letter**, is an essential step in applying for a job. Your letter of application provides you with the chance to present yourself as articulate, interesting, and professional. It also allows you to put a personal face on the factual content of the résumé. Letters of application follow the general format of all business letters; see figure 44.4 for a sample letter of application.

Return address and date

Joseph F. Delaney III
138 Main Street, Apt. 10D
Cityville, PA 16800
June 4, 2013

Name and address of recipient

Mr. Jim Konigs, Human Resource Director
E. G. Hickey Technical Enterprise
333 Cumberville State Road, Suite 110
West Cumberville, PA 19428-2949

Greeting

Dear Mr. Konigs:

Body of letter

I am applying for the position of project manager posted on Monster.com. I graduated on May 15 with a B.S. degree in information sciences and technology from Pennsylvania State University. I believe that my in-depth research and education in information technology make me an ideal candidate for this position.

I have completed the required coursework and an internship in information technology, consulting, and security, working under such distinguished professors as James Wendle and David Markison. I am currently a teaching instructor with Dr. Markison, responsible for student evaluation and advising. I have served as a project team leader in database management; my team created Rabble Mosaic Creator, a website that allows users to create mosaics out of images.

In addition, I have applicable experience as a member of the student government's Academic Committee, which analyzes students' problems in light of policy before presenting the issues to the dean and professor in charge. I have also worked in the Penn State libraries.

I would appreciate the opportunity to talk with you about the position and my interest in risk and project management. I am available for an interview and can be reached at the phone number or e-mail address at the top of my résumé.

Closing

Sincerely,

Signature

Joseph F. Delaney

Joseph F. Delaney III

Enclosure line

Encl.: résumé

Figure 44.4. Model letter of application.

TIPS FOR WRITING LETTERS OF APPLICATION

- Address your letter to a specific person. If you are responding to an ad that mentions a department without giving a name, call the company and find out who will be doing the screening. If you cannot obtain a specific name, use an appropriate title such as *Human Resources Director*.

- Be brief. You can assume that the recipient will be screening many applications, so keep your letter to one easy-to-read page.

- Mention that you are enclosing a résumé or refer to it but do not summarize it. Your goal is to attract the attention of a busy person (who will not want to read the same information in both your letter and your résumé).

- Indicate why you are interested in working for the company or organization to which you are applying. Demonstrating that you already know something about the company and the position indicates your seriousness and motivation.

- In your closing, be sure to specify how and where you can be reached and emphasize your availability for an interview.

44f Oral presentations with PowerPoint

Oral reports accompanied by PowerPoint presentations are commonplace in business. Such reports can be either internal (for supervisors and colleagues) or external (for clients or investors). They may take the form of project status reports, demonstrations of new equipment or software, research reports, or recommendations.

Keep in mind the following guidelines as you compose an oral report and create PowerPoint slides to accompany it.

> ## ELEMENTS OF A STANDARD ORAL PRESENTATION
>
> - **Introduction.** The introduction provides an outline of your main points so that listeners can easily follow your presentation. In no more than one-tenth of your overall presentation time (for example, one minute of a ten-minute presentation), mention who you are, your qualifications, your topic, and the relevance of that topic to your audience.
> - **Body.** Make sure the organization of your presentation is clear through your use of transitions. You can number each point, use cause-and-consequence transitions, or use chronological transitions. Provide internal summaries to remind your listeners where you have been and where you are going. Offer comments to help your audience sense the weight of various points.
> - **Conclusion.** Rather than restating the main ideas, make your conclusion memorable by ending with a proposal for action, a final statistic, recommendations, or a description of the benefits of a certain course of action. Conclusions should be even shorter than introductions.

Student Emily Cohen and fellow group members created PowerPoint slides to accompany an oral presentation in a business class in which they were writing a business plan. Figure 44.5 shows two of those slides.

Figure 44.5. A dark background with white type is appropriate for a presentation given in a well-lit room. A precise title and concise bulleted points help audience members skim the upper slide, letting them focus more on what the presenter is saying. Using contrasting colors on the lower slide makes the information stand out.

TIPS FOR INCORPORATING POWERPOINT INTO AN ORAL PRESENTATION

- Design your slides for your audience, not for yourself. If you need speaking notes for your talk, write them on note cards or type them into the notes section provided below each slide.
- Be aware of the limitations of PowerPoint. Use no more than five lines of text per slide. Tell your audience where they can find more details.
- In general, keep text and visuals separate. Alternating predominantly visual slides with slides of text will keep your audience's attention. Let visuals (charts, pictures, or graphs) stand alone with just a heading or a title. Use text slides to define terms, to present block quotations, and to list your main points.
- Time your speaking with your presentation of the slides so that the two components are synchronized.

44g   Business reports

Certain elements are common to all business reports.

ELEMENTS OF A STANDARD BUSINESS REPORT

- **Front matter.** This may include a title page, a table of contents, a list of illustrations, and an abstract.
- **Introduction.** This section identifies the problem addressed by the report, presents background information, and includes a purpose statement and a description of the scope of the report.
- **Discussion.** In the body of the report, research findings are presented, which may be accompanied by charts and graphs. Use clear headings for subsections; for a shorter report, use paragraph breaks.
- **Conclusion(s).** This section presents conclusions deduced from the data presented in the body of the report.
- **Recommendation(s).** Not always necessary, this section outlines what should be done with or about the findings.
- **Back matter.** Back matter may include a glossary, a list of the references cited, and one or more appendixes.

Answers to Even-Numbered Exercises

Exercise 17.1, page 254

2. If (conjunction-subordinating) you (pronoun) are (verb), you (pronoun) should (verb-auxiliary) join (verb) the (article-definite) University Anime and Manga Club (noun-proper).

4. Memberships (noun-common) are (verb) free (adjective); however (conjunction-adverbial [also called conjunctive adverb]), donations (noun-common) are (verb) always (adverb) welcome (adjective).

Exercise 17.2, page 257

A slash separates the subject and predicate in each sentence. The complement is underlined and identified in square brackets.

2. He / showed <u>slides of mountain lakes and heather meadows</u>. [direct object]

4. Mountaineers and artists / consider <u>the North Cascades</u> <u>the most dramatic mountains in the range</u>. [direct object, object complement]

6. Many volcanoes / are in the Cascades. [no complement, "in the Cascades" is an adverbial prepositional phrase]

8. Many visitors to this area / hike <u>the Pacific Crest Trail</u>. [direct object]

10. The trail / begins in southern California, passes through Oregon and Washington, and ends in British Columbia. [no complement, "in southern California," "through Oregon and Washington," and "in British Columbia" are adverbial prepositional phrases]

Exercise 17.3, page 264

2. <u>The Charter of the United Nations</u> [noun phrase] <u>was written</u> [verb phrase] <u>in 1945</u> [prepositional phrase].

4. <u>The United Nations</u> [noun phrase] devotes most of its energies to <u>protecting human rights</u> [verbal phrase: gerund], <u>maintaining peace</u> [verbal phrase: gerund], and <u>encouraging social development</u> [verbal phrase: gerund].

6. <u>Its blue flag easily recognized everywhere</u> [absolute phrase], the United Nations now includes <u>193 member states</u> [noun phrase].

Exercise 17.4, page 267

Sentence 2.   1. if you make your living by swallowing swords [adverbial]
              2. However: adverbial conjunction / if: subordinating conjunction
Sentence 4.   1. No dependent clauses
              2. and: coordinating conjunction
Sentence 6.   1. No dependent clauses
              2. No conjunctions

Exercise 18.1, page 272

Sentences 2, 3, 4, 6, 7, 9, 10, 12, and 13 are fragments.
Answers will vary. The following is one possible revision of the paragraph.

One of the most popular rides at any county fair or amusement park is the Ferris wheel. The original Ferris wheel, designed by George Washington Gale Ferris, Jr., for a national exposition in 1893, rose to a height of 264 feet and accommodated 2,140 passengers. Ferris's goal was to build something that would surpass in effect the Eiffel Tower, which was constructed just a few years earlier. Though Ferris's plans were not immediately accepted, once they were, and the wheel opened to the public, it became an immediate success, at times carrying thirty-eight thousand passengers a day. Since the nineteenth century, engineers have designed taller and taller Ferris wheels. The 541-foot Singapore Flyer holds the record, but the Beijing Great Wheel, currently under construction, will be over a hundred feet taller.

Exercise 19.1, page 277

Answers will vary. The following are possibilities.

2. He mentions, for example, research showing that measurements of happiness in the United States have not risen much in the last fifty years: people are responding to survey questions about their levels of happiness in much the same way as they did in 1960.

4. Bok believes that people become accustomed to higher standards of living, not realizing how quickly they adapt, and so they do not become happier.
6. CORRECT

Exercise 20.1, page 282

2. ended   4. led   6. might have lost, had not fished

Exercise 20.2, page 286

Answers will vary depending on the tense chosen. All the sentences in the following paragraph are in the past tense.

I **had** already **been walking** for a half hour in the semi-darkness of Amsterdam's early-morning streets when I **came** to a red light. I **was** in a hurry to get to the train station and no cars **were** out yet, so I **crossed** over the cobblestones, passing a man waiting for the light to change. I never **looked** back when he **scolded** me for breaking the law. I **had** a train to catch. I **was** going to Widnau, in Switzerland, to see Aunt Marie. I **had** not **seen** her since I **was** in second grade.

Exercise 20.3, page 288

2. active   4. active   6. passive

Exercise 20.4, page 290

2. Superstitious people think that if NASA <u>had changed</u> the number of the mission, the astronauts would have had a safer journey.
4. The crew used the lunar module as though it <u>were</u> a lifeboat.
6. If NASA ever <u>planned</u> a space mission on Friday the Thirteenth again, the public would object.

Exercise 20.5, page 296

2. include   4. is   6. know

Exercise 21.1, page 304

Answers will vary. The following are possibilities.

[1]When my brother and I were in middle school, we formed a band with our friends Jason and Andrew. [2]My grandmother had given Jake a guitar and me a drum kit for Christmas. [3]We practiced either alone or together for the rest of the winter. [4]Then, in the spring, we met

up with Jason, whom we had known for years. [5]He and his cousin Andrew, who we later called Android, were excited to join Jake and me. [6]Jason already had a guitar, and Andrew could sing. [7]After we played together one afternoon, we decided to call ourselves *The Crash*. [8]Jason and Andrew came over to our house to jam whenever their parents let them—which was most of the time. [9]Our parents did not mind our noise at all. [10]My dad said our playing reminded him of his own teenage garage band.

Exercise 21.2, page 304

2. They also recommended our hiring someone with extensive experience in statistical analysis.
4. CORRECT

Exercise 21.3, page 307

Answers will vary. The following are possibilities.
2. People should have the right to participate in a study only if they feel comfortable doing so.
4. Participants should be guaranteed that the information they provide will remain confidential.

Exercise 21.4, page 309

Answers will vary. The following are possibilities.
2. Because her father worked for the United Nations Education, Scientific and Cultural Organization (UNESCO), Baez lived in many different countries as a young girl.
4. Baez and her younger sister, Mimi Fariña, also a singer-songwriter, sometimes toured together.

Exercise 21.5, page 310

Answers will vary. The following are possibilities.
2. The issue was ignored until gas prices started to rise dramatically.
4. Nonetheless, the ratings can never be exact, given that driving habits differ from individual to individual.

Exercise 21.6, page 312

Answers will vary. The following are possibilities.

2. For example, orangutans, African elephants, and Atlantic bottlenose dolphins should roam freely rather than be held in captivity.
4. Like humans, animals such as these show emotions, self-awareness, and intention.
6. Clearly, they have the right to freedom.

Exercise 22.1, page 315

2. really   4. quietly

Exercise 22.2, page 317

2. less frequently   4. closest

Exercise 22.3, page 319

Answers will vary. The following are possibilities.

2. Hitchcock was identified with thrillers only after making his third movie, *The Lodger*.
4. Although his movies are known for suspense, sometimes moviegoers also remember Hitchcock's droll sense of humor.
6. Originally a British citizen, Alfred Hitchcock was knighted by Queen Elizabeth II in 1980.

Exercise 22.4, page 321

Answers will vary. The following are possibilities.

2. In determining an appropriate challenge, climbers must consider safety precautions.
4. Although adding extra weight, a first-aid kit should be in every climber's pack.

Exercise 23.1, page 327

Answers will vary. The following are possibilities.

2. President Obama argued for the spending cuts.
4. Brown and Edwards described the improvements that had been made to the old building.

Exercise 23.2, page 330

Answers will vary. The following are possibilities.

2. He drew a generic male face with metal teeth and long red ribbons of hair falling in front of it.

4. The evil visage of Darth Maul was so horrible that McCaig added elegant black feathers to balance the effect.

Exercise 24.1, page 334

Answers will vary. The following are possibilities.

The Lummis, a tribe in the Northwest, believe that grief is a burden that should not be carried alone. After the terrorist attack on the World Trade Center, Lummi carvers, wanting to help shoulder the burden of grief felt by others, crafted a healing totem pole for the citizens of New York, many of whom had family members who were killed in the terrorist attacks. The Lummis do not believe that it is the pole itself that heals but rather the prayers and songs said over it. For them, healing is not the responsibility of a single person; it is the responsibility of the community.

Exercise 24.2, page 336

Answers will vary. The following are possibilities.

2. Duct tape was originally called "duck tape" because, like ducks, it was waterproof and because it was made of cotton duck, a durable, tightly woven material.

4. Although many new colorful forms of duct tape are available, they are more expensive and less practical than standard silver.

Exercise 25.1, page 339

Answers will vary. The following are possibilities.

2. When she hired new employees for her department, she looked for applicants who were accomplished, hardworking, and articulate.

4. In her annual report, she wrote that her most important achievements were attracting new majors and increasing scholarship donations.

6. Whether planning for department meetings or conventions, Helen prepared her remarks in advance.

Exercise 26.1, page 343

Answers will vary. The following are possibilities.

2. Rudolph's Olympic achievement is impressive, but even more spectacular is her victory over a crippling disease.

4. Her determination was essential to her recovery, as were her siblings' willingness to help and her mother's vigilant care.

Exercise 27.1, page 347

Answers will vary. The following is a possibility.

2. With ideologies that could not be more different, both men see the Bible as the foundation from which the moral well-being of the United States should be reconstructed.

Exercise 27.2, page 348

Answers will vary. The following are possibilities.

2. After he pasted a map onto a piece of wood, he used a fine-bladed saw to cut around the borders of the countries.

4. Because the wooden pieces were cut by hand, the original puzzles were quite expensive.

6. After he recovered, built up his strength, and gained self-confidence, Lee's passion became mountain biking.

8. What kinds of activities can help survivors of traumatic brain injury toward recovery? Advocates believe that reviewing and practicing conversation and people skills are both essential to success.

Exercise 28.1, page 353

Answers will vary. The following are possibilities.

2. Parents should read to their small children.

4. For six years, he worked as a mail carrier in a small town.

Exercise 29.1, page 358

Answers will vary. The following are possibilities.

2. start over: She reconsidered the experiment and started over to ensure accurate results.

4. fulfill an obligation with minimal effort: Because their contract for the project expires soon, the agency works with minimal effort.

Exercise 30.1, page 363

Answers will vary. The following are possibilities.
2. Before the ceremony, he had not received an award.
4. The fans watching the television made a lot of noise.
6. Registering early is important.

Exercise 31.1, page 367

Answers will vary. The following are possibilities.
2. In general, people notice goose bumps on their forearms, but some people also report having goose bumps on their legs.
4. The German and Italian languages also have words that refer to goose flesh, but French and Spanish translations refer to hens.
6. Not only humans experience piloerection, but other mammals do as well.

Exercise 31.2, page 368

2. Although sound cannot be seen, people have described it this way for a long time.
4. Envisioning waves in the air, he hypothesized that sound would not be able to pass through a vacuum because there would be no air to transmit it.
6. In 1654, Otto von Guericke found that he could not hear a bell ringing inside the vacuum he had created. [The comma after "1654" is optional.]
8. However, although most sound reaches us through the air, it travels faster through liquids and solids.

Exercise 31.3, page 372

2. The largest cat on record, for example, was forty-eight inches long.
4. Most Maine Coons have exceptionally high intelligence for cats, which enables them to recognize language and even to open doors.
6. According to a legend, later proven to be false, Maine Coons are descendants from Turkish Angora cats owned by Marie Antoinette.

Exercise 31.4, page 374

2. On February 15, 1527, Cabeza de Vaca was appointed to an expedition headed for the mainland of North America.
4. Devastated by misfortune, the expedition dwindled rapidly.
6. His endurance now tested, Cabeza de Vaca lived as a trader and healer among Native Americans of the Rio Grande Basin, learning from them and eventually speaking on their behalf to the Spanish crown.

Exercise 32.1, page 376

2. The game is called soccer only in Canada and the United States; elsewhere it is known as football.
4. In amateur matches, players can be substituted frequently; however, in professional matches, the number of substitutions is limited.

Exercise 32.2, page 379

2. The process consists of six stages: recognizing a need or desire, finding information, evaluating options, deciding to purchase, purchasing, and assessing purchases.
4. The post-purchase assessment has one of two basic results: satisfaction or dissatisfaction with the product or service.

Exercise 33.1, page 383

2. an hour's drive
4. the eyewitness's report
6. Pat and Alan's new book
8. the neighbor's spying

Exercise 33.2, page 385

2. Hanson's book was published in the early 1920s.
4. Few students enrolled during the academic year '13–'14.
6. They hired a rock 'n' roll band for their engagement party.
8. You'll have to include the ISBNs of the books you're going to purchase.

Exercise 34.1, page 389

2. Negroponte starts his article with a problem: "Innovation is inefficient" (2).

4. "The biggest challenge in stimulating a creative culture," asserts Negroponte, "is finding ways to encourage multiple points of view" (2).

6. According to the author, "More than ever before, in the new 'new economy,' research and innovation will need to be housed in those places where there are parallel agendas and multiple means of support" (3).

Exercise 35.1, page 398

2. Encouraging cultural diversity, fostering intercultural discussions, and promoting peace—these are just a few of UNESCO's goals.

4. According to a recent policy statement, the "Millennium Summit of Heads of States [New York, September 2010] recognized the value of cultural diversity for the enrichment of humankind..." (UNESCO 4).

Exercise 36.1, page 403

2. desirable, readable, traceable, knowledgeable

Exercise 36.2, page 406

2. a forty-eight-inch television screen

4. a seventeenth-century painting

6. a food-borne virus

Exercise 37.1, page 410

[1]Swimmer **M**ichael **P**helps holds the record as the most decorated **O**lympian. [2]By the end of the 2012 **O**lympics in **L**ondon, **E**ngland, he had earned twenty-two medals (**t**he previous record holder had eighteen). [3]In the 2008 **S**ummer **O**lympic **G**ames in **B**eijing, China, **P**helps finished first eight times. [4]Afterwards, with a bonus he was given by the sports company **S**peedo, **P**helps established a **f**oundation to promote healthy lifestyles and the sport of swimming, especially among children. [5]According to **P**helps, the swimming pool provided a place for him "**t**o have fun, stay healthy, set goals, work hard and gain confidence."

Exercise 38.1, page 413

2. The Frye Art Museum features three of the paintings that were on display: *The Birch Grove*, *Lady Curzon*, and *The Duel*.
4. Another exhibit at the Frye featured paintings, such as *Sorrow* and *No. 21*, commissioned to accompany music inspired by Joyce's poetry.
6. *Interactive* is a key word for describing this exhibit, as there were also shelves of artifacts for people to examine.

Exercise 39.1, page 418

2. The original canal was 363 miles long, running between Albany and Buffalo.
4. DeWitt Clinton, U.S. senator from New York, found support for the construction of the canal in the state legislature.
6. The Corridor is over five hundred miles long and runs through twenty-three counties of upstate New York.

Glossary of Usage

By learning about usage in this glossary, you will increase your ability to use words effectively.

Agreement on usage occurs slowly—often after a period of debate. An asterisk (*) before an entry indicates that a new usage has been reported by dictionary editors. This usage, however, might not yet be accepted by everyone.

a lot of   *A lot of* is conversational for *many*, *much*, or *a great deal of*: They do not have ~~a lot of~~ much time. *A lot* is sometimes misspelled as *alot*.

a while, awhile   *A while* means "a period of time." It is often used with the prepositions *after*, *for*, and *in*: We rested for **a while**. *Awhile* means "a short time." It is not preceded by a preposition: We rested **awhile**.

accept, except   The verb *accept* means "to receive": I **accept** your apology. The verb *except* means "to exclude": The policy was to have everyone wait in line, but mothers and small children were **excepted**. The preposition *except* means "other than": All **except** Joe will attend the conference.

advice, advise   *Advice* is a noun: They asked their attorney for **advice**. *Advise* is a verb: The attorney **advised** us to save all relevant documents.

affect, effect   *Affect* is a verb that means "to influence": The lobbyist's pleas did not **affect** the politician's decision. The noun *effect* means "a result": The **effect** of his decision on the staff's morale was positive and long lasting. When used as a verb, *effect* means "to produce" or "to cause": The activists believed that they could **effect** real political change.

all ready, already   *All ready* means "completely prepared": The rooms are **all ready** for the conference. *Already* means "by or before the time specified": She has **already** taken her final exams.

* **all right**   *All right* means "acceptable": The students asked whether it was **all right** to use dictionaries during the exam. *Alright* is not yet a generally accepted spelling of *all right*, although it is becoming more common in journalistic writing.

all together, altogether   *All together* means "as a group": The cast reviewed the script **all together**. *Altogether* means "wholly, thoroughly": That game is **altogether** too difficult.

allude, elude   *Allude* means "to refer to indirectly": The professor **alluded** to a medieval text. *Elude* means "to evade" or "to escape from": For the moment, his name **eludes** me.

allusion, illusion   An *allusion* is a casual or indirect reference: The **allusion** was to Shakespeare's *Twelfth Night*. An *illusion* is a false idea or an unreal image: His idea of college is an **illusion**.

alot   See **a lot of**.

already   See **all ready, already**.

alright   See **all right**.

altogether   See **all together, altogether**.

* **among, between**   To follow traditional usage, use *among* with three or more entities (a group): The snorkelers swam **among** the fish. Use *between* when referring to only two entities: The rivalry **between** the two teams is intense. Current dictionaries also note the possibility of using *between* to refer to more than two entities, especially when these entities are considered distinct: We have strengthened the lines of communication **between** the various departments.

amount of, number of   Use *amount of* before nouns that cannot be counted: The **amount of** rain that fell last year was insufficient. Use *number of* with nouns that can be counted: The **number of** students attending college has increased.

and/or   This combination denotes three options: one, the other, or both: a parent **and/or** a teacher. These options can also be presented separately with *or*: The student's application should be signed by a parent, a teacher, **or** both.

* **angry at, angry with**   Both *at* and *with* are commonly used after *angry*, although according to traditional guidelines, *with* should be used when a person is the cause of the anger: She was **angry with** me because I was late.

another, other, the other   *Another* is followed by a singular noun: **another** book. *Other* is followed by a plural noun: **other** books. *The other* is followed by either a singular or a plural noun: **the other book**, **the other books**.

anymore, any more   *Anymore* meaning "any longer" or "now" most frequently occurs in negative sentences: Sarah doesn't work here **anymore**. Its use in positive sentences is considered conversational; *now* is generally used instead: All he ever does ~~anymore~~ **now** is watch television. As two words, *any more* appears with *not* to mean "no more": We do not have **any more** time.

anyone, any one   *Anyone* means "any person at all": We did not know **anyone**. *Any one* refers to one of a group: **Any one** of the options is better than the current situation.

* **anyplace, everyplace, someplace**   These words are becoming increasingly common in academic writing. However, according to traditional usage rules, they should be replaced by *anywhere*, *everywhere*, and *somewhere*.

as   Conversational when used after such verbs as *know*, *say*, and *see*. Use *that*, *if*, or *whether* instead: I do not know ~~as~~ **whether** my application is complete. Also considered conversational is the use of *as* instead of *who*, *which*, or *that*: Many of the performers ~~as~~ **who** have appeared on our program will be giving a concert this evening.

* **as, like**   According to traditional usage, *as* begins either a phrase or a clause; *like* begins only a phrase: My brother drives too fast, just ~~like~~ **as** my father did. Current dictionaries note the informal use of *like* to begin clauses after verbs such as *look* and *sound*.

assure, ensure, insure   *Assure* means "to state with confidence, alleviating any doubt": The flight attendant **assured** us that our flight would arrive on time. *Ensure* and *insure* are usually interchangeable to mean "make certain," but only *insure* means "to protect against loss": The editor **ensured** [OR **insured**] that the reporter's facts were accurate. Physicians must **insure** themselves against malpractice suits.

awhile   See **a while, awhile**.

bad   Unconventional as an adverb; use *badly* instead. The team played **badly**. However, the adjective *bad* is used after sensory verbs such as *feel*, *look*, and *smell*: I feel **bad** that I forgot to return your book yesterday.

being as, being that   Unconventional; use *because* instead. ~~Being as~~ **Because** the road was closed, traffic was diverted to another route.

* **beside, besides**   According to traditional usage, these two words have different meanings. *Beside* means "next to": The president sat **beside** the prime minister. *Besides* means "in addition to" or "other than": She has written many articles **besides** those on political reform. Professional writers regularly use *beside* to convey this meaning, as long as there is no risk of ambiguity.

better, had better   *Better* is conversational. Use *had better* instead: We ~~better~~ **had better** finish the report by five o'clock.

between   See **among, between**.

* **can, may**   *Can* refers to ability, and *may* refers to permission: You **can** [are able to] drive seventy miles an hour, but you **may** not [are not permitted to] exceed the speed limit. In contemporary usage, *can* and *may* are used interchangeably to denote possibility or permission, although *may* is used more frequently in formal contexts.

capital, capitol   *Capital* means either "a governing city" or "funds": The **capital** of Minnesota is St. Paul. An anonymous donor provided the **capital** for the project. As a modifier, *capital* means "chief" or "principal": This year's election is of **capital** importance. It may also refer to the death penalty: **Capital** punishment is legal in some states. A *capitol* is a statehouse; the *Capitol* is the U.S. congressional building in Washington, DC.

cite, site, sight   *Cite* means "to mention": Be sure to **cite** your sources. *Site* is a location: The president visited the **site** for the new library. As a verb, *site* also means "to situate": The builder **sited** the factory near the freeway. *Sight* means "to see": The crew **sighted** land. *Sight* also refers to a view: What an incredible **sight**!

climactic, climatic   *Climactic* refers to a climax, or high point: The actors rehearsed the **climactic** scene. *Climatic* refers to the *climate*: Many environmentalists are worried about the recent **climatic** changes.

coarse, course   *Coarse* refers to roughness: The jacket was made of **coarse** linen. *Course* refers to a route: Our **course** to the island was indirect. *Course* may also refer to a plan of study: I want to take a **course** in nutrition.

compare to, compare with   *Compare to* means "to regard as similar," and *compare with* means "to examine for similarities and/or differences": She **compared** her mind **to** a dusty attic. The student **compared** the first draft **with** the second.

complement, complementary, compliment, complimentary   *Complement* means "to complete" or "to balance": Their personalities **complement** each other. They have **complementary** personalities. *Compliment* means "to express praise": The professor **complimented** the students on their first drafts. Her remarks were **complimentary**. *Complimentary* may also mean "provided free of charge": We received **complimentary** tickets.

* **compose, comprise**   *Compose* means "to make up": That collection is **composed** of medieval manuscripts. *Comprise* means "to consist of": The anthology **comprises** many famous essays. Dictionary editors have noted the increasing use of *comprise* in the passive voice to mean "to be composed of."

conscience, conscious, consciousness   *Conscience* means "the sense of right and wrong": He examined his **conscience** before deciding whether to join the protest. *Conscious* means "awake": After an hour, the patient was fully **conscious**. After an hour, the patient regained **consciousness**. *Conscious* may also mean "aware": We were **conscious** of the possible consequences.

continual, continually, continuous, continuously   *Continual* means "constantly recurring": **Continual** interruptions kept us from completing the project. Telephone calls **continually** interrupted us. *Continuous* means "uninterrupted": The job applicant had a record of ten years' **continuous** employment. The job applicant worked **continuously** from 2000 to 2009.

could of   *Of* is often mistaken for the sound of the unstressed *have*: They **could** ~~of~~ **have** [OR might **have**, should **have**, would **have**] gone home.

couldn't care less   *Couldn't care less* expresses complete lack of concern: She **couldn't care less** about her reputation. *Could care less* is considered unconventional in academic writing.

council, counsel A *council* is an advisory or decision-making group: The student **council** supported the new regulations. A *counsel* is a legal adviser: The defense **counsel** conferred with the judge. As a verb, *counsel* means "to give advice": She **counsels** people with eating disorders.

criteria, criterion *Criteria* is a plural noun meaning "a set of standards for judgment": The teachers explained the **criteria** for the assignment. The singular form is *criterion*: Their judgment was based on only one **criterion**.

* **data** *Data* is the plural form of *datum*, which means "piece of information" or "fact": When the **data are** complete, we will know the true cost. However, current dictionaries also note that *data* is frequently used as a mass entity (like the word *furniture*), appearing with a singular verb.

desert, dessert *Desert* can mean "a barren land": Gila monsters live in the **deserts** of the Southwest. As a verb, *desert* means "to leave": I thought my friends had **deserted** me. *Dessert* refers to something sweet eaten at the end of a meal: They ordered apple pie for **dessert**.

device, devise *Device* is a noun: She invented a **device** that measures extremely small quantities of liquid. *Devise* is a verb: We **devised** a plan for work distribution.

differ from, differ with *Differ from* means "to be different": A bull snake **differs from** a rattlesnake in a number of ways. *Differ with* means "to disagree": Senator Brown has **differed with** Senator Owen on several issues.

* **different from, different than** *Different from* is generally preferred for use with nouns, pronouns, and noun phrases: This school was **different from** most others. It may also be used with a noun clause: The school was **different from** what we had expected. *Different* is also commonly used with adverbial clauses in which *than* is the conjunction: We are no **different than** they are.

discreet, discrete *Discreet* means "showing good judgment or self-restraint": His friends complained openly, but his comments were quite **discreet**. *Discrete* means "distinct": The participants in the study came from three **discrete** groups.

disinterested, uninterested *Disinterested* means "impartial": A **disinterested** observer will give a fair opinion. *Uninterested* means "lacking interest": She was **uninterested** in the outcome of the game.

distinct, distinctive *Distinct* means "easily distinguishable or perceived": Each proposal has **distinct** advantages. *Distinctive* means "characteristic" or "serving to distinguish": We studied the **distinctive** features of hawks.

* **due to** Traditionally, *due to* was not synonymous with *because of*: ~~Due to~~ Because of holiday traffic, we arrived an hour late. However, dictionary editors now consider this usage of *due to* acceptable.

effect See **affect, effect**.

elicit, illicit *Elicit* means "to draw forth": He is **eliciting** contributions for a new playground. *Illicit* means "unlawful": The newspaper reported their **illicit** mishandling of public funds.

elude See **allude, elude**.

emigrate from, immigrate to *Emigrate* means "to leave one's own country": My ancestors **emigrated from** Ireland. *Immigrate* means "to arrive in a different country to settle": The Ulster Scots **immigrated to** the southern United States.

ensure See **assure, ensure, insure**.

especially, specially *Especially* emphasizes a characteristic or quality: Some people are **especially** sensitive to the sun. *Especially* also means "particularly": Wildflowers are abundant in this area, **especially** during May. *Specially* means "for a particular purpose": The classroom was **specially** designed for music students.

etc. Abbreviation of *et cetera*, meaning "and others of the same kind." Use only within parentheses: Be sure to bring appropriate camping gear (tent, sleeping bag, mess kit, **etc.**). Because *and* is part of the meaning of *etc.*, avoid using the combination *and etc.*

everyday, every day *Everyday* means "routine" or "ordinary": These are **everyday** problems. *Every day* means "each day": I read the newspaper **every day**.

everyone, every one *Everyone* means "all": **Everyone** should attend. *Every one* refers to each person or item in a group: **Every one** of you should attend.

everyplace   See **anyplace, everyplace, someplace**.

except   See **accept, except**.

explicit, implicit   *Explicit* means "expressed clearly and directly": Given his **explicit** directions, we knew how to proceed. *Implicit* means "implied or expressed indirectly": I mistakenly understood his silence to be his **implicit** approval of the project.

farther, further   Generally, *farther* refers to geographic distance: We will have to drive **farther** tomorrow. *Further* means "more": If you need **further** assistance, please let me know.

* **feel**   Traditionally, *feel* was not synonymous with "think" or "believe": I ~~feel~~ think that more should be done to protect local habitat. Dictionary editors now consider this use of *feel* to be a standard alternative.

fewer, less   *Fewer* occurs before nouns that can be counted: **fewer** technicians, **fewer** pencils. *Less* occurs before nouns that cannot be counted: **less** milk, **less** support. *Less than* may be used with measurements of time or distance: **less than** three months, **less than** twenty miles.

* **first, firstly; second, secondly**   Many instructors prefer the use of *first* and *second*. However, according to current dictionaries, *firstly* and *secondly* are also well-established forms.

former, latter   Used together, *former* refers to the first of two; *latter* to the second of two. John and Ian are both English. The **former** is from Manchester; the **latter** is from Birmingham.

further   See **farther, further**.

get   Considered conversational in many common expressions: The weather ~~got better~~ improved overnight. I did not know what he ~~was getting at~~ meant.

good, well   *Good* is an adjective, not an adverb: He pitched ~~good~~ well last night. *Good* in the sense of "in good health" may be used interchangeably with *well*: I feel **good** [OR **well**] this morning.

had better   See **better, had better**.

half   *A half a* or *a half an* is unconventional; use *half a/an* or *a half*: You should be able to complete the questionnaire in **a half ~~an~~** hour.

hanged, hung   *Hanged* means "put to death by hanging": The prisoner was **hanged** at dawn. For all other meanings, use *hung*: He **hung** the picture above his desk.

has got, have got   Conversational; omit *got*: I **have** ~~got~~ a meeting tomorrow.

he/she, his/her   Although used as a solution to the problem of sexist language, these combinations are not universally accepted. Consider using *he or she* and *his or her* or transforming the sentence with the plural *they* or *their*. See **28b**.

herself, himself, myself, yourself   Unconventional as subjects in a sentence. Joe and ~~myself~~ I will lead the discussion.

* **hopefully**   According to traditional usage, *hopefully* means "with hope," not "it is hoped": **Hopefully**, the negotiators discussed the proposed treaty. However, dictionary editors have started to accept the use of *hopefully* as a sentence modifier: **Hopefully**, the treaty will be ratified. If your instructor prefers you to follow traditional usage, use *I hope* in such a sentence: **I hope** the treaty will be ratified.

hung   See **hanged, hung**.

i.e.   Abbreviation of *id est*, meaning "that is." Use only within parentheses: All participants in the study ran the same distance (**i.e.**, six kilometers). Otherwise, replace *i.e.* with the English equivalent, *that is*: Assistance was offered to those who would have difficulty boarding, ~~i.e.,~~ that is, the elderly, the disabled, and parents with small children. Do not confuse *i.e.* with *e.g.,* meaning "for example."

illicit   See **elicit, illicit**.

illusion   See **allusion, illusion**.

immigrate   See **emigrate from, immigrate to**.

* **impact**   Though *impact* is commonly used as a verb in business writing, many instructors still use it as a noun only: The new tax ~~impacts~~ affects everyone.

implicit   See **explicit, implicit**.

imply, infer   *Imply* means "suggest without actually stating": Though he never mentioned the statistics, he **implied** that they were questionable. *Infer* means "draw a conclusion based on evidence": Given the tone of his voice, I **inferred** that he found the work substandard.

in regards to   See **regard, regarding, regards**.

inside of, outside of   Drop *of* when unnecessary: Security guards stood **outside ~~of~~** the front door.

insure   See **assure, ensure, insure**.

irregardless   Unconventional; use *regardless* instead.

its, it's   *Its* is a possessive form: The committee forwarded **its** recommendation. *It's* is a contraction of *it is*: **It's** a beautiful day.

kind of a, sort of a   The word *a* is unnecessary: This **kind of ~~a~~** book sells well. *Kind of* and *sort of* are not conventionally used to mean "somewhat": The report was **~~kind of~~ somewhat** difficult to read.

later, latter   *Later* means "after a specific time" or "a time after now": The concert ended **later** than we had expected. *Latter* refers to the second of two items: Of the two versions described, I prefer the **latter**.

lay, lie   *Lay* (*laid, laying*) means "put" or "place": He **laid** the book aside. *Lie* (*lay, lain, lying*) means "rest" or "recline": I had just **lain** down when the alarm went off. *Lay* takes an object (to **lay** something), while *lie* does not. These verbs may be confused because the present tense of *lay* and the past tense of *lie* are spelled the same way.

lead, led   As a noun, *lead* means "a kind of metal": The paint had **lead** in it. As a verb, *lead* means "to conduct": A guide will **lead** a tour of the ruins. *Led* is the past tense of the verb *lead*: He **led** the country from 1949 to 1960.

less, less than   See **fewer, less**.

lie   See **lay, lie**.

like   See **as, like**.

literally   Conversational when used to emphasize the meaning of another word: I was **~~literally~~ nearly** frozen after I finished shoveling the sidewalk. *Literally* is conventionally used to indicate that an expression is not being used figuratively: My friend **literally** climbs the walls after work; his fellow rock climbers join him at the local gym.

lose, loose   *Lose* is a verb: She does not **lose** her patience often. *Loose* is chiefly used as an adjective: A few of the tiles are **loose**.

lots, lots of   Conversational for *many* or *much*: He has **~~lots of~~ many** friends. We have **~~lots~~ much** to do before the end of the quarter.

mankind   Considered sexist because it excludes women: All ~~mankind~~ humanity will benefit from this new discovery.

may   See **can, may**.

may of, might of   See **could of**.

maybe, may be   *Maybe* is an adverb: **Maybe** the negotiators will succeed this time. *May* and *be* are verbs: The rumor **may be** true.

* **media, medium**   According to traditional definitions, *media* is a plural word: The **media** have sometimes created the news in addition to reporting it. The singular form is *medium*: The newspaper is one **medium** that people seem to trust. The use of *media* as a collective noun taking a singular verb, although frequent, is still considered conversational.

most   Unconventional to mean "almost": We watch the news ~~most~~ almost every day.

myself   See **herself, himself, myself, yourself**.

nothing like, nowhere near   Unconventional; use *not nearly* instead: Her new book is ~~nowhere near~~ not nearly as mysterious as her previous novel.

number of   When the expression *a number of* is used, the reference is plural: **A number of** positions **are** open. When *the number of* is used, the reference is singular: **The number of** possibilities **is** limited. See also **amount of, number of**.

off of   Conversational; omit *of*: He walked **off** ~~of~~ the field.

on account of   Conversational; use *because of*: The singer canceled her engagement ~~on account of~~ because of a sore throat.

* **on the other hand**   If you use *on the one hand* to introduce the first of two contrasting points, make sure that *on the other hand* introduces the second. However, *on the other hand* may be used to introduce a contrasting point even if it is not preceded by *on the one hand*.

other   See **another, other, the other**.

passed, past   *Passed* is the past tense of the verb *pass*: Deb **passed** the other runners right before the finish line. *Past* means "beyond a time or location": We walked **past** the high school.

per   In ordinary contexts, use *a* or *an*: You should drink at least six glasses of water ~~per~~ a day.

percent, percentage   *Percent* (also spelled *per cent*) is used with a specific number: **Sixty percent** of the students attended the ceremony. *Percentage* refers to an unspecified portion: The **percentage** of students attending college has increased in recent years.

perspective, prospective   *Perspective* means "point of view": We discussed the issue from various **perspectives**. *Prospective* means "likely to become": **Prospective** journalists interviewed the editor.

phenomena, phenomenon   *Phenomena* is the plural form of *phenomenon*: Natural **phenomena** were given scientific explanations.

* **plus**   *Plus* joins nouns or noun phrases to make a sentence seem like an equation: Her endless curiosity **plus** her boundless energy makes her the perfect camp counselor. Note that a singular form of the verb is required (e.g., *makes*). In the past, *plus* was not used to join clauses: The candidate had three advanced degrees. ~~Plus~~ In addition, she had experience working abroad. The use of *plus* at the beginning of a clause is now considered acceptable by some dictionaries.

precede, proceed   To *precede* is to "go ahead of": A moment of silence **preceded** the applause. To *proceed* is to "go forward": After stopping for a short rest, we **proceeded** to our destination.

prejudice, prejudiced   *Prejudice* is a noun: They were unaware of their **prejudice**. *Prejudiced* is an adjective: She accused me of being **prejudiced**.

pretty   *Pretty* means "attractive," not "rather" or "fairly": We were ~~pretty~~ fairly tired after cooking all day.

principal, principle   As a noun, *principal* means "chief official": The **principal** greeted the students every day. It also means "capital": The loan's **principal** was still quite high. As an adjective, *principal* means "main": Tourism is the country's **principal** source of income. The noun *principle* refers to a rule, standard, or belief: She explained the three **principles** supporting the theory.

proceed   See **precede, proceed**.

prospective   See **perspective, prospective**.

quotation, quote   In academic writing, *quotation* refers to a repeated or copied sentence or passage: She began her speech with a ~~quote~~ quotation from *Othello*. *Quote* expresses an action: My coach **quotes** lines from television commercials.

raise, rise   *Raise* (*raised, raising*) means "to lift or cause to move upward, to bring up or increase": Retailers **raised** prices. *Rise* (*rose, risen, rising*) means "to get up" or "to ascend": The cost of living **rose** sharply. *Raise* takes an object (to **raise** something); *rise* does not.

real, really   *Really* rather than *real* is used to mean "very": He is from a ~~real~~ really small town. To ensure this word's effectiveness, use it sparingly.

* **reason why**   Traditionally, this combination was considered redundant: No one explained **the reason ~~why~~** the negotiations failed. [OR No one explained **~~the reason~~ why** the negotiations failed.] However, dictionary editors report its use by well-known writers.

regard, regarding, regards   Be sure to use the correct forms of these words: *in regard to, with regard to, as regards,* and *regarding* [NOT *in regards to, with regards to,* or *as regarding*].

* **relation, relationship**   According to traditional definitions, *relation* is used to link abstractions: We studied the **relation** between language and social change. *Relationship* is used to link people: The **relationship** between the two friends grew strong. However, dictionary editors now label as standard the use of *relationship* to connect abstractions.

respectfully, respectively   *Respectfully* means "showing respect": The children learned to treat one another **respectfully**. *Respectively* means "in the order designated": We discussed the issue with the chair, the dean, and the provost, **respectively**.

rise   See **raise, rise**.

should of   See **could of**.

sight   See **cite, site, sight**.

sit, set   *Sit* means "to be seated": Jonathan **sat** in the front row. *Set* means "to place something": The research assistant **set** the chemicals on the counter. *Set* takes an object (to **set** something); *sit* does not.

site   See **cite, site, sight**.

so   Instead of using *so* to mean "very," find a precise modifier: She was ~~so~~ intensely focused on her career.

someplace   See **anyplace, everyplace, someplace**.

sometime, sometimes, some time   *Sometime* means "at an unspecified time": They will meet **sometime** next month. *Sometimes* means "at times": **Sometimes** laws are unfair. *Some time* means "a span of time": They agreed to allow **some time** to pass before voting on the measure.

sort of a   See **kind of a, sort of a**.

specially   See **especially, specially**.

stationary, stationery   *Stationary* means "in a fixed position": Traffic was **stationary** for an hour. *Stationery* means "writing paper and envelopes": The director ordered new department **stationery**.

supposed to, used to   Be sure to include the frequently unsounded *d* at the end of the verb form: We are **supposed to** leave at 9:30 a.m. We **used to** leave earlier.

than, then   *Than* is used in comparisons: The tape recorder is smaller **than** the radio. *Then* refers to a time sequence: Go straight ahead for three blocks; **then** turn left.

their, there, they're   *Their* is the possessive form of *they*: They will give **their** presentation tomorrow. *There* refers to location: I lived **there** for six years. *There* is also used as an expletive (see **30a(3)**): **There** is no explanation for the phenomenon. *They're* is a contraction of *they are*: **They're** leaving in the morning.

theirself, theirselves   Unconventional; use *themselves*. The students finished the project by ~~theirselves~~ themselves.

then   See **than, then**.

to, too, two   *To* is an infinitive marker: She wanted **to** become an actress. *To* is also used as a preposition, usually indicating direction: They walked **to** the memorial. *Too* means either "also" or "excessively": I voted for her **too**. They are **too** busy this year. *Two* is a number: She studied abroad for **two** years.

toward, towards   Although both are acceptable, *toward* is preferred in American English.

try and   Conversational for *try to*: The staff will **try ~~and~~ to** finish the project by Friday.

uninterested   See **disinterested, uninterested**.

* **unique**   Traditionally, *unique* meant "one of a kind" and thus was not preceded by a qualifier such as *more*, *most*, *quite*, or *very*: Her prose style is ~~quite~~ unique. However, *unique* is also widely used to mean "extraordinary."

use, utilize   In most contexts, *use* is preferred to *utilize*: We ~~utilized~~ used a special dye in the experiment. However, *utilize* may suggest an effort to employ something for a purpose: We discussed how to **utilize** the resources we had been given.

used to   See **supposed to, used to**.

very   To ensure this word's effectiveness, use it sparingly. Whenever possible, choose a stronger word: She was ~~very satisfied~~ delighted with her new digital camera.

ways   Conversational when referring to distance; use *way* instead: It's a long ~~ways~~ way from home.

well   See **good, well**.

where . . . at, where . . . to   Conversational; omit *at* and *to*: **Where** is the library ~~at~~? **Where** are you moving ~~to~~?

with regards to   See **regard, regarding, regards**.

would of   See **could of**.

your, you're   *Your* is a possessive form: Let's meet in **your** office. *You're* is a contraction of *you are*: **You're** gaining strength.

yourself   See **herself, himself, myself, yourself**.

Glossary of Terms

This glossary provides brief definitions of frequently used terms. Consult the index for references to terms not listed here.

absolute phrase   A sentence-like structure containing a subject and its modifiers. Unlike a sentence, an absolute phrase has no verb marked for person, number, or tense: *The ceremony finally over*, the graduates tossed their mortarboards in the air. See **17d(6)**.

acronym   A word formed by combining the initial letters or syllables of a series of words and pronounced as a word rather than as a series of letters: *NATO* for North Atlantic Treaty Organization. See chapter **39**.

active voice   See **voice**.

adjectival clause   A dependent clause, also called a **relative clause**, that modifies a noun or a pronoun. See **17e**.

adjective   A word that modifies a noun or a pronoun. Adjectives typically end in suffixes such as *-able, -al, -ant, -ative, -ic, -ish, -less, -ous*, and *-y*. See **17a** and chapter **22**. **Coordinate adjectives** are two or more adjectives modifying the same noun and separated by a comma: a *brisk, cold* walk. See **31d**.

adverb   A word that modifies a verb, a verbal, an adjective, or another adverb. Adverbs commonly end in *-ly*. Some adverbs modify entire sentences: *Perhaps* the meeting could be postponed. See **17a** and chapter **22**.

adverbial clause   A dependent clause that modifies a verb, an adjective, or an adverb. See **17e(2)**.

adverbial conjunction   A word such as *however* or *thus* that joins one independent clause to another; also known as a **conjunctive adverb**. See **17a(7)**. COMPARE: **conjunction**.

agreement   Grammatical correspondence in number, person, or gender between pronouns and their antecedents and subjects and their verbs. See **20f** and **21c**.

antecedent   A word or group of words referred to by a pronoun. See **17a(3)**, **21a**, and **21c**.

appositive   A pronoun, noun, or noun phrase that identifies, describes, or explains an adjacent pronoun, noun, or noun phrase. See **17a** and **21b(4)**.

article   A word used to signal a noun. *The* is a definite article; *a* and *an* are indefinite articles. See **17a(4)**.

auxiliary verb, auxiliary   A verb that combines with a main verb. *Be*, *do*, and *have* are auxiliary verbs when they are used with main verbs. Also called **helping verbs**. **Modal auxiliaries** include *could*, *should*, and *may* and are used for such purposes as expressing doubt or obligation and making a request. See **17a**, **17d**, and **20a**.

Boolean operators   Words used to broaden or narrow database searches. These include *or*, *and*, *not*, and *near*. Also called logical operators. See **9b**.

case   The form of a noun or a pronoun that indicates its relationship to other words in a sentence. Nouns and pronouns can be subjects or subject complements (**subjective case**), objects (**objective case**), or markers of possession and other relations (**possessive case**). See **21b**.

claim   A statement that a writer wants readers to accept; also called a **proposition**. See **5b**, **6c**.

clause   A sequence of related words forming an independent unit (**independent clause** or **main clause**) or an embedded unit (**dependent clause** used as an adverb, adjective, or noun). A clause has both a subject and a predicate. See **17e**.

collective noun   A noun that refers to a group: *team*, *faculty*, *committee*. See **17a(2)**.

colloquial   A label for any word or phrase that is characteristic of informal speech. *Kid* is colloquial; *child* is used in formal contexts. See **28a(2)**.

common noun   A noun referring to any or all members of a class or group (*woman*, *city*, *holiday*) rather than to specific members

(*Susan, Reno, New Year's Day*). COMPARE: **proper noun**. See **17a(2)**.

complement   A word or words used to complete the meaning of a verb. A **subject complement** is a word or phrase that follows a linking verb and categorizes or describes the subject. An **object complement** is a word or phrase that categorizes or describes a direct object when it follows such verbs as *make, paint, elect,* and *consider.* See **17c**.

compound predicate   A predicate that has two parts joined by a connecting word such as *and, or,* or *but*; each part contains a verb: Clara Barton *nursed the injured during the Civil War* and *later founded the American Red Cross.* See **17b**.

compound subject   Two subjects joined by a connecting word such as *and, or,* or *but*: *Students* and *faculty* are discussing the issue of grade inflation. See **17b**.

compound word   Two or more words functioning as a single word: *ice cream, double-check.* See chapter **36**.

conjunction   A word used to connect other words, phrases, clauses, or sentences. **Coordinating conjunctions** (*and, but, or, nor, for, so,* and *yet*) connect and relate words and word groups of equal grammatical rank. See **17a(7)**. A **subordinating conjunction** such as *although, if,* or *when* begins a dependent clause and connects it to an independent clause. See **17a(7)** and **17e(2)**. COMPARE: **adverbial conjunction**.

conjunctive adverb   See **adverbial conjunction**.

coordinate adjective   See **adjective**.

coordinating conjunction   See **conjunction**.

coordination   The use of grammatically equivalent constructions to link or balance ideas. See chapter **24**.

correlative conjunctions, correlatives   Two-part connecting words such as *either . . . or* and *not only . . . but also.* See **17a(7)**.

count nouns   Nouns naming things that can be counted (*word, student, remark*). See **17a(2)**. COMPARE: **noncount nouns**.

dangling modifier   A word or phrase that does not clearly modify another word or word group. See **22e**. COMPARE: **misplaced modifier**.

dangling participial phrase A verbal phrase that does not clearly modify another word or word group.

demonstrative pronouns Four words (*this*, *that*, *these*, and *those*) that distinguish one individual, thing, event, or idea from another. Demonstratives may occur with or without nouns: *This law* will go into effect in two years. *This* will go into effect in two years. See **21a(6)**.

dependent clause Also called *subordinate clause*. See **clause**.

determiner A word that signals the approach of a noun. A determiner may be an article, a demonstrative, a possessive, or a quantifier: *a reason, this reason, his reason, three reasons.*

direct object See **object**.

direct quotation See **quotation**.

ellipsis points Three spaced periods that indicate either a pause or the omission of material from a direct quotation. See **35g**.

elliptical construction (clause) A construction, usually a clause, missing one or more words that are assumed to be understood. See **17e, 21b(7), 30b**.

essential element A word or word group that modifies another word or word group, providing information that is essential for identification. Essential elements are not set off by commas, parentheses, or dashes: The woman *who witnessed the accident* was called to testify. Also called a **restrictive element**. COMPARE: **nonessential element**. See **17e, 21a(4)**, and chapter **31**.

ethos One of the three classical appeals; the use of language to demonstrate the writer's trustworthy character, good intentions, and substantial knowledge of a subject. Also called an **ethical appeal**. See **6e**. See also **logos** and **pathos**.

expletive A word signaling a structural change in a sentence, usually used so that new or important information is given at the end of the sentence: *There* were over four thousand runners in the marathon. See **30a**.

genre A literary category, such as drama or poetry, identified by its own conventions.

gerund A verbal that ends in *-ing* and functions as a noun: *Snowboarding* is a popular winter sport. See **17d(3)**.

gerund phrase A verbal phrase that employs the *-ing* form of a verb and functions as a noun: Some students prefer *studying in the library.* See **17d(3)**.

helping verb See **auxiliary verb**.

homophones Words that have the same sound and sometimes the same spelling but differ in meaning: *their*, *there*, and *they're* or *capital* meaning "funds" and *capital* meaning "the top of a pillar." See chapter **36**.

idiom An expression whose meaning often cannot be derived from its elements. *Burning the midnight oil* means "staying up late studying." See **29c**.

indefinite pronoun A pronoun such as *everyone* or *anything* that does not refer to a specific person, place, thing, or idea. See **21a(7)** and **21c**.

independent clause See **clause**.

indirect object See **object**.

indirect question A sentence that includes an embedded question, punctuated with a period instead of a question mark: My friends asked me *why I left the party early.* See chapter **35**.

indirect quotation See **quotation**.

infinitive A verbal that consists of the base form of the verb, usually preceded by the infinitive marker *to.* An infinitive is used chiefly as a noun, less frequently as an adjective or adverb: My father likes *to golf.* See **17d(3)**.

infinitive phrase A verbal phrase that contains the infinitive form of a verb: They volunteered *to work at the local hospital.* See **17d(3)**.

inflection A change in the form of a word that indicates a grammatical feature such as number, person, tense, or degree. For example, *-ed* added to a verb indicates the past tense, and *-er* indicates the comparative degree of an adjective or adverb.

intensifier See **qualifier**.

intensive pronoun See **reflexive pronoun**.

interjection A word expressing a simple exclamation: *Hey! Oops!* When used at the beginnings of sentences, mild interjections are set off by commas. See **17a(8)**.

linking verb　A verb that relates a subject to a subject complement. Examples of linking verbs are *be, become, seem, appear, feel, look, taste, smell,* and *sound.* See **17a(1)** and **20a**.

logos　One of the three classical appeals; the use of language to show clear reasoning. Also called a **logical appeal**. See **6e**. See also **ethos** and **pathos**.

main clause　Also called **independent clause**. See **clause**.

misplaced modifier　A descriptive or qualifying word or phrase placed in a position that confuses the reader: I read about a wildfire that was out of control *in yesterday's paper.* [The modifier belongs after *read.*] See **22d**.

mixed construction　A confusing sentence that is the result of an unintentional shift from one grammatical pattern to another: When police appeared who were supposed to calm the crowds showed up, most people had already gone home. [The sentence should be recast with either *appeared* or *showed up*, not with both.] See **23c**.

mixed metaphor　A construction that includes parts of two or more unrelated metaphors: Her *fiery* personality *dampened* our hopes of a compromise. See chapter **23**.

modal auxiliary　See **auxiliary verb**.

modifier　A word or word group that describes, limits, or qualifies another. See chapter **22**.

mood　A set of verb forms or inflections used to indicate how a speaker or writer regards an assertion: as a fact or opinion (**indicative mood**); as a command or instruction (**imperative mood**); or as a wish, hypothesis, request, or condition contrary to fact (**subjunctive mood**). See **20e**.

nominalization　Formation of a noun by adding a suffix to a verb or an adjective: *require, requirement; sad, sadness.*

nominative case　Also called **subjective case**. See **case**.

noncount nouns　Nouns naming things that cannot be counted (*architecture, water*). See **17a(2)**. COMPARE: **count nouns**.

nonessential element　A word or word group that modifies another word or word group but does not provide information essential for identification. Nonessential elements are set off by commas, parentheses, or dashes: Carol Murphy, *president of the* *university*, plans to meet with alumni representatives. Also called a **nonrestrictive element**. See **17e** and chapter **31**. COMPARE: **essential element**.

nonrestrictive element See **nonessential element**.

noun A word that names a person, place, thing, idea, animal, quality, event, and so on: *Alanis, America, desk, justice, dog, strength, departure*. See **17a(2)**. See also **collective noun**, **common noun**, **count noun**, **noncount noun**, and **proper noun**.

noun clause A dependent clause used as a noun. See **17e**.

noun phrase A noun and its modifiers. See **17d(1)**.

number The property of a word that indicates whether it refers to one (**singular**) or to more than one (**plural**). Number is reflected in the word's form: *river/rivers, this/those, he sees/they see*. See **20b**, **20f**, **21b**, and **21c**.

object A noun, pronoun, noun phrase, or noun clause that follows a preposition or a transitive verb or verbal. A **direct object** names the person or thing that receives the action of the verb: I sent the *package*. An **indirect object** usually indicates to whom the action was directed or for whom the action was performed: I sent *you* the package. See **17c**. The **object of a preposition** follows a preposition: I sent the package to *you*. See **17d(4)**.

object complement See **complement**.

objective case See **case**.

participial phrase A verbal phrase that includes a participle and serves as a modifier: The stagehand *carrying the trunk* fell over the threshold. See **17d**. See also **participle** and **phrase**.

participle A verb form that may function as part of a verb phrase (had *determined*, was *thinking*) or as a modifier (a *determined* effort; the couple, *thinking* about their past). A **present participle** is formed by adding *-ing* to the base form of a verb. A **past participle** is usually formed by adding *-ed* to the base form of a verb (*walked, passed*); however, many verbs have irregular past-participle forms (*written, bought, gone*). See **20a**.

particle A word such as *across, away, down, for, in, off, out, up, on*, or *with* that combines with a main verb to form a phrasal verb: *write down, look up*. See **20a**.

parts of speech   The classes into which words may be grouped according to their forms and grammatical relationships. The traditional parts of speech are verbs, nouns, pronouns, adjectives, adverbs, prepositions, conjunctions, and interjections. See **17a**.

passive voice   See **voice**.

past participle   See **participle**.

pathos   One of the three classical appeals; the use of language to stir the feelings of an audience. Also called an **emotional appeal** or a **pathetic appeal**. See **6e**. See also **ethos** and **logos**.

perfect progressive tense   The form a verb takes to indicate that an action, condition, or event originating in the past is ongoing or incomplete (*he is talking*; *the brakes were failing*; *her film will be showing*). See **20b**.

perfect tense   The form a verb takes to indicate actions performed or events completed before a particular time (*I have read that book already*; *The film had begun*; *By next term, I will have finished my internship*). See **20b**.

person   The property of nouns, pronouns, and their corresponding verbs that distinguishes the speaker or writer (**first person**), the individuals addressed (**second person**), and the individuals or things referred to (**third person**). See **20b, 21b**.

personal pronoun   A pronoun that refers to a specific person, place, thing, and so on. Pronoun forms correspond to three cases: subjective, objective, and possessive. See **21a(1)**.

phrasal verb   A grammatical unit consisting of a verb and a particle such as *after, in, up, off*, or *out*: *fill in, sort out*. See **20a**.

phrase   A sequence of grammatically related words that functions as a unit in a sentence but lacks a subject, a predicate, or both: *in front of the stage*. See **17d**.

point of view   The vantage point from which a topic is viewed; also, the stance a writer takes: objective or impartial (third person), directive (second person), or personal (first person). See **21e**.

possessive case   See **case**.

predicate   The part of a sentence that expresses what a subject is, does, or experiences. It consists of the main verb, its auxiliaries, and any complements and modifiers. The **simple predicate**

consists of only the main verb and any accompanying auxiliaries. See **17b** and **17c**. COMPARE: **subject**.

preposition A word such as *at, in, by,* or *of* that relates a pronoun, noun, noun phrase, or noun clause to other words in the sentence. See **17a(6)**.

prepositional phrase A preposition with its object and any modifiers: *at* the nearby airport, *by* the sea. See **17d(4)**.

present participle See **participle**.

primary source A source that provides firsthand information. See **9a**. COMPARE: **secondary source**.

progressive tense The form a verb takes to indicate that an action or condition is in progress (*he is talking; the brakes were failing; her film will be showing*). See **20b**.

pronoun A word that takes the position of a noun, noun phrase, or noun clause and functions as that word or word group does: *it, that, he, them.* See **17a** and chapter **21**.

proper noun The name of a specific person, place, organization, and so on: *Dr. Pimomo, Fargo, National Education Association.* Proper nouns are capitalized. See **17a(2)**. COMPARE: **common noun**.

proposition See **claim**.

qualifier A word that intensifies or moderates the meaning of an adverb or adjective: *quite* slowly, *somewhat* reluctant. Words that intensify are sometimes called **intensifiers**. See **20a(5)**.

quotation A **direct quotation** (also called **direct discourse**) is the exact repetition of someone's spoken or written words. An **indirect quotation** is a report of someone's written or spoken words not stated in the exact words of the writer or speaker. See **11d** and chapter **34**.

reflexive pronoun A pronoun that ends in *-self* or *-selves* (*myself* or *themselves*) and refers to a preceding noun or pronoun in the sentence: *He* added a picture of *himself* to his web page. When used to provide emphasis, such a pronoun is called an **intensive pronoun**: The president *herself* awarded the scholarships. See **21a**.

refutation A strategy for addressing opposing points of view by discussing those views and explaining why they are unsatisfactory. See **6d(2)** and **6f**.

relative clause   See **adjectival clause**.

relative pronoun   A word (*who, whom, that, which,* or *whose*) used to introduce an **adjectival clause**, also called a **relative clause**. An antecedent for the relative pronoun can be found in the main clause. See **17e**.

restrictive element   See **essential element**.

Rogerian argument   An approach to argumentation that is based on the work of psychologist Carl R. Rogers and that emphasizes the importance of withholding judgment of others' ideas until they are fully understood.

secondary source   A source that analyzes or interprets firsthand information. See **9a**. COMPARE: **primary source**.

signal phrase   A short phrase that identifies the source of a quotation: *according to Jones, Jones claims.* See **11c**.

simple tense   Present (*she talks*), past (*it failed*), or future (*I will dare*) forms of verbs. See **20b**.

split infinitive   The separation of the two parts of an infinitive form by at least one word: *to completely cover.* See **17d(3)**.

squinting modifier   A modifier that is unclear because it can refer to words either preceding it or following it: Proofreading *quickly* results in missed spelling errors. See **22d**.

subject   The pronoun, noun, or noun phrase that carries out the action or assumes the state described in the predicate of a sentence. Usually preceding the predicate, the subject includes the main noun or pronoun and all modifiers. A **simple subject** consists of only the main noun or pronoun. See **17b**. COMPARE: **predicate**.

subject complement   See **complement**.

subjective case   See **case**.

subordinating conjunction   See **conjunction**.

subordination   The connection of a grammatical structure to another, usually a dependent clause to an independent clause: *Even though customers were satisfied with the product,* the company wanted to improve it. See chapter **24**.

tense   The form of a verb that indicates time and sometimes completeness or duration of an action, an event, or a state of being. See chapter **20**.

thesis statement   The central point or main idea of an essay. See **2b**, **8d**.

tone   The writer's attitude toward the subject and the audience, usually conveyed through word choice and sentence structure.

topic   The specific, narrowed main idea of an essay. See **2b**.

topic sentence   A statement of the main idea of a paragraph. See **3a**.

Toulmin model   A system of argumentation developed by philosopher Stephen Toulmin in which a claim and supporting reasons or evidence depend on a shared assumption. See **5b**.

transitions   Words, phrases, sentences, or paragraphs that relate ideas by linking sentences, paragraphs, or larger segments of writing. See **3d(2)** and **19b(5)**.

verb   A word denoting action, occurrence, or existence (state of being). See **17a(1)** and chapter **20**.

verb phrase   A main verb and any auxiliaries. See **17a** and **20d**.

verbal phrase   A verb form functioning as a noun, an adjective, or an adverb. See **17a**. See also **gerund**, **infinitive**, and **participle**.

voice   A property of a verb that indicates the relationship between the verb and its subject. The **active voice** is used to show that the subject performs the action expressed by the verb; the **passive voice** is used to show that the subject receives the action. See **20d**.

warrant   According to the **Toulmin model**, the underlying assumption connecting a claim and data. See **5b**.

Index

Numbers and letters in **color** refer to chapters and sections in the handbook; other numbers refer to pages. Page numbers in *italics* indicate a glossary of usage term.

543

CITATION MAPS

Use these maps to help you quickly cite commonly used kinds of sources.

SPECIAL TOPICS FOR MULTILINGUAL WRITERS

REVISION SYMBOLS

ab	abbreviation **39a–c**		*main*	main idea **3a**
ac	acronym **39d**		*MLA*	MLA format **13**
adj	adjective **17a(4), 22a–b, 22d**		*mod*	modifier **22**
adv	adverb **17a(5), 22a–b**		*n*	number **33c, 39e–f**
agr	agreement **20f, 21c**		*^*	omission
APA	APA format **14**		*¶*	paragraph **3**
ʾ	apostrophe **33**		*//*	parallelism **25**
arg	argument **6**		*( )*	parentheses **35e**
awk	awkward		*.*	period **34c(1), 35a**
cap	capital **37**		*pl*	plural **36c(5)**
CMS	CMS format **15**		*pro*	pronoun **21, 24a(2)**
coh	coherence **4a, 22d–e**		*?*	question mark **34c(3), 35b**
:	colon **32b, 34c(2)**		*" "*	quotation marks **34**
,	comma **31, 34c(1)**		*red*	redundant **30a(1)**
con	conciseness **30**		*ref*	reference **21d**
coor	coordination **24b–c**		*rep*	repetition **25b, 26c**
cred	source credibility **10**		*;*	semicolon **32a, 34c(2)**
cs	comma splice **19**		*sg*	singular
CSE	CSE format **16**		*/*	slash **35h**
—	dash **34c(3), 35d**		*sp*	spelling **36a–d**
ɣ	delete		*sub*	subordination **24a, 24c**
dev	development **3**		*[ ]*	square brackets **35f**
...	ellipsis points **35g**		*t*	tense **20b**
evid	evidence **6d**		*thesis*	thesis statement **2b**
!	exclamation point **34c(3), 35c**		*trans*	transition **3d(4)**
frag	fragment **18**		*∽*	transpose
fs	fused sentence **19**		*u*	unity **4a, 23**
hy	hyphenation **36e**		*usg*	usage **Glossary of Usage**
inc	incomplete		*var*	variety **27**
irreg	irregular verb **20a**		*v*	verb **20**
ital	italics **38**		*wc*	word choice **23e–g, 28a–b**
log	logic **6d–e**		*w*	wordiness **30a**
lc	lowercase **37**		*ww*	wrong word **29a–c**

Contents